Movies We Love

Movies We Love

100 Collectible Classics

By Frank Miller
Foreword by Robert Osborne

Turner Publishing, Inc.
ATLANTA

James Stewart and Katharine Hepburn find the love we all crave in *The Philadelphia Story*.

This book is dedicated to
my mother,
Helen Miller,
a classic if ever there was one.

Acknowledgments

Like the great films of Hollywood's Golden Age, this book was far from a solo effort. I will always be thankful to the many people at Turner Publishing who have helped me mold a career as a writer, particularly Michael Reagan, Karen Smith, Marty Moore, and Michael Walsh. Special thanks in this area are due the three people who did the most to help me shape this book: my editor, Alan Axelrod; project coordinator, Zodie Spain; and research assistant Woolsey Ackerman, who unearthed most of the photos and sent me much-valued packets of films and press clippings. In addition, I would like to thank Katherine Evans, Mary Katherine Fiorillo, and Carrie Ellis of Turner Classic Movies for their support on this project.

For research assistance I am indebted to Linda Maher, Robert Cushman, and all of the staff at the Margaret Herrick Library of the Academy of Motion Picture Arts and Sciences, and the staffs of the Georgia State University Library and the Fulton County Public Library. Finally, I wish to acknowledge the invaluable assistance of my good friend David Tucker of the DeKalb County Public Library. Not only did David locate research materials for me from the DeKalb County libraries and his own private collection, but he generously read through the final text to help me check facts.

Library of Congress Cataloging-in-Publication Data

Miller, Frank.
Moves we love: 100 collectible classics/by Frank Miller.—1st ed.
p. cm.
ISBN 1-57036-276-9 (alk. paper)
1. Motion pictures—Catalogs. 2. Video recordings—Catalogs.
I. Title.
PN1998.M42 1996
791.43—dc20 95-46282
CIP

Published by Turner Publishing, Inc.
A Subsidiary of Turner Broadcasting System, Inc.
1050 Techwood Drive, NW
Atlanta, Georgia 30318

Distributed by Andrews and McMeel
A Universal Press Syndicate Company
4900 Main Street
St. Louis, Missouri 64112

First Edition
10 9 8 7 6 5 4 3 2 1

Printed in the U.S.A.

Table of Contents

Foreword by Robert Osborne

Host of Turner Classic Movies

Everyone loves the movies, and for a myriad of reasons. Why do I love movies? Let me count the ways.

I love them because they entertain me, excite me, enlighten me, educate me. I'd even go so far as to say movies have taught me most of what I know. I first became aware of India because of the movies (*Gunga Din*). And the Civil War (*Gone With the Wind*). From the movies I learned the simplest things (how to behave in public, why one should avoid apes in New York named "Kong") and the more complicated stuff (why they call it Pasteurized milk, what happened in the Tower of London). Someone I know once said I probably wouldn't have known there was a Vietnam War if John Wayne hadn't made *The Green Berets*. Not quite true, but close. I certainly learned more about the French Revolution from *A Tale of Two Cities* than I did through my textbooks at Martha Washington Grade School in Colfax, Washington. It was *The Good Earth* that made me aware of China (and locusts). *The Life of Emile Zola* taught me about the ramifications of the Dreyfus Affair and Devil's Island.

Of course, not all the knowledge I gained from movies was accurate. I found out later that the silver screen at the Rose Theater in Colfax had probably provided more misinformation than truth—like the promise there would always be happy endings for everyone and the theory that good always triumphs (although, I must admit, I still do basically believe in the latter; it's the "always" I've had to discard). Along with the other misinformation I gleaned from the movies is that crime doesn't pay (alas, it sometimes seems to) and that the girl next door would look like June Allyson, and grandma would be like Jane Darwell. For me, it was the other way around: the girl next door where I lived looked a lot like Ma Joad in *The Grapes of Wrath,* and my grandmother was more like June A.

Like many people, I fell in love with movies at a young age. The earliest moment in a movie I can recall seeing is the Prince kissing Snow White and awakening her from the dead. Great trick! And I have vivid recollections of Edward G. Robinson—at least I *think* it was Robinson, although it could have been John Garfield—blasting someone with a machine gun.

For years I also remembered an image of a girl sitting in a convertible, deliberately parked on a railroad track, while she very nervously lit a cigarette as a train approached. For years the scene haunted me: What was the movie? Who was the girl? Why was she on that track? So I have an added personal reason to thank heaven for Turner Classic Movies. One day, quite by accident, on TCM I saw an MGM oldie called *These Glamour Girls,* and there was the girl (Marsha Hunt) with the shaking hands and the cigarette and, barreling down on her, the train. For the record, she was on those tracks, chucking it all, because she'd been snubbed by some nasty sorority girls at the local college. (*Another* lesson from the movies: watch out for sorority girls.)

I'd like to think that, as I've grown older, my movie tastes have upgraded a bit—but I'm not sure they have, or that I've really wanted them to change. A grade B, or even a C-minus, movie can still grab my interest and bring me to attention if the timing's right. However, it's movies such as *The Adventures of Robin Hood, An American in Paris, The Shop Around the Corner, Murder, My Sweet*—and others covered in this magnificent roundup of *Movies We Love*—that really get the adrenaline pumping.

It's hard to fathom these days that there was a time—not too long ago—when no one except the die-hard buffs paid attention to "old" movies. There were no VCRs, no video rentals, no movie societies or film schools, no Turner Classic Movies on cable. And very few books were available about Hollywood's past, either. So, truly, count us all lucky to be living in a more enlightened time, in which we not only can read fascinating details about many of the movies we love but also can watch them on the tube, uninterrupted and commercial-free. Or—maybe the best part—we have the opportunity to collect them on tape and watch them any time we choose.

Picking one or one hundred of anything is always a matter of personal taste, of course. That's a given. But if your favorite film isn't included among the group celebrated within these pages, I'm sure you'll find it difficult—be honest!—to figure out which one or two or three of the hundred that have been selected you'd drop in favor of another choice.

One more thing: Enjoy the photographs here, peruse the copy, because Frank has included much fascinating information on each and every one of the films spotlighted. (Did you know, for instance, that Marlon Brando, Rock Hudson, and Burt Lancaster were all early choices to play Ben-Hur in William Wyler's 1959 version? And Charlton Heston, who finally was cast in the title role, had originally been set to play Messalla, the villain of the piece? Or that Spencer Tracy's Oscar for *Boys Town* was sent out to be engraved and came back incorrectly inscribed "to Dick Tracy"?) I've always been a firm believer that the more one knows about a movie, the more fascinating that film is to watch.

And that's the bottom line: Do watch the movies. You can look at photographs from movies, you can read about the films, but the important thing is to see them. That's why they were created, to be watched and enjoyed as *motion* pictures. It's the only way to get the full impact of a *Casablanca*, a *King Kong,* or a *Red Badge of Courage*. It's the only way to understand fully why all of the one hundred classic movies covered here are movies we truly cherish and love.

Adam's Rib

"Vive la Différence!"

1949. CAST: Spencer Tracy (Adam Bonner), Katharine Hepburn (Amanda Bonner), Judy Holliday (Doris Attinger), Tom Ewell (Warren Attinger), David Wayne (Kip Lurie), Jean Hagen (Beryl Caighn). Producer: Lawrence Weingarten; Director: George Cukor; Screenplay: Ruth Gordon, Garson Kanin; Photography: George J. Folsey; Music: Miklos Rosza; Song ("Farewell Amanda"): Cole Porter. RUNNING TIME: 100 minutes.

The battle of the sexes has rarely been waged as mercilessly, or to such hilarious effect, as in *Adam's Rib,* the sixth film to bring together one of the screen's most popular romantic teams, Spencer Tracy and Katharine Hepburn. It may not have been their best vehicle (most critics would probably vote for *Pat and Mike*), but it certainly is their most fondly remembered. Viewed from the perspective of almost fifty years, the film seems a lighthearted echo of the team's off-screen relationship.

Their first meeting was none too promising. When producer Joseph L. Mankiewicz introduced them on the MGM lot, Hepburn was wearing three-inch platform shoes. "I'm afraid, Mr. Tracy, I may be a little tall for you," she said. "Don't worry," quipped Mankiewicz, "he'll cut you down to size." Yet their partnership actually raised both to new heights. His on-screen simplicity helped her develop a more controlled, less affected style, while the unmasked ardor with which she viewed him on-screen made him seem more romantic.

After a strong start together in *Woman of the Year,* Tracy and Hepburn had trouble finding the ideal vehicle. Few people then or now could look at films like *Without Love* and *The Sea of Grass* with unalloyed delight. Then, Kanin and his actress-writer wife, Ruth Gordon, came up with the script for *Adam's Rib*—the first script specifically written for the team since *Woman of the Year.*

The script was more than just a vehicle for its two stars. It also contained four strong supporting roles that Tracy, Hepburn, and Cukor hoped to fill with promising newcomers from the stage. David Wayne was cast as a fey songwriter enamored of Hepburn. Tom Ewell made his screen

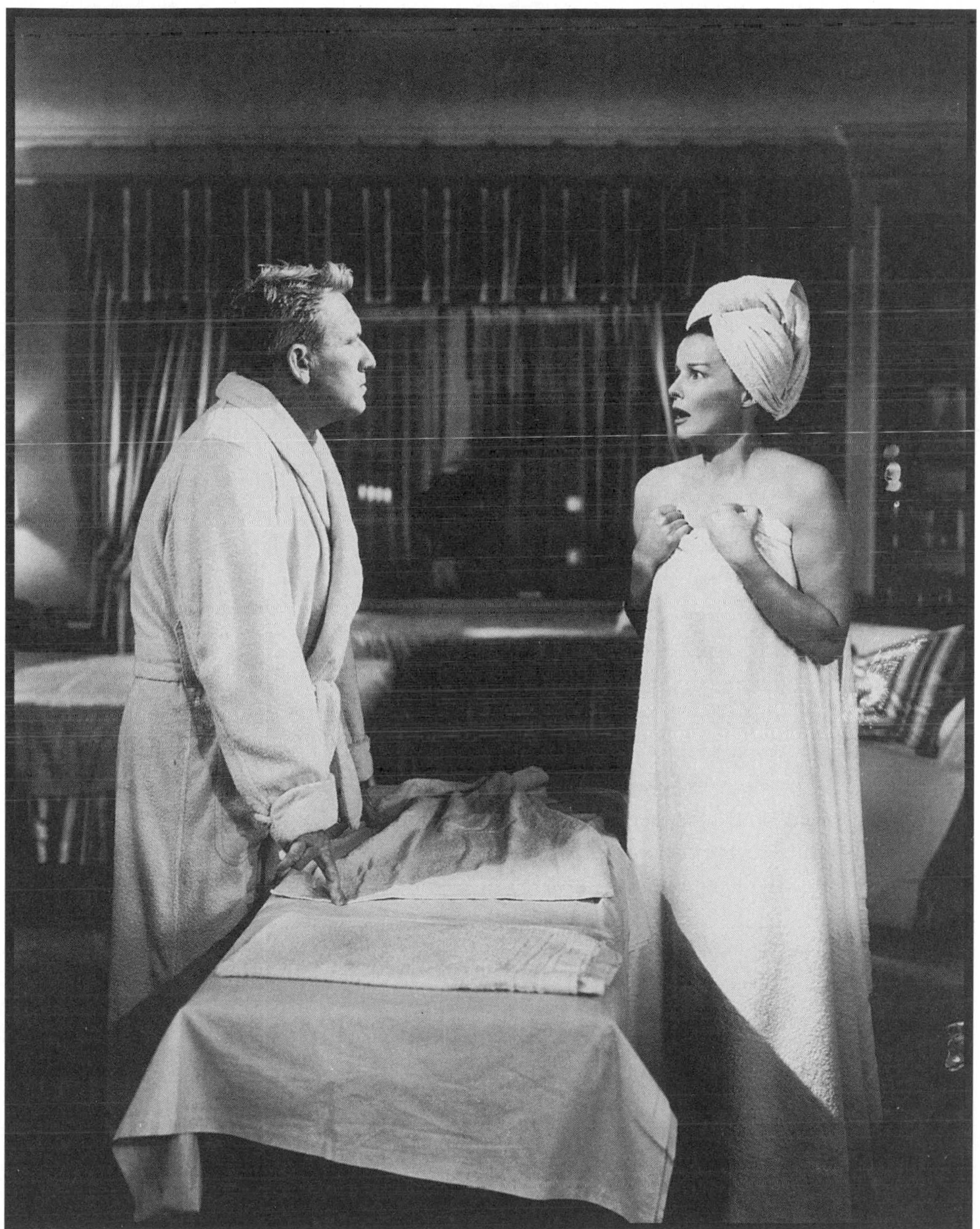

The screen's favorite couple face off: Spencer Tracy and Katharine Hepburn.

debut as the straying husband shot by his desperate wife. Jean Hagen (later Lina Lamont in *Singin' in the Rain*) was his girlfriend. And to play the wife, the juiciest of the four roles, they chose Judy Holliday.

This last bit of casting was a calculated maneuver, particularly on Hepburn's part. Holliday had just scored a major hit on Broadway by stepping in at the last minute to replace departed star Jean Arthur in Kanin's play *Born Yesterday*. Holliday dearly wanted to play the role on screen also, but producer Harry Cohn, who had bought the rights, wanted no part of her. With the help of Cukor, who was set to direct *Born Yesterday* as well and had used Holliday in a small role in his 1944 *Winged Victory*, Hepburn turned *Adam's Rib* into an elaborate screen test for Holliday.

Adam's Rib opens with Holliday tracking her husband to his love nest and shooting him by accident while trying to take out his girlfriend. Her first major dialogue scene was a long interview with Hepburn—a virtual monologue for the newcomer. Tracy and Cukor planned the scene so that only Holliday would be shown full-face. Hepburn spent most of her time with her back to the camera for over-the-shoulder shots of her costar or in profile for long shots. Legend has it that she even refused to shoot closeups, thus throwing the entire scene to Holliday.

Once the sequence was assembled, Hepburn and Cukor sent it to Harry Cohn. He had even taken time to test a young unknown named Marilyn Monroe. The scene opened his eyes to Holliday's screen potential. Not only did she win the chance to re-create her role in *Born Yesterday*, she began a career in film that eventually brought her the Oscar for Best Actress.

Tracy and Hepburn got a lot more out of Holliday's casting than just the satisfaction of helping out a screen newcomer. They also got a wonderful supporting performance that added texture and depth to an already solid film. *Adam's Rib* was a big hit for the studio and proof positive that the two stars were still one of the screen's most bankable—and lovable—teams.

THE TRACY-HEPBURN COLLECTION

Woman of the Year ***(MGM, 1942)***
Keeper of the Flame ***(MGM, 1942)***
Without Love ***(MGM, 1945)***
The Sea of Grass ***(MGM, 1947)***
State of the Union ***(MGM, 1948)***
Adam's Rib ***(MGM, 1949)***
Pat and Mike ***(MGM, 1952)***
The Desk Set ***(20th Century-Fox, 1957)***
Guess Who's Coming to Dinner ***(Columbia, 1967)***

The Adventures of Robin Hood

"Only a Rainbow Can Duplicate Its Brilliance!"

1938. CAST: Errol Flynn (Sir Robin of Locksley), Olivia de Havilland (Maid Marian), Basil Rathbone (Sir Guy of Gisbourne), Claude Rains (Prince John), Patric Knowles (Will Scarlett), Eugene Pallette (Friar Tuck), Alan Hale (Little John). Producer: Hal Wallis; Directors: Michael Curtiz, William Keighley; Screenplay: Norman Reilly Raine, Seton I. Miller (Based on ancient Robin Hood legends); Photography: Sol Polito, Tony Gaudio (Technicolor); Music: Erich Wolfgang Korngold. RUNNING TIME: 102 minutes.

When *Star Wars* burst on the screen in 1977, audiences thrilled to the derring-do of Luke Skywalker and Han Solo, the dazzling escapes, the light-saber battles, and the crashing chords of John Williams's score. To some, this high-spirited adventure may have seemed new. But producer-director George Lucas had wisely turned for inspiration to one of the most invigorating adventures of all time, Warner Bros.' 1938 *The Adventures of Robin Hood*.

The film represented the studio's biggest investment to that time—more than $2 million in an era when most movies were made for a quarter of that price. It was Warner's second film in the three-strip Technicolor process, which had made its feature debut only three years earlier. In addition, it cemented Errol Flynn's status as the screen's greatest adventure star and clearly established him and Olivia de Havilland as one of the industry's great romantic duos. And, as with so many of Hollywood's greatest films, none of those accomplishments were part of the studio's original plans.

Warner's had considered a new film version of *Robin Hood* in 1929. With the coming of sound, they hoped to capitalize on the name recognition from Douglas Fairbanks's hit 1922 silent version. But little was done with the project until 1935, when Dwight Franklin, who was working as a period consultant on Flynn's first starring vehicle, *Captain Blood,* suggested a new version of the classic tale. But it wasn't Flynn's heroism that had inspired him. Rather, he had seen James Cagney as Bottom in *A Midsummer Night's Dream*. Most of the Warner's stock company (including Frank McHugh, Allen Jenkins, and Hugh Herbert) had been cast as the "rude mechanicals," and Franklin suggested casting them as Cagney's "merry men."

As plans began to take shape, Cagney walked out on his Warner's contract. In his place, the studio

Olivia de Havilland during a color check for one of her most famous films.

decided to use Flynn. Originally his costar was to have been Anita Louise, who also had been the first choice to team with him in *Captain Blood*. But the Flynn–de Havilland duo was fast becoming a fan favorite, so the studio decided to team them for a third time.

From the moment location shooting started in Bidwell Park, a huge forest 350 miles north of Hollywood, there were delays. Director William Keighley painstakingly set up the first scene—Robin's meeting with Little John—only to have fog roll in as they were about to start shooting. The fog remained for three days.

Once Flynn discovered the local watering holes in nearby Chico, there were more delays as the star showed up hung over and barely able to remember his lines. His misbehavior may have been a response to his thwarted romantic inclinations toward de Havilland. One night, he even stormed de Havilland's hotel room—in full costume. The actress and her stand-in had to enlist their neighbors to carry him off.

"Kneel and swear this oath: That you, the free men of this forest, swear to despoil the rich only to give to the poor, to shelter the old and the helpless, and to protect all women, rich or poor, Norman or Saxon. Swear to fight for a free England, to protect her loyalty until the return of our king and sovereign, Richard the Lionhearted. And swear to fight to the death against our oppressors."

—Errol Flynn brings revolution to Sherwood Forest in The Adventures of Robin Hood

To make matters worse, producer Hal Wallis was not happy with the footage coming back from location. He thought the action scenes lacked punch, and reportedly some of the scenes of Robin and his men in the woods looked to him like a gay camping trip. Slowly he began laying plans to replace Keighley with Michael Curtiz, who had already directed Flynn in *Captain Blood* and *Light Brigade*. By the time he made the switch, two months into shooting, the film was already fifteen days behind schedule.

Flynn reportedly was not happy with the change in directors. He had disliked Curtiz since they worked together on the actor's first Warner's film, *The Case of the Curious Bride*. He also was a good friend of Keighley's. When Curtiz showed up to direct his first scene, the banquet in Nottingham Castle, the star reportedly spit a mouthful of prop wine at him. Yet the filming moved along more quickly under Curtiz, and the picture was completed following a marathon session, three and a half months after shooting had begun.

The Adventures of Robin Hood was the studio's top moneymaker of the year. It established Flynn as a major box-office star, and was one of three films—the others were *Angels with Dirty Faces* and *Four Daughters*—that made Curtiz the top director on the lot.

An American in Paris

The Lion Roars in French

1951. CAST: Gene Kelly (Jerry Mulligan), Leslie Caron (Lise Bouvier), Oscar Levant (Adam Cook), George Guetary (Henri Baurel), Nina Foch (Milo Roberts). Producer: Arthur Freed; Director: Vincente Minnelli; Screenplay: Alan Jay Lerner; Photography: Alfred Gilks; Ballet Photography: John Alton (Technicolor); Musical Direction: John Green, Saul Chaplin; Music and Lyrics: George and Ira Gershwin. RUNNING TIME: 115 minutes.

When the British rock group ABC wanted to reach the MTV generation with "The Look of Love" in the early eighties, they modeled their video on the ballet from MGM's 1951 *An American in Paris*. The choice was natural. The musical number, which featured Gene Kelly and Leslie Caron dancing out their courtship in scenes inspired by the French Impressionist painters, had a look of love all its own.

An American in Paris was one of the most important musicals in MGM's history. The surprise Oscar winner showed just how far producer Arthur Freed had brought the genre in taste and style. Indeed, his work at MGM put the studio's musicals far ahead of the competition.

The idea for *An American in Paris* was born when Freed heard the piece at a 1949 concert. Gene Kelly had earlier suggested a film about an American GI who stays in Paris to paint after the war, and this seemed the perfect match of music and story. For $158,750, MGM picked up the rights to the title and other selections from the Gershwin catalog.

Most of the production team fell into place naturally. Kelly, of course, would star and choreograph. Vincente Minnelli, who had studied art in Paris and been a close friend of the Gershwins in New York, was tapped as director. And to costar as Kelly's acerbic sidekick, Freed picked another Gershwin friend, Oscar Levant, who had devoted much of his career as a concert pianist to Gershwin's music.

Production on the MGM backlot started before Minnelli, Freed, and Kelly had worked out all of the details for the "American in Paris" ballet. In fact, the rest of the film was completed almost a month before the ballet started shooting. Initially, MGM's executives balked at even approving the sequence. After all, the film worked perfectly well without it. And the ballet was budgeted at over $400,000,

Gene Kelly nurses his broken heart just before the "American in Paris" ballet.

enough to make a small-scale feature. But Freed had studio head Louis B. Mayer's backing, and Mayer convinced new production chief, Dore Schary, to get behind the ballet as well.

To help conceptualize the sequence, they hired costume designer Irene Sharaff. Minnelli had already decided to film the ballet in the style of such great painters as Renoir, Dufy, Van Gogh, and Toulouse-Lautrec. Sharaff listened to the original Gershwin piece repeatedly to determine which artist fit which part of the music best. Then, she created costumes and backdrops for each sequence.

The rehearsal and construction for the ballet took so much time that Minnelli was able to make another film in the interim, *Father's Little Dividend,* the sequel to his popular *Father of the Bride*. He then returned to film the "American in Paris" ballet. The final cost of the ballet sequence—$542,000.

Even the few critics who thought the rest of the film just another boy-meets-girl story were enthralled with the ballet. The fans loved it, too, to the tune of more than $8 million at the box office.

There was one more triumph in store for *An American in Paris,* however. When the Oscar nominations for 1951 came out, everybody was surprised to learn that the film had scored in eight categories. They were more surprised Oscar night when the picture won for Best Costumes, Best Adapted Score, Best Art Direction, Best Cinematography, Best Screenplay—there was even a special award for Kelly's choreography and the Irving G. Thalberg Award to Freed.

Surely that was it, everybody thought. It could never win Best Picture over such highly favored dramatic contenders as *A Streetcar Named Desire* or *A Place in the Sun*. Then, film pioneer Jesse Lasky opened the envelope and announced that *An American in Paris* had been voted Best Picture of 1951. There was an audible gasp from the audience, but nobody was more surprised than the people from MGM. The next day, they took out a trade ad to celebrate the victory with a picture of Leo the Lion saying, "Honestly, I was just standing in the sun waiting for a streetcar."

Director Vincente Minnelli and Gene Kelly.

THE WIT AND WISDOM OF OSCAR LEVANT (AS WRITTEN BY ALAN JAY LERNER)

***On character:* "It's not a pretty face, I grant you, but underneath its flabby exterior is an enormous lack of character."**

***On music:* "I'm a concert pianist. That's a pretentious way of saying I'm unemployed at the moment."**

***On the equality of the sexes:* "I told you this sponsoring business was complicated. See what happens today? Women act like men and want to be treated like women."**

Angels with Dirty Faces

"Let's Go Say a Prayer for a Boy Who Couldn't Run as Fast as I Could"

1938. CAST: James Cagney (Rocky Sullivan), Pat O'Brien (Jerry Connelly), Humphrey Bogart (James Frazier), Ann Sheridan (Laury Ferguson), George Bancroft (Mac Keefer), Billy Halop (Soapy), Leo Gorcey (Bim). Producer: Sam Bischoff; Director: Michael Curtiz; Screenplay: John Wexley, Warren Duff (Based on a story by Rowland Brown); Photography: Sol Polito; Music: Max Steiner. RUNNING TIME: 97 minutes.

The forces of good and evil locked in a battle over the souls of the young—it's a morality tale as old as storytelling itself. Yet when told well—and it is certainly well told in *Angels with Dirty Faces*—it has all the urgency of today's headlines.

Angels with Dirty Faces features James Cagney's best performance of the thirties: he won both an Oscar nomination and the New York Film Critics Award. But the role also mirrors the controversies at the heart of his career as a screen gangster. Just as childhood friend Father Connelly (Pat O'Brien) fights Cagney's influence over a group of street toughs (played by the Dead End Kids), so censors of the day feared that Cagney's hyperkinetic, very human gang leader would inspire younger viewers to crime. The battle still rages as congressional leaders ponder the alleged links between violent entertainment and violence in the real world.

The film starts with Rocky and Jerry as youngsters already involved in crime. When they flee from a robbery, Rocky gets caught because he is too slow. As a result, he becomes a career criminal, while Jerry takes up the priesthood and tries to reform their old neighborhood—including a teen gang whose members idolize Rocky. When the gangster is sentenced to die for murder, Jerry begs him to turn yellow at the end so the kids will stop looking up to him.

As perfect as the story was for the team of Cagney and O'Brien, who made eight films together, it was actually written as a vehicle for the Dead End Kids, a group of young actors who had made a popular debut in 1937's slum drama *Dead End* and would go on to star in several low-budget film series. When Warner's signed the kids in 1938, the studio asked writer Rowland Brown to create a story for them. But the finished product was so good, he decided he could get more for it elsewhere.

A crook at the top and a crook on the way up: Humphrey Bogart visits James Cagney.

Cagney joined the project when Brown sold the story to Grand National Pictures, where the star was making films during a brief walk-out from his Warner's contract. When Grand National went bust, Cagney returned to Warner's—and brought the story with him.

To play Rocky Sullivan, Cagney drew on his memories of growing up in New York's Hell's Kitchen. His chief inspiration was a drug-addicted pimp who stood on a street corner all day hitching his trousers, twitching his neck, and repeating, "Whadda ya hear! Whadda ya say!" It made for a great performance, but those mannerisms haunted Cagney. "I did those gestures maybe six times in the picture," he would write in his autobiography. "That was over thirty years ago—and the impressionists have been doing me doing him ever since."

The Dead End Kids were the terror of the set. They threw other actors off with their ad-libbing and once cornered costar Humphrey Bogart and stole his pants. But they hadn't reckoned with

James Cagney and Pat O'Brien (third and second from right) face the last mile together.

Cagney's street-bred toughness. The first time Leo Gorcey pulled an ad-lib on Cagney, the star stiff-armed the young actor right above the nose. From then on, the gang behaved.

The heated on-screen battle between Cagney and O'Brien was matched offscreen by the studio's battles with the censors. Under the Production Code, Warner's had to remove anything that made Rocky too glamorous or dramatized the means of committing crimes. Production Code head Joe Breen was particularly upset with the execution scene; he thought it made the character too heroic. Cagney and Curtiz played the scene ambiguously—an artistic choice, not just a sop to the censors. But that wasn't enough in some areas.

The Chicago censors cut Cagney and O'Brien's scene before the execution, so there was no other explanation but that Rocky had chickened out. Australia and New Zealand went even further, cutting the breakdown scene and the Dead End Kids' reaction to it. And with continuing controversy over gangster films around the world, the film was banned outright in Denmark, China, Poland, Finland, and parts of Switzerland and Canada.

The controversy could not keep people away from a movie they wanted to see, however. *Angels with Dirty Faces* was Cagney's highest grossing film to that time, with $1.7 million in profits.

EVOLUTION OF A BOWERY BOY

From troubled teens to overgrown adolescent clowns, the young actors who first entered filmmaking as the Dead End Kids in 1937 kept box offices hopping for more than two decades. At various times their membership included Billy Halop, Huntz Hall, and Gabriel Dell, but the force behind their later low-budget comedies was tough-talking Leo Gorcey. Here's a quick look at the line of descent from Dead End Kid to Bowery Boy:

1935—Dead End Kids created in Sidney Kingsley's social problem play **Dead End*****. Halop, Hall, Dell, and Gorcey team for the first time.***

1937—Screen debut in film version of **Dead End.**

1938–39—Six films for Warner Bros. as the Dead End Kids.

1938–43—Splinter group makes nine films for Universal as the Little Tough Guys.

1940–45—Another group makes twenty-two films at Monogram as the East Side Kids.

1946–58—With a new format partially engineered by Gorcey, The Bowery Boys make forty-eight films for Monogram.

The Band Wagon

"The World Is a Stage, the Stage Is a World of Entertainment"

1953. CAST: Fred Astaire (Tony Hunter), Cyd Charisse (Gaby Gerard), Oscar Levant (Lester Marton), Nanette Fabray (Lily Marton), Jack Buchanan (Jeffrey Cordova). Producer: Arthur Freed; Director: Vincente Minnelli; Screenplay: Betty Comden, Adolph Green; Photography: Harry Jackson (Technicolor); Musical Direction: Adolph Deutsch; Music and Lyrics: Howard Dietz, Arthur Schwartz; Choreography: Michael Kidd.

RUNNING TIME: 112 minutes.

World and stage mirrored each other a hundred times over in *The Band Wagon*, one of the four or five best musicals ever made at MGM. The plot was loosely inspired by the careers of star Fred Astaire and writers Betty Comden and Adolph Green. And just as the film depicted the physical and emotional chaos surrounding the production of a Broadway hit, its production was attended by physical and emotional suffering for almost everybody involved.

The Band Wagon started out as an attempt to duplicate the success of two previous Arthur Freed hits, *An American in Paris* and *Singin' in the Rain*. Each film had been written around the song catalog of a single composer—George Gershwin for the former and Freed himself for the latter. Third time out, the producer chose the works of another noted tunesmith, Arthur Schwartz, who, with MGM vice president Howard Dietz, had written some of the stage's wittiest musicals of the twenties and thirties.

Although Gene Kelly had scored personal triumphs in the earlier films, Freed knew that the material was better suited to another dancer on the MGM contract roster—Fred Astaire. In fact, Astaire had teamed with his sister, Adele, for the last time in the 1931 Dietz-Schwartz musical from which the film would take its name. That was just about all Freed gave writers Comden and Green to work with. The pair tried and rejected a number of story pegs before coming up with something that lit their creative fires. They would make *The Band Wagon* the ultimate "puttin' on a show" musical, drawing on their own experience working on Broadway and their knowledge of stage legend.

With that in mind, director Vincente Minnelli suggested that Comden and Green model the male

lead, Tony Hunter, on the Astaire of a few years earlier, when the star had considered retiring. But would Astaire go for it? To their pleasant surprise, he bought the concept and even suggested other ways the script could mirror his career.

Astaire was hardly the only model for the film's characters. Comden and Green based the Broadway impressario Jeffrey Cordova (Jack Buchanan) on José Ferrer, who had made headlines recently by producing four Broadway hits while starring in a fifth. They even drew on themselves to create the husband-and-wife writing team played by Nanette Fabray and Oscar Levant.

For leading lady, Freed and Minnelli decided it was time to give one of MGM's supporting

Fred Astaire, Nanette Fabray, and Jack Buchanan perform "Triplets."

A SHINE ON YOUR SHOES

Cyd Charisse was not Fred Astaire's only dancing partner in* The Band Wagon. *For his big number in the 42nd Street penny arcade, "A Shine on Your Shoes," he was joined by a tap-dancing bootblack. To cast the role, MGM went for the real thing. LeRoy Daniels's shoe shines were the hit of downtown Los Angeles because of the "boogie woogie" rhythms he gave every brushstroke. He was the perfect choice to work with Astaire, but it was not his first brush with the world of entertainment: Three years earlier his spirited approach to his craft had inspired a hit recording by Bing Crosby, "Chattanooga Shoe Shine Boy."

players a big break. Cyd Charisse had been at the studio since 1944, impressing most of the executives with her beauty and her balletic dancing. But that one big picture had eluded her.

First, however, she had to win Fred Astaire's approval. He had no problems with her dancing. But he was concerned that she might be too tall for him. On their first meeting, he surreptitiously got as close as possible so he could size her up. When he told Comden and Green what he'd done, they put the incident in the script.

Although *The Band Wagon* was conceived as frothy, lighthearted entertainment, the atmosphere on the set was anything but lighthearted. Astaire was nursing his wife through the illness that would eventually claim her life. Minnelli was consumed with worry about ex-wife Judy Garland's increasingly erratic behavior on the set of *A Star Is Born*. And Oscar Levant was recovering from a heart attack he had suffered just six weeks before shooting began. He required a stand-in for some scenes and had to be replaced by Buchanan in the strenuous "Triplets" number with Astaire and Fabray. To make matters worse, Levant masked his insecurities by constantly picking on Fabray.

None of this showed on screen, of course. What audiences saw was a witty, sophisticated musical containing all the elements that set Freed's musicals apart from standard Hollywood fare. The film featured some of Astaire's best numbers, including his romantic pas de deux with Charisse to "Dancing in the Dark" and the Mickey Spillane takeoff, "The Girl Hunt Ballet."

The latter was in the works for weeks, with choreographer Michael Kidd, Minnelli, Astaire, Charisse, and production designer Oliver Smith all involved in story conferences. The sequence took seven days to shoot—not as long as the "American in Paris" ballet, but a significant amount of time for a single musical number. Its cost represented $314,475 of the film's $2.1 million budget. But with box-office returns topping $5.6 million, nobody complained.

THE UNKINDEST CUTS

***The Band Wagon** has one of the most extensive scores of any screen musical—twenty numbers in all. But there could have been more. Here are the four complete numbers and one fragment that were shot, then cut for time purposes:*

"Sweet Music"—duet for Nanette Fabray and Oscar Levant, performed at the backers' audition.

"You Have Everything"—duet for Fred Astaire and Cyd Charisse as each practices in adjoining rehearsal rooms.

"Got a Bran' New Suit"—sung by Fabray, danced by Astaire in a sequence designed to show the development of a musical number. Ironically, after Astaire performs the number, he is informed that it has been cut from the show.

"Two-Faced Woman"—danced by Charisse to dubbed vocal track by India Adams. Later the vocal track was used for the Joan Crawford musical **Torch Song.**

"Telephone Duet"—danced by Astaire and Charisse as part of "The Girl Hunt Ballet," with the stars using movement to convey the essence of a telephone conversation.

Battleground

"Bastogne Must Be Taken"

1949. CAST: Van Johnson (Holly), John Hodiak (Jarvess), Ricardo Montalban (Rodrigues), George Murphy (Pop Stazak), Marshall Thompson (Jim Layton), James Whitmore (Kinnie), and the original "Screaming Eagles" of the 101st Airborne Division. Producer: Dore Schary; Director: William A. Wellman; Screenplay: Robert Pirosh; Photography: Paul C. Vogel; Music: Lennie Hayton. RUNNING TIME: 118 minutes.

When the Germans demanded surrender from the U.S. troops under siege at Bastogne in 1944, General Anthony C. McAuliffe made headlines around the world with his one-word reply: "Nuts!" MGM's new vice president in charge of production, Dore Schary, might have been tempted to issue the same terse rejoinder in the face of two different studio administrations opposed to his telling the GI's side of World War II.

Schary began work on *Prelude to Love,* a realistic story about American GIs in France, while serving as production chief at RKO. For writer, he picked Robert Pirosh, a World War II veteran whose infantry unit had helped raise the siege of Bastogne.

A research trip back to Bastogne, where he found an empty K-ration box he'd discarded three years earlier, gave Pirosh the idea of focusing the film almost entirely on the GIs. Schary loved the idea but had not reckoned with the more traditional tastes in Hollywood. When he tried to borrow Van Johnson and Ricardo Montalban from MGM for the film, executives there told him the script was a stinker. Then eccentric tycoon Howard Hughes bought RKO. One of his first corporate actions was to cancel production on the film, which by then had been retitled *Battleground.* That and other signs that Hughes would not let Schary run the studio his own way led the production executive to resign. Schary didn't ask for severance pay. All he wanted was the chance to buy the rights to *Battleground* after he resettled.

It didn't take him long to find a new home at MGM. The studio had been suffering under a management crisis since Irving G. Thalberg's death in 1936, and Nicholas Schenck—president of the studio's parent company, Loew's, Inc.—wanted to bring in some new blood, someone like Schary.

As vice president in charge of production, Schary's first official act was to purchase the rights to

John Hodiak and Van Johnson (both seated) survey the terrain.

Battleground. Again he met with opposition. Mayer thought people were tired of the war and would not pay to see a grimly realistic treatment of it. His concerns reached Schenck, who also tried to discourage the project. But Schary had already left one studio over *Battleground,* and he told them he wouldn't hesitate to leave another.

There was little star treatment during the filming of *Battleground*. To get the feel for their military roles, the actors were put through two weeks of basic training. Uniforms were issued, just as in the army. The actors lined up and took their chances. If it didn't fit, it didn't fit.

To complete the transformation of studio into combat zone, MGM secured the services of twenty paratroopers from the famed 101st Airborne Division, who had been at Bastogne. Not only did they train with the actors and serve as living research libraries, the soldiers also appeared in the film. Schary considered it a high compliment when Major General Laurence S. Kuter, head of the Berlin airlift, visited the set and said, "They all look alike to me. Which are the actors?"

THE WOMAN IN QUESTION

The only woman prominently featured in* Battleground *was French singer-actress Denise Darcel. Ironically, she was the only one of the film's stars to have experienced anything like the siege of Bastogne in real life. While still a teenager, she watched helplessly as the Nazis occupied her homeland and even took over the family house. Before long, she was part of the resistance, working in a department store by day and laboring in an underground munitions factory by night. She even used a job scrubbing floors for the enemy as a front for ferreting out secrets. In danger of being caught there, she escaped by locking herself in a bathroom and pretending to take a bath. Little wonder her performance was so strong that, after seeing her first scene, Wellman asked that the part be built up.

Director William A. Wellman shot the film in sequence and kept the production running with near military efficiency. He got a lot of help from the weather. For the first scene, which called for foggy countryside, Mother Nature obliged with an uncharacteristically overcast day. For the final scenes, in which the fog around Bastogne lifts so that the Air Force can drop much needed supplies and ammunition, there was a return to the sunny skies of Southern California.

As a result, the production came in days ahead of schedule and $100,000 under budget. But the savings were unnecessary. *Battleground* was MGM's biggest hit since the war, grossing $4.5 million on its initial release. It brought the studio its first Oscar nomination for Best Picture since 1946, with Oscars going to Pirosh's script and Paul C. Vogel's cinematography.

For the time, at least, the studio seemed to be back on its feet, and the siege on Dore Schary had been lifted. On the strength of *Battleground*'s success, Schary got approved for other projects that departed from MGM's glamorous tradition, including *The Asphalt Jungle, Intruder in the Dust,* and *The Red Badge of Courage*. The honeymoon would not last forever—Schary would be fired in 1956—but while it was on, it made for some great filmmaking.

MARCHING ONTO THE HIT PARADE

For a gritty wartime drama,* Battleground *scored a success in a surprising arena—the hit parade. During the war, America's GIs had developed a series of chants that kept them in step but avoided monotonous repetition of "Hut, two, three, four."* Battleground *was the first film to feature these marching songs—in an admittedly sanitized version—that eventually would become a staple of World War II movies. They even inspired a hit record.

SERGEANT: *They signed you up for the length of the war.*
TROOPS: *I never had it so good before!*
SERGEANT: *But the best you'll get on a bivouac—*
TROOPS: *Is a whiff of cologne from a passing WAC!*
SERGEANT: *Sound off!*
TROOPS: *One, two.*
SERGEANT: *Sound off!*
TROOPS: *Three, four.*
SERGEANT: *Cadence count!*
TROOPS: *One, two, three, four, one, two . . . three-four!*

Ben-Hur

The Intimate Epic

1959. CAST: Charlton Heston (Judah Ben-Hur), Jack Hawkins (Quintus Arrius), Stephen Boyd (Messala), Haya Harareet (Esther), Hugh Griffith (Sheik Ilderim), Martha Scott (Miriam). Producer: Sam Zimbalist; Director: William Wyler; Screenplay: Karl Tunberg (Based on the novel by Lew Wallace); Photography: Robert Surtees (Camera 65, Panavision, Technicolor); Music: Miklos Rozsa; Associate Directors: Andrew Marton, Yakima Canutt, Mario Soldati. RUNNING TIME: 212 minutes.

It may just have been the biggest gamble in Hollywood history. The once-great MGM, now in financial difficulties, put all its assets behind a single motion-picture epic. The budget started out twice that of the average film, ultimately reaching more than seven times the average. They entrusted the film to a director best known for intimate, personal dramas. And still they came out a winner!

MGM was in dire straits in the fifties due to the inroads of television and the Supreme Court decision that forced the major studios to sell off their theater chains. Nicholas Schenck, president of parent company Loew's, Inc., didn't seem to have the answers, so a corporate shake-up ended with Joseph R. Vogel at the helm. After looking at the success other studios were having with epic productions, he made a daring decision. MGM would put the bulk of its assets into the creation of the epic to end all epics.

Ben-Hur had been the hit that put MGM on the map back in 1925, but because of a complicated deal for the rights to Lew Wallace's mammoth novel, the film had actually lost money for the studio. Still, the box-office appeal of the plot, which combined the fictional story of rebellious Hebrew prince Judah Ben-Hur with the life of Christ, was undeniable.

Producer Sam Zimbalist, who had helped edit the silent version, was assigned to shepherd the production along. The obvious choice to direct would have been Cecil B. DeMille, who had just scored the biggest hit of his career with *The Ten Commandments*. Instead, Zimbalist went to William Wyler, the very serious director of such dramas as *Wuthering Heights* and *The Best Years of Our Lives*. Wyler, too, had a connection with the silent *Ben-Hur;* he had worked as an assistant director on the chariot race.

Charlton Heston fights to survive *Ben-Hur*'s famous chariot race.

Nobody was more surprised with the choice than Wyler himself, and initially he turned down the offer. Zimbalist assured him that spectacular scenes like the chariot race and the battle at sea would be handled by the second unit. He needed a director like Wyler to keep the human element in perspective, to make the film "Hollywood's first intimate epic," as Wyler would later call it.

Next came the quest to find the perfect Ben-Hur. Marlon Brando turned them down. Rock Hudson's home studio, Universal, did not want its biggest star tied up for almost a year on an outside picture. And Burt Lancaster decided that, as an atheist, he couldn't play the simple Christian story.

To play the villainous Messala, Wyler had cast Charlton Heston, whom he was currently directing in the western *The Big Country*. As other actors refused the film's title role, Wyler suggested that Heston switch roles, then badgered the MGM brass until they agreed.

Although the silent *Ben-Hur* had moved production from Rome to Hollywood to save costs, by the late fifties the opposite journey proved more economical. MGM took over the Cinecitta studios in Rome, spending a year to build the arena for the chariot race on eighteen acres of ground and constructing a small lake at one end of the filmmaking complex for the naval battles.

It took three months, on and off, to shoot the twenty-minute chariot race, which had a thirty-five-page script. Former stuntman Yakima Canutt trained Heston, Boyd, and the six stuntmen involved for six weeks before the cameras rolled. Initially, Heston was concerned about how he would look competing with experienced stuntmen in the race, but Canutt assured him, "Never you mind, Chuck. You just drive the chariot. I guarantee you'll win the damn race."

In fact, Heston did very well for himself in the race. Others on the production were less fortunate. Several people were felled during the Italian summer. Production manager Henry Henigson was forced to take a vacation in Capri to escape the stress of production. Worst of all, Zimbalist left the set one day complaining of chest pains. Twenty minutes later, he was dead. Production was so rushed at this point that there was only time for Wyler to deliver a brief eulogy before resuming shooting.

Finally on January 7, 1959, they finished the film. Two hours later, Heston and Wyler were on a plane to London for the British premiere of *The Big Country*. As they left the studio, Wyler's last official words to Heston were, "Well, thanks, Chuck. I hope I can give you a better part next time!"

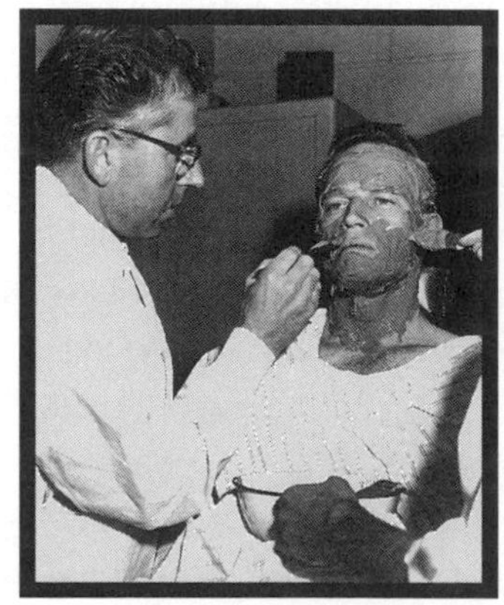

Charlton Heston in makeup.

With the picture finished, MGM's publicity department sprang into action. The cost of newspaper ads reached $1.5 million. Merchandising tie-ins included everything from toy swords and chariots for the kiddies to "Ben-His" and "Ben-Hers" towels, to Roman-style tiaras, to a Ben-Hur candy bar. By the time the film premiered on November 18, 1959, its title was a household word.

And the gamble had paid off—in spades. *Ben-Hur* was not just the top-grossing film of the year: Its $80 million in worldwide film rentals made it the second highest-grossing film of all time. That was more than enough to save the financially troubled studio.

When Oscar night rolled around, *Ben-Hur* became the all-time Oscar champ. Out of twelve nominations, the film won eleven awards, including Best Picture, Best Director, and Best Actor for Heston. As they stood backstage after the awards ceremony, Heston turned to his director, who had won previously for *Mrs. Miniver* and *The Best Years of Our Lives,* and said, "I guess this is old hat to you." "Chuck," Wyler replied, "it never gets old hat!"

The Big Parade

"The Whole Gang's Going Over!"

1925. CAST: John Gilbert (James Apperson), Renée Adorée (Melisande), Hobart Bosworth (Mr. Apperson), Claire McDowell (Mrs. Apperson), Claire Adams (Justyn Reed), Robert Ober (Harry), Karl Dane (Slim). Director: King Vidor; Screenplay: Harry Behn (Based on a story by Lawrence Stallings); Titles: Joseph W. Farsham; Photography: John Arnold; Music: William Axt, David Mendoza. RUNNING TIME: 141 minutes.

MGM's "boy wonder" vice president, Irving Thalberg, bucked the odds when he set out to create a realistic view of World War I. He even went against his boss and mentor, studio head Louis B. Mayer, to get the film done his way. It would not be the first time his tenacity paid off in a big way. With *The Big Parade* and *Ben-Hur* both released in 1925, MGM, in its first full year of operations, established itself as a major player in the filmmaking business. Not only did those films help establish MGM's reputation as "the Tiffany's of Hollywood studios," but Thalberg's commitment to getting things right, no matter what the cost, also earned the studio another nickname: "Retake Valley."

The Big Parade came about because one of Thalberg's most valued directors, King Vidor, was tired of churning out program pictures. When Vidor expressed his ambition to direct a film that would do more than just play a week and be forgotten, Thalberg asked him what subjects he thought were important. "War, wheat, or steel!" was Vidor's reply. With little faith in the cinematic potential of the latter two, Thalberg set out to find a great war story for his director.

The first possibility was *What Price Glory?*, the hit play by Maxwell Anderson and Lawrence Stallings. Thalberg was enthralled when he saw it on Broadway, but disappointed to learn that Fox Studios had already snapped up the rights. If he couldn't get the play, he thought, he could at least get one of the authors. So, he hired Stallings, who had based the story on his own experiences as a marine in World War I.

They took the train back to Hollywood together and used the cross-country trip to hammer out a five-page story. It would follow three men—a millionaire, a riveter, and a bartender—as they signed up for duty, traveled to France, cavorted with the locals, and then experienced the grim horrors of battle. The two working-class men would die in battle. The young millionaire would

Above: King Vidor (second from left) directs John Gilbert and Renée Adorée. *Right:* Renée Adorée and John Gilbert.

THE UNKINDEST CUTS

For all his faith in The Big Parade, *Irving Thalberg was not above a bit of judicious pruning to cut the running time. After the film was completed, he even ordered it recut without the director's approval. King Vidor was so appalled at this new version of his film that he searched the MGM Editing Department to find and restore the lost footage.*

Vidor also faced a hefty cut in his paycheck. His original contract for the film called for him to take a percentage of the profits. When Louis B. Mayer realized the film was a potential blockbuster, he did not want to share the wealth. So, he got the studio's lawyers to convince Vidor that the profits would not really be very big and offered him a lump payment instead. Later, Vidor realized that he could have been a millionaire, had he stuck to his original deal.

lose a leg, as Stallings had during the war.

To play the latter role, Thalberg cast MGM's hottest young romantic star, John Gilbert. But not without a struggle. Vidor had worked with Gilbert earlier and considered him "too sophisticated, too hard to handle." For his part, Gilbert was far from interested in playing a role that would require him to appear without makeup and without his trademark mustache. But Thalberg overruled their objections. He convinced Gilbert that the role was a good career move and on the first day of filming personally escorted his star to the set.

Thalberg also had to deal with objections from above. Mayer insisted that nobody would want to see a realistic depiction of the Great War and tried to block the film. But Thalberg went over his head to the management of MGM's parent company, Loew's, Inc., to get the project approved. As a result, the film triggered a rift between the two that would never heal.

But as filming continued, Mayer soon realized the picture's potential. Few sources agree on exactly how *The Big Parade* was upgraded from wartime romance to military epic, but at some point Mayer helped Thalberg win approval from MGM's New York management to increase the picture's budget from $200,000, an average cost for that period, to $382,000.

One boost to the film's authenticity was the strong presence of World War I veterans among the film's extras. As a result, Vidor did not need to send his cast into military training to look convincing as soldiers. They already were. This did make for one problem, however. After watching film of a wartime funeral, Vidor decided he wanted the march into the Belleau Woods to have the same deadly pace. He used a metronome to determine the pace of the funeral march, then had a drummer beat out the same tempo on the set, instructing the cast to make all their moves to the beat. This almost triggered a rebellion among the veterans in the cast, who thought he was turning their experiences into some kind of ballet. But Vidor got his way and created one of the most memorable battle sequences in film history.

Indeed, everything about *The Big Parade* was memorable. The film opened to critical acclaim and record attendance, playing six months at Grauman's Egyptian Theater in Hollywood and almost two years at the Astor Theater in New York. It ultimately grossed more than $15 million, making it not just MGM's most profitable silent film but, in the opinion of some historians, the most profitable silent of all time.

The Big Sleep

"A Lot Depends on Who's in the Saddle"

1946. CAST: Humphrey Bogart (Philip Marlowe), Lauren Bacall (Vivian Sternwood), John Ridgely (Eddie Mars), Louis Jean Heydt (Brody), Elisha Cook Jr. (Jones), Regis Toomey (Bernie Ohls), Martha Vickers (Carmen Sternwood), Dorothy Malone (Girl in Bookshop), Charles Waldron (General Sternwood). Producer-Director: Howard Hawks; Screenplay: William Faulkner, Jules Furthman, Leigh Brackett (Based on the novel by Raymond Chandler); Photography: Sidney Hickox; Music: Max Steiner. RUNNING TIME: 114 minutes.

One critic called it a new high in on-screen decadence and violence. Nobody—not even the original author—could figure out whodunnit to each of the story's seven murder victims. And the two stars were living through one of the worst crises in their lives. Yet with the right man in the saddle, producer-director Howard Hawks, *The Big Sleep* became a classic film noir and, in the eyes of many a critic, the definitive Warner Bros. thriller.

The movie came into being to satisfy Warner's need for a vehicle to reteam Humphrey Bogart and Lauren Bacall. The latter had made a sizzling screen debut opposite Bogie in Hawks's *To Have and Have Not*. The picture was so hot, a second match-up was inevitable.

The answer was *The Big Sleep,* in which private eye Philip Marlowe gets mixed up with the wealthy, decadent Sternwood sisters. Warner Bros. gave Hawks $50,000 for the rights, which ended up costing him only $5,000. He then assigned the script to William Faulkner—the great American novelist whose only other film credit was *To Have and Have Not*—and fledgling screenwriter Leigh Brackett.

Reshaping Chandler's novel for the screen proved a major challenge. To begin with, there was no suitable role for Bacall. Of the two Sternwood daughters, Carmen is the more vicious—a drug-addicted nymphomaniac who poses for pornographic photos, commits several of the book's murders, and, in her own father's description, likes to pull the wings off flies. This role would go to a recent Warner contract player named Martha Vickers. Carmen's sister, Vivian, twice divorced and once widowed—by her own hand—was the role the writers cleaned up for Bacall.

But Hawks still was not happy with the script, and he eventually wound up rewriting it on the set, which contributed to the picture's extended, seventy-six-day shooting schedule. At one point, production shut down for two days as everybody tried to figure out who had killed the Sternwood chauffeur. They even wired Chandler, but he didn't know either, writing back: "The butler did it!"

As the mystery unfolded before the cameras, the stars were going through turmoil in their private lives. Bogie and Bacall had fallen in love while shooting *To Have and Have Not*, but he was still married to actress Mayo Methot. The triangle remained unresolved as shooting began. Throughout production Bogart and Bacall repeatedly split up so that Bogie could give his alcoholic wife one more chance. Then they got back together in secret when they couldn't stand being apart. By the time production ended, the Bogart-Methot marriage was finished for good. Before *The Big Sleep* was released, Bogie and his Baby were man and wife.

Lauren Bacall

It helped, of course, that the picture sat on the shelf for almost a year. Immediately after completing *The Big Sleep*, Bacall made *Confidential Agent*, a film Warner executives decided to release first because of its war-related story. Unfortunately, Bacall's performance without Bogart and Hawks lacked the magic she had displayed in her screen debut. As damage control, Warner's decided to reshoot parts of *The Big Sleep* to emphasize the kind of insolent sexual banter the stars had played so well in *To Have and Have Not*. Several brief scenes between Bogart and the Sternwood butler were reshot with Bacall. A scene in Marlowe's office that nobody much liked was replaced by the famous

A HORSE IS A HORSE, OF COURSE, OF COURSE

***VIVIAN:** Well, speaking of horses, I like to play them myself—but I like to see them work out a little first, see if they're front-runners or come from behind, find out what their hole-card is, what makes them run.*

***MARLOWE:** Find out mine?*

***VIVIAN:** I think so.*

***MARLOWE:** Go ahead.*

***VIVIAN:** I'd say you don't like to be rated. You like to get out in front, open up a lead, take a little breather in the backstretch and then come home free.*

***MARLOWE:** You don't like to be rated yourself.*

***VIVIAN:** I haven't met anyone yet that could do it. Any suggestions?*

***MARLOWE:** Well, I can't tell till I've seen you over a distance of ground. You've got a touch of class, but I don't know how—how far you can go.*

***VIVIAN:** A lot depends on who's in the saddle. Go ahead, Marlowe. I like the way you work. In case you don't know it, you're doing all right.*

—HUMPHREY BOGART AND LAUREN BACALL IN THE BIG SLEEP

"horse-racing" scene, in which the detective and Vivian have a seductive conversation ostensibly about the sport of kings.

With these changes, the film was finally ready for release. Some wondered if they could get by with a mystery that barely made sense, but with *The Big Sleep,* style—and the cleverly handled suggestion that there was more going on sexually than met the eye—carried the day. The film proved another big winner for Warner's, Hawks, and Bogart, and it made Bacall one of Hollywood's top female stars.

Lauren Bacall and Humphrey Bogart get the drop on one of the film's many shady characters.

THE GIRL WHO PULLED THE WINGS OFF FLIES

For all Lauren Bacall's glamour, many critics consider Martha Vickers, who played the thumb-sucking murderess Carmen, the most striking actress in* The Big Sleep. *With reviewers comparing her to the young Bette Davis, her future should have been assured. But as would happen with many another talented actress, the timing was never right. The studio didn't realize the impact of her performance until it was too late. During the delay between* The Big Sleep's *filming and its release, Warner Bros. cast her as a virginal heiress in the musical* The Time, the Place, and the Girl. *From there, her roles got smaller and smaller. She made headlines by becoming Mickey Rooney's third wife, but with the decline in studio filmmaking, there just weren't many opportunities for her. She died in 1971 at the age of forty-six, one of many gifted actresses who somehow or other failed to conquer Hollywood.

The Blackboard Jungle

"One, Two, Three O'Clock, Four O'Clock Rock"

1955. CAST: Glenn Ford (Richard Dadier), Anne Francis (Anne Dadier), Louis Calhern (Jim Murdoch), Margaret Hayes (Lois Judby Hammond), John Hoyt (Mr. Wasnaki), Richard Kiley (Joshua Y. Edwards), Sidney Poitier (Gregory W. Miller), Vic Morrow (Artie West). Producer: Pandro S. Berman; Director-Screenplay: Richard Brooks (Based on the novel by Evan Hunter); Photography: Russell Harlan; Music: Charles Wolcott. RUNNING TIME: 101 minutes.

MGM embraced the new Hollywood of gritty realism and social problem pictures when it tackled juvenile delinquency in *The Blackboard Jungle.* A canny mixture of current affairs and old-fashioned plotting, the film scored heavily at the box office while igniting controversy among educators and censors alike. And just to add to the mix, it was the first Hollywood film to put the new rock 'n' roll music on its soundtrack, introducing Bill Haley and the Comets' rousing "Rock Around the Clock."

When Evan Hunter first published his novel about juvenile delinquency in an inner-city vocational school, some educators claimed he had exaggerated the problem. Others saw the book as a much-needed exposé of social ills. For MGM production chief Dore Schary, it provided yet another opportunity for the kind of moviemaking he loved most—a gripping story with great entertainment value that also took a stand on social issues.

He gave the film to writer-director Richard Brooks, a man who was no stranger to controversy. In fact, his first big splash in Hollywood had come when his novel *The Brick Foxhole,* about the murder of a homosexual, reached the screen as *Crossfire,* an exposé of anti-Semitism. Brooks had made his film-directing debut at MGM with the international thriller *Crisis* in 1950, but he had yet to tackle the kind of story that seemed best-suited to his talents—until *The Blackboard Jungle* came along.

Casting the students presented a special problem. Schary and Berman didn't want standard Hollywood juveniles, so they instructed Al Altman, MGM's East Coast talent executive, to find them some new faces. After hundreds of interviews, Altman screen-tested nine young men, from whom Berman and Brooks picked the six principal teen players, including Vic Morrow, Jameel

Farrah (who would later change his name to Jamie Farr), and Rafael Campos. All of the actors chosen for juvenile roles in *The Blackboard Jungle* were in their late teens or early twenties with one exception. Sidney Poitier, then thirty-one and already a veteran of such acclaimed films as *No Way Out* and *Cry, the Beloved Country,* had not even been considered for the film at first. Altman called him and asked him to recommend younger black actors to be interviewed. Poitier obliged, then weeks later was called in to discuss other possibilities for the role. When the actor arrived for the meeting, Altman admitted he had really wanted to see if Poitier still looked young enough to play a teenager. He did.

With a combination of stage-trained youngsters and experienced film actors like Glenn Ford, Louis Calhern, and John Hoyt, Brooks filmed *The Blackboard Jungle* in near-record time, particularly for MGM. Only three months passed between script completion and the film's premiere.

With the film's release, the debate over the story's accuracy and fairness was renewed with a vengeance. There was even an investigation of conditions at the Bronx Vocational High School because of rumors that the book had been based on Hunter's experiences as a substitute teacher there.

Equally hot was the question of whether or not films like *The Blackboard Jungle* should be exported. Along with several violent gangster pictures released at the same time, the movie had some politicians concerned that Hollywood was giving anti–U.S. propagandists ammunition. MGM dealt with the problem by adding a prologue to the film's international prints: "The scenes and events depicted here are fictional. The United States is fortunate in having a school system that is a tribute to its faith in youth."

That was not enough for U.S. Ambassador to Italy Clare Boothe Luce, however. Officials at the Venice Film Festival invited MGM to send *The Blackboard Jungle* for an out-of-competition screening. When Ambassador Luce got wind of this, she pressured the board to withdraw the invitation. Schary was outraged, and Loew's International president Arthur Loew lodged a complaint with the State Department, which disavowed any prior knowledge of her actions. But it was too late to get back into the festival.

Yet, ultimately, the controversy worked in the film's best interests. *The Blackboard Jungle* was already doing strong business domestically. With the free publicity generated by Ambassador Luce's protests, it went on to solid international business as well, topping the box office in Australia, Egypt, Hong Kong, Chile, and Belgium. By the end of its first release, it had returned well over $5 million at the box office, making it MGM's highest-grossing film since *Ivanhoe,* two years earlier.

ARE YOU NOW OR HAVE YOU EVER BEEN . . .?

The Blackboard Jungle *was a big break for Sidney Poitier, helping him land later roles in the features* Goodbye, My Lady *and* Something of Value. *He almost lost the chance when MGM's legal department asked him to sign a loyalty oath. The practice had evolved in reaction to the House Un-American Activities Committee's investigations of alleged Communist infiltration of the entertainment industry, but it did not sit well with the liberal young actor, so he postponed signing the oath, and nothing more was said.*

During filming, however, director Richard Brooks told him that the studio's front office had a complete dossier on the actor. Poitier's friendships with controversial black actors Paul Robeson and Canada Lee, and his work with Actors Equity to obtain equal treatment for black actors had branded him a subversive in some circles.

Sidney Poitier on his way to the head of the class.

Blow Up

"England Swings Like a Pendulum Do"

1966. CAST: David Hemmings (Thomas), Vanessa Redgrave (Jane), Sarah Miles (Patricia), Jane Birkin, Gillian Hills (Teenagers), Peter Bowles (Ron). Producer: Carlo Ponti; Director: Michelangelo Antonioni; Screenplay: Michelangelo Antonioni, Tonino Guerra, Edward Bond (Based on a story by Julio Cortazar); Photography: Carlo di Palma (Metrocolor); Music: Herbie Hancock, The Yardbirds. RUNNING TIME: 111 minutes.

When Italian director Michelangelo Antonioni received a special Oscar in 1995, viewers were treated to the astonishing spectacle of one of the world's most original filmmakers being applauded by studio executives who probably would be fired for trying to make pictures like his. For Antonioni is the master of ennui. His films make alienation tangible. Some find his work totally engrossing. Others have labeled it pretentious and boring. The controversy hit Hollywood in 1966 when MGM and Antonioni kicked off a three-picture deal with *Blow Up*.

The Italian director had started his career making documentaries in the forties, but if he drew any conclusions from his attempts to capture reality on film, it was that reality was essentially unknowable. He first hit the big time with *L'Avventura,* the story of a socialite's mysterious disappearance. When it premiered at the Cannes Film Festival, half of the audience stood up and cheered. The rest shouted their disapproval.

As Antonioni's star rose, Hollywood was looking for ways to survive competition from television. One thing they could not ignore was the popularity of foreign films on the art-house circuit. So MGM decided to take a chance on Antonioni.

For his first MGM film, Antonioni decided to adapt an Argentine short story called "Las Babas del Diablo." The plot centered on a fashion photographer (David Hemmings) who discovers a murder in the background of one of his pictures. When the film vanishes, he questions his own perceptions of reality.

On receiving the script, Hollywood's self-censorship bureau, the Production Code Administration, carped about several infractions. Two scenes seemed to call for nudity. The photographer

The depersonalized mod world of *Blow Up.*

THE CRITICS ARE NOT UNANIMOUS

"Antonioni, like his fashion-photographer hero, is more interested in getting pretty pictures than in what they mean. But for reasons I can't quite fathom, what is taken to be shallow in his hero is taken to be profound in him. Maybe it's because of the symbols: do pretty pictures plus symbols equal art?" —PAULINE KAEL, NEW REPUBLIC

"This movie seems to me one of the finest, most intelligent, least hysterical expositions of the modern existential agony we have yet had on film."

—RICHARD SCHICKEL, LIFE

*"**Blow Up** should not be dismissed as mere cheap-jack pornography (beautifully color-photographed). . . . It is degeneracy become militant. . . . Since the young lack the knowledge that humanity has gone through such amoral nihilism many times before, and always found it a form of suicide, both social and individual, the young, and primarily the intellectual young, will be damaged the most by it, and by the esthetic gabble with which perverts and the Left—what an unholy alliance that is—will seek to promote this cinematically worthless, and socially deleterious film."* —HENRY HART, FILM IN REVIEW

"Try to understand . . . this film has been made by one of the most intelligent Italian directors. It is an attempt to portray world society represented by its London manifestations. It is in a certain sense anticipatory to the life toward which humanity is advancing. Antonioni shows a deep humanity toward that which the Gospel calls 'sins against the Holy Spirit.' " —L'OSSERVATORE ROMANO

urged a fashion model writhing on the floor to "Make it come." Later, he watches a married couple make love, and the woman uses his presence to heighten her sexual response. Antonioni refused to make any changes, however. The world he had created on screen, in which total sensual satisfaction drove people to a state of ennui, was too important to the film as a whole. Nor did he have to alter the film. His contract with MGM gave him final cut.

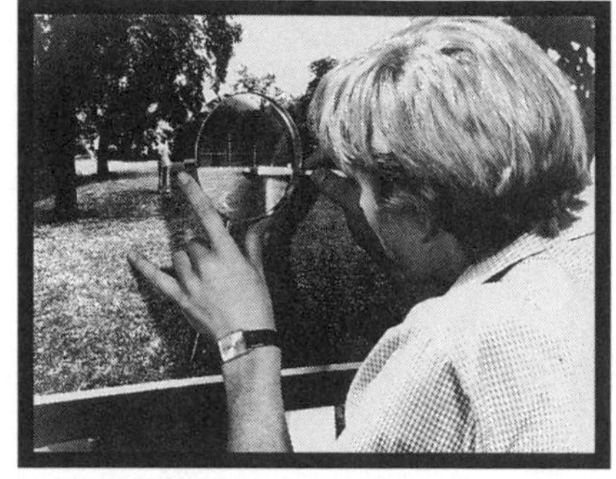

David Hemmings on the trail of mystery.

The Production Code Administration's refusal to approve *Blow Up* put MGM in a quandary. Although the days had passed when the Breen office (as it was called when run by the much stricter Joseph Breen) could keep a film out of first-run theaters, the major Hollywood studios, which were all members of the Motion Picture Association, still couldn't release a film without Code approval. So MGM released *Blow Up* through a subsidiary called Premiere Pictures.

This, however, was hardly the end of the censorship battles. *Blow Up*'s portrait of swinging London—it was the first Hollywood film with a modern orgy scene—brought it a condemned rating from the National Catholic Office of Motion Pictures (which had replaced the Legion of Decency) and an obscenity trial in Antonioni's native Italy (the censors lost). Cuts demanded by the censors in Argentina, where the original story was written, were so extensive that MGM refused to release the film there.

At the same time, however, the film picked up some powerful defenders among the clergy. The Vatican's daily paper, *L'Osservatore Romano,* gave the picture a glowing front-page review. A Presbyterian minister in Brooklyn even took his parishioners to see the film in lieu of his Sunday morning sermon.

When the film previewed in Los Angeles, it was met with open hostility. The trade paper *Variety* predicted that MGM would find *Blow Up* a big bust, and the studio was ready to dump the picture in art-houses and college towns. But instead the film turned out a surprise winner, grossing $7 million in the U.S. alone. The cost was only $1.6 million.

Blow Up eventually became Antonioni's most profitable film, but it did not trigger a major American career for the Italian director. The second film in his three-picture deal with MGM was *Zabriskie Point,* a notorious box-office loser often derided as one of the worst movies ever made. There was no third film. Antonioni returned to Italy, where he made fewer, but better, films, including *The Passenger,* with Jack Nicholson. But for all of the acclaim they drew, none of his later films has had the impact of the scandalous, confusing, and often quite brilliant *Blow Up*.

Boys Town

"There's No Such Thing as a Bad Boy"

1938. CAST: Spencer Tracy (Father Edward Flanagan), Mickey Rooney (Whitey Marsh), Henry Hull (Dave Morris), Leslie Fenton (Dan Farrow), Addison Richards (The Judge), Bobs Watson (Pee Wee). Producer: John W. Considine Jr.; Director: Norman Taurog; Screenplay: John Meehan, Dore Schary (Based on a story by Dore Schary and Eleanore Griffin); Photography: Sidney Wagner; Music: Edward Ward.

RUNNING TIME: 96 minutes.

The great films of Hollywood's Golden Age have maintained their hold on audiences for decades, but only a handful of them can still make headlines more than fifty years after their premieres—*Gone With the Wind, The Wizard of Oz, Citizen Kane,* and *Casablanca* among them. *Boys Town* joined that list in 1994, following a surprising turnabout on the American political scene.

With the landslide that gave the Republican Party control of both the House and the Senate, Georgia congressman and Speaker-elect Newt Gingrich was in the news, particularly in opposition to welfare. One solution Gingrich proposed for dealing with the rising tide of illegitimate births among low-income families was a return to orphanages. And his ideal was Boys Town, the Nebraska home for delinquent boys founded by Father Edward Flanagan. But it was not so much the Boys Town in Nebraska he claimed as inspiration, as the one created in Hollywood for MGM's classic 1938 biography of Father Flanagan.

In many ways, *Boys Town* was a blockbuster after the fact. When a secretary at MGM suggested Father Flanagan's crusade might make a good film, nobody at the studio expected anything special. The project was given an average budget for the period, $800,000, and put on the assembly line for the standard two-month shooting schedule. Of course, what was average for MGM was pretty high-toned by most other standards. Even on a relatively low budget, the studio allowed for an unprecedented three weeks of location work at the real Boys Town, at a time when most films were shot on studio back lots.

Spencer Tracy was Father Flanagan's immediate choice for the starring role, though the assignment frightened the actor so much that he turned it down and went on a three-day bender. Tracy's father had always wanted him to become a priest. Although he had played one successfully in *San Francisco* (1936), it had brought up a lot of guilt about disappointing his dad. Now he was confronted with playing not just a priest, but one of the most famous and revered priests in the world. It took several meetings with Flanagan to convince Tracy that he could do justice to the role.

To play someone he considered "the greatest man I ever met," Tracy pared away all of his actor's tricks and mannerisms. On the set, he spent most of his time discussing religious issues with the film's technical advisor, Father John O'Donald. The result was a simple, sincere performance that helped make Tracy one of the screen's most popular actors and put him on the annual list of top box-office stars for the first time in his career.

At Oscar time, Tracy was an obvious nominee for Best Actor, but there was some doubt as to whether or not he would win. He had won the year before for *Captains Courageous,* and this time out his friend James Cagney seemed to be the favorite for *Angels with Dirty Faces*. But win he did, becoming the only performer to win back-to-back Best Actor Oscars until Tom Hanks duplicated the feat in 1993 and 1994 (Luise Rainer still holds the distaff record with Best Actress trophies in 1936 and 1937). Tracy gave a generous acceptance speech, crediting his success entirely to the influence of Father Flanagan: "If you have seen him through me, then I thank you."

In the thirties, the ballots were counted in time for the winners' names to be engraved on the awards. They must have been a little rushed that year, because the name on the statue was "Dick Tracy." When the real Tracy returned the award to have it corrected, an overzealous press agent at MGM announced that the star was having it engraved to Father Flanagan and would donate the trophy to Boys Town. This announcement did not please Tracy, however. "I won it, I want to keep it," he protested. To save face, the studio convinced the Academy to issue a second Oscar so that they could send one to the orphanage and have another for the star.

THE SPEAKER SPEAKS—NEWT GINGRICH ON BOYS TOWN

What We Can Learn from Father Flanagan: "You have to love people enough to want to change them, not just feel their pain."

On the Film's Underlying Morality: "If you had no spiritual sense of yourself, if you didn't think you were endowed by your creator, no wonder you became a criminal or an addict or an alcoholic."

On the Message It Has for Today's Audience: "Government, by its own internal definitions, can't be a friend. So you have to ask yourself, when you see these children on the evening news, how are we going to build a system where once again they have a friend? That's an important question that comes out of Boys Town."

Top: Mickey Rooney runs afoul of Spencer Tracy once again. *Bottom:* Bobs Watson and Mickey Rooney.

THE WAGES OF FAME

One would think the success of Boys Town would have given Father Flanagan's home for delinquent boys invaluable free publicity, but, for a while, the film actually hurt the charity, triggering a major drop in donations. Flanagan blamed the decline on the picture's image of a prosperous, thriving Boys Town. Viewers thought the home was doing so well that it didn't need any help. As contributions continued to decline, Louis B. Mayer took to the airwaves to solicit funds for Flanagan's dream: "Boys Town does need your money, so keep it coming, Americans."

Bringing Up Baby

"I've Just Gone Gay—All of a Sudden!"

1938. CAST: Katharine Hepburn (Susan Vance), Cary Grant (David Huxley), Charles Ruggles (Major Horace Applegate), May Robson (Aunt Elizabeth), Barry Fitzgerald (Mr. Gogarty), Walter Catlett (Constable Slocum), Asta (George, the Dog), Nissa (Baby, the Leopard). Producer-Director: Howard Hawks; Screenplay: Dudley Nichols, Hagar Wilde (Based on a story by Hagar Wilde); Photography: Russell Metty; Music: Roy Webb.

RUNNING TIME: 102 minutes.

Bringing Up Baby has become so ingrained a part of our movie-made culture as one of the funniest films ever, that it's hard for today's audiences to believe it was actually a bust at the box office. Or that Katharine Hepburn's expert playing of the picture's screwball heroine marked her first out-and-out comic role. Or that any actor, much less six of Hollywood's most talented stars, would have said no to the costarring role eventually played by Cary Grant.

The film was a last-ditch effort by RKO Studios to broaden Hepburn's appeal to the moviegoing public. She had burst on the scene with moving, distinctive performances in *A Bill of Divorcement* (1932) and *Little Women* (1934), but after a flurry of publicity and an Oscar for *Morning Glory,* she had alienated fans with her eccentric off-screen behavior, strange script choices, and sometimes mannered acting.

Then Hepburn scored a surprise hit in *Stage Door,* which demonstrated her flair for comedy, so production head Pandro S. Berman decided to put her into *Bringing Up Baby* with director Howard Hawks, a master of fast-paced comedy.

The part of the ineffectual paleontologist did not seem strong enough for most Hollywood leading men. Ronald Colman, Leslie Howard, Fredric March, Ray Milland, and Robert Montgomery all said no. So did Cary Grant at first, claiming that he just did not understand how to play such a role. He changed his mind when Hawks suggested that he model his performance on bespectacled silent screen comic Harold Lloyd and play the man as an "innocent abroad."

Initially, Hawks had trouble communicating with Hepburn. The problem was her approach to comedy. In early scenes, she took the whole thing as a lark, often laughing at her own imagined

Cary Grant with his two favorite sets of bones. The one with skin is Katharine Hepburn.

STALKING LEOPARDS IN WILDEST HOLLYWOOD

The title role in **Bringing Up Baby** *was played by a film star as professional and experienced as either of her two costars. Nissa, the leopard who played Baby, had been nursed during infancy by trainer Madame Olga Celeste. The animal even played hide-and-seek with its owner. But tame as Nissa seemed, the studio wasn't taking any chances. Several of Nissa's key scenes were process shots created in the editing room. If you look closely at the scene in which Hepburn drags the wild leopard into the jailhouse, you will notice that the rope she's holding doesn't always move the same way as the rope around the leopard's neck.*

For some scenes, however, the cat had to be filmed with the actors. Most of the cast was terrified of her, except for Hepburn. Just to keep on the safe side, the star had her shoes coated with resin so she wouldn't slip and startle Nissa with any unexpected movements. But she also wore a perfume that Madame Celeste had advised would make the animal more playful. When Nissa's role was completed, her trainer told the press, "I think if Miss Hepburn should ever decide to leave the screen, she could make a very good animal trainer. She has control of her nerves."

cleverness. Hawks tried to explain the need for a more serious approach, but he just couldn't get through to her. Finally, he suggested she consult with comic Walter Catlett, an old friend of his. Catlett saw the problem immediately and acted out one of her scenes with Grant—played dead serious. Not only did Hepburn get the point, she insisted that Hawks write Catlett into the film, so he would be around to help her.

Hawks encouraged improvisation from his cast. When Hepburn broke a heel during one scene, she quickly added the line, "I was born on the side of a hill." Grant even got one by the Production Code censors that way. At one point, he is forced to wear a woman's negligee. Hepburn's aunt (May Robson) asks him if he dresses like that all the time. The script called for a simple denial: "I don't own one of these." But Grant's improvised, "I've just gone gay—all of a sudden!" marked Hollywood's only on-screen use of the word "gay" in a sexual context until the sixties.

But for all the gaiety on screen, there was little in the RKO executive suites. The studio heads did not understand the film at all. They asked for more romance and less slapstick, and they demanded that Grant stop hiding behind the character's glasses. With the film completed, they even contemplated shelving it.

At the time, the executives seemed right. Despite glowing reviews from some sources, the picture lost $365,000. Part of the problem was Hawks's perfectionism. His attention to detail had pushed the budget over the $1 million mark at a time when the average picture cost $800,000.

As a result of *Bringing Up Baby*'s poor box office, RKO fired Hawks, handing his next project, *Gunga Din,* to George Stevens. Hepburn decided to buy out her contract, eventually returning to Broadway to rebuild her career.

But that was hardly the end for *Bringing Up Baby*. With the sale of the film to television in the fifties and the rise of repertory cinemas in the sixties, new generations discovered it. By that time, the Hollywood romanticism of the thirties had been tempered by a more realistic approach, and moviegoers could appreciate *Bringing Up Baby* for what it was—one of the most outrageously funny films ever made.

WHAT'S UP, BABY?

With* Bringing Up Baby*'s continued popularity, imitation was inevitable. Director Peter Bogdanovich was only too happy to acknowledge the film's influence on his own* What's Up, Doc?** *In fact, the critic-turned-director, had shown early rushes to Howard Hawks, who advised him to screen* Bringing Up Baby** for stars Barbra Streisand and Ryan O'Neal so that they could learn how to play farce seriously. Hawks was delighted with the homage to his work, but scolded Bogdanovich for admitting that he stole* What's Up, Doc?** from the earlier film: "I never told 'em where I stole it from."

Cabin in the Sky

Taking a Chance

1943. CAST: Ethel Waters (Petunia Jackson), Eddie "Rochester" Anderson (Little Joe), Lena Horne (Georgia Brown), Louis Armstrong (The Trumpeter), Rex Ingram (Lucius/Lucifer Jr.), Kenneth Spencer (Rev. Green/The General). Producer: Arthur Freed; Director: Vincente Minnelli; Screenplay: Joseph Schrank (Based on the play by Lynn Root, John Latouche, and Vernon Duke); Photography: Sidney Wagner; Musical Adaptation: Roger Edens; Musical Director: Georgie Stoll; Music and Lyrics: John Latouche and Vernon Duke, E. Y. Harburg and Harold Arlen.

RUNNING TIME: 100 minutes.

The MGM musical took a major leap forward in 1943 when Arthur Freed put his musical production unit behind a stage show that had scored with the critics, if not with audiences. *Cabin in the Sky* was notable as only the second all-black feature in MGM history (the first was 1929's *Hallelujah*). It marked the film debut of one of the screen's greatest musical directors, Vincente Minnelli. In addition, the intelligence with which Freed and Minnelli approached the picture pointed to the type of imaginative, sophisticated musicals that would soon become MGM's stock in trade.

With the start of World War II, many producers and writers saw better treatment of African Americans on screen as a way of helping the country pull together behind the war effort. For Freed, the answer was to produce an all-black musical. When George Gershwin's folk opera *Porgy and Bess* proved unavailable, he turned to *Cabin in the Sky*, which had run for six months on Broadway. Despite a strong score, including "Taking a Chance on Love," the production only made a profit because of the price MGM paid for the film rights.

Freed had brought Minnelli to Hollywood in 1940 to train the young stage designer and director for film. After offering advice on other pictures, Minnelli was ready to make a picture of his own. But despite the promise Minnelli had already shown, Freed still had to fight to get him assigned to *Cabin in the Sky*. For insurance, he assigned a more experienced director, Andrew Marton, to help him with his first feature.

Minnelli and Freed turned to the team of E. Y. Harburg and Harold Arlen, who had worked on

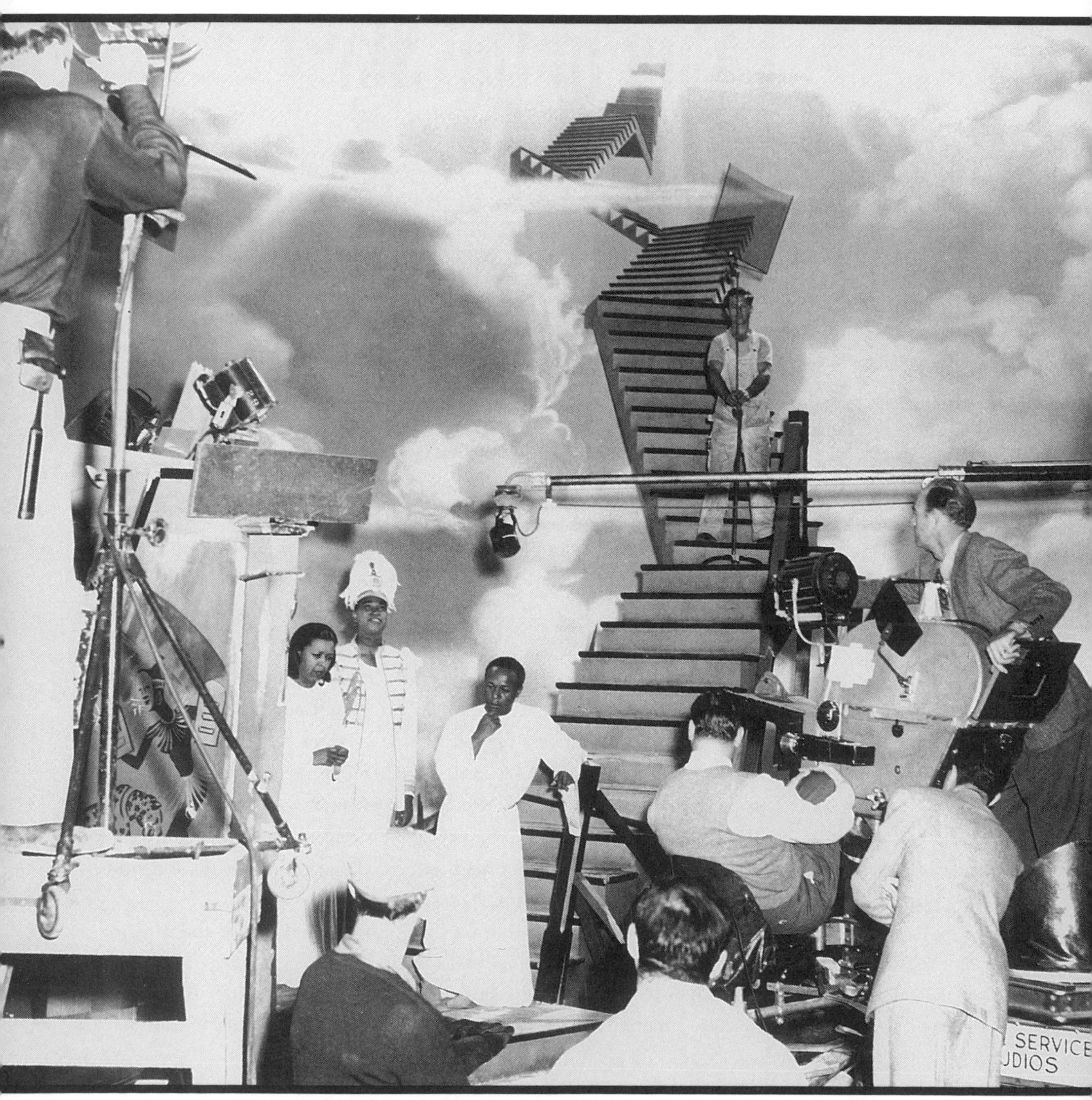

Filming one of the fantasy sequences, with Ethel Waters, Kenneth Spencer, and Eddie "Rochester" Anderson.

The Wizard of Oz, to add some new songs to the score. One of them, "Happiness Is a Thing Called Joe," became the biggest hit of the picture.

Ethel Waters was the only choice for the role of Petunia, who tries to keep her husband on the straight-and-narrow. She had scored a triumph in the role on Broadway, despite the fact that she'd originally turned it down because she didn't like the play's treatment of religion or the limited size of her role.

To play Georgia Brown, whom the Devil hires to lead Petunia's husband astray, Minnelli cast his protégée Lena Horne. Horne had arrived at MGM a year earlier, but her only appearances had been brief "guest-star" roles. With her sensual song stylings, she was the first black woman in a major studio film to be presented as a sex symbol.

But Horne's casting caused problems on the set. Her friends had warned her that Waters had trouble relating to other women, particularly if she saw them as competition. That had posed no problem on Broadway, where Georgia had been a dancing role. Now there was another female singer threatening to steal Petunia's thunder. During one of their first scenes together, Horne hurt her foot. When Waters decided her rival's injury was getting too much attention, she staged a memorable tantrum. After that the two women would not even speak to each other.

None of those problems interfered with the film's success. The picture won rave reviews, though the trade papers noted the commercial problems of releasing an all-black film during an era of continuing racial prejudice. For all the on-screen quality, however, Freed had kept the cost down to around $600,000, admittedly by underpaying most of the black cast. As a result, it still made a profit, despite a modest domestic return of $1.6 million.

Although the film did not trigger a spate of all-black films, it did a great deal to bolster Horne's screen career. In addition, *Cabin in the Sky* started Minnelli's rise to the top at MGM. After the minor Red Skelton musical *I Dood It,* he would direct the first of his truly great pictures, *Meet Me in St. Louis.* That movie would fulfill the promise of *Cabin in the Sky,* helping make MGM's musicals the best in Hollywood.

BREAKING THE COLOR BARRIER

Before **Cabin in the Sky,** *the major studios had produced only three other films with all-black casts:*

Hallelujah (MGM, 1929)—*King Vidor directed this pioneering black musical, which, like* **Cabin in the Sky,** *featured an allegorical story about the struggle between good and evil. To get studio approval for the film, Vidor had to lay his salary on the line.*

Hearts in Dixie (Fox, 1929)—*Billed as the first "All-Shuffling, All-Coonshouting Musical," this imitation of* **Hallelujah** *starred Stepin Fetchit and Clarence Muse.*

The Green Pastures (WB, 1936)—*The film version of Marc Connelly's Pulitzer Prize–winning retelling of Old Testament stories, with Rex Ingram as "de Laud," ignited protests from the black community over its stereotyped images.*

Camille

"I Always Look Well When I'm Near Death"

1937. CAST: Greta Garbo (Marguerite), Robert Taylor (Armand), Lionel Barrymore (Monsieur Duval), Elizabeth Allen (Nichette), Jessie Ralph (Nanine), Henry Daniell (Baron de Varville). Producer: Irving G. Thalberg; Director: George Cukor; Screenplay: Zoe Akins, Frances Marion, James Hilton (Based on the novel and play *La Dame aux Camelias* by Alexandre Dumas fils); Photography: William Daniels; Music: Herbert Stothart. RUNNING TIME: 108 minutes.

Death was never far from the set of MGM's *Camille*. Not only did the title character die in the end (a normal occurrence for Greta Garbo's heroines), but the director's mother and the producer passed away during filming. Earlier the star had lost a sister to tuberculosis, the same disease that would end her character's life. Far from hindering the production, however, the presence of death enhanced the emotional resonance of a film that would become one of Garbo's and the studio's crowning triumphs.

MGM production chief Irving G. Thalberg had been a devoted fan of Alexandre Dumas's *La Dame aux Camelias* since he read the novel at the age of twelve. He had even checked a medical encyclopedia to see if his own delicate health might be the result of tuberculosis.

The project was first broached as early as 1933, shortly after Garbo had finished filming *Queen Christina*. When the star fell ill on a trip home to Sweden, the film was postponed, not starting production until 1936. But the time was well spent working out problems with the script.

At least nine writers took a stab at the script, including *Grand Hotel* author Vicki Baum and Garbo's sometime lover Mercedes de Acosta. Among the problems they had to deal with were deemphasizing the material rewards of Marguerite's life of sin and making the hero's father a believable—rather than laughable—voice of morality. The final script was credited to Zoe Akins, Frances Marion, and James Hilton.

Director George Cukor had met Garbo only a few times before taking on the assignment of directing her in *Camille*. He had not been all that impressed with her, telling friends that he found her pretentious and self-consciously gloomy. Other directors cautioned him that the only way to

Director George Cukor confers with Greta Garbo.

THE MAN THAT ALMOST GOT AWAY

George Cukor almost didn't get a chance to finish making* Camille. *Shortly after his mother's death, the director, who usually kept his private life quite private, was arrested for propositioning a young man on the street. But no morals charge was strong enough to keep MGM from turning out a film a week, so the studio's legal department got the charges dropped while the publicity department kept them out of the papers. They did such a good job that, years later, Cukor's biographers found no official record of the incident, although almost everybody who was in Hollywood at the time remembered hearing of it.

survive a picture with her was to get tough early and stay that way. But toughness was not exactly in the director's vocabulary.

After only a few days of shooting, Thalberg congratulated Cukor for getting more out of Garbo than any other director had. Cukor couldn't understand the praise; they had only done a few simple shots of her sitting in a theater box. When he ran some of her earlier films and then looked at his footage again, he realized that there was a difference. With other directors, Garbo always had seemed a little guarded, aloof from the characters she played. With Cukor, she was more relaxed and totally open. Before, her work had been merely excellent. In *Camille,* it was great.

Tragedy struck the set twice during filming. First, Cukor's mother died of stomach cancer shortly before he had to film Marguerite's death scene. Although terribly affected by his mother's passing, that did not stop the director from using his observations of her last days as a source of details for Garbo's death scene. Shortly after that, Thalberg died of pneumonia. Again, this was a great blow to Cukor, who respected the boy wonder more than any other producer. He had even called Thalberg the only Hollywood producer who was an artist in his own right.

Camille's premiere was a triumph for almost everyone involved. Garbo made a rare public appearance for the film's Hollywood bow as a gesture of respect to Thalberg. Even those critics who had previously seemed immune to her charms hailed her work as superior acting, on a par with that of the great ladies of the stage. There were even fans who swore that, when Marguerite died, they saw Garbo's soul leave its body. She won her third Oscar nomination for the role (losing to Luise Rainer in MGM's *The Good Earth*) and her second Best Actress award from the New York Film Critics Circle (her first had been for *Anna Karenina*).

A BOUQUET OF CAMILLES ON SCREEN

Sarah Bernhardt (1912)

Clark Kimball Young (1915)

Theda Bara (1917)

Nazimova (1920, with Rudolph Valentino as Armand)

Pola Negri (1921, in German)

Norma Talmadge (1927, with Gilbert Roland as Armand)

Yvonne Printemps (1934, in French)

Teresa Stratas (1982, opera* La Traviata*, filmed in Italy)

Greta Scacchi (1984, for television)

Captain Blood

In Like Flynn

1935. CAST: Errol Flynn (Dr. Peter Blood), Olivia de Havilland (Arabella Bishop), Lionel Atwill (Colonel Bishop), Basil Rathbone (Captain Levasseur), Ross Alexander (Jeremy Pitt). Producer: Hal B. Wallis; Director: Michael Curtiz; Screenplay: Casey Robinson (Based on the novel by Rafael Sabatini); Photography: Hal Mohr, Ernest Haller; Music: Erich Wolfgang Korngold. RUNNING TIME: 119 minutes.

Warner Bros. found an actor who seemed born to buckle his swash when the studio cast relative newcomer Errol Flynn in its first big-budget costume adventure. Before moving into acting—as the screen's first Fletcher Christian in the Australian film *In the Wake of the Bounty*—Flynn had worked as a prospector in the South Pacific, a plantation manager in New Guinea, and a sailor. No wonder he seemed such a perfect choice, even if *Captain Blood* was only his fifth film.

During the early thirties, Warner Bros. was just about the last Hollywood studio you'd expect to produce a lavish eighteenth-century epic. Not only was it best know for topical dramas "torn from the day's headlines," but also the management was distinctly opposed to historical films, having suffered through several costly disasters in the past. As other studios scored with period pieces like *Treasure Island* and *The Count of Monte Cristo,* however, Warner's finally decided to follow suit. They already owned the screen rights to Rafael Sabatini's novel, which had been filmed by Vitagraph in 1924, so it seemed a natural choice.

Their first pick for the title role was Robert Donat, the English actor who had just scored a hit in *The Count of Monte Cristo*. Sources differ as to why Donat turned the film down. The official story was that he suffered from asthma and feared a recurrence should he undertake the strenuous role. Others suggest that either he could not reach terms with the notoriously cheap Jack Warner or he did not want to leave his mistress behind in London.

Just about everybody on the lot claims credit for casting Flynn in *Captain Blood*. According to Jack Warner, Flynn's wife, Lili Damita, urged him to test the actor. Production chief Hal Wallis claimed he got the idea from his sister Minna, who happened to be Flynn's agent. And Curtiz said

Two stars—and a great screen team—are born: Errol Flynn and Olivia de Havilland.

"His sword carved his name across the continents—and his glory across the seas!"

—AD LINE FOR CAPTAIN BLOOD

that he had spotted the actor's potential when he directed him as a corpse in the Perry Mason mystery *The Case of the Curious Bride*.

By the time somebody actually suggested Flynn for the role, they already had test footage of him as Blood. Like most beginning actors, Flynn earned his keep playing opposite other performers being considered for film roles. He had tested in scenes from *Captain Blood* with Jean Muir, Anita Louise, and Olivia de Havilland. In fact, he may have helped newcomer de Havilland win the role. When he tested with the other actresses, he hardly looked at them, distracting them so much they could barely remember their lines. But he was entranced with the nineteen-year-old de Havilland, giving her his full attention.

With other options exhausted, Warner decided the property was so strong that it could support two newcomers, and Flynn won the role. Hedging his bets, however, he reduced the budget from $1 million, as originally planned, to just $700,000.

Flynn started the film on his best behavior, but before long he started showing up late and hung-over from all-night drinking bouts with his friends or fights with his wife. Curtiz, whose mangled, Hungarian-accented English was a standing joke on the lot, would scream at him, "I picked you up from a corpse and made you a hero. And now from a hero I'll put you back to a corpse, and you'll be a bum again."

As it was, Curtiz did his part in contributing to the production delays. He was notorious for his slow working methods, particularly on action scenes. When the director persisted in shooting extra angles of the battles at sea, even though everything else had been completed, Wallis shut the film down. By then, the budget had climbed to $995,000.

Warner's made the money back in no time, however, once the fans discovered their new hero. *Captain Blood* made a $900,000 domestic profit, $1.5 million with international rentals added. In addition, the studio had a new star, with critics hailing Flynn as the successor to Douglas Fairbanks Sr.'s crown as the screen's great swashbuckler. Flynn's success helped all involved with *Captain Blood*. He and de Havilland would team for seven more films. And though the director never learned to pronounce his name, always calling him "Earl Fleent," Curtiz would work with him ten more times.

THE WRONG SCORE

Composer Erich Wolfgang Korngold started a long association with Warner Bros. in 1935 when he adapted Felix Mendelssohn's incidental music to* A Midsummer Night's Dream *for the studio's only foray into Shakespearean territory.* Captain Blood *was to have been his first original film score, but the rushed production schedule left him only three weeks in which to compose it. When the studio needed still more music, they cribbed a bit of Franz Liszt to fill in the gap. Outraged, Korngold insisted his credit be changed from "Music by" to "Musical Arrangements by," even though he had written the vast majority of the score.

Captains Courageous

"My God! It's Harpo Marx!"

1937. CAST: Freddie Bartholomew (Harvey), Spencer Tracy (Manuel), Lionel Barrymore (Disko), Melvyn Douglas (Mr. Cheyne), Charles Grapewin (Uncle Salters), Mickey Rooney (Dan). Producer: Louis D. Lighton; Director: Victor Fleming; Screenplay: John Lee Mahin, Marc Connelly, Dale Van Every (Based on the novel by Rudyard Kipling); Photography: Harold Rosson; Music: Franz Waxman. RUNNING TIME: 116 minutes.

Leo the Lion took to the seas for this atypical nautical adventure. Not only were there no roles for the studio's stable of female stars, but the gentlemen on display were sailors worn by too much sea and sun, hardly what one would have expected from Hollywood's house of glamour. Yet this tear-jerker for men, as some critics dubbed it, went on to become the studio's top moneymaker of 1937.

Despite its lack of glamour, Rudyard Kipling's story dovetailed nicely with the MGM approach to filmmaking. Its story of a spoiled rich boy who becomes a man when he falls off a luxury liner and is picked up by a New England tuna boat was the type of family fare Louis B. Mayer loved—a simple story with a solid lesson in traditional family values. *Captains Courageous* also offered the kinds of roles that would further the careers of the studio's contract talent. Although it meant lowering the male lead's age from fifteen to eleven, the picture provided a perfect vehicle for juvenile star Freddie Bartholomew, who had made his MGM debut as the young David Copperfield and would reach the peak of his popularity in *Captains Courageous*.

The film also contained what executives thought was the perfect role for an actor fast becoming the studio's dramatic mainstay, Spencer Tracy. As Manuel, the Portuguese fisherman who takes a paternal interest in the boy, Tracy would get to extend his range on camera while also demonstrating the warmth that charmed audiences. Unfortunately, Tracy didn't see it that way. In his opinion, *Captains Courageous* was primarily the boy's picture, even after the role of Manuel was built up for him. He also was not thrilled about having to sing on screen or learn a Portuguese accent. Finally, his wife, Louise, convinced him to make the picture, pronouncing it one of the best he had ever been offered.

There was still the matter of the hair, however. After one session with the stylist, Tracy

Spencer Tracy may have hated singing, but it made for a great scene (with Freddie Bartholomew).

WHATEVER BECAME OF . . .

Freddie Bartholomew was at the height of his popularity in **Captains Courageous**, *but, like most child stars, he would not stay on top for long. With the success of the Andy Hardy films a year later, Mickey Rooney, who had a supporting role in* **Captains Courageous**, *soon became MGM's top child actor, while Bartholomew found himself consigned to less exciting roles. At the same time, his aunt, who served as his legal guardian in the U.S., alienated MGM management by suing to get him out of his contract. By 1942, Bartholomew had to take a smaller role in one of Rooney's star vehicles,* **A Yank at Eton**. *That marked the end of the British juvenile's MGM contract. After service in World War II, he tried to restart his career as an adult, but there were few roles available for him. After a period as a television star in the late forties and early fifties, he moved into advertising, eventually becoming a top executive at Benton and Bowles in New York. Later he also served as producer for the daytime drama* **As the World Turns**. *Bartholomew died in 1992 at the age of sixty-eight.*

quipped, "It's a wonder they don't use perfume on me," while telling other friends, "If my father had lived to see it, this would have killed him." To make matters worse, Joan Crawford took one look at him on the back lot and yelled, "My God! It's Harpo Marx!"

Once location work started off the Catalina coast, however, Tracy's mood improved markedly. Most of the film was shot on the 110-foot schooner *Ortha F. Spinney,* an authentic Gloucester fishing boat rechristened *We're Here* when MGM bought it for the film. Tracy pestered Captain J. M. Hersey with questions about sailing and requests to take the wheel himself. Toward the end of filming, Tracy bought his own yacht.

Tracy also loved working with his costars. Lionel Barrymore had long been his idol, as much for his legendary stage work in the twenties as for his simple, unpretentious film acting. After his concerns over working with Bartholomew, Tracy decided the kid was okay. The young actor was as much of a perfectionist as Tracy, enduring long hours in wet clothing to get his scenes just right.

Once the picture was completed, however, Tracy returned to denigrating his performance. Even after he won an Oscar nomination for the role, he persisted in telling the press that he hadn't done anything special on screen. Tracy also threatened to stay home from the awards. Ultimately, events beyond his control kept him away. Torrential rains forced the Academy to postpone the ceremonies for a week, by which time Tracy was in the hospital with appendicitis.

On Oscar night, Tracy sent his wife to represent him, but even though she was the first to arrive, nobody recognized her. When Tracy was announced as the Best Actor winner, Louis B. Mayer got up to accept, then asked Mrs. Tracy to come up and say a few words. Most of the audience had not caught her name and wondered who this unfamiliar woman was. Her simple acceptance speech—"I accept this award on behalf of Spencer, Susie, Johnny, and myself" —brought down the house, however.

HARPO'S REVENGE

Shortly after completing Captains Courageous, Spencer Tracy made his only film with Joan Crawford, Mannequin. On the set, he often annoyed his costar by chewing garlic or whispering rude comments in her ear during love scenes. Some might have considered his behavior an attempt to upstage the actress, whose love affair with the camera would last for five decades. In truth, however, he was trying to help her performance by forcing her to concentrate as never before. Crawford caught on quickly and found her work improving tremendously under Tracy's influence. She also found herself falling in love with him. They started a brief affair, but she called it off when she realized he would never leave his wife for her. All heartache aside, however, Tracy's growing popularity and the new, improved Joan Crawford worked box-office magic, making Mannequin her highest grossing film in years.

Casablanca

"Louis, I Think This Is the Beginning of a Beautiful Friendship"

1942. CAST: Humphrey Bogart (Richard "Rick" Blaine), Ingrid Bergman (Ilsa Lund Laszlo), Paul Henreid (Victor Laszlo), Claude Rains (Captain Louis Renault), Conrad Veidt (Major Heinrich Strasser), Sydney Greenstreet (Señor Ferrari), Peter Lorre (Ugarte), Dooley Wilson (Sam). Producer: Hal B. Wallis; Director: Michael Curtiz; Screenplay: Julius J. and Philip G. Epstein and Howard Koch (Based on the play *Everybody Comes to Rick's* by Murray Burnett and Joan Allison); Photography: Arthur Edeson; Music: Max Steiner. RUNNING TIME: 102 minutes.

The beautiful friendship between *Casablanca* and film audiences began with the picture's release in December 1942. Since then, the film's popularity has actually grown, making it one of a handful of movies that has achieved legendary status. Like other such films—*Gone With the Wind, The Wizard of Oz,* and *Citizen Kane* among them—it is as much talked about for what happened off-screen as for what has enthralled audiences for decades on-screen. And, like many a Hollywood legend, between what really happened and what people think happened there is a great gulf fixed. So, let's look at a few *Casablanca* legends in the hope of once and for all setting the record straight.

LEGEND #1: *Casablanca* was inspired by one of the biggest flops in Broadway history, a play so bad the film's writers only kept the setting and a few character names.

Everybody Comes to Rick's, the play on which *Casablanca* was based, was hardly the biggest flop in Broadway history for one simple reason—it never reached Broadway. Producers Martin Gabel and Carly Wharton optioned it in 1940, but disagreed with authors Murray Burnett and Joan Allison over rewrites. The authors' agent suggested shopping it around Hollywood, where Warner Bros. picked up the rights in late 1941.

LEGEND #2: Ronald Reagan was the first choice to play Rick Blaine.

There is actually evidence to support this legend. Shortly after producer Hal Wallis decided to call his new film *Casablanca,* the studio publicity department sent out a press release announcing that the new film would star Ronald Reagan, Ann Sheridan, and Dennis Morgan. Yet the earliest memos Wallis himself wrote about casting indicate that he had Humphrey Bogart in mind from the start.

LINES CONSIDERED FOR THE FINAL FADE-OUT OF CASABLANCA

The last line of Casablanca is heard over the shot of Rick and Louis walking off into the fog. Since their backs are to the camera, it was dubbed in three weeks after shooting stopped. Among the choices producer Hal Wallis considered as Rick's response to the news that Louis will acompany him to the Free French garrison in Brazaville were:

"Louis, I begin to see a reason for your sudden attack of patriotism. While you defend your country, you also protect your investment."

"If you ever die a hero's death, Heaven protect the angels!"

"Louis, I might have known you'd mix your patriotism with a little larceny."

"Louis, I think this is the beginning of a beautiful friendship."

LEGEND #3: Humphrey Bogart only got the role of Rick Blaine because George Raft turned it down.

There is no evidence supporting this rumor, though it's easy to see how it got started. Raft was under contract to Warner's at the time, but he seemed to spend more time refusing roles than playing them. Two roles he turned down, Sam Spade in *The Maltese Falcon* and Mad Dog Earle in *High Sierra*, helped boost Bogie to stardom.

LEGEND #4: Production of *Casablanca* was so chaotic that Ingrid Bergman never knew until the last day of shooting which leading man she would end up with.

Casablanca was indeed filmed under chaotic conditions, with the script being put together daily by Wallis and director Michael Curtiz from several different versions. At one time, there was even talk of changing the ending so that Bogart would get the girl. When word of this possibility reached the set, Ingrid Bergman started asking which way the film was going, so that she would know whether her character loved Rick or Victor more. Curtiz suggested she "Play it in between," which worked out well by keeping the audience in suspense. Bergman finally saw how the scene would be played the night before it was filmed, when the eagerly awaited script pages finally arrived. But (and this is a very important but), the film's final scene was far from the last one shot. Like most movies, *Casablanca* was filmed out of sequence. After flying off to Lisbon with Paul Henreid, Bergman worked on the film for eleven more days, during which time she shot some of her most important scenes.

Claude Rains, Humphrey Bogart, and Paul Henreid relax between takes.

LEGEND #5: *Casablanca* was an instant classic, loved by all.

Casablanca did well at the box office, placing fifth for 1943, but it was nobody's idea of a classic at the time. It was praised as an entertaining film with a few rousing scenes and some good performances, but it was also dismissed by many critics as a typical product of the Hollywood assembly line.

Will she or won't she?—Ingrid Bergman literally caught between Paul Henreid and Humphrey Bogart.

Cat on a Hot Tin Roof

"Maggie the Cat Is Alive!"

1958. CAST: Elizabeth Taylor (Maggie Pollitt), Paul Newman (Brick Pollitt), Burl Ives (Big Daddy Pollitt), Jack Carson (Gooper Pollitt), Judith Anderson (Big Mama Pollitt), Madeleine Sherwood (Mae Pollitt). Producer: Lawrence Weingarten; Director: Richard Brooks; Screenplay: Richard Brooks and James Poe (Based on the play by Tennessee Williams); Photography: William Daniels (Metrocolor). RUNNING TIME: 108 minutes.

Elizabeth Taylor proved herself alive and then some, despite the tragedy and scandal that attended her appearance in *Cat on a Hot Tin Roof*. Along the way she also demonstrated a new maturity as a dramatic actress, while handing MGM its biggest moneymaker of the year. And, as was true of the decade's other Tennessee Williams adaptations, the film helped set new standards for what was acceptable on-screen.

Cat on a Hot Tin Roof was hardly the most shocking of Williams's plays, but its story of a woman trying to get her husband to make love to her was still strong enough to create major censorship problems. It took so long to work out an acceptable screenplay that MGM lost its first two choices to star in the film—Grace Kelly and James Dean. They also lost the first director under consideration when George Cukor decided that no screenplay could remain true to Williams's vision and pass the Production Code. That left the door open for Richard Brooks, one of MGM's fastest-rising directors and playwrights. And just to guarantee the film's success, the studio decided to team its hottest young actress, Elizabeth Taylor, with Paul Newman, an actor who seemed to have inherited James Dean's smoldering intensity (not to mention a few of the roles planned for the late star).

The film represented a turning point for Taylor, both personally and professionally. After two failed marriages, she had finally found wedded bliss with producer Mike Todd. She was even considering retiring from acting to devote all her time to the marriage. In March 1958, Todd had to fly to New York to accept an award as "Showman of the Year." Ill with a virus, Taylor couldn't accompany him. Todd's private plane, *The Lucky Liz,* crashed, killing all on board.

Brooks and company shot around Taylor as she tried to cope with her almost unendurable grief.

Elizabeth Taylor and the screen's most provocative brass bed.

Elizabeth Taylor and Paul Newman rehearse.

Three weeks after the funeral, she asked if she could visit the set. That visit was all she needed. She resumed working, just afternoons at first, but eventually for full days. Gradually, playing the role helped her regain her equilibrium.

Taylor found comfort from another source as well. Todd's best friend was singer Eddie Fisher, then married to MGM star Debbie Reynolds. Fisher became an almost constant visitor in Taylor's home. Sometime during post-production, the two began an affair. When Reynolds announced she was filing for divorce, the press turned on Taylor, transforming her from tragic widow to brazen homewrecker in nothing flat.

Thanks to the notoriety—and quality work from all concerned—*Cat on a Hot Tin Roof* became MGM's top-grossing film of 1958, taking in almost $9 million. It also scored six Oscar nominations.

Cat People

"Kiss Me and I'll Claw You to Death!"

1942. CAST: Simone Simon (Irena Dubrovna), Kent Smith (Oliver Reed), Tom Conway (The Psychiatrist), Jane Randolph (Alice Moore), Jack Holt (Commodore), Alan Napier (Carver), Elizabeth Russell (The Cat Woman). Producer: Val Lewton; Director: Jacques Tourneur; Screenplay: DeWitt Bodeen; Photography: Nicholas Musuraca; Music: Roy Webb. RUNNING TIME: 73 minutes.

Horror became respectable when producer Val Lewton launched a series of thoughtful low-budget fright films at RKO in 1942. By all rights, his films were too gentle, too intelligent to succeed with wartime audiences. But thanks to strong advertising campaigns, and the producer's ability to make audiences think they had seen more than they had, it turned into a surprise hit, helping save the studio from bankruptcy.

RKO was in dire financial straits in 1942, when studio head Charles Koerner decided to cash in on the success Universal was enjoying with their Frankenstein and werewolf films. Was it desperation that made him turn to the one man in Hollywood least likely to produce horror films? Lewton was a soft-spoken, decidedly nonaggressive character, who never would have considered shocking people in person. He couldn't even tell off a rude waiter.

But for all his quietness, Lewton had attracted considerable attention during eight years as a story editor for David O. Selznick. He quickly earned a reputation for his strong story sense and his skills as a script doctor. Even though he had warned Selznick not to take a chance on *Gone With the Wind* (Lewton thought *War and Peace* would do better business), he had written one of the film's most famous scenes, Scarlett's visit to the Atlanta train station.

When Lewton took his new job at RKO, he had to work under certain limitations. His films had to cost less than $150,000, they had to run no more than seventy-five minutes, and he would have to work with market-tested titles dictated by the front office. Within those restrictions, however, he could make his movies any way he liked. To him, that meant putting something really frightening on screen—the dark side of the human mind.

For his first film, Lewton was handed the title *Cat People*. At first he was so embarrassed that he

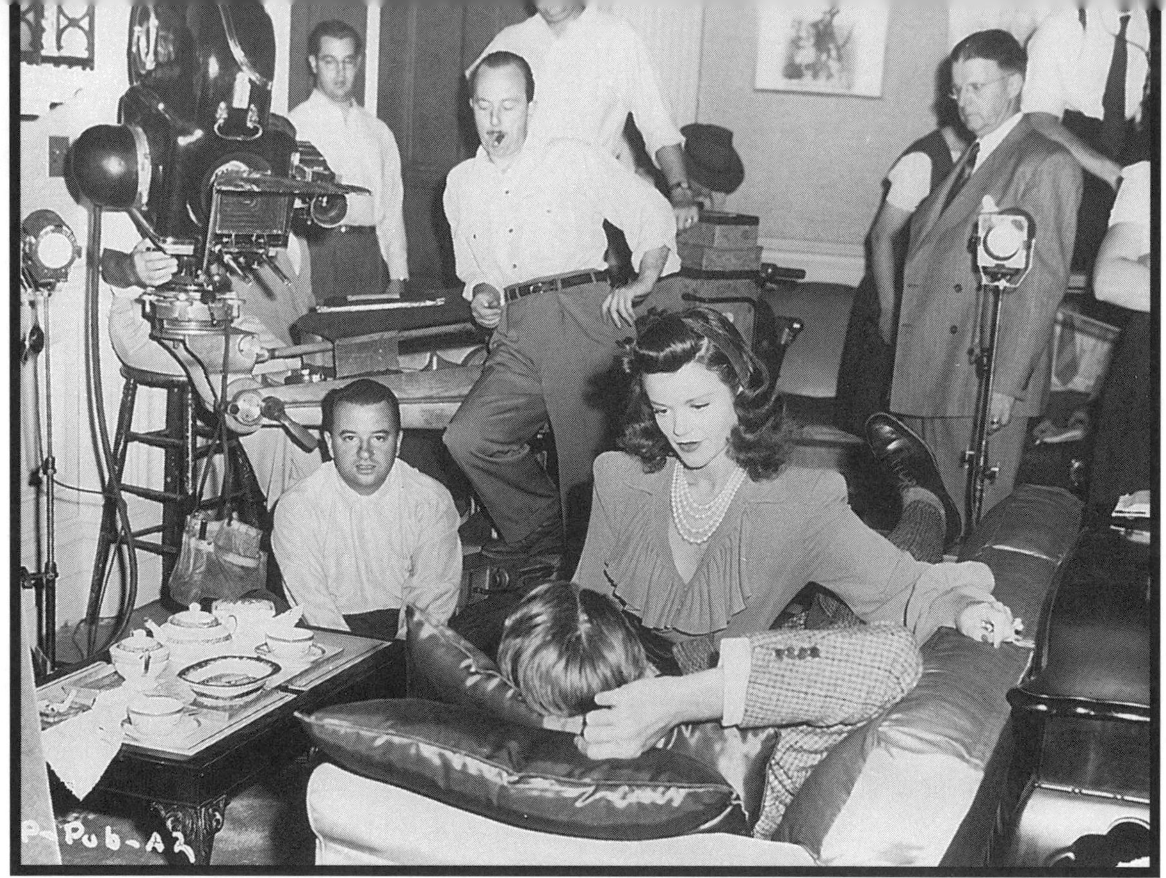

Above: **Simone Simon and Kent Smith (back of head) on the set.**

Right: **The advertising art for *Cat People* depicts Simone Simon more explicitly than the film itself.**

offered to release writer DeWitt Bodeen from his contract. But then Lewton's creative juices started flowing, and he came up with the story of a sexually repressed fashion designer (Irena, played by Simone Simon) who fears that romantic passion will turn her into a cat. When her fears jeopardize her marriage to a naval architect (Kent Smith), she begins stalking his former girlfriend.

To cut costs and make the film look more expensive, Lewton had it shot almost entirely on sets from other films. The zoo in Central Park was a standing set that had been used in the Fred Astaire–Ginger Rogers musical *Shall We Dance*. The front hallway in Irena's apartment building was actually the staircase from *The Magnificent Ambersons*.

Nobody expected *Cat People* to do any more than fill out a double bill for a week or two. Then something amazing happened. Though the picture had gotten only mixed reviews, word of mouth spread, and business started building. In Hollywood it played thirteen weeks at one theater—longer than many big-budget films. Eventually the film did well enough to save the studio from bankruptcy. It also put Lewton on solid footing at RKO, where he would soon use his influence to further the directing careers of Robert Wise and Mark Robson.

THE LEWTON COLLECTION: RESHAPING THE WORLD OF HORROR

I Walked with a Zombie *(1943)—Jane Eyre goes calypso in this tale of a nurse in the West Indies whose patient may be the victim of a voodoo curse.*

The Leopard Man *(1943)—A runaway leopard inspires a psychopathic killer.*

The Seventh Victim *(1943)—A neurotic woman falls prey to a group of sophisticated satanists in Manhattan.*

The Ghost Ship *(1943)—The pressures of his job turn a ship's captain into a homicidal maniac.*

The Curse of the Cat People *(1944)—In a loose sequel to* **Cat People**, *Oliver's young daughter retreats into a fantasy world.*

The Body Snatcher *(1945)—Boris Karloff stars as a grave robber who starts creating some corpses of his own.*

Isle of the Dead *(1945)—As a Greek general, Karloff fears a local plague has been caused by a vampire.*

Bedlam *(1946)—This time, Karloff is the unscrupulous keeper of an eighteenth-century London madhouse.*

Citizen Kane

"This Is the Biggest Toy Train Set Any Boy Ever Had"

1941. CAST: Orson Welles (Charles Foster Kane), Joseph Cotten (Jedediah Leland), Dorothy Comingore (Susan Alexander), Everett Sloane (Mr. Bernstein), Ray Collins (Boss J. W. "Big Jim" Gettys), George Coulouris (Walter Parks Thatcher), Agnes Moorehead (Mrs. Mary Kane), Ruth Warrick (Mrs. Emily Norton Kane). Producer-Director: Orson Welles; Screenplay: Herman J. Mankiewicz, Orson Welles; Photography: Gregg Toland; Music: Bernard Herrmann. RUNNING TIME: 119 minutes.

Once Orson Welles got his hands on the best that RKO Studios had to offer—"the biggest toy train set any boy ever had," as he called it—he astounded the cynics by producing, directing, co-writing, and starring in a film often called the best ever made. Whether or not *Citizen Kane* deserves that honor, it is clearly one of the most influential films of all time. Gregg Toland's shadowy, deep-focus camera work was a major influence on the development of film noir. In addition, *Citizen Kane* has become a beacon for critics promoting the use of film as a medium for personal expression and, as such, inspired generations of young artists to move into filmmaking.

In July 1939, Welles signed an unprecedented contract with RKO. After attracting national attention with his Mercury Theatre on Broadway and radio, particularly when he panicked a nation with a documentary-like adaptation of H. G. Wells's *The War of the Worlds,* he had been approached by several Hollywood studios. But only RKO offered him almost complete artistic control.

While developing projects at the studio, Welles continued producing the radio version of the Mercury Theatre, with Herman J. Mankiewicz providing many of their scripts. Before long, the two were working on a project initially called *American,* about the rise and fall of a publishing tycoon. This script would become *Citizen Kane*.

Although Welles's inexperience at filmmaking made him a pariah to much of Hollywood, it proved a boon in attracting the perfect cameraman for *Citizen Kane*. Toland was already acknowledged as one of the best in the business when he offered his services to Welles, saying, "You don't know what can't be done."

Work began the first week in June 1940. During this period, Welles and his production team

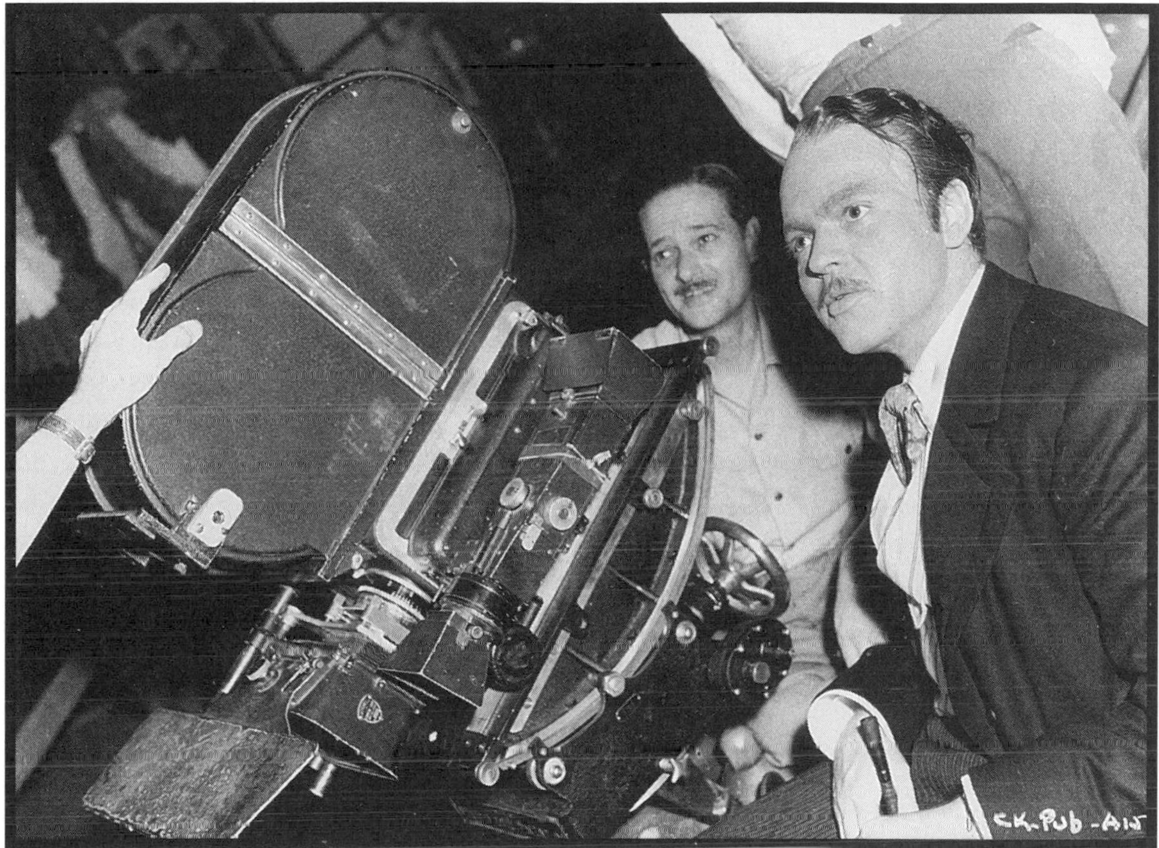

Cameraman Gregg Toland and Orson Welles set up a shot—"like two kids in a sandbox," according to costar Ruth Warrick.

BEYOND ROSEBUD: THE FUTURE OF *CITIZEN KANE*'S DREAM CAST

Ray Collins became a television fixture as Lieutenant Tragg on Perry Mason.

Dorothy Comingore was blacklisted when she refused to name names before the House Un-American Activities Committee. Like Susan Alexander Kane, she ended up telling her life's story to anybody who would buy her a drink.

Joseph Cotten built a solid career as a leading man in such pictures as Shadow of a Doubt, Portrait of Jennie, *and* The Third Man.

George Coulouris went on to more great roles in films like Watch on the Rhine *and* For Whom the Bell Tolls.

Agnes Moorehead became one of the industry's most respected character actresses with roles in The Magnificent Ambersons *and* Johnny Belinda, *but perhaps became best known as Endora on television's* Bewitched.

Everett Sloane turned his film debut as Mr. Bernstein into a long career of character roles, including Rita Hayworth's husband in Welles's The Lady from Shanghai.

Ruth Warrick became one of the great soap opera stars as Phoebe Tyler Wallingford on All My Children.

settled on the visual elements that would make *Citizen Kane* such a departure from standard studio filmmaking—deep focus, high-contrast lighting with deep shadows, low-angle shots that required putting ceilings on the sets and long takes with extensive camera movement. In addition, Welles used special effects to keep costs down by creating the illusion that there were bigger sets and larger crowds than RKO could afford. Some scholars have estimated that as many as 80 percent of the shots were achieved through some effects process.

The film finished shooting in January 1941 and was slated for a debut on Valentine's Day, February 14. And that's when William Randolph Hearst stepped in. During production, Welles had kept the story under wraps, but once previews started, Hearst realized the film was about him. Threats to sue for libel forced repeated postponements of the film's premiere and about three minutes worth of cuts. In addition, Hearst refused to have the film mentioned in any of his newspapers.

Welles countered by giving the film more preview screenings for filmmakers and members of the press. Eventually, public pressure became so strong that RKO had to open the film, which it did on May 1, 1941, to rave reviews.

Still, pressure from Hearst and the studio heads kept the film out of many theaters. To make matters worse, the film proved too sophisticated for general audiences. Although it did well in downtown theaters in the major cities, it fared poorly in the small towns and neighborhood theaters on which most of Hollywood depended for profits. By the time it had played out its initial run, it posted a loss of about $150,000. When the film won only one Academy Award—to Mankiewicz and Welles for Best Screenplay—RKO withdrew it from circulation.

But *Citizen Kane* wouldn't stay hidden forever. With the end of World War II, the film went into European release, drawing raves from some of that continent's most influential critics. In 1956, RKO became the first of the major studios to sell its library to television. As a result, *Citizen Kane* suddenly became available around the world and virtually around the clock. At the same time, Welles made a highly publicized return to Broadway to star in Shakespeare's *King Lear*. Prompted by renewed interest in his career, RKO rereleased the film. This attracted the attention of a new generation of American critics, who began hailing *Citizen Kane* as one of the medium's greatest achievements.

More than fifty years after its initial release, *Citizen Kane* remains one of the most viewed, discussed, and acclaimed films of all time. It is the most studied film in colleges worldwide. In fact, when the American Film Institute polled professors on which films they used in class, *Citizen Kane* was named twice as often as the second-ranked picture, Sergei Eisenstein's *Battleship Potemkin*.

Crossfire

Playing with Dynamite

1947. CAST: Robert Young (Finlay), Robert Mitchum (Keeley), Robert Ryan (Montgomery), Gloria Grahame (Ginny), Paul Kelly (The Man), Sam Levene (Joseph Samuels).
Producer: Adrian Scott (for Dore Schary); Director: Edward Dmytryk; Screenplay: John Paxton (Based on the novel *The Brick Foxhole* by Richard Brooks); Photography: J. Roy Hunt; Music: Roy Webb.
RUNNING TIME: 86 minutes.

Hollywood faced a long-forbidden subject—anti-Semitism—in a 1947 film, an unlikely source. *Crossfire* was a gamble for RKO. The studio had not attempted anything groundbreaking since it signed and then fired Orson Welles earlier in the decade. Then Dore Schary took over as vice president in charge of production. Schary was a man with a mission and a message. He believed that movies could entertain while also enlightening the audience about society's problems. With *Crossfire,* his first film as head of RKO, he showed exactly what that philosphy meant.

Crossfire was adapted from *The Brick Foxhole,* a novel by future filmmaker Richard Brooks about stateside GIs facing boredom during the last days of World War II. What attracted the attention of RKO producer Adrian Scott was a subplot in which a bigot murders a homosexual. The story would have been impossible on screen under the Production Code, but Scott saw the opportunity to tackle bigotry of another sort by transforming the victim into a Jew. The story fit right in with Schary's filmmaking philosophy. It didn't hurt either that the studio's hottest director—Edward Dmytryk, who had scored a hit with the film noir *Murder, My Sweet*—was eager to direct the project.

Schary gave the film a budget of just $500,000, which was low for an A feature at the time. To keep costs down, Scott decided to shoot on sets built for other films. Schary even helped by juggling production schedules so the sets would be available to him. Dmytryk also settled on a dark, shadowy camera style with long takes to hold costs down even more.

The one thing they didn't economize was the cast. Screen veteran Robert Young starred as the district attorney investigating the murder. Fast-rising leading man Robert Mitchum was the marine who helps him find the killer. Gloria Grahame was borrowed from MGM to play a prostitute who provides an alibi for one suspect.

The key role in the film, however, was Montgomery, the sadistic bigot who turns out to be the killer. Robert Ryan was another of the studio's most promising young leading men. He had served in the marines with Brooks, and as soon as he read the novel, told the author he wanted to play the role. He attacked the part with frightening intensity, winning a well-deserved Oscar nomination for his efforts. But the vicious role would come to haunt the liberal-minded actor. In later years, he would refuse to discuss the part.

Dmytryk brought *Crossfire* in three days ahead of schedule. He had worked so efficiently that after the movie was edited, there were only two hundred feet of film left unused. That did not, however, endear him to more conservative executives, who were sure the subject matter would repel audiences. The cynics dubbed the film "Backfire," predicting that it would end Schary's reign at the studio.

When the film opened in July 1947, the reviews and box-office returns bore out Schary's faith in the project. While praising the film for its civic virtues, critics were quick to point out that the social message was couched in a fast-moving, compelling murder mystery. From the start, business was strong, with *Crossfire* eventually earning back more than twice its cost. Insiders began predicting that *Crossfire* would earn RKO its first Best Picture Oscar since *Cimmaron* in 1931.

Then the subpoenas started to arrive. The House Un-American Activities Committee was just starting its investigation of alleged Communist infiltration of the motion picture industry for years. Scott and Dmytryk were members of the "Hollywood Ten," a group of suspected Communists who refused to testify for the HUAC, claiming the investigation violated their First Amendment rights. On November 24, 1947, they were cited for contempt of Congress (Dmytryk would serve six months in prison; Scott, a year). Four days later, Schary was forced to fire them.

But even as Scott and Dmytryk faced an uncertain future on the blacklist, *Crossfire* was helping bring Hollywood into a new era. The studio heads could turn their backs on the film's creators, but not on its success. As a result, it got a little easier to tackle social issues in Hollywood, with future pictures taking on racism (*Home of the Brave* and *Lost Boundaries*), juvenile delinquency (*The Blackboard Jungle*), and drug addiction (*The Man with the Golden Arm*).

THE PROOF OF THE PUDDING

After finishing work on Crossfire, Edward Dmytryk was approached by a crew member with a question: "It's such a fine suspense story. Why did you have to bring in all that anti-Semitism?" The man went on to add, "There's no anti-Semitism in America. If there were, why is all the money in America controlled by Jewish bankers?" All Dmytryk could say was, "That's why we made the film."

Robert Young questions Robert Mitchum and friend.

SEE NO EVIL, HEAR NO EVIL

Transforming the murder victim from a homosexual to a Jew was not the only change demanded by Hollywood's Production Code censors. They also insisted that Gloria Grahame's character never be clearly identified as a prostitute. For one scene, in which it seemed that her former pimp was trying to win her back, they demanded that the man be made a deserted husband trying to patch up his broken marriage to the girl. This was a little much for the production team, however. Though they wrote the lines the censors wanted, actor Paul Kelly played the character in such a way that the audience could only assume that he was lying. Happy to see the dialogue rewritten, the Production Code Administration passed the film nonetheless.

Dark Victory

"I'll Have a Large Order of Prognosis Negative"

1939. CAST: Bette Davis (Judith Traherne), George Brent (Dr. Frederick Steele), Humphrey Bogart (Michael O'Leary), Geraldine Fitzgerald (Ann King), Ronald Reagan (Alec Hamin), Henry Travers (Dr. Parsons). Producers: Hal B. Wallis, David Lewis; Director: Edmund Goulding; Screenplay: Casey Robinson (Based on the play by George Emerson Brewer Jr. and Bertram Bloch); Photography: Ernest Haller; Music: Max Steiner. RUNNING TIME: 106 minutes.

Bette Davis got just what the career doctor ordered—despite massive opposition from Jack L. Warner—in this heart-wrenching 1939 romance. Of course, Davis usually had to fight for what she believed in, from scripts to acting choices to a fair break financially. With *Dark Victory*, she even went to war with herself for a while.

The story of a glamorous society woman humanized by her fight with terminal illness had been a Broadway flop starring Tallulah Bankhead in 1934. But despite the play's unimpressive run, it captured Hollywood's attention. David O. Selznick considered buying the rights for Greta Garbo at MGM before he committed himself to a remake of *Anna Karenina*. After he set up shop as an independent producer, he bought the screen rights for $50,000, at various times considering the project for Merle Oberon, Janet Gaynor, and Katharine Hepburn. But he just couldn't get the script right.

By 1938, Selznick had pretty much given up on the project and sold it to Warner Bros. for $27,500. They wanted it as a vehicle for Kay Francis, who was making mostly low-budget features, but she had a superstitious fear of playing death scenes and refused it. Barbara Stanwyck campaigned for the role, but by that time Bette Davis had gotten wind of the property.

Davis had only recently returned to Warner's after walking out on her contract in a quest for better roles and better money. She had scored a series of hits, capped by 1938's *Jezebel,* for which she won her second Oscar. *Dark Victory* seemed the perfect step in her rise to stardom—a tremendous acting challenge and a film with strong box-office appeal.

But Jack Warner didn't see it that way. He thought the story was maudlin and depressing and would alienate Davis's growing legion of fans. "Who wants to see some dame go blind?" was his

"Deep in the heart of every actress lives the ideal role she longs to play—a role that embodies every talent she possesses. Now such a role has come to Bette Davis in Dark Victory. Not a 'character' part, but a natural, normal woman who faces all that fate can offer—all the sweet and bitter of life—all the joy and pain of love—and comes through the dark with colors gloriously flying. Eight years she has waited to play this role. We sincerely believe it's her greatest screen performance."

—Warner Bros. ad copy for Dark Victory

Bette Davis, as desperate onscreen as she was offscreen.

judgment, to which Davis replied, "Only half the women in America." When she enlisted producers Hal Wallis and David Lewis and one of the studio's top directors, Edmund Goulding, Warner finally gave in. "Okay, go hang yourself!" he said.

By the time shooting started, that's exactly what Davis thought she was doing. Although still married to her first husband, Ham Nelson, she had just had a very painful affair with director William Wyler. On the rebound, she had a fling with Howard Hughes, but the relationship ended when Nelson bugged one of their trysts and tried to blackmail them. Refusing any offer of help from Hughes, Davis borrowed $70,000 from Warner's to pay off her soon-to-be-ex-husband.

The strain actually helped her performance. The day after her husband's blackmail attempt, she had to do a photo session with legendary glamour photographer George Hurrell. Stunned by her air of vulnerability, he took some of her most beautiful portraits, portraits that became an integral part of the film's advertising campaign.

But all Davis could feel was the strain. After one week, she called Wallis in tears, "I think you should replace me. I'm sick!" "I've seen the first week's rushes," he shot back. "Stay sick!" Before long, she found the role a haven from her problems. She also found a haven in the arms of leading man George Brent. She had been attracted to Brent since they made their first film together in 1932. Back then, she was married, and he was about to marry dramatic star Ruth Chatterton. By the time they made *Dark Victory,* however, Brent was a free man, and Davis was on the road to divorce. They embarked on an affair that lasted for a year after they finished filming.

When *Dark Victory* premiered in April 1939, Davis was almost universally hailed for giving her best performance ever. In addition, the film proved to be one of her biggest hits: Its profits paid for three new sound stages on the Warner

Bros. lot. Exhibitors voted Davis the number two female attraction at the box office for 1939, right behind Shirley Temple. In 1940, she would rise to number one.

The day after *Dark Victory* opened, Davis entered the Warner's commissary to a sea of compliments. She maintained her composure throughout lunch, but inwardly she was on fire. As she told interviewers toward the end of her life, she wanted to shout, "By damn, I was right! Everyone in America wants to see a story where the heroine dies in the end!"

LITTLE RONNIE REAGAN

Dark Victory *was the only film Bette Davis made with the future president of the United States, a fact neither of them seemed to regret. Ill-matched artistically, temperamentally, and politically, they kept a wary distance from each other for years. After Reagan was elected governor of California, Davis started telling interviewers that his nickname at Warner's had been "Lit-tle Ron-nie Reagan." She was particularly displeased when he showed up late at a dinner to honor Jack Warner. When his entrance forced everyone to stand, she accused him of trying to upstage their former boss.*

Bette Davis and George Brent grasp at happiness.

David Copperfield

"I Am Born"

1935. CAST: W. C. Fields (Micawber), Lionel Barrymore (Dan Peggotty), Maureen O'Sullivan (Dora), Madge Evans (Agnes), Edna May Oliver (Aunt Betsy), Lewis Stone (Mr. Wickfield), Frank Lawton (David as Man), Freddie Bartholomew (David as Child), Roland Young (Uriah Heep), Basil Rathbone (Mr. Murdstone), Elsa Lanchester (Clickett). Producer: David O. Selznick; Director: George Cukor; Screenplay: Howard Estabrook, Hugh Walpole (Based on the novel by Charles Dickens); Photography: Oliver T. Marsh; Music: Herbert Stothart. RUNNING TIME: 132 minutes.

A new approach to filming the classics was born when producer David O. Selznick turned a faithful adaptation of one of Charles Dickens's most popular novels into a box-office winner. It took considerable determination to get the project past studio executives, who didn't think the classics worked on screen. But determination was one quality Selznick possessed in abundance.

Filming *David Copperfield* was a personal cause for Selznick. His father, Lewis Selznick, had used the book to learn English when he first emigrated from Russia, then read the story to his sons every night. For years, David had dreamed of filming the book as a tribute to his father. With the success of RKO's 1933 adaptation of *Little Women,* a project Selznick had helped get started before he left that studio for MGM, the time finally seemed right. But first he had to overcome the "expertise" of his boss and father-in-law, Louis B. Mayer. Conventional wisdom held that classics like *David Copperfield* were unfilmable. They were too sprawling to be brought to the screen faithfully, and cutting them for the new medium would unleash a flood of complaints. Selznick thought he saw a way to compromise. He felt that an adaptation could maintain all the high spots and most of the characters from the original, while getting rid of extraneous episodes and shortening what remained.

Selznick bombarded Mayer with memos for a year before the studio head gave in. The hits he had scored with *Dinner at Eight* and *Viva Villa* were strong arguments in the producer's favor. So was the thought of casting MGM's resident child star, Jackie Cooper, as the young David.

Selznick, however, considered Cooper too pert and American for the role and convinced Mayer to let him find an unknown. An extensive talent hunt followed during which Selznick saw nine

THE PERFECT LOCATION

Director George Cukor joined David O. Selznick on a month-long tour scouting locations in England. He visited all the locales that had inspired Dickens's novel and secured the services of novelist and Dickens expert Hugh Walpole, whose commitment to spend a few weeks as a consultant on the film turned into a full-fledged writing assignment. Ultimately, Cukor shot the film on the MGM back lot, with the art department creating reasonable facsimiles of Dickens's London. One set Cukor actually considered an improvement. To duplicate the White Cliffs of Dover, where David lived with his Aunt Betsy, Cukor shot in Malibu. He told the press that the U.S. location actually improved on the original, calling his cliffs "better, whiter, and cliffier."

Basil Rathbone (with Violet Kemble-Cooper, Freddie Bartholomew, and Elizabeth Allan) establishes his credentials as a screen villain.

thousand boys and generated reams of publicity. Then Selznick's director, George Cukor, who also had done *Little Women*, met Freddie Bartholomew, a young English actor vacationing in America. Cukor dressed the boy as David and took him to meet Selznick. "Mr. Selznick, I am David Copperfield, sir," said the boy. "Right you are," replied Selznick.

Maureen O'Sullivan with signed script.

There was a little more trouble casting Mr. Micawber, the genial father figure whose sentence to debtors' prison inspires David's heroic trek from London to Dover to live with his aunt. Selznick considered both Charles Laughton and W. C. Fields for the role, finally settling on Laughton because of his box-office pull in England.

As he usually did, Laughton researched the role extensively, planning the character's look to match the book's original illustrations. Cukor was astounded at his resemblance to the drawings, but dismayed by his insecurity. Laughton usually had trouble finding his character during the first few days of filming, but always came through in the end. This time, however, he seemed completely lost. He agonized between takes and could hardly retain his lines.

After three days, Laughton asked to be removed from the film. He even suggested they replace him with Fields and issued press statements taking all the responsibility on himself.

Fields turned out to be inspired casting. Contrary to his reputation for terrorizing children on the set (he once spiked child-star Baby LeRoy's formula), he got along fine with Bartholomew, praising the child's professionalism. He also improvised some inspired comic bits for the character.

When *David Copperfield* was finished, Selznick presented the MGM hierarchy with a 132-minute film, an unusually long picture for the day. Executives considered releasing it in two parts. Mayer even tried cutting Lionel Barrymore's role down to cameo length. But Selznick mustered support from English teachers, whose complaints convinced Mayer to release the film uncut.

Surprisingly, the film's running time was viewed as a virtue. Critics praised Selznick and company for getting so much of Dickens's novel onto the screen. And American audiences loved it. As a result of *David Copperfield*'s success, Hollywood became much more open to classic adaptations. Selznick had done more than just produce a great picture—he had set the stage for his later adaptations of *Anna Karenina, A Tale of Two Cities*, and *Gone With the Wind*.

LONG ENOUGH FOR ME

Faced with producer David O. Selznick's refusal to cut* David Copperfield, *Nicholas Schenck—president of MGM's parent company, Loew's, Inc.—asked, "How long can it be?" "How long is it good?" was Selznick quick reply. As the fans proved, the film was just fine at its original 132-minute length.

The Dawn Patrol

"Hoorah for the Next Man Who Dies!"

1938. CAST: Errol Flynn (Courtney), David Niven (Scott), Basil Rathbone (Major Brand), Donald Crisp (Phipps), Melville Cooper (Watson), Barry Fitzgerald (Bott). Producers: Hal B. Wallis, Robert Lord; Director: Edmund Goulding; Screenplay: Seton I. Miller, Dan Totheroh (Based on the story "The Flight Commander" by John Monk Saunders); Photography: Tony Gaudio; Music: Max Steiner. RUNNING TIME: 103 minutes.

Warner Bros. went to war three years before the Japanese attacked Pearl Harbor with this thrilling, often heartbreaking tale of men-at-arms. By the late thirties, the studio had pretty much abandoned their once-popular run of topical melodramas "torn from the headlines." Yet this remake of one of the studio's first big hits proved that they could still respond quickly to changes in world affairs.

The Dawn Patrol had started with independent producer Samuel Goldwyn as a vehicle for his top male star, Ronald Colman. Following the great success of Paramount's *Wings*—the first movie to win the Oscar for Best Picture—Goldwyn hired director Howard Hawks to develop a World War I flying drama of his own.

Goldwyn ultimately passed on the story, and Hawks finally sold the project to Warner Bros. The 1930 original starred Richard Barthelmess as Courtney, the cynical flyer promoted to flight commander; Neil Hamilton as Brand, who precedes Courtney in the job; and Douglas Fairbanks Jr. as Scott, Courtney's best friend. The film's success established Hawks as a major film director and propelled Fairbanks to stardom.

By 1938, Europe was gearing up for another major war. Seeing the growing interest in military subjects, executives in Warner Bros'. London office asked to reissue *The Dawn Patrol*. Instead, production chief Hal Wallis suggested a remake. One of the first film's writers, Seton I. Miller, was still under contract and could whip up a new script in no time. In fact, Miller used so much of the original that he requested his earlier collaborator, Dan Totheroh, be given a cowriting credit. The studio could reuse the original aerial footage while reshooting the other scenes on relatively few sets. As Wallis put it, "We should be able to remake the picture for a 'quarter.'"

As an added bonus the remake would promote the studio's male contract stars, particularly Errol Flynn, who was always Wallis's first choice for the lead. For Brand, they chose Basil Rathbone, a stage actor who had faced off with Flynn successfully in *Captain Blood* and *The Adventures of Robin Hood*.

After considering several studio players for Scott, Wallis decided to borrow David Niven from Goldwyn Studios, where he had mostly played suave man-about-town roles. He would later credit his role in *The Dawn Patrol* with helping him grow up on screen. Beyond that,

FLY THE FRIENDLY SKIES OF WARNER BROS.

Even though most of the aerial footage in The Dawn Patrol came from the film's 1930 incarnation, Warner's still needed shots of the planes taking off and landing. So they assembled a squadron of seventeen vintage World War I aircraft, most of them Nieuports. Flying them proved just as hazardous as in World War I. By the time filming ended, stunt flyers had crashed fifteen of them.

David Niven takes off for stardom, with a little help from offscreen friend Errol Flynn.

the film was both a source of professional happiness and personal dismay for Niven. The happiness came from finally getting to work with director Edmund Goulding, a recent arrival at Warner's from MGM. When Niven was new in Hollywood and looking for work, Goulding had taken an interest in the young actor and set up a screen test for him at MGM.

David Niven and Errol Flynn's daring escape.

WITH FRIENDS LIKE THESE

One fact contributing to David Niven's disenchantment with Errol Flynn was the latter's lack of sympathy for the suffering of others. Once, while chopping ice on board Flynn's yacht, the Sirocco, Niven slipped and impaled his hand with the ice pick. When he called Flynn for help, his friend advised him not to move, he wanted to see how their dates would react to the sight. Another time, Niven was water skiing when Flynn became so preoccupied with his female companion that he cut his friend loose. The man had to paddle back to shore using one of the skis as a raft. When they met up again, Niven complained that he'd almost been eaten by a shark. "Wish I'd seen that," was the closest Flynn came to an apology. Little wonder that in his memoirs Niven paid tribute to Flynn as follows: "The greatest thing about Errol was that you always knew exactly where you stood with him because he always let you down. He let himself down, too. . . ."

But the film also marked the end of Niven's friendship with Flynn. The two had met through French actress Lili Damita, who would marry Flynn. During one rift in their stormy marriage, he and Niven shared a bachelor house by the ocean, which they nicknamed Cirrhosis-by-the-Sea. They also had a great time costarring together in *The Charge of the Light Brigade.* By the time they went to work on *The Dawn Patrol,* both men had changed. Niven was beginning to tire of his bachelor days and had outgrown Flynn's playboy adventures. He had also developed a more serious approach to his work, realizing that his performance was just part of the team effort required to make a film successful. Flynn's prima donna behavior—particularly the disdainful way he treated crew members and extras—appalled the younger actor.

Critics praised the film for its combination of aerial pyrotechnics (few noticed that they had been borrowed from the 1930 version) and an antiwar message. With the conflict in Europe heating up, *The Dawn Patrol* would become one of Hollywood's last antiwar films of the thirties. Although some plot elements would be borrowed for Warner's 1941 Ronald Reagan film *International Squadron,* there would be no attempt to duplicate the spirit of *The Dawn Patrol* until the late forties, when MGM released *Command Decision* and Fox scored a major hit with *Twelve O'Clock High.*

Dinner at Eight

Repent at Leisure

1933. CAST: Marie Dressler (Carlotta Vance), John Barrymore (Larry Renault), Wallace Beery (Dan Packard), Jean Harlow (Kitty Packard), Lionel Barrymore (Oliver Jordan), Lee Tracy (Max Kane), Billie Burke (Mrs. Oliver Jordan). Producer: David O. Selznick; Director: George Cukor; Screenplay: Frances Marion, Herman J. Mankiewicz, Donald Ogden Stewart (Based on the play by George S. Kaufman and Edna Ferber); Photography: William Daniels.

RUNNING TIME: 113 minutes.

In 1933, MGM welcomed producer David O. Selznick with the swankiest, most glamorous soirée the screen had ever seen. True, the guests of honor never showed, the host was about to lose his shirt and his health, and one of the guests was plotting his host's financial ruin. But it was exactly that no-holds-barred take on society that made *Dinner at Eight* a hit on both stage and screen.

MGM's production chief, Irving G. Thalberg, picked up the rights to the long-running Broadway hit in hopes of turning it into a follow-up to the studio's first all-star blockbuster, *Grand Hotel*. His instincts were true, but ill health forced him to give up the project. So, studio head Louis B. Mayer convinced his son-in-law, David O. Selznick, to leave RKO Pictures for MGM, where his first project would be *Dinner at Eight*.

The cast Selznick assembled for *Dinner at Eight* was a who's who of the MGM contract list, including Marie Dressler, the top star at the box office at that time; Lionel Barrymore, one of Mayer's favorite stars; and Wallace Beery.

Selznick had to fight to get the director he wanted, George Cukor, who had done outstanding work for him at RKO. The conservative Mayer disliked Cukor because he was a homosexual, but Selznick won out. *Dinner at Eight* would mark the beginning of a long association between Cukor and the studio.

He also had to fight for Jean Harlow and John Barrymore. Selznick felt that Barrymore was perfect for fading matinee idol Larry Renault, a role with more than a few similarities to the Great Profile himself. Studio executives were concerned about his drinking and erratic behavior, but had to give in to Selznick's demands. Mayer was also hesitant to cast Harlow as Beery's social-climbing wife. He feared

Jean Harlow relaxes between takes in her white-on-white negligee.

"ME MUSSOLINI, YOU JANE"

As originally filmed, Marie Dressler's dog in Dinner at Eight was named Mussolini, as it had been in the Kaufman-Ferber play. When the Italian government objected to this canine allusion to "Il Duce," the star had to redub her lines. At least the change gave MGM a chance to plug its own product. They renamed the dog "Tarzan."

the actress would be out of her depth among the more experienced cast members, but Cukor, who had admired her work in *Red Dust,* insisted that she could pull her weight.

As it turned out, those two casting choices were among the most successful in the film. Barrymore embraced the similarities between himself and his character, allowing the writers to insert references to his profile and his three divorces. Despite his reputation for giving directors a hard time, he got along beautifully with Cukor, who was a close friend of his sister Ethel. When George Bernard Shaw visited the set, Barrymore even pulled Cukor aside and offered to make some mistakes on the set so Cukor could correct him in front of their guest.

Harlow always credited the director with helping her find herself as a comedienne. According to Cukor, however, the talent had always been there. He was surprised to discover that the real Harlow—a soft-spoken, gracious woman who would send people presents in gratitude for the simplest courtesies—was far different from her brassy screen image. He also discovered that her greatest comic gift was the ability to deliver lines as though she didn't quite know what they meant.

The critics were ecstatic. Most considered the film an improvement over the play, particularly the last scene, written by Donald Ogden Smith. As Harlow and Dressler prepare to go in to dinner, the former mentions she's been reading a book. "It's a screwy sort of book," she says, "all about the future. This man thinks that someday machines will take the place of every known profession." "My dear," warbles Dressler, "that's something you need never worry about."

The film's $1 million profit gave Selznick the clout he needed to get difficult projects like *David Copperfield* approved and eventually helped him secure backers when he became an independent producer. But the biggest winner was probably Jean Harlow. Not only did critics marvel at her newfound comic abilities, but she made such a strong impression in her final costume that people began referring to white satin evening dresses as "Jean Harlow gowns."

A WHITE SHADE OF PALE

The designers for* Dinner at Eight, *Hobe Erwin and Fred Hope, defied Hollywood convention by creating an all-white bedroom for Jean Harlow. In truth, they used eleven different shades of white, then worked with cameraman William Daniels to use shadows for further variation. With the white-on-white bedroom, however, they had to be particularly careful of Jean Harlow's costumes. Anything would show through. So the platinum blonde had to dye her pubic hair to match her trademark tresses. When even that didn't help, Harlow's hairdresser designed a white "wiglet" to cover the area.

The Dirty Dozen

"There's No Such Thing as a Nice War"

1967. CAST: Lee Marvin (Major Reisman), Ernest Borgnine (General Worden), Charles Bronson (Joseph Wladislaw), Jim Brown (Robert Jefferson), John Cassavetes (Victor Franko), Richard Jaeckel (Sergeant Bowden), George Kennedy (Major Max Armbruster), Ralph Meeker (Captain Stuart Kinder), Robert Ryan (Colonel Everett Dasher-Breed). Producer: Kenneth Hyman; Director: Robert Aldrich; Screenplay: Lukas Heller, Nunnally Johnson (Based on the novel by E. M. Nathanson); Photography: Edward Scaife (70mm, Metrocolor); Music: Frank DeVol. RUNNING TIME: 150 minutes.

Director Robert Aldrich played both sides against the middle with *The Dirty Dozen,* giving MGM the biggest hit of the year and setting a new standard for the grisly depiction of modern warfare. It was nothing new for the master of the politics of brutality, but certainly a far cry from the studio's days of glamorous, idealized family entertainment.

He discovered E. M. Nathanson's novel while it was still in outline form. Even then he could smell a hit in its story of a renegade World War II general forced to train twelve stockade cases for a suicide mission behind German lines. At the time, however, he wasn't in any position to buy his own material. Instead, MGM picked up the rights, assigning accomplished screenwriter Nunnally Johnson to adapt the story. When the studio brought in Kenneth Hyman, whose 7-Arts Productions had backed *Whatever Happened to Baby Jane,* Aldrich became the logical choice to direct.

Casting proved a problem. Although Aldrich's contract gave him cast approval, the studio went behind his back to offer the starring role to John Wayne. This was a big mistake in Aldrich's view. It wasn't that he questioned Wayne's politics. He just saw Major Reisman as a less heroic figure than he would have been in Wayne's hands, preferring Lee Marvin for the role.

MGM was spared any possible embarrassment when Wayne withdrew to devote more time to directing and starring in *The Green Berets.* Aldrich cast Marvin in his place, which turned out to be a major boon when the actor's career took off with an Oscar for *Cat Ballou* and a major hit in *The Professionals.* For the rest of the cast, Aldrich picked several actors with whom he'd worked previously, including Charles Bronson, Ernest Borgnine, George Kennedy, and Ralph Meeker.

The Dirty Four plus one: convicts Jim Brown, John Cassavetes, Telly Sevalis, and Charles Bronson, with officer George Kennedy.

For location shooting, the company moved to MGM's Borehamwood Studios in England. But the English weather caused so many delays that the film went $1 million over its $4 million budget. In addition, the German chateau set caught fire under mysterious circumstances. Fortunately, most of the scenes there had been shot already.

For all the problems, however, MGM never lost faith in the film. The studio even paid to have the print blown up from the original 35mm to 70mm to take advantage of the picture's dazzling special effects. MGM's confidence was fully vindicated when *The Dirty Dozen* opened to strong box office, grossing $7.5 million in just five weeks. Eventually, the film would become the number-one picture of 1967, posting more than $20 million in rentals.

But *The Dirty Dozen*'s box-office success was matched by the controversy it evoked. Even in a year of surprisingly violent films—including *Bonnie and Clyde* and *Point Blank*—Aldrich's work stood out. Though some critics applauded him for taking a strong antiwar stance, others claimed that it was impossible to use violence to denounce violence. One writer even tried to blame the film for that summer's Detroit race riots. Aldrich was quick to defend his work, stating that, "The whole nature of war is dehumanizing. There's no such thing as a nice war." He also got support from a surprising source. Deposed scripter Nunnally Johnson defended Aldrich's use of violence: "War is a dreadful thing, and if people are going to be killed and their bones broken and their heads burst open, you have to go along with that."

Dr. Jekyll and Mr. Hyde

"There Are Bounds Beyond Which One Should Not Go"

1932. CAST: Fredric March (Dr. Henry Jekyll/Mr. Hyde), Miriam Hopkins (Ivy Pearson), Rose Hobart (Muriel Carew), Holmes Herbert (Dr. Lanyon), Edgar Norton (Poole), Halliwell Hobbes (Brigadier General Carew). Producer-Director: Rouben Mamoulian; Screenplay: Samuel Hoffenstein, Percy Heath (Based on the novel *The Strange Case of Dr. Jekyll and Mr. Hyde* by Robert Louis Stevenson); Photography: Karl Struss.

RUNNING TIME: 97 minutes.

For an audience new to sound, what we would consider the clichés of the horror genre—sudden screams, inexplicable laboratory apparatus, warnings that "there are things man was not meant to know"—were revelations. They set the stage for a battle between good and evil so terrifyingly primal, people actually worried about the effect such films would have on children and pregnant women. Before there was splatter, horror films could aspire to art. But few early horror pictures rose to the level of Rouben Mamoulian's definitive rendering of the Jekyll-Hyde legend.

Director Rouben Mamoulian saw *Dr. Jekyll and Mr. Hyde* as a comment on the repressive nature of conventional morality. For him, Hyde wasn't a force of evil, but rather a vehicle for primitive passions too long held in check. To make the proper contrast between the good and evil in his main character, he insisted on casting a young, attractive Jekyll. This was a departure from Stevenson's original, in which Hyde is fifty-five. Mamoulian's insistence on casting Fredric March was another surprise. The young actor was primarily known for romantic comedy roles.

One of the most astonishing scenes in the film is Jekyll's first transformation into Hyde. The camera pans between his hand and his face, with the features noticeably altered each time they're seen. Then the camera whirls around the room before coming to rest on Hyde as he looks at his new face in the mirror. The first part of the transformation was achieved through makeup, lights, and jump cuts. To make Jekyll transform on camera, makeup artists put red shadows on March's face. These were blocked out by a red filter on the camera. When the filter was removed, the shadows appeared. For the rest of the transformation, the rapid pans between March's hand and face concealed jump cuts, during which the actor went through several stages of makeup.

Fredric March contemplates things "man was not meant to know."

A NIGHTINGALE SANG AT PARAMOUNT

Mamoulian had one problem with the scene in which Jekyll spontaneously transforms into Hyde after watching a cat pounce on a singing nightingale. There were no nightingales in America. He could dummy up a convincing bird, but nothing in this country sang quite like a true English nightingale. He sent out an assistant to see if he could find a bird anywhere in the area, but the man returned with a rather large Englishwoman instead. "Where's the nightingale?" Mamoulian asked, to which the woman replied, "I am your nightingale." She then explained that she was an expert on birdcalls. Still skeptical, Mamoulian asked her to demonstrate the nightingale's song. When she asked, "The northern nightingale or the Welsh nightingale?" he knew he'd solved his problem.

Dr. Jekyll and Mr. Hyde was a tremendous success, winning Fredric March the only acting Oscar for a horror film until Anthony Hopkins won for *The Silence of the Lambs* in 1992. During the ceremonies, ballot counters discovered that Wallace Berry had come within one vote of March for his performance in *The Champ*. After the last scheduled award was given out, they called Beery to the dais and gave him the evening's second Best Actor Oscar. March would later quip that it was ironic that, since both men had just adopted children, they should be honored for best male performance.

In 1935, Paramount was faced with a product shortage and decided to reissue *Dr. Jekyll and Mr. Hyde*. By that time, Hollywood had adopted stricter censorship regulations under the Production Code, requiring the studio to cut some of Miriam Hopkins's hottest scenes as the sluttish barmaid Ivy. In addition, the studio shortened the film so it could play more easily in double bills.

Sixty years later, MGM, which had bought all rights to the film when they remade it with Spencer Tracy and Ingrid Bergman in 1941, managed to find all but three minutes of the lost footage. They failed to recover Hyde's first trip outside the laboratory, during which he tramples a young child, which some scholars think may have been cut during previews. But even with that scene missing, the restored, "uncensored" print brought new attention to the screen's best version of Stevenson's classic tale.

Fredric March in makeup tests for his transformation.

Doctor Zhivago

"Somewhere, My Love"

1965. CAST: Omar Sharif (Yuri Zhivago), Julie Christie (Lara), Geraldine Chaplin (Tonya), Rod Steiger (Komarovsky), Alec Guinness (Yevgraf), Tom Courtenay (Pasha). Producer: Carlo Ponti; Director: David Lean; Screenplay: Robert Bolt (Based on the novel by Boris Pasternak); Photography: Freddie Young (B.S.C.); Music: Maurice Jarre.

RUNNING TIME: 180 minutes.

Some films make their mark solely through box-office performance, others develop cult followings through repeated theatrical revivals and television screenings, but only a handful, like *Doctor Zhivago,* leave behind a cultural legacy lasting long after the final fade-out.

Director David Lean's epic romance was more than just the first major western film to capture the turmoil of the Russian Revolution. It had a significant effect on the culture at large—influencing everything from fashion to music to the way people named their children.

Boris Pasternak's magical tale of the poet-doctor Yuri Zhivago, the beautiful Lara, and their struggles to remain together through the turmoil of the Russian Revolution became an international bestseller in 1957, despite the Soviet government's efforts to suppress the novel for its "hatred of Socialism." Italian producer Carlo Ponti won the film rights in 1963 after fierce competition, then contracted with MGM to release the picture. He also hired director David Lean and gave him complete artistic control on the strength of his recent success with *Lawrence of Arabia.*

Filming in the Soviet Union was out of the question, so Lean settled on Spain, a major location for international film production. The Moscow street sets were constructed just outside Madrid, while the mountains three hundred miles to the north served as the location for Zhivago's country estate and the train scenes.

Initially, Lean had hoped to get Peter O'Toole, the star of *Lawrence of Arabia,* to play Zhivago. But O'Toole was reluctant to undertake another arduous location shoot and turned the film down. Instead, Lean chose Egyptian actor Omar Sharif, who had moved into western filmmaking with *Lawrence of Arabia*. For his leading ladies, Lean bypassed established female stars in favor of two

Julie Christie in tests to develop the "mod" look of revolutionary Russia.

relative unknowns: Charles Chaplin's daughter Geraldine and British actress Julie Christie.

Because of the production's size and Lean's desire to capture the different seasons during which the story took place, shooting was set for ten months. The schedule grew even longer because of weather delays that added $2.5 million to the final budget. *Doctor Zhivago* was shot during one of the mildest winters in Spanish history. Winter scenes were postponed so often that many had to be shot during the summer, and costume designer Phyllis Dalton had to keep strict watch over the film's extras to be sure they didn't remove too many layers of clothing.

The weather wreaked havoc on the film's sets as well. The production crew had planted seven thousand daffodil bulbs for spring scenes near Zhivago's country estate, but the winter was so mild they started blooming in January. The crew had to dig up the bulbs, pot them for cold storage, and replant them. Meanwhile, the landscape, which had turned green before the winter scenes could be shot, had to be treated with white paint, plaster dust, and even white plastic sheets to create the illusion of snow-filled vistas.

Yet all the effort proved worthwhile when *Doctor Zhivago* became one of MGM's biggest hits ever. By the end of its first year in release, the film had grossed $16 million.

Helping tremendously was the popularity of Maurice Jarre's score, particularly "Lara's Theme (Somewhere, My Love)." From a guitar rendition he once heard on a Venetian gondola, to a performance on tribal instruments in Central Africa, to countless music boxes, the chart-topping melody has followed Jarre around the world.

But "Lara's Theme" was far from the only legacy left by *Doctor Zhivago*. The "Zhivago Look" inspired designers like Yves St. Laurent and Christian Dior to incorporate fur trim, silk braiding, and boots in their collections. In addition, the film revived the popularity of mustaches and beards. *Doctor Zhivago*'s influence even extended to the way people named their children. Suddenly, Lara, a name formerly used only in Russia, started turning up on birth announcements.

CAST OF THOUSANDS—SOME *DOCTOR ZHIVAGO* STATISTICS

Length of Original Novel	*512 pages*
Projected Length of a Film Incorporating Entire Novel	*72 hours*
Film's Running Time at Premiere	*3 hours, 17 minutes*
Number of Sets Built for Film	*117*
Length of Main Moscow Street	*1/2 mile*
Number of Extras in Film	*10,000*
Number of Extras in Moscow Street Scenes	*3,500*
Size of Orchestra Required to Record Score	*110*
Number of Balalaika Players Used to Record Score	*22*

Easter Parade

"It Only Happens When I Dance with You"

1948. CAST: Judy Garland (Hannah Brown), Fred Astaire (Don Hewes), Peter Lawford (Jonathan Harrow III), Ann Miller (Nadine Hale), Jules Munshin (François), Clinton Sundberg (Mike the Bartender). Producer: Arthur Freed; Director: Charles Walters; Screenplay: Francis Goodrich, Albert Hackett, Sidney Sheldon, Guy Bolton (Based on a story by Goodrich and Hackett); Photography: Harry Stradling Sr. (Technicolor); Musical Direction: Johnny Green, Roger Edens; Music and Lyrics: Irving Berlin.

RUNNING TIME: 103 minutes.

It almost didn't happen at all. One of Hollywood's most delightful, carefree musicals reached the screen only after the replacement of two stars, a director, and the studio for which the production had been planned in the first place.

The project was inspired by Paramount's 1946 hit *Blue Skies,* a combination of new and vintage songs by Irving Berlin, starring Fred Astaire and Bing Crosby. Berlin decided that he'd like to do another film built around his song catalog and approached Joseph Schenck at 20th Century–Fox—which had produced their own Berlin musical, *Alexander's Ragtime Band,* in the thirties. Schenck loved the idea and the title—*Easter Parade*—but Fox executives weren't keen on paying Berlin a percentage of the gross. So, Berlin shopped the idea around to other studios, finally getting what he wanted out of MGM.

Naturally, the project went to Arthur Freed, MGM's best musical producer. He and the writing team of Frances Goodrich and Albert Hackett came up with the plot hook: when his dancing partner moves on to solo stardom, an experienced vaudevillian trains and falls in love with her replacement, all between Easter 1911 and Easter 1912. The story was set for Judy Garland, Gene Kelly, and Cyd Charisse, with Garland's husband, Vincente Minnelli, directing.

Then the defections started. Garland's previous film had been *The Pirate,* also with Kelly and Minnelli. At the time, the director and dancer's close collaboration had made her jealous. After the film, Garland suffered a breakdown and was still under psychiatric supervision when she returned to the studio. Five days into rehearsal, her psychiatrist called Freed, advising him that Garland

Fred Astaire thinks partner Ann Miller will be "Hard to Replace," until he falls for Judy Garland.

FIFTH AVENUE, CALIFORNIA

At the close of* Easter Parade*, audiences gasped at the panoramic shot of New York's Fifth Avenue in 1912, which combined the grandeur of St. Patrick's Cathedral with buildings long since torn down. MGM spared no expense for the scene, using seven hundred extras and more than one hundred vintage automobiles. But they weren't about to send the company on location—or into the past. Art director Jack Martin Smith built the bottom ten feet of the cathedral and just two blocks on one side of Fifth Avenue. The rest was painted in by the special effects department. To make the effect even more spectacular, it was the first such shot to use a moving camera.

should not be working with her husband at this time. So Freed replaced Minnelli with Charles Walters, a former dancer whose only other directing credit had been *Good News,* with June Allyson.

About this time, Cyd Charisse broke her leg. Mayer had just signed Ann Miller, so Freed assigned her to the film. Since Miller's brassy style was a far cry from Charisse's more balletic dancing, they needed a new solo number for the character. Musical director Roger Edens suggested "Shaking the Blues Away," which became one of the film's highlights.

SMILE AND SHOW YOUR DIMPLE

"Easter Parade" was introduced in the 1933 Broadway musical* As Thousands Cheer *but actually had been written fifteen years earlier. As "Smile and Show Your Dimple," it had not gone over well with audiences, but Irving Berlin liked the melody and filed it away for future use. Years later, when he needed a song for a musical revue based on the sections of a newspaper, he refurbished the song to go with the Sunday color fashion page. Berlin always likened a hit song to a successful marriage between music and lyrics. In the case of "Easter Parade," he often said, "It took a divorce and second marriage to bring about the happiest of unions."

Then Kelly broke his ankle playing touch football. Freed considered the young Gene Nelson but decided he needed a box-office name to match with Garland. That's when he called Fred Astaire.

Astaire had announced his retirement after completing *Blue Skies* two years earlier, but the prospect of working with Garland was just too good. He called Kelly and asked him three questions: "Will this hurt your career?" "Do you think I can learn the dances?" and "Is there any chance you could do the picture?" Kelly finally said, "As one hoofer to another, I'd like to see you back in pictures." When *Easter Parade* opened in July 1948, it became MGM's top-grossing film of the year, taking in more than $6.8 million on an investment of $2.5 million. It not only brought Astaire back into musicals as a member of the MGM stock company but also set Ann Miller on the road to stardom at the studio.

For Garland, it was her last great MGM musical. The film also gave her one of her signature tunes—the tramps' duet, "A Couple of Swells." Starting with her smash appearance at the Palace in 1951, the number became a part of the Garland repertoire, often followed by a poignant rendition of "Over the Rainbow," still in tramp costume.

Executive Suite

"Eight Stars in a Boardroom"

1954. CAST: William Holden (McDonald Walling), June Allyson (Mary Blanchard Walling), Barbara Stanwyck (Julia O. Tredway), Fredric March (Loren Phineas Shaw), Walter Pidgeon (Frederick Y. Alderson), Shelley Winters (Eva Bardeman), Paul Douglas (Josiah Walter Dudley), Louis Calhern (George Nyle Caswell), Dean Jagger (Jesse W. Grimm), Nina Foch (Erica Martin). Producer: John Houseman; Director: Robert Wise; Screenplay: Ernest Lehman (Based on the novel by Cameron Hawley); Photography: George Folsey. RUNNING TIME: 104 minutes.

The world of boardroom battles and back-stabbing came to life as never before when MGM presented filmgoers with their first inside look at corporate America. In addition, *Executive Suite*'s colorful characters offered the studio its first opportunity for all-star casting in years.

Novelist Cameron Hawley had been a business executive before leaving the rat race to concentrate on writing. His experience inspired the story of a corporation torn apart by infighting and treachery when its powerful president dies without naming a successor. MGM's head of production, Dore Schary, quick to spot the entertainment value, assigned the project to producer John Houseman, a former associate of Orson Welles. Houseman was determined not to use any of the studio's contract writers for the film. He wanted a fresh perspective, somebody who wasn't steeped in the studio's glamorous traditions. His assistant suggested the young Ernest Lehman, who'd made a hit with the short story "The Sweet Smell of Success." *Executive Suite* would be his first major script assignment, to be followed by Oscar nominations for *North by Northwest* and *Who's Afraid of Virginia Woolf?*

Since *Executive Suite* climaxed with a long board meeting to elect the new president, Houseman felt he needed a director with a strong editing sense to keep things moving. His choice was Robert Wise, who had started out as an editor at RKO, working on *Citizen Kane* and *The Magnificent Ambersons* before turning to directing.

With the story's focus on several main characters, Houseman and Schary decided to return to the kind of all-star cast MGM had used for such classics as *Dinner at Eight* and *Grand Hotel,* but it

Barbara Stanwyck and Fredric March prepare for the climactic boardroom battle.

required a bit of schedule shuffling. They had to convince Fredric March to return from a Greek vacation early, wait for June Allyson to finish *The Glenn Miller Story* at Universal, and fly Shelley Winters to Hollywood from a film location in Canada.

One star whose schedule couldn't be adjusted was Henry Fonda, Houseman's first choice to play the idealistic production manager fighting to keep the company honest. Fonda had committed to star in a Broadway musical and needed the time to develop his singing voice. In his place, Houseman cast William Holden.

Holden's casting yielded another bonus when it helped Houseman attract Barbara Stanwyck, who had wanted to work with the actor since he made his starring debut opposite her in 1939's *Golden Boy*. The role of Julia Tredway, the embittered mistress of the company's late president, was hardly the largest in her career. It would only require seven days work from the star. But the role and the chance to reteam with Holden were too good to turn down.

Because the script leaned heavily on dialogue, Houseman filled the cast with stage veterans. When Wise called for extra rehearsals, most of them were delighted at the chance to get into their roles. Knowing the level of work he could expect from such a cast, Holden made sure he knew the entire script before the first rehearsal.

Unfortunately, Allyson didn't. Coming directly from another film, she arrived late for the first rehearsal with script still in hand. The other actors were appalled, and Stanwyck told her off to her face. That night, Allyson's agent called Houseman to complain that the rest of the cast didn't like her and made her feel persecuted. The producer smoothed things over, and the next day his star was on time and letter-perfect.

Executive Suite garnered strong reviews and set a box-office record during its first weekend at New York's Radio City Music Hall. As a result, Houseman was the hero of the hour at MGM, where he would continue to turn out solid films like *Lust for Life* and *The Cobweb* until he left to found the American Shakespeare Festival in Stratford, Connecticut, in 1956.

> **"Today . . . you meet the exciting women behind the scheming men who struggle for power in MGM's Executive Suite.**
>
> **"THE LONELY HEIRESS . . . haunted by her secret love!**
>
> **"THE OFFICE WIFE . . . her kisses could kill a man's chances!**
>
> **"THE YOUNG WIFE . . . fearful of losing her man!**
>
> **"THE PRIVATE SECRETARY . . . knows all the answers—and there's plenty to know!"**
>
> **—Ad copy for Executive Suite**

Father of the Bride

"I Always Used to Think That Marriage Was a Simple Affair"

1950. CAST: Spencer Tracy (Stanley T. Banks), Joan Bennett (Ellie Banks), Elizabeth Taylor (Kay Banks), Don Taylor (Buckley Dunstan), Billie Burke (Doris Dunstan), Leo G. Carroll (Mr. Massoula), Rusty [later Russ] Tamblyn (Tommy Banks), Roger Moore (Bit). Producer: Pandro S. Berman; Director: Vincente Minnelli; Screenplay: Frances Goodrich, Albert Hackett (Based on the novel by Edward Streeter); Photography: John Alton; Music: Adolph Deutsch. RUNNING TIME: 93 minutes.

Real life gave MGM an unexpected publicity boost when Elizabeth Taylor took her first husband just a few weeks before *Father of the Bride* premiered in June 1950. The film was so well made that it probably didn't need much help at the box office, but the headlines generated by her wedding, not to mention the frenzy into which it sent her fans, certainly didn't hurt.

MGM production chief Dore Schary assigned the film to producer Pandro S. Berman, who gave the script to one of the studio's top screenwriting teams, Frances Goodrich and Albert Hackett. Berman had just had a very good experience working with Vincente Minnelli on *Madamae Bovary,* so he offered the director his first shot at a comedy. At the time, Minnelli was waiting for production to begin on *An American in Paris*. He had been scheduled to direct Robert Walker in *The Skipper Surprised His Wife,* but found Streeter's story of the indignities suffered by a father preparing to give away his only daughter much better suited to his tastes.

Berman and Minnelli were in agreement from the first on the perfect actor for the title role. Only Spencer Tracy, in their opinion, could keep the audience laughing while also being true to the mixed emotions Stanley Banks, like most fathers, felt on watching his little girl leave home. Before they could settle the casting, however, Schary ran into radio comedian Jack Benny at a party. Benny wanted to play the role desperately, and Schary agreed to give him a shot at it. Minnelli and Berman were horrified. Benny's style of comic playing, however expert, was totally wrong for the story. To make matters worse, once Tracy heard that the studio was testing actors for the role, he decided he didn't want it. Minnelli got Katharine Hepburn to arrange a dinner for the two at which the director convinced his star that the film just wouldn't work without him.

> *"The bride gets the thrills! Father gets the bills!"*
>
> —Ad line for Father of the Bride

Elizabeth Taylor was the natural choice for Kay Banks. At the time she was announced for *Father of the Bride,* Taylor made an announcement of her own—she was considering marrying William Pawley and retiring from the screen. As she told the press, the thought of planning her own wedding and playing a young bride at the same time was "positively drooly."

First, though, she had to fulfill a loan-out to Paramount Pictures, where she would join Montgomery Clift for *A Place in the Sun*. Pawley grew tired of waiting for her to work through her studio commitments, and the wedding was canceled. But Liz wouldn't be alone for long. Before the film was finished, she started dating hotel heir Nicky Hilton. When he popped the question, they set the wedding for May 6, 1950—just weeks before the projected premiere of *Father of the Bride*.

Production proceeded smoothly. Minnelli enjoyed working with all of the cast—which included Joan Bennett, Billie Burke, and Leo G. Carroll—and he particularly liked working with cinematographer John Alton, who was just graduating from low-budget films. Alton's ability to work quickly helped the film stay on budget, while his facility with shadows and light helped Minnelli create a special look for the film, adding some film noir touches to hint at the more serious side of the story.

MGM was pretty happy, too. Halfway through production, the story department registered the title *Now I'm a Grandfather,* and the studio negotiated with Streeter to buy sequel rights for $10,000. The sequel, in which Taylor has her first child, was finally made as *Father's Little Dividend* later that year. After completing *Father of the Bride,* Minnelli went on to shoot most of *An American in Paris*. While Gene Kelly was choreographing and rehearsing the film's ballet, Minnelli went back to make the sequel.

Father of the Bride was one of the big box-office winners of 1950, ranking sixth on the list of top grossers with $4.1 million in rentals on a budget of about $1 million. The sequel did a surprising $3.9 million in business. There would be a failed television series starring Leon Ames in the sixties and a successful big-screen remake in 1991, followed by a 1995 sequel, both with Steve Martin in Tracy's role and Diane Keaton as his wife.

Elizabeth Taylor walks down the aisle.

Flesh and the Devil

"Sometimes I Felt I Was Intruding"

1926. CAST: John Gilbert (Leo Van Harden), Greta Garbo (Felicitas von Eltz), Lars Hanson (Ulrich von Kletzingk), Barbara Kent (Hertha Prochvitz), William Orlamond (Uncle Kutowski), George Voss (Pastor Voss). Director: Clarence Brown; Screenplay: Benjamin F. Glazer (Based on the novel *Es War; Roman in Zwei Banden* by Herman Sudermann); Titles: Marian Ainslee; Photography: William Daniels. RUNNING TIME: 112 minutes.

Moviegoers shared director Clarence Brown's assessment of the love scenes in this silent romance. Working together for the first time, Greta Garbo and John Gilbert quickly became the screen's premier romantic team—on-screen and off. And just as their romance would lead to on-screen tragedy in their first film together, so it would also contribute to the unhappy fate of the biggest male star in silent pictures.

Flesh and the Devil was only Garbo's third film in America. The sleek Swedish star was considered prime vamp material and generated considerable electricity playing shady ladies in her first two MGM pictures, *The Torrent* and *The Temptress*. Fan mail was pouring in, with a considerable amount suggesting she team with MGM's top male star, John Gilbert.

Shortly after casting was announced, Gilbert ran into Garbo at the studio and decided to introduce himself. But when he said, "Hello, Greta," she looked down and replied, "It is Miss Garbo," then walked off. When Garbo refused to show up at preliminary meetings on the film, Gilbert seethed.

On the first day of shooting, director Clarence Brown realized that Garbo was actually terrified of meeting Gilbert. Brown went to Gilbert and asked him to come meet his costar. But he'd been stung once too often. "To hell with her," he said. "Let her come to meet me." So, Brown brought Garbo to Gilbert's dressing room. He quickly realized how shy she was, and before the meeting had ended he was enchanted with her. Within a few days, they were lovers. Within a few weeks, she'd moved into his mansion.

The love affair provided a special boost to the film. The stars' clinches continued long after Brown yelled, "Cut!" After some scenes, the director simply motioned the crew to move quietly to

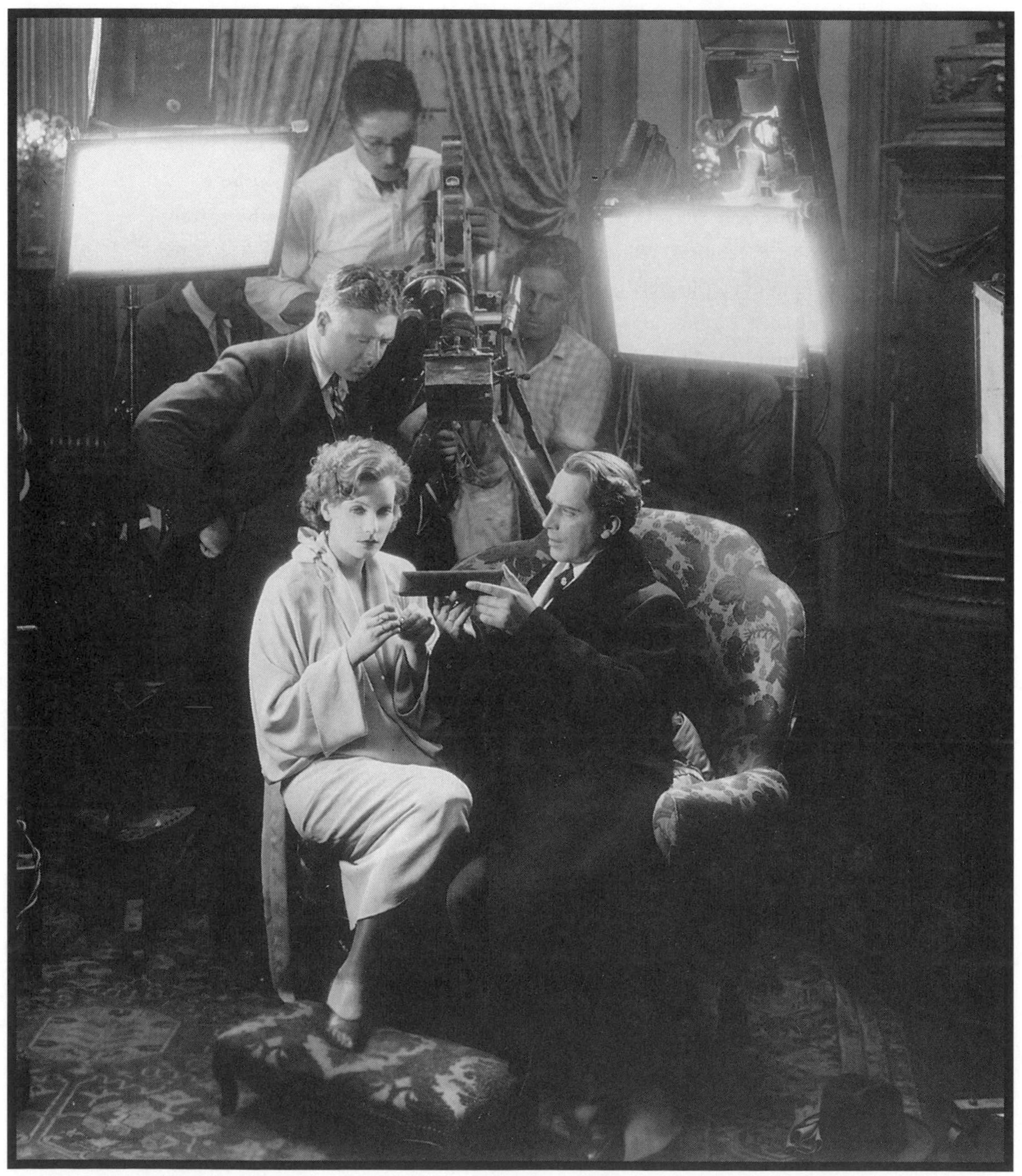

Director Clarence Brown (standing) "eavesdrops" on Greta Garbo and John Gilbert.

another part of the set. And when the stars weren't kissing in a scene, they could barely keep their hands off each other.

The result was a box-office bonanza. MGM's next project for Garbo was *Love,* an adaptation of *Anna Karenina* to costar Ricardo Cortez. When the project was announced, fans flooded the studio with mail demanding that she and Gilbert be reteamed, and they were. As a result, marquees around the nation spread the news, "Gilbert and Garbo in *Love*" (originally the title was to have been *Heat* until writer Frances Marion pointed out how bad that would look).

By this time, however, the affair had begun to cool. Garbo had repeatedly turned down Gilbert's marriage proposals. Once he had gotten her as far as city hall, only to watch her flee down the steps at the last minute. Two years later, their friends King Vidor and actress Eleanor Boardman were planning their own wedding, and Gilbert suggested making it a double ceremony. Garbo agreed, to everyone's surprise. On the morning of the event, however, she didn't show. Gilbert was already upset enough when Mayer made a crude comment about the relationship. The star snapped and started to strangle their boss. After the guests pulled them apart, Mayer hissed, "You're finished, Gilbert. I'll destroy you if it takes a million dollars."

With the coming of sound, he may have done just that. Some in Hollywood hinted that Mayer had deliberately sabotaged the soundtrack of Gilbert's first talkie, *His Glorious Night,* to make the actor's light tenor voice sound ridiculous. Others suggested that he simply kept Gilbert from getting the best scripts.

Garbo, who had become a bigger star than ever with the arrival of sound, tried to help by demanding he costar with her in *Queen Christina,* but it was too little, too late. Her former lover sank into alcoholism and despair, dying of a heart attack in 1936 at the age of forty-one. His fate makes the love scenes he and Garbo shared, particularly in the flush of first love while making *Flesh and the Devil,* even more poignant.

TIMELESS PASSION

Like most silent films, **Flesh and the Devil** *was withdrawn from circulation with the coming of sound. Despite its legendary status, the film was little seen for decades. With the growing interest in film preservation and restoration in the eighties, however, a revival was inevitable.*

Fortunately, MGM's executives had the foresight to store most of the studio's films under optimal conditions. This made it possible for the studio to supply a new print, as good as the original, when the London Film Festival booked it in 1982. Carl Davis wrote a new score, performed live at each screening, and Gilbert's daughter, Leatrice Gilbert Fountain, introduced the film. The three performances sold out quickly. Although the audience had to adjust to the conventions of silent-film acting at the start, by the end they were enthralled. Ushers reported that even teens in the audience were visibly moved, rushing to wipe tears from their eyes as the house lights came up.

Footlight Parade

"1,000 Surprises! 300 Beauties! 20 Big Stars!"

1933. CAST: James Cagney (Chester Kent), Joan Blondell (Nan Prescott), Ruby Keeler (Bea Thorn), Dick Powell (Scotty Blair), Guy Kibbee (Silas Gould), Ruth Donnelly (Harriet Bowers Gould). Director: Lloyd Bacon; Screenplay: Manuel Seff, James Seymour; Photography: George Barnes; Musical Director: Leo F. Forbstein; Music and Lyrics: Harry Warren and Al Dubin, Sammy Fain and Irving Kahal; Choreography: Busby Berkeley. RUNNING TIME: 104 minutes.

The ads for *Footlight Parade* may have exaggerated the film's lineup of great stars, but they were far from wrong in their other claims. The last of three trendsetting musicals released by Warner Bros. in 1933, the picture was easily the most dazzling, thanks to some of Busby Berkeley's most imaginative musical numbers ever and the surprise choice of James Cagney to star.

Of course, taps were much more familiar to Cagney than the gats of his gangster films. He had started his career as a dancer, a skill he picked up to keep out of trouble growing up in New York's Hell's Kitchen. But his early success as Tom Powers in *Public Enemy*, only his fifth film, forever typed him as a tough-talking gangster star.

Cagney quickly grew tired of such roles, rightly seeing how much they were limiting his career. When he heard of plans for *Footlight Parade,* he fought to play Chester Kent, the Broadway producer who meets the competition from talking pictures by converting his operation to produce live musical "prologues" for movie theatres.

The film put Cagney in strong company. It was the third teaming for Ruby Keeler and Dick Powell, both of whom the star admired tremendously. It also marked his sixth picture with Joan Blondell, who had recently married the picture's cameraman, George Barnes.

More important, it gave him a chance to work with the man who had turned the film musical into something more than just filmed stage shows—Busby Berkeley. Berkeley had rescued the genre from the box-office doldrums with eye-popping numbers in *42nd Street* and *Gold Diggers of 1933*. With *Footlight Parade* he went even further, climaxing the film with three intricate musical numbers in a row.

CRACKING WISE

While Dick Powell, Ruby Keeler, and even James Cagney carried the musical numbers in **Footlight Parade,** *Joan Blondell helped keep the film's first hour afloat as Cagney's secretary and romantic interest. In her best scene, she gets rid of a gold digger (Clare Dodd) out to cash in on his new success. "As long as they've got sidewalks," Blondell snaps, "you've got a job." The line would be cut by censors when the film was reissued in 1935 (after Hollywood started enforcing the Production Code) and not return until the picture's 1970 reissue, complete with G rating.*

Pioneering dance director Busby Berkeley contemplates some of the chorus girls' chief assets.

A CLICHÉ IS BORN

Great lines seemed to follow Ruby Keeler around like adoring fans. In *Footlight Parade,* she starts out as one of Cagney's secretaries, wearing horn-rimmed glasses for the role. Romance blossoms when Dick Powell takes off her specs and marvels, "Why, Miss Thorn, you're beautiful." It was a movie moment that would be repeated for decades to come.

"Honeymoon Hotel" featured Dick Powell and Ruby Keeler singing and dancing their dreams of wedded bliss, as they are chased through the halls of a New Jersey resort by assorted relatives and well-wishers. At the end of the piece, Powell ends up in bed not with Keeler, but with a lascivious overgrown baby played by Billy Barty. The number was considered so risqué that parts of it were cut by local censorship boards.

Berkeley was at his most spectacular in the second number, "By a Waterfall." More than one hundred chorus girls swam, slid, and posed in a series of swimming pools, platforms, and caverns while water flowed at the rate of twenty thousand gallons per minute.

Dick Powell and Ruby Keeler.

It took two weeks of rehearsal and six days of shooting to film the routine, at a cost of $250,000 (half the film's budget). Berkeley even designed special rubber bathing suits and caps for the chorus girls to give the illusion that they were almost naked. The results were so spectacular that Broadway showman Billy Rose asked Berkeley to stage his Aquacade for the Texas State Fair, an assignment Berkeley had to refuse because of his commitments at Warner Bros.

The film's final number may seem the strangest by our standards, but was a big hit in 1933. Filling in for a drunken actor, Cagney sings and dances "Shanghai Lil" as a sailor searching for his lost girl in a Chinese brothel. After he introduces the song, it's picked up by the chorus as the camera moves through what is clearly an opium den (this number, too, was heavily cut by censors). Finally, he finds his Asian sweetheart—in the form of Ruby Keeler. After they dance together on the table tops, there's a barroom brawl. The sailors then march out, stopping to form some patriotic images for the overhead camera, with Keeler now dressed as a tar, so she can be with her lover.

Footlight Parade received mixed reviews, with some critics calling it the best of Warner's first three Berkeley musicals and others calling it the least. It did not do as well at the box office as *42nd Street* or *Gold Diggers,* but it still made a $1 million profit. With the nostalgia craze of the seventies, United Artists, which had bought Warner's pre-1948 library, reissued the film on a double bill with *Gold Diggers of 1935* (which includes Berkeley's famous "Lullaby of Broadway" number).

Forbidden Planet

"O Brave New World"

1956. CAST: Walter Pidgeon (Doctor Morbius), Anne Francis (Alta), Leslie Nielsen (Commander Adams), Warren Stevens (Lieutenant "Doc" Ostrow), Jack Kelly (Lieutenant Farman), Richard Anderson (Chief Quinn), Earl Holliman (Cook). Producer: Nicholas Nayfack; Director: Fred McLeod Wilcox; Screenplay: Cyril Hume (Based on a story by Irving Block, Allen Adler); Photography: George Folsey (CinemaScope, Eastmancolor); Electronic Tonalities: Louis and Bebe Barron.

RUNNING TIME: 98 minutes.

While Ed Wood Jr. dreamed of pie-plate flying saucers over Hollywood, and Roger Corman pitted teen heroes against men in rubber suits, MGM made its only large-scale foray into the science-fiction craze of the fifties. Even though it was treated as a lesser production by the studio, *Forbidden Planet* benefited from the craftsmanship of MGM's many filmmaking departments to emerge as the best science-fiction film of the decade and, in the opinion of many, the best sci-fi flick of all time.

The story of space travelers set upon by a monster from the Id when they try to rescue a lost mission's last survivor—a wizard-like scientist living alone with his daughter—originated with special effects artist Irving Block and writer Allen Adler. Initially, they thought it best suited for a low-budget studio, but their agent thought it might have a chance at MGM. He arranged for them to present the story to producer Nicholas Nayfack. Production chief Dore Schary was already interested in taking advantage of the science-fiction craze. The high literary tone of Block and Adler's conception, combining the plot of William Shakespeare's *The Tempest* with Freudian psychology, suggested that this might be the perfect way to do so while maintaining the studio's elevated reputation.

Initially, *Forbidden Planet* was budgeted at a modest $500,000, and scripter Cyril Hume was told to avoid any costly scenes, but as the studio's art direction and special effects departments got to work, Schary's interest quickened and he raised the budget to almost $1.9 million.

Art director Arthur Lonergan was chiefly responsible for the production design, including the interior of United Planets Cruiser C-57D, the flying saucer on which Nielsen and his space crew

BLAST OFF FOR THE BOOB TUBE: THE MIGRATION FROM *FORBIDDEN PLANET* TO TELEVISION

Walter Pidgeon	MGM Parade
Anne Francis	Honey West, Riptide
Leslie Nielsen	The New Breed, Peyton Place, The Protectors, Bracken's World, Police Squad
Warren Stevens	Tales of the 77th Bengal Lancers, The Richard Boone Show, Bracken's World
Jack Kelly	Maverick, Get Christie Love, The Hardy Boys Mysteries
Richard Anderson	The Lieutenant, Perry Mason, Dan August, The Six Million Dollar Man, The Bionic Woman, Cover Up
Earl Holliman	Hotel de Paree, The Wide Country, Police Woman

arrive on Altair-4, and the planet's exteriors, which used a 10,000-square-foot cyclorama to create a world of green skies. Special effects chief A. Arnold Gillespie supervised the creation of the planet's interior, filled with machinery built by Altair-4's long-vanished inhabitants, the Krel. The set combined walkways for the actors with matte paintings and animation to create the illusion that the machinery extended to the core of the planet.

Gillespie's greatest creation was Robby the Robot, the film's version of Shakespeare's Ariel. The metal and plastic automaton was actually a costume. Two technicians took turns operating it from inside while a battery of crew members ran the various lights, dials, and other apparatus. For Robby's voice, they hired one of the most prolific voice-over artists of television's early days, Marvin Miller, who also played Michael Anthony on the popular series *The Millionaire*.

Helping with the special effects was a team of animators from the Walt Disney Studios, under the supervision of Joshua Meador, who had created the animation for the "Rite of Spring" sequence in *Fantasia*. Their chief assignment was to create the Monster from the Id, an invisible creature only glimpsed when it passes through the force field surrounding the flying saucer or gets hit by the crew's energy weapons.

One of the most distinctive elements in *Forbidden Planet* is its electronic score. Louis and Bebe Barron were experimenting with electronic music in New York when they approached Schary just as he was trying to decide how to handle the film's score. For $25,000, about the cost of scoring the film by traditional methods, they created a series of taps, whoops, and gurgles Schary called "electronic tonalities" to avoid problems with the musicians' union. It was the first electronic score ever used for a feature film.

Forbidden Planet opened to mixed reviews, with most critics admiring the effects but labeling it kid stuff. With the emergence of such serious science-fiction hits as *2001: A Space Odyssey* and television's *Star Trek* series, however, *Forbidden Planet* was taken more seriously. Some critics have even suggested the film as an inspiration for *Star Trek,* with its portrait of an intergalactic starship whose crew is organized along military lines. And even with bona fide sci-fi blockbusters like *Star Wars* and *E.T.* from which to choose, many fans continue to point to *Forbidden Planet* as the greatest science-fiction movie of them all—a tribute both to the imagination of Block and Adler and to MGM's ability to commit itself to a new type of film.

FORBIDDEN INTERPLANETARY STATISTICS

Size of Cyclorama for Altair-4 Exterior	*10,000 square feet*
Height of Robby the Robot	*6 feet, 11 inches*
Robby's Weight	*100 pounds*
Number of Electric Motors Required to Operate Robby	*6*
Amount of Electrical Wiring in Robby	*2,600 feet*
Amount of Electrical Wiring in Space Ship	*27 miles*
Amount of Neon Tubing in Krel Laboratory	*2,500 feet*
Number of Individual Switches Needed to Operate Laboratory	*119*
Number of Technicians Needed to Operate Laboratory	*15*
Amount of Bourbon Robby Creates for Ship's Cook	*60 gallons*

Robby the Robot looks on as Anne Francis and a surprisingly serious Leslie Nielsen prepare to learn the secrets of the Krel from a dying Warren Stevens.

Fort Apache

"For the Honor of the Regiment"

1948. CAST: John Wayne (Captain Kirby York), Henry Fonda (Lieutenant Colonel Owen Thursday), Shirley Temple (Philadelphia Thursday), Ward Bond (Sergeant-Major Michael O'Rourke), John Agar (Lieutenant Michael "Mickey" O'Rourke), George O'Brien (Captain Sam Collingwood). Producers: John Ford, Merian C. Cooper; Director: John Ford; Screenplay: Frank S. Nugent (Based on the story "Massacre" by James Warner Bellah); Photography: Archie J. Stout; Music: Richard Hageman.

RUNNING TIME: 127 minutes.

Director John Ford nudged the western into a new era with his 1948 study of the effect a vainglorious, by-the-books commander has on a frontier outpost surrounded by hostile Indians. It hardly sparked the kind of revolution triggered by such provocative films as *The Gunfighter, High Noon,* and *Broken Arrow,* but Ford's revisionist view of the Indian Wars may very well have made those films possible.

When Ford first described the project to writer Frank S. Nugent, he said he wanted to develop a relatively untapped element of western lore—the life of the cavalryman. In most films, including the director's own *Stagecoach,* the cavalry simply rode to the rescue, then vanished before the fade-out. Ford wanted to show what it meant to these men and their families to commit themselves to the defense of a new frontier. The idea was so strong that eventually he developed it through three films—critics have called them his "Cavalry Trilogy"—*Fort Apache, She Wore a Yellow Ribbon,* and *Rio Grande,* all adapted from the fiction of James Warner Bellah.

At the same time, Ford realized the American Indian had been given a raw deal in most westerns, treated either as a shadowy monster or as a stereotyped comedy figure. Ford wasn't quite ready to deal with the Indian as victim of U.S. expansion—that would have to wait until he made *Cheyenne Autumn* in 1964—but with the Cavalry Trilogy he tried to suggest that they had just reason for rebelling. The true enemy in *Fort Apache* is the corrupt federal agent trying to make a fortune at their expense.

Completing his revisionist vision is the film's ending. Lieutenant Colonel Thursday's foolishness

The forces of civilization come to Fort Apache with the arrival of Shirley Temple and Henry Fonda.

leads to a massacre in which most of his regiment is killed. In the original short story, he escapes, then returns to the site to commit suicide. For the film, Ford had him die with his men. Then his second-in-command, the more experienced cavalryman played by John Wayne, hides the truth, turning Thursday into a hero.

As usual, Ford filled the cast with actors with whom he had worked before—some would call them the John Ford Stock Company—including John Wayne, Henry Fonda, Victor McLaglen, Ward Bond, Anna Lee, and Pedro Armendariz. George O'Brien even came out of retirement for the picture.

> ***"The pay is $13 a month. The diet, beans and eggs—may be horsemeat before this campaign is over. They fight over cards or rot-gut whiskey, but share the last drop in their canteens. The faces may change. Names. But they're there. They're the regiment—the regular Army—now and fifty years from now."***
>
> —JOHN WAYNE EULOGIZING HIS LOST COMRADES IN FORT APACHE

To play Fonda's daughter, Ford turned to Shirley Temple, whom he had directed in one of her best pictures as a child star, *Wee Willie Winkie*. Some sources have reported that the director browbeat her on the set, fighting to get a mature performance out of her. But that was nothing compared to Ford's treatment of her husband, John Agar. Agar was making his film debut in *Fort Apache*, and Ford reportedly didn't want to cast him. But the publicity bonus was too hard to refuse. Through the early days of filming, Ford attacked the beginner whenever he didn't have his lines down pat or betrayed his insecurity in the saddle. He even took to calling him "Mr. Temple."

Finally, the ill treatment got to be too much, and Agar packed his bags. But Wayne got to him first and assured him that Ford always treated the least experienced cast member that way. Wayne got Agar to stay, helped him with his lines, and even gave him riding lessons.

Fort Apache got mixed reviews. Ford was still a favorite with the critics, many of whom applauded his telling eye for detail and his ability to provide a solid dramatic background for the action scenes. Others thought the first half of the film dragged, particularly during some Irish humor involving McLaglen and the love scenes between Temple and Agar. Later critics would complain that Ford had not gone far enough in presenting the Indians' point of view.

Yet nobody could deny the power of the film's final scenes, particularly the negotiations with Cochise and Thursday's misguided charge. *Fort Apache* brought in a $445,000 profit and even added a new phrase to the language. In time, "Fort Apache" became associated with any location surrounded by hostile forces, as in the 1981 Paul Newman film *Fort Apache, the Bronx*.

42nd Street

"You've Got to Come Back a Star"

1933. CAST: Warner Baxter (Julian Marsh), Bebe Daniels (Dorothy Brock), George Brent (Pat Denning), Una Merkel (Lorraine Fleming), Ruby Keeler (Peggy Sawyer), Guy Kibbee (Abner Dillon), Dick Powell (Billy Lawler), Ginger Rogers (Ann "Anytime Annie" Lowell). Producer: Darryl F. Zanuck; Director: Lloyd Bacon; Screenplay: James Seymour, Rian James (Based on the novel by Bradford Ropes); Photography: Sol Polito; Musical Director: Leo F. Forbstein; Music and Lyrics: Al Dubin, Harry Warren. RUNNING TIME: 89 minutes.

New stars, both on-camera and off, and a new approach to a genre everybody thought was dead were the results of Warner Bros.' biggest gamble since its first experiments with talking pictures. Although their pioneering work in the new medium had turned the Brothers Warner into major Hollywood players, by 1932 they had overextended themselves to the point that the studio posted a $6 million loss. *42nd Street* was their last chance to come out on top, and when the film opened, everyone involved, from newcomer Ruby Keeler to choreographer Busby Berkeley, had to come out stars or die trying.

When sound had first arrived with Warner's part-talkie *The Jazz Singer*, all the studios in Hollywood had rushed to create musicals of their own. As a result, the form soon became a glut on the market. After a while, theater owners started putting "Not a Musical" on marquees in an effort to win back customers.

Then Warner Bros.' head of production, Darryl F. Zanuck, got his hands on the galleys of a novel about the production of a Broadway musical. MGM had just scored a major hit with its first all-star drama, *Grand Hotel*, and, oddly enough, that glossy romance served as the inspiration for Zanuck's decision to buy the rights to *42nd Street*. Like *Grand Hotel*, the novel focused on a variety of characters who would provide juicy roles for a large cast of well-known actors.

Initially, Zanuck saw the film as a straight comedy with the musical numbers simply in the background. His initial casting preferences included such distinctly nonmusical types as Kay Francis, for the stage star sidelined by a broken ankle, and Loretta Young, for the youngster who goes on in her

The chorus taps its way through a stage set modeled on 42nd Street.

place. But the producer knew that the right kinds of numbers would put the film over as never before. So he called the only man he could trust with the choreography, Busby Berkeley. After eight films in Hollywood, the one-time actor was about to return to New York, a refugee from the decline of the musical.

Zanuck anchored his cast with experienced stars like Warner Baxter, who had won the second Best Actor Oscar for *In Old Arizona*, and Bebe Daniels. To play the show's young singing star, he chose a recently signed contract player who made only two other films, Dick Powell. Joan Blondell had been slotted to play one of the chorus girls, a fast-mover dubbed "Anytime Annie" ("The only time she said, 'No,' she didn't hear the question"), but she was too busy, so he signed the young Ginger Rogers, who was free-lancing at the time.

But that still left the ingenue uncast. One of Warner's biggest stars at the time was Al Jolson, and he had a problem. His wife since 1928, former Broadway hoofer Ruby Keeler, was bored stiff. He didn't want her back East on Broadway, so, he asked his employers to give her a screen test. She had the right qualities for the role, and, more important, she could dance.

More than a huge hit—*42nd Street* was a phenomenon. It became only the tenth film in Warner's history to post more than $2 million in rentals, the dividing line between a success and a blockbuster at the time. Keeler and Powell came out stars and for years were one of the studio's most popular teams.

But the real hero of *42nd Street* was Busby Berkeley, who pretty much had a free hand at Warner's for years. As musical styles changed, he moved to other studios, most notably MGM, where he helped shape the careers of the young Judy Garland and Mickey Rooney.

Time and frequent imitation put *42nd Street* out of fashion. The plot and even the lines were used so often they sounded hopelessly corny. With the nostalgia craze of the seventies, however, the film staged a comeback, playing to packed houses in repertory cinemas around the country. It inspired the Broadway revival of *42nd Street* in 1971, which reunited Keeler and Berkeley, then reached Broadway itself in 1980, winning the Tony Award for Best Musical.

CENSORS OVER BROADWAY

Long before the real 42nd Street became the center for much of New York City's vice traffic, the film **42nd Street** *caused some problems with censors around the world. With its wisecracking, hard-as-nails approach to the realities of theatrical life, the film had more than its share of off-color remarks and situations. In Australia, they had to cut the name of Ginger Rogers's character, "Anytime Annie," while Ohio cut Rogers's remark about a girl who "makes forty-five dollars a week and sends her mother a hundred of it."*

Risqué business posed problems in Pennsylvania, where censors cut the end of the "Shuffle Off to Buffalo" number, in which Ruby Keeler reaches through the curtains of her berth to put her slippers on the floor, then drops them as her off-screen husband initiates lovemaking. Massachusetts cut some shots in which Bebe Daniels showed too much bosom, and just to uphold the modesty of both sexes, Quebecois censors deleted the scene in which Keeler walks in on Powell in his underwear.

Yet the film couldn't hold a candle to the original novel for rawness. Zanuck's writers had to soften several details, including Peggy Sawyer's transition into a screaming diva, Dorothy Brock's nymphomania, and a love affair between director Julian Marsh and boy singer Billy Lawler.

Ruby Keeler, tapping her way to stardom.

ANOTHER STAR IS BORN

42nd Street *was such a big hit that one actress didn't even have to appear in the film to get a career boost out of it. To publicize the picture, Warner's sent the "42nd Street Express" on a cross-country tour, bringing stars to big cities and whistle-stops across the nation. Since most of the film's players were already tied up making* **Gold Diggers of 1933**, *the studio used the stunt to garner publicity for its other contract players—including the young Bette Davis. The publicity she got from the tour, especially the "Local Girl Makes Good" headlines when the train reached her native New England, helped raise her stock at the studio considerably.*

Freaks

"We Accept You, One of Us!"

1932. CAST: Wallace Ford (Phroso), Leila Hyams (Venus), Olga Baclanova (Cleopatra), Roscoe Ates (Roscoe), Henry Victor (Hercules), Harry Earles (Hans), Daisy Earles (Frieda). Producer-Director: Tod Browning; Screenplay: Willis Goldbeck, Leon Gorden, Edgar Allen Woolf, Al Boasberg (Based on the short story "Spurs" by Ted Robbins); Photography: Merritt B. Gerstad. RUNNING TIME: 64 minutes.

If ever a film was treated as though it were not "one of us," it was *Freaks*. Almost from its inception, Tod Browning's sensitive yet horrifying tale of sideshow performers in a European circus was ostracized at MGM, the last studio anybody would expect to produce such a story. Only in recent years has the film found its audience and risen to acclaim as one of the all-time great horror films.

Browning knew the film's title characters from firsthand experience, having run away to join the circus at the age of eighteen. There he witnessed the lives of the little people, Siamese twins, limbless wonders, bearded ladies, pinheads, and others who had few alternatives at the time beyond performing. The humanity he saw in them up close contrasted severely with the reactions of the sideshow audience, who viewed them with revulsion and disdain.

When Browning began directing films, he drew on his circus experience to create some of his most notable successes, particularly such Lon Chaney classics as the silent *The Unholy Three* and *The Unknown*. He also built a strong relationship with young production executive Irving G. Thalberg, whom he would follow to MGM.

With the coming of sound, the horror film enjoyed a renaissance. *Dracula,* which Browning directed on loan-out in 1931, saved Universal from bankruptcy. It would be followed by a string of horror hits, starting with the 1932 *Frankenstein*. Before long, every studio in Hollywood wanted to get on the horror bandwagon.

And here was MGM with a horror expert of its own. There are conflicting stories about how *Freaks* found its way to the MGM production schedule. In one version, Thalberg discovered Ted Robbins's story "Spurs" and handed it to Browning, saying, "I want something that out-horrors

The wedding banquet at which Olga Baclanova (left of center, in evening gown) reveals her true character.

ONE OF A KIND

For all the complaints raised about Freaks *on its initial release and even on reissue, it is certainly more sympathetic than most Hollywood attempts to deal with deformity. Here's a sampling of other films starring real-life "wonders of nature":*

The Terror of Tiny Town *(1938)—An exploitation quickie billed as the world's first all-midget western, now considered one of the worst movies ever made.*

The Brute Man *(1946)—Rondo Hatton starred in a horror-film version of his life story (the once-handsome actor was hideously deformed by acromegaly), which embarrassed executives at Universal so much they sold it to poverty-row studio PRC.*

Chained for Life *(1950)—Daisy and Violet Hilton of* Freaks *starred in this sorry tale of Siamese twins, one of whom commits murder.*

House of the Damned *(1961)—More sympathetic is this haunted-house tale, in which the ghosts turn out to be a family of circus freaks trying to escape from the world.*

Mutations *(1973)—Back to exploitation as Donald Pleasance's genetics experiments create a circus filled with sideshow freaks.*

The Sentinel *(1976)—As if this story of a New York apartment house built on the gates of Hell weren't bad enough, director Michael Winner's use of the deformed and handicapped to play the "legions of hell" provoked complaints about exploitation (some of the extras claimed they didn't realize until they got to the set how they were to be used).*

The Elephant Man *(1980)—The only film to approach* Freaks *in emotional power, with director David Lynch making poetry out of the true story of John Merrick (John Hurt), whose deformities made him the toast of Victorian London.*

Frankenstein." According to other sources, midget Harry Earles, who had starred for Browning in *The Unholy Three,* brought the story to the director's attention.

In "Spurs," a sideshow midget marries a beautiful bareback rider, only to be humiliated when she continues her affair with the circus strong man. Browning and his writers fleshed the story out with some telling glimpses of life among the sideshow characters and changed the ending to have the other freaks take their revenge on the adulterous couple, who are plotting to murder the woman's husband.

> ***"Can a full-grown woman truly love a midget? Here is the strangest romance in the world—the love of a giant, a siren and a midget!"***
>
> **—AD LINE FOR THE ORIGINAL RELEASE OF FREAKS**
>
> ***"Do Siamese twins make love? What sex is the half-man, half-woman?"***
>
> **—AD LINE FOR 1933 REISSUE AS NATURE'S MISTAKES**

From the start, almost everyone at MGM except Thalberg shunned the production. Studio chief Louis B. Mayer tried to block the film not once, but twice: before it went into production and later when Browning's cast first showed up for work. The director had assembled his sideshow performers from circuses around the country, then had to put them up in trailers on the studio back lot. Before long a committee of executives got Mayer to bar the cast from the studio commissary. Their presence was making people sick.

Then came the first preview. Women reportedly fled screaming from the theater, and the manager complained about having to clean up after patrons who had become physically ill. Thalberg tried adding a happy ending, showing Earles reunited with his midget sweetheart (played by the actor's sister, Daisy), but even that wasn't enough. Eventually, MGM withdrew the film at a loss of $164,000 on an investment of $316,000.

Yet Thalberg continued to have faith in the production. He ordered a reissue under a new title, *Nature's Mistakes,* in 1933, but it still didn't work. The film was banned in England for thirty years and eventually fell into the hands of Dwain Esper, an exploitation filmmaker and distributor who sent it out under the titles *Forbidden Love* and *The Monster Show.*

Even though the film was extremely difficult to find over the next few decades, its reputation grew, particularly in Europe. In 1962, *Freaks* was invited to the Cannes Film Festival for a special screening. The favorable response there helped get the British ban lifted and led to requests to show the film in revival houses, where it became a popular item, particularly among student audiences in the late sixties and early seventies.

Browning did not live to see *Freaks* find its audience. He had followed the box-office disaster with only three films before retiring from the screen to live off his considerable earnings. He died in October 1962, just as the *Freaks* revival was beginning.

Gaslight

"The Strange Drama of a Captive Sweetheart"

1944. CAST: Charles Boyer (Gregory Anton), Ingrid Bergman (Paula Alquist), Joseph Cotten (Brian Cameron), Dame May Whitty (Miss Thwaites), Angela Lansbury (Nancy Oliver), Barbara Everest (Elizabeth Tompkins). Producer: Arthur Hornblow Jr.; Director: George Cukor; Screenplay: John Van Druten, Walter Reisch, John Balderston (Based on the play *Angel Street* by Patrick Hamilton); Photography: Joseph Ruttenberg; Music: Bronislau Kaper. RUNNING TIME: 114 minutes.

When MGM released the quintessential gothic melodrama *Gaslight* in 1944, the studio painted it as a strange story of "Love Clouded by Evil." The result was a box-office blockbuster that helped make Ingrid Bergman one of the top stars of the forties. Yet for all the glory the film brought her, Bergman might well have felt like the "captive sweetheart" of the film's ads, trying to survive a contract with independent producer David O. Selznick that almost cost her one of her most famous roles.

Selznick had brought Bergman to America after one of his associates saw her in the Swedish version of *Intermezzo*. She made her American film debut to stunning reviews in Selznick's remake of the story. But after that, she spent most of her time on loan to other studios, with Selznick charging the studios much more than he was required to pay his star.

As soon as Bergman saw *Angel Street* on stage, she knew she wanted to play Paula Alquist, the woman almost driven mad by her husband. MGM had bought the rights for its own European sensation, Hedy Lamarr, but she turned the role down. Just as Warner Bros. had done when casting *Casablanca,* the studio next turned to Bergman. But Selznick almost blew the deal for her.

MGM had already signed Charles Boyer to play Paula's husband, and his contract stipulated top billing. Selznick insisted that Bergman be top-billed. But Bergman pleaded with Selznick to give in, crying that billing didn't matter to her when the role was this good.

Finally, Selznick did give in. In return for his concession on billing, he got the studio to build up a supporting role in *Gaslight,* the police detective who saves Paula, so that he could loan them another of his contract players, Joseph Cotten. MGM paid $253,750 for Bergman, of which she got just over $75,000.

Charles Boyer torments his "captive sweetheart" (Ingrid Bergman) to an Oscar-winning performance.

To research her role, Bergman visited a mental hospital, where she studied one patient in particular to learn the symptoms of a nervous breakdown. But once she saw the first rushes, her confidence faded. "I look so healthy," she complained to George Cukor. He reassured her that that would add to the suspense by keeping the audience guessing; they wouldn't be sure themselves if Boyer could break down such a physically robust woman.

Not all of Cukor's dealings with Bergman were as easy as that. The director thought it important to remind Bergman before every scene exactly where it fit in the progression of her mental condition. But Bergman soon tired of this repetition. Finally, she snapped, "You know, I'm not stupid. You told me that before."

Cukor apologized and left her alone for a few days. But it was clear from the rushes that she did indeed need help placing her scenes in context. She looked too sane. Cukor got himself so worked up that he stormed into her dressing room and told her off. After slamming the door and leaving, he returned and gave it to her again, finishing off with an order to, "Piss on that!" Her performance improved markedly.

One performer Cukor had little trouble with was Angela Lansbury, who was making her film debut as the sexually provocative maid who unwittingly adds to Bergman's torment. Lansbury had never acted before but proved to be a natural in front of the cameras and, as Cukor described her, "a pro from the day one." But like Bergman, she would soon feel hemmed in by her long-term contract. Despite strong performances in *Gaslight, The Picture of Dorian Gray,* and other MGM films, she would not realize her full potential until she moved to Broadway in the sixties to star in the musical *Mame.*

"If I were not mad, I could have helped you. Whatever you had done, I could have pitied and protected you. But, because I am mad, I hate you. Because I am mad, I have betrayed you. And because I am mad, I'm rejoicing in my heart without a shred of regret, watching you go with glory in my heart."

—Ingrid Bergman turning the tables on Charles Boyer after his arrest in *Gaslight*

Not only did *Gaslight* score with critics and audiences, but Bergman seemed a shoo-in for an Oscar. Despite their differences, the actress thanked Selznick and Cukor profusely. For *Gaslight* pushed Bergman into the top ranks of dramatic actresses. Its popularity—along with that of *Casablanca, The Bells of St. Mary's,* and *Spellbound*—made her one of Hollywood's top box-office draws. She would enjoy that position for only a few years, however. The image those films created for Bergman, as the virgin saint of Hollywood, proved her undoing in 1948, when she traveled to Italy to make a film with Italian director Roberto Rossellini and ended up pregnant by him while still married to another man.

Gigi

"What Miracle Has Made You the Way You Are?"

1958. CAST: Leslie Caron (Gigi), Maurice Chevalier (Honoré Lachaille), Louis Jourdan (Gaston Lachaille), Hermione Gingold (Mme. Alvarez), Eva Gabor (Liane D'Exalmans), Jacques Bergerac (Sandomir). Producer: Arthur Freed; Director: Vincente Minnelli; Screenplay: Alan Jay Lerner (Based on the play *Gigi,* dramatized by Anita Loos from the novel by Colette); Photography: Joseph Ruttenberg (CinemaScope, Metrocolor); Music: Frederick Loewe; Musical Director: André Previn. RUNNING TIME: 116 minutes.

That MGM would even attempt a witty, sophisticated, expensive musical during a period of financial instability was wonder enough. That it would succeed at a time when audiences were generally rejecting the genre was even more surprising. And that the movie would go on to become the biggest hit of Hollywood's greatest musical producer, breaking the Oscar record set by *Gone With the Wind* two decades earlier, was almost beyond belief.

Colette's story of a young girl raised to be a courtesan was published in the late forties. In 1951, a stage version adapted by Anita Loos brought Audrey Hepburn to Broadway for the first time. MGM first considered an adaptation of *Gigi* that year but ran into problems with Hollywood's self-censorship board, the Production Code Administration, so the studio let matters drop.

By 1954, Anita Loos had decided to create a musical version of her play. Hoping it would merit a film sale, she wrote Freed to ask for copies of the PCA correspondence. He sent the letters but also started thinking about doing the production on his own. By that time, Breen had retired, replaced by the more liberal Geoffrey Shurlock. Freed thought he could stick with the original and concentrate on Gigi's innocence in an overly sophisticated world, and Shurlock finally agreed.

To direct and write, Freed went to the team that had made *An American in Paris,* Vincente Minnelli and Alan Jay Lerner. The latter had just opened *My Fair Lady* on Broadway and asked his collaborator on the songs, composer Frederick Loewe, to join him.

Freed's first choice to play Gigi was Audrey Hepburn, but she wasn't interested in returning to the role, so they cast Leslie Caron, who not only had starred in *An American in Paris,* but also had played Gigi recently in London. Gaston—Gigi's adult friend, potential sponsor, and eventual husband

Leslie Caron and Louis Jourdan relaxing *sur la plage* (above) and back in Paris (left).

GIGI AND OSCAR

Best Picture
Best Director: Vincente Minnelli
Best Adapted Screenplay: Alan Jay Lerner
Best Color Cinematography: Joseph Ruttenberg
Best Art and Set Decoration: Cedric Gibbons, Preston Ames, and Keogh Gleason
Best Song: "Gigi" by Alan Jay Lerner and Frederick Loewe
Best Scoring of a Musical Motion Picture: André Previn
Best Costume Design: Cecil Beaton
Best Film Editing: Adrienne Fazan

—was somewhat harder to cast. There was nobody in Hollywood who was right for the role. British actor Dirk Bogarde was interested, but he couldn't get out of his contract with J. Arthur Rank Studios. Almost at the last minute, they decided to cast Louis Jourdan.

Freed managed to convince MGM's management that they needed to shoot most of the film on location in France. Many of the interiors used were historical buildings not constructed for filmmaking. For Honoré's bedroom, they shot in a museum, where they had to put the lights on platforming outside the windows.

The company finished location shooting the first week in September and, after a week off, resumed filming in Hollywood. Because of weather delays, the film was already over budget, so Minnelli decided to shoot the beach scenes in California rather than France. Minnelli raced through the scenes but needed one more shot of Gigi riding a donkey with Gaston. The light was already beginning to go when Ruttenberg noticed a fog bank moving in. Minnelli was busy coaching the actors and didn't hear Ruttenberg's first requests to get on with it. At the last moment, the cameraman yelled, "Vincente! We're shooting!" The director ducked out of the way, and Ruttenberg got his shot.

With other musicals failing at the box office, Freed insisted on making *Gigi* a special event by opening it not in a movie theater but in a Broadway house—the Shuberts' Royale. The film opened to tremendous reviews, playing six months at the Royale, then moving to another first-run house for almost a year. It grossed more than $7 million on its first run, on an investment of $3.3 million.

When Oscar night rolled around, the film broke *Gone With the Wind*'s record eight Academy Awards by taking home nine honors, plus a special award for Chevalier. In fact, *Gigi* was the first major Oscar winner to capture every award for which it was nominated.

CONTRIBUTIONS ABOVE AND BEYOND

Not only did Maurice Chevalier's performance in Gigi set the film's style and tone, but his remarks on accepting the role inspired one of the film's best songs. In his first meeting with Lerner and Loewe, the dapper Frenchman said, "At seventy-two, I am too old for women, too old for the extra glass of wine, too old for sports. All I have left is the audience, but I have found that quite enough." Those comments stuck with Lerner, eventually leading him to write "I'm Glad I'm Not Young Any More."

Gold Diggers of 1933

"Everybody on Stage for the 'Forgotten Man' Number"

1933. CAST: Warren William (J. Lawrence Bradford), Joan Blondell (Carol King), Aline MacMahon (Trixie Lorraine), Ruby Keeler (Polly Parker), Dick Powell (Brad Roberts/Robert Trent Bradford), Guy Kibbee (Faneuil H. Peabody), Ginger Rogers (Fay Fortune). Producer: Robert Lord; Director: Mervyn LeRoy; Screenplay: Erwin Gelsey, James Seymour, David Boehm, Ben Markson (Based on the play *Gold Diggers of Broadway* by Avery Hopwood); Photography: Sol Polito; Music: Leo F. Forbstein; Choreography: Busby Berkeley; Music and Lyrics: Harry Warren, Al Dubin. RUNNING TIME: 96 minutes.

With the success of *42nd Street,* Hollywood jumped back on the musical bandwagon. But the other studios had to wait until *42nd Street* opened and scored a hit to start imitating it, while Warner's knew they had a smash halfway through production. As a result, everybody was back on stage as soon as the other film was finished.

As a follow-up, the studio turned to a remake of *Gold Diggers of Broadway,* a story about three chorus girls mixed up with high society that had served the studio well as a silent and as a talking picture. Busby Berkeley was back on board as choreographer, with even more creative control than before, along with Ruby Keeler, Dick Powell, Guy Kibbee, and Ginger Rogers.

Berkeley set out to top *42nd Street* by creating four dazzling production numbers for the new film. To cheer up Depression-weary audiences, he decided to open the film with "We're in the Money," in which Ginger Rogers leads a chorus clad in oversized coins. The novelty of the number was Rogers's delivery of the second verse in pig Latin, an early thirties fad. Berkeley hadn't planned the bit originally, but when he heard Rogers do it to entertain the other dancers during a break, he decided to add it to the picture.

For the "Pettin' in the Park" number, the camera roams through a make-believe Central Park, observing lovers at play during the four seasons. When a sudden storm drenches the women, they change behind a screen, casting shadows that clearly reveal they are naked. They then emerge in metal dresses to confound their amorous beaus. At the close, midget Billy Barty, who has cavorted

MAKE IT AGAIN, JACK: THE OTHER VERSIONS OF *GOLD DIGGERS*

The Gold Diggers *(1923)—The silent version, produced by stage giant David Belasco, who had presented Avery Hopwood's original play on Broadway. The two gold diggers in the original were played by Louise Fazenda and Hope Hamilton.*

The Gold Diggers of Broadway *(1929)—The sound version added a third gold digger and songs, including "Tiptoe Through the Tulips" and "Painting the Clouds with Sunshine." Starring were Nancy Welford, Ann Pennington, and Winnie Lightner.*

Painting the Clouds with Sunshine *(1951)—Virginia Mayo, Virginia Gibson, and Lucille Norman were the chorines this time, with the story set in Las Vegas. In addition to numbers from the 1929 version, the songs included "With a Song in My Heart" and "Birth of the Blues."*

through the number dressed in baby clothes, hands Dick Powell a can opener. The number was heavily censored by local boards around the country.

Berkeley's biggest number was "The Shadow Waltz," in which blonde-wigged chorines dance while playing violins wired with neon tubing. During filming, Hollywood was hit with a strong earthquake that caused a blackout on the Warner's lot. Berkeley was almost thrown from the camera boom, forced to swing by one hand until he could get back on. Many of the chorus girls were dancing on a thirty-foot platform when the quake hit. Berkeley yelled for them to sit down until they could get the soundstage doors open and let some light in.

Joan Blondell

The film's finale is one of the strangest in all of Berkeley's musicals. "Remember My Forgotten Man" carries a strong social protest message. Dressed as a streetwalker, Joan Blondell (a strange choice in itself, as she couldn't sing) speaks the first verse and chorus, about the plight of World War I veterans ("You put a shotgun in his hand") now marching on the unemployment line. The tune is then picked up by singer Etta Moten (some sources erroneously list Marian Anderson as the singer or claim she dubbed Blondell's voice). Following a montage depicting the transition from front line to bread line, the number ends with Blondell center screen, backed by silhouettes of men in uniform, while the hordes of unemployed reach out to her.

Berkeley's inspiration was the May 1932 "Bonds March" on Washington in which World War I veterans appealed to get their benefits early so they could get back on their feet. That it was filmed at all is a testament to the studio's faith in Berkeley's vision. Once Jack Warner and production chief Hal B. Wallis saw the number, they decided to make it the film's finale, a slot originally planned for "Pettin' in the Park."

Depression-weary Americans wished that they, like the chorus here, could sing "We're in the Money."

The film received, if anything, even better reviews than *42nd Street,* thanks largely to the more careful pacing of musical numbers throughout the picture and the stronger emphasis on romance as rich-boy-turned-songwriter Powell woos Keeler, and his stuffy brother (William) falls for Blondell. *Gold Diggers of 1933* also improved on its predecessor's profits by almost $1 million, assuring that the musical was back to stay. Indeed, the genre would continue to be one of Hollywood's surest sources of income for two decades.

AND THE REST OF THE *GOLD DIGGERS* SERIES

Gold Diggers of 1935 *(1935)—Dick Powell, Adolph Menjou, Glenda Farrell, and Alice Brady star, with Berkeley turning in his best work ever on the "Lullaby of Broadway" number (the song won an Oscar). Also featured was "The Words Are in My Heart," with a line of chorus girls playing dancing pianos.*

Gold Diggers of 1937 *(1937)—Powell and Joan Blondell are back, this time with Victor Moore as comic foil. The main musical treat is "Plenty of Money and You," which also bore the title "The Gold Digger's Song."*

Gold Diggers in Paris *(1938)—Rudy Vallee took over for Powell in the final* Gold Diggers *film, this time leading his musical revue to Paris where they have mistakenly entered a ballet competition.*

Gone With the Wind

"A Land of Cavaliers and Cotton Fields"

1939. CAST: Clark Gable (Rhett Butler), Leslie Howard (Ashley Wilkes), Olivia de Havilland (Melanie Wilkes), Vivien Leigh (Scarlett O'Hara), Hattie McDaniel (Mammy), Thomas Mitchell (Gerald O'Hara). Producer: David O. Selznick; Director: Victor Fleming; Screenplay: Sidney Howard (Based on the novel by Margaret Mitchell); Photography: Ernest Haller, Lee Garmes (Technicolor); Music: Max Steiner. RUNNING TIME: 222 minutes.

Gone With the Wind has become the emblem for Hollywood's Golden Age, a romantic era that now seems as distant as the Old South the film idealized. It was a product of the old studio system, in which producers with vision shaped the dreams of millions of Americans. In print, Scarlett O'Hara was the heroine of Depression women. On screen, Scarlett quickly became the stand-in for a generation caught up in World War II (the film was a big hit in France after the liberation). And the story has retained its hold for more than fifty years, thanks largely to the vision of one man—David O. Selznick.

"It stinks, and I don't know why I bother with it, but I've got to do something with my time."

—Margaret Mitchell

Margaret Mitchell created her one great literary achievement while recuperating from an accident. When an editor from the Macmillan Publishing Company came to Atlanta scouting new talent, a friend told the agent about Mitchell's novel. Mitchell reluctantly handed over the manuscript, then had second thoughts, but it was too late. The editor had gotten hooked on the story. Soon all of America would be hooked, too. The book topped the bestseller list for twenty-one months and brought Mitchell a Pulitzer Prize.

"No Civil War picture ever made a nickel." —Irving G. Thalberg

The book's galleys started making the rounds in Hollywood before it was published, but nobody was biting. There hadn't been a successful Civil War film since *The Birth of a Nation*. MGM passed. Then Selznick's East Coast story editor, Katherine Brown, recommended it. At first, Selznick hesitated. But his board chairman, John Hay Whitney, threatened to buy the rights himself, and

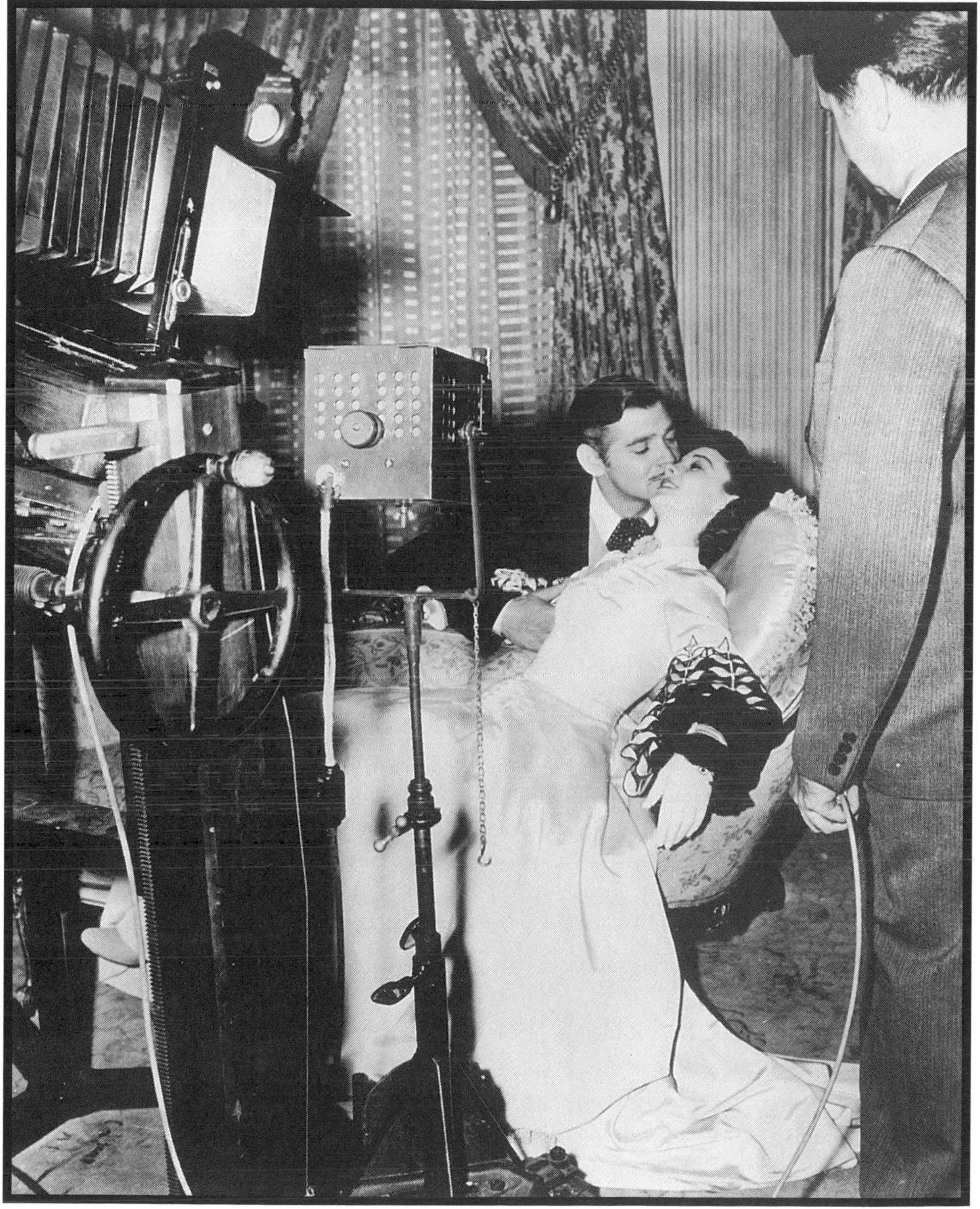

It looks like love, but stars Clark Gable and Vivien Leigh didn't really get along: In this scene she probably objected to the smell of his dentures.

Selznick finally gave in, getting the fee reduced to $50,000. Selznick went on vacation to read the novel and returned to discover he'd just bought the nation's biggest bestseller.

Selznick searched the country and tested half of Hollywood to find the perfect Scarlett. With the role still uncast, Selznick went into production on December 10, 1938, with the burning of Atlanta. Among the guests viewing the fire were Selznick's brother, agent Myron Selznick, and a client he'd just signed—Vivien Leigh. A few days later, she signed for the role.

Principal photography started on January 26, 1939, and there were problems from the start. Director George Cukor disagreed with Selznick about how to play certain scenes. Star Clark Gable felt Cukor, best known as a "woman's director," was devoting too much time to costars Leigh and Olivia de Havilland. When Cukor started rewriting the script on the set, Selznick decided it was time to find another director. Selznick fired him on February 13, replacing him with MGM director Victor Fleming, who was a close friend of Gable's.

"It is really very miserable and going terribly slowly. I am such a fool to have done it."

—Vivien Leigh

That hardly stopped the problems. Now Leigh and de Havilland felt they were being neglected. On weekends, they sneaked over to Cukor's mansion to get coaching on their roles. The strain of the production was telling on Fleming, too. In April, he walked off the film, claiming to have had a nervous breakdown. Selznick replaced him with director Sam Wood until Fleming returned.

"It's a great thing—this benefit for David O. Selznick."

—Bob Hope, hosting the Academy Awards

Gone With the Wind received mostly glowing reviews. On Oscar night, it became the Academy's biggest winner to date, with honors going to the film, Leigh, supporting actress Hattie McDaniel, director Fleming, and adapter Sidney Howard, among others—eight Oscars in all. In addition, Selznick received the Irving G. Thalberg Award as the year's outstanding producer, and another special Oscar went to designer William Cameron Menzies, who had overseen the production's look.

"Hollywood itself is practically dead, but Gone With the Wind *goes on forever."*

—Time

Gone With the Wind grossed $945,000 in its first week, $14 million in its first year. By 1943, the film had grossed $32 million. Not only was it the highest-grossing picture ever, but it would hold that position until *The Sound of Music* came out in 1965. The film continued to do solid business with reissues in 1961, 1967, and 1989. Adjusted for inflation, it's international grosses are more than $2 billion, making it the most profitable film of all time.

The Good Earth

"To Catch the Soul of China"

1937. CAST: Paul Muni (Wang Lung), Luise Rainer (O-Lan), Walter Connolly (Uncle), Tilly Losch (Lotus), Charley Grapewin (Old Father), Jessie Ralph (Cuckoo), Keye Luke (Elder Son). Producers: Irving G. Thalberg, Albert Lewin; Director: Sidney Franklin; Screenplay: Talbot Jennings, Tess Schlesinger, Claudine West (Based on the novel by Pearl Buck); Photography: Karl Freund; Music: Herbert Stothart.

RUNNING TIME: 138 minutes.

MGM production chief Irving G. Thalberg showed just how far Hollywood could go in bringing movie audiences the world with this lavish film version of Pearl Buck's acclaimed novel. Before the film could be completed, however, the strain of fighting to make MGM Hollywood's greatest studio felled the boy wonder, who died of pneumonia in September 1936. Although Thalberg had always eschewed any on-screen credit for himself, studio head Louis B. Mayer insisted on adding a special card preceding the film's titles: "To the memory of Irving Grant Thalberg we dedicate this picture—his last great achievement."

The Good Earth was a publishing phenomenon, spending two years on the bestseller list, winning the Pulitzer Prize in 1931, and contributing significantly to author Pearl Buck's receiving the Nobel Prize a few years later. Thalberg paid $50,000 for the film rights, despite objections from Mayer, who screamed, "The public won't buy pictures about American farmers, and you want to give them Chinese farmers?"

At first, the film was assigned to George Hill, who traveled to China for location footage. After arranging for his location manager, Frank Messenger, to shoot there, Hill returned to the U.S. He never lived to see the results of his labors. Hill was a recovering alcoholic. On his return, he fell off the wagon. Shortly afterward, he committed suicide.

Meanwhile, the location shoot in China was not going well. Tired of continued resistance and feeling a distinct coolness from the government, Messenger returned to Hollywood with little usable footage.

More successful was merchant Jimmy Lee, a Cantonese who spent three years purchasing props, costumes, farm animals, even entire farmhouses, and sending them back to MGM. In all, he procured eighteen tons of materials for the production. And that was just the start of the film's scale. MGM bought five hundred acres in the San Fernando Valley, forty miles outside Los Angeles, and converted it into a Chinese farming province and a small city. They even built a river and irrigation system.

The one sequence that caused Franklin and Thalberg the most trouble was the climactic locust attack. For the first attempt, they intercut shots of the actors with location footage of locusts swarming in Africa, but the results were far from convincing. Special-effects artist A. Arnold Gillespie tried using a combination of pickled grasshoppers, burnt cork, and bits of wood, which were blown at the actors on location and also filmed against a blank screen at the studio. But again, Thalberg felt there just weren't enough locusts. Then word reached him that Utah had been hit with a plague of nineteen-year grasshoppers. He sent a camera crew that returned with more than just footage; they brought back barrels full of live grasshoppers. These were shot in close-up and used in scenes with the actors. Finally, with all these pieces put together, Thalberg was satisfied.

Ultimately, filming took eleven months, with Thalberg's death coming just as the picture was about to be edited. By the time the film premiered, its budget had climbed to $2.8 million, the highest since the silent version of *Ben-Hur*. In fact, the budget was so high that, despite solid reviews and Oscars to Rainer and cameraman Karl Freund, the film failed to recoup its cost on initial release, posting a loss of almost $500,000. With subsequent reissues and television sales, *The Good Earth* eventually moved into the black and acquired a reputation as one of Hollywood's most dazzling productions and a fitting testament to its creator.

TRANSFIGURED—NOT!

Irving G. Thalberg's dream of making* The Good Earth *one of his greatest accomplishments even extended to the film's score. After hearing some of Arnold Schönberg's early compositions on the radio, Thalberg decided to offer the scoring assignment to the great composer of* Transfigured Night*, who recently had arrived in Hollywood after fleeing Hitler's Germany.

But Schönberg was not interested in the way Hollywood used music. At first, he tried setting his price so high that Thalberg would have to give up, but instead the executive agreed to pay him $50,000. Then Thalberg shifted to the hard sell: "Think of it! A terrific storm is going on. The wheat field is swaying in the wind, and suddenly the earth begins to tremble! In the midst of an earthquake, O-Lan gives birth to a baby! What an opportunity for music!" "With all that going on," Schönberg wondered, "why do you need music?"

Finally, the composer asked for the one thing Thalberg would not give him—total artistic control. Not only did he insist that not one note of his score be changed, but he wanted to set the actors' line readings so their pitch and rhythm would fit with the music. That prospect was enough to get Thalberg to assign the score to studio composer Herbert Stothart.

Paul Muni tries out the other side of the camera.

Goodbye, Mr. Chips

The Sun Never Sets on the MGM Empire

1939. CAST: Robert Donat (Charles Chipping), Greer Garson (Katherine Ellis), Terry Kilburn (John/Peter Colley), John Mills (Peter Colley as a Young Man), Paul Henreid (Max Staefel), Judith Furse (Flora). Producer: Victor Saville; Director: Sam Wood; Screenplay: W. C. Sheriff, Claudine West, Eric Maschwitz, Sidney Franklin (Based on the novel by James Hilton); Photography: Frederick A. Young; Music: Richard Addinsel. RUNNING TIME: 114 minutes.

MGM invaded England, then conquered the hearts of America when it set up production in a small studio in Denham. The idea was simple. Because the British government imposed a quota system on film imports (which could only represent a given proportion of home-grown productions), why not purchase a studio over there from which to produce British films with an American touch? The idea appealed to studio head Louis B. Mayer's Anglophilia and, to nobody's surprise, led to three major hits before World War II forced a temporary shutdown.

In 1938, MGM launched its Denham operations with *A Yank at Oxford,* starring Robert Taylor as a brash American student and Maureen O'Sullivan and Vivien Leigh as the good and bad girls he's torn between. *The Citadel* followed, with Robert Donat as a dedicated doctor led astray by riches and social prestige. The picture was such a hit, and Donat's performance so well received, that he beat out Brian Aherne and Charles Laughton to win the role of Chips.

James Hilton's twenty-thousand-word novella had been a surprise hit back in 1934, a surprise even in the author's eyes. He had churned it out in four days to meet a magazine deadline. The story attracted little notice until it fell into the hands of critic-columnist Alexander Woollcott. In contrast to his acidic comments on the arts and personalities of the day—Woollcott was the model for Sheridan Whiteside in Kaufman and Hart's *The Man Who Came to Dinner*—the critic had a sentimental streak. He began touting the book on his weekly radio broadcasts, which is how MGM production chief Irving G. Thalberg got wind of it.

Thalberg got MGM to pick up the film rights and scheduled the film to follow such projects as *The Good Earth, Camille,* and *Marie Antoinette*. But before any of them could be completed, he died

The world's greatest actor? Many thought so after seeing Robert Donat's Oscar-winning performance.

of pneumonia. This was one project in which Thalberg and Mayer had been in total agreement, so the studio head switched the project to MGM's Denham studio.

Only one problem remained: Who would play Chips's wife, Kathy? It required an actress with just the right mix of gentility and high spirits to capture a character whose spirit turns Chips's life around and enchants his stuffy academic colleagues. During production of *A Yank at Oxford,* Mayer had visited England to work out production problems and scout talent. One night, he attended a period melodrama called *Old Music* and became enraptured with the leading lady, a beautiful redhead of Irish-Scottish descent named Greer Garson. The next day he met with her mother, who managed the twenty-nine-year-old's career, and offered them both contracts (Mrs. Garson would serve as a script consultant).

LET IT SNOW

Technicians labored for three weeks to create a convincing snowstorm for* Goodbye, Mr. Chips. *The day they finally finished the snow scenes, England was hit by one of its worst blizzards ever.

But at first Mayer had nothing for her to do. She took classes, posed for photographs, dieted and exercised, but that was all. Garson was ready to return to England for good when the director of *Goodbye, Mr. Chips,* Sam Wood, viewed her screen test. Garson returned to England all right, but as the star of her first film.

To create the world of a boys' school, MGM built the largest set yet created in a British film studio. The production also visited the Repton School, founded in 1557, for location shooting. This was both an event and a great honor; never before had a major American studio made a film about life in one of England's famous public schools. Students and faculty alike gave up their summer holidays to appear in crowd scenes and otherwise help with the production.

Goodbye, Mr. Chips was the third hit in a row from MGM's British unit. It made Garson one of the studio's top stars, winning her an Oscar nomination for Best Actress (she lost to Vivien Leigh). Her debut was almost overshadowed by Donat's touching performance, during which he ages from twenty-five to eighty-three. Paul Muni hailed him as the world's greatest actor, and the Motion Picture Academy honored him with the Oscar for Best Actor. Because of poor health and extreme selectiveness about film assignments, Donat never really capitalized on the Oscar. But his performance remains one of the most beloved in Hollywood history.

Sam Wood (center) directs Greer Garson, Robert Donat, and the boys.

Grand Hotel

"People Come. People Go. Nothing Ever Happens."

1932. CAST: Greta Garbo (Grusinskaya), John Barrymore (Baron Felix von Geigern), Joan Crawford (Flaemmchen), Wallace Beery (General Director Preysing), Lionel Barrymore (Otto Kringelein), Lewis Stone (Dr. Otternschlag). Director: Edmund Goulding; Screenplay: William A. Drake (Based on the play and novel *Menschen im Hotel* by Vicki Baum and the American version by William A. Drake); Photography: William Daniels. RUNNING TIME: 113 minutes.

Contrary to Lewis Stone's wry observation at the end of the picture, there was a lot happening at the Grand Hotel, just as there was a lot going on at MGM at the time. With *Grand Hotel* the studio with "more stars than there are in the heavens" introduced the all-star feature in 1932.

The genius behind this towering edifice was MGM production chief Irving G. Thalberg, who went after the film rights after hearing of the German stage version of Vicki Baum's novel *Menschen im Hotel*. But plans had already started to bring the play to New York, in a new version called *Grand Hotel* by William A. Drake. Since the production was still looking for backers, MGM bought in for $15,000 in return for movie rights. When *Grand Hotel* ran for 444 performances, MGM actually made some money on the deal and suddenly had a project with name recognition.

Because *Grand Hotel*'s multiple plot lines spread the focus among five major characters, Thalberg decided to cast the film with the five biggest stars under contract to MGM. Of course, not all the stars agreed with his casting. At twenty-seven, Greta Garbo feared she was too old to play the ballerina Grusinskaya. Nor was she pleased when Thalberg reneged on a promise to cast her former costar and lover John Gilbert as the Baron, a jewel thief who falls in love with Grusinskaya when he breaks into her room to rob her.

Thalberg briefly considered studio newcomer Clark Gable for the Baron, but then he noticed the wonderful work John and Lionel Barrymore were doing for MGM in *Arsene Lupin,* another tale of a chic jewel thief. The two were so eager to work together again that when Thalberg mentioned *Grand Hotel* to them, John Barrymore readily signed a three-picture deal with the studio.

Joan Crawford was less intrigued by the production, fearing that she couldn't hold her own in

Is Joan Crawford sizing up the competition posed by Barrymores Lionel and John?

THE *GRAND HOTEL* CHAIN

1945—MGM remake, Weekend at the Waldorf, *with Ginger Rogers in Garbo's role, Lana Turner as Crawford, and Walter Pidgeon as John Barrymore.*

*1958—*At the Grand, *stage musical premieres in Los Angeles and flops, with Paul Muni as Kringelein, Cesare Danova as the Baron, and Joan Diener as Grusinskaya.*

1959—West German film based on Menschen im Hotel *with Michele Morgan as Grusinskaya and Gert Frobe (the future Goldfinger) as Preysing.*

1972—MGM breaks ground for world's largest hotel in Las Vegas, to be called, naturally, the MGM Grand.

1976—MGM announces plans for a Grand Hotel *remake that never takes place.*

*1989—*Grand Hotel: The Musical *opens on Broadway, with Michael Jeter winning a Tony Award as Kringelein.*

such a high-powered cast, particularly against accomplished scene-stealers like the Barrymore brothers. Early in the shooting she laid down the law to them: "All right, boys, but don't forget that the American public would rather have one look at my back than watch both of your faces for an hour."

John Barrymore and Joan Crawford.

The biggest holdout, however, was Wallace Beery, who hated the role of Preysing, the corrupt industrialist. Thalberg finally won him over by agreeing to let him play the part with a German accent. Not only did the choice separate Preysing from the more homespun characters Beery had been playing in films like *The Champ,* it also appealed to the ham in him.

Director Edmund Goulding's job was far from easy. By the time he was through, he had a new nickname on the lot: "The Lion Tamer." Although the MGM publicity department churned out reams of releases about how well the stars worked together, most of them did not get along. Beery tried to throw Crawford off by ad-libbing until Goulding insisted that he stop. Crawford annoyed the cast by playing maudlin German love songs on her record player at top volume. Beery countered by getting some of his drinking buddies to serenade Crawford with "Marching through Georgia."

Yet there were also moments of camaraderie. Crawford and Lionel Barrymore admired each other's work and became good friends. Garbo was equally thrilled to be working with John Barrymore. When he showed up hung over, a frequent state for the hard-drinking star, she gave him a secret Swedish remedy that cured him in no time. After one particularly demanding scene, she impulsively kissed him and exclaimed, "You have no idea what it means to play opposite so perfect an artist."

Grand Hotel opened to rave reviews, with critics at a loss to decide who took top acting honors. In its first year, it grossed more than $2.5 million, accounting for a hefty portion of MGM's $8 million profit for 1932. The film gave the young Crawford a major career boost, while sticking Garbo with the line most often associated with the reclusive star: "I vahnt to be alone."

It was also the only film to win the Oscar for Best Picture without scoring any other nominations. Historians have also pointed to this as a sign of the film's greatest strength. Thalberg had created such a seamless celebration of Hollywood glamour that no one element stood out more than any other.

THE INIMITABLE GRETA GARBO

Before Grand Hotel's premiere at Grauman's Chinese in Hollywood, impresario Sid Grauman informed the audience that they were in for a rare treat. The usually reclusive Garbo would appear on stage after the film. The news gave the well-crafted film added suspense. Then, at the end, Grauman brought out Wallace Beery—in full drag, including long blonde wig. The audience was not amused. There was hardly any laughter as they filed out, impressed with the film, if not with Grauman's sense of humor.

Greed

Slash and Burn

1925. CAST: Gibson Gowland (McTeague), ZaSu Pitts (Trina), Jean Hersholt (Marcus Schouler), Chester Conklin (Mr. Sieppe), Sylvia Ashton (Mrs. Sieppe), Oscar Gottell, Otto Gottell (The Sieppe Twins). Producer: Erich von Stroheim; Director: Erich von Stroheim; Screenplay: Erich von Stroheim, June Mathis; Photography: Ben F. Reynolds, William H. Daniels, Ernest B. Schoedsack; Music: Arranged by James Bradford, using the *Greed* theme by Louis Kempinsky.

RUNNING TIME: 140 minutes.

One of the great "lost masterpieces" of Hollywood history, *Greed* has achieved legendary status as much for what audiences will never see of it as for what remains. Even though producer-director-writer Erich von Stroheim considered the picture his masterpiece, it became a victim of the corporate mergers that created MGM. The studio's new production chief, Irving G. Thalberg, had three-quarters of the director's cut removed, and he burned the negative to recover its silver content.

Thalberg and von Stroheim had clashed before, when they both worked at Universal, where von Stroheim started his directing career after years of work as an actor specializing in Teutonic villains.

His three films at Universal were box-office bonanzas, but von Stroheim's extravagance—insisting on realistic details most audiences would never notice and spending as much as a year to film one picture—kept the profit margins low. With his third picture, *Foolish Wives,* Thalberg took the cutting away from von Stroheim. Six weeks into von Stroheim's next film, *Merry Go Round,* Thalberg fired him for going over budget.

Within two months, von Stroheim signed with the Goldwyn Studios. Then he went to work on a project he'd dreamed of for years, a film version of Frank Norris's novel *McTeague*—about a San Francisco dentist whose life is ruined when his wife wins a lottery and is driven mad by greed.

Determined to make the most faithful possible rendition of the novel, von Stroheim shot in real locations in San Francisco. This meant working in tight spaces. In some cases the camera had to be placed on scaffolding outside windows when rooms were too small to accommodate cast and crew.

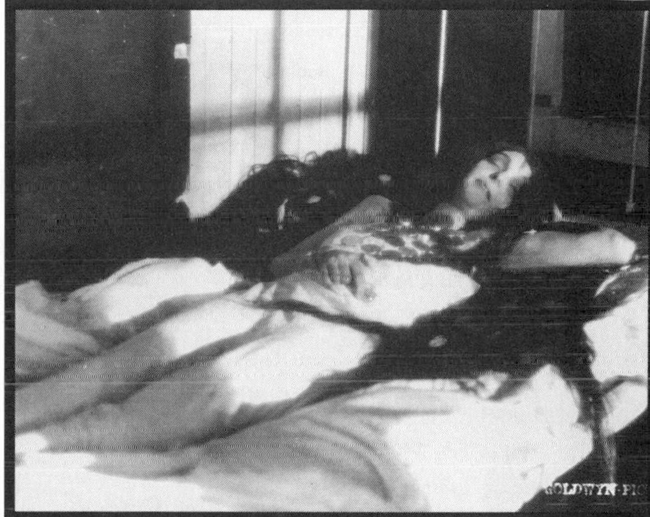

ZaSu Pitts, with Gibson Gowland on their wedding night (above left), and later as a slave to gold (above right)

THE WHOLE PICTURE: A BRIEF OVERVIEW OF WHAT WAS CUT FROM *GREED*

- *The film's prologue, depicting McTeague's family life in a mining town, intended to show the hereditary and environmental forces shaping his character. At almost two hours, the sequence represents von Stroheim's principal addition to the novel.*
- *Subplot involving the charwoman who sells Trina the lottery ticket and a junk man seduced by her stories of family wealth. He marries her to get his hands on the money, has an eerie dream in which he exhumes family caskets in search of gold, then kills the woman and drowns himself.*
- *Subplot relating the courtship of two elderly boarders living in the same house as McTeague; intended to balance the sordidness of the main plot.*
- *Details of Trina's relationship with Marcus and her marriage to McTeague.*
- *McTeague's journey from San Francisco back to his hometown and then to Death Valley after he kills Trina. The deletion of this material causes the most abrupt jump in the film.*

CRITICAL TO A FAULT

"If a contest were to be held to determine which has been the filthiest, vilest, most putrid picture in the history of the motion picture business, I am sure that Greed would walk away with the honors."

—HARRISON REPORTS

"Von Stroheim is a genius—Greed established that beyond all doubt—but he is badly in need of a stop-watch."

—ROBERT E. SHERWOOD, LIFE

"Imagine any girl keeping company with a young fellow urging her to see Greed when she knows the night that she sits through it he is going to sour on any thought that has to do with marriage?"

—VARIETY

"The most important picture yet produced in America. . . . When the 'movies' can produce a Greed, they can no longer be sneered at."

—RICHARD WATTS, NEW YORK HERALD TRIBUNE

When the director decided he wanted to capture action on the street outside, they had to knock out walls to get the right camera angle.

After months in San Francisco, von Stroheim took his crew to Death Valley for the film's climax, in which McTeague's enemy, Marcus, tracks him down in the desert after Trina's murder. For almost a month they worked in the desert, where temperatures climbed as high as 161° F. Of the forty-two men on the crew, fourteen had to be replaced because of illness. The company cook, who suffered from high blood pressure, died.

After nine months of shooting, von Stroheim locked himself up in an editing suite with a studio guard stationed to keep intruders out and the director in. His rough cut came in at forty-two reels—approximately nine hours of film. The few people he showed it to were overwhelmed. There was no hope of distributing it in its original length, so von Stroheim set about cutting it down to about twenty-four reels—a mere five hours.

That's when Thalberg entered. The boy wonder was horrified at von Stroheim's self-indulgence, and the film's sordidness. He demanded that *Greed* be cut to ninety minutes, the average length for a feature at that time.

When von Stroheim failed to cut it enough, Thalberg handed the film over to title writer Joseph Farnham, who reduced it to ten reels and created titles to bridge the gaps. The result was a powerful mess. Although some critics saw von Stroheim's genius, Farnham had cut out much of the story's development, leaving the film to lurch from one big moment to the next.

Von Stroheim produced one more hit for MGM (they had to use him under his contract), *The Merry Widow,* but even that film's success couldn't wipe out the loss on *Greed*. It was his last hit as a director. Later films were taken over by their studios, and the man's directing career ended in 1932.

Yet *Greed*'s reputation continued to grow. In 1952, it placed seventh in an international critics' poll naming the greatest films of all time. Ten years later, Britain's *Sight and Sound* magazine conducted a similar poll, in which *Greed* placed fourth—higher than any other silent film.

Gunga Din

"You're a Better Man Than I Am . . . "

1939. CAST: Cary Grant (Sergeant Cutter), Victor McLaglen (Sergeant MacChesney), Douglas Fairbanks Jr. (Sergeant Ballantine), Sam Jaffe (Gunga Din), Eduardo Cianelli (Guru), Joan Fontaine (Emmy Stebbins). Producer: Pandro S. Berman; Director: George Stevens; Screenplay: Joel Sayre, Fred Guiol (Based on the story by Ben Hecht and Charles MacArthur, suggested by the poem by Rudyard Kipling); Photography: Joseph H. August; Music: Alfred Newman.
RUNNING TIME: 117 minutes.

Adventure had three names in 1939, and they were Cutter, Ballantine, and MacChesney. RKO set out to imitate Warner Bros.' swashbuckling Errol Flynn adventures with this spirited improvisation on Rudyard Kipling's famous poem. They even used the location from Flynn's *The Charge of the Light Brigade*. The result was one of the screen's most popular, energetic, and enduring adventure stories.

Gunga Din had only been filmed once before—a silent version in 1911 that only lasted fifteen minutes, which is about all the material present in the Kipling poem. MGM tried molding a script to go with the poem in 1928 but couldn't seem to get it right, nor could they arrive at a satisfactory agreement on the rights. In 1936, independent producer Edward Small paid Kipling's widow £5,000 for screen rights. When Small signed on as a producer at RKO, he also sold them the film rights.

Originally, the studio intended to give the film to Howard Hawks, who had just signed with great fanfare to direct *Bringing Up Baby*. Hawks assigned the team of Ben Hecht and Charles MacArthur to create a story line, which they did, drawing on another Kipling story, "Soldiers Three," as well as their own stage and screen hit *The Front Page*. In their story, British colonial officers Cutter and MacChesney conspire to keep their partner in adventure, Sergeant Ballantine, from leaving the service for marriage, just as Walter Burns, the newspaper editor in *The Front Page,* plotted to keep his star reporter from leaving the paper to marry a society girl.

When Hawks went over budget on *Bringing Up Baby,* however, the studio fired him and took George Stevens, one of their most promising directors, off *Room Service* for *Gunga Din*. Stevens had directed Laurel and Hardy two-reelers during his early years in Hollywood. He picked one of his

Cary Grant, Victor McLaglen, and Douglas Fairbanks Jr. fight for queen and country.

gagwriters from those days, Fred Guiol, to turn the story into a script.

> *"Thrills for a thousand movies plundered for one mighty show!*
>
> *"Romance aflame through dangerous days and nights of terror! In a land where anything can happen—most of all to a beautiful girl alone!"*
>
> —AD LINES FOR GUNGA DIN

The studio signed Victor McLaglen and Cary Grant to star, with the latter set as the romantic young Ballantine. At first, they were going to cast Jack Oakie as Cutter. When he wasn't available, they cast Douglas Fairbanks Jr. But Grant saw more comic possibilities in Cutter than he did in his own, larger role. He suggested the swap to Stevens and RKO production chief Pandro S. Berman, who were both amenable. Fairbanks agreed to decide the casting on a coin toss, which Grant won. The role of Cutter gave Grant a chance to draw on both his natural athleticism (he had started out as a vaudeville acrobat) and his Cockney background.

On location, Stevens proved as much of a perfectionist as Hawks had been, leading to production delays and budget overruns. Moreover, with the script still unfinished, he encouraged the three stars to improvise throughout the movie.

Gunga Din was shot largely on location in Lone Pine, California, two hundred miles north of Los Angeles in the middle of the Sierra Nevadas. Temperatures rose to 115°F almost every day, while a constant wind nearly drove the company mad. With no hotels nearby, RKO hired the same contractors who had built the workers' accommodations near Boulder Dam to construct a city of seventy-two tents, including a commissary, twelve two-bed cabins (for the stars), and an open-air movie theater.

After seventy-five days on location and another month in the studio, *Gunga Din* was ready, forty days over schedule and half a million dollars over budget. The film opened to strong press and solid business. Because of its high cost—more than $1.9 million, the highest budget in RKO history—*Gunga Din* failed to turn a profit during initial release, although some sources list it with the second-highest gross of 1939.

With its 1941 reissue, it moved into the black. By that time, however, it was a slightly shorter film. Stevens had featured actor Reginald Sheffield as Kipling, but the writer's widow thought the scenes ludicrous. Before the film's British premiere, his scenes were cut, and he was matted out of Gunga Din's funeral. RKO kept the cuts in all later prints. With that slight change, *Gunga Din* entered the ranks of the screen's most popular adventure films.

Filming a street scene.

How the West Was Won

Raising the Western to New Widths

1962. CAST: Spencer Tracy (Narrator), Carroll Baker (Eve Prescott), Henry Fonda (Jethro Stewart), Gregory Peck (Cleve Van Valen), George Peppard (Zeb Rawlings), Robert Preston (Roger Morgan), Debbie Reynolds (Lilith Prescott), James Stewart (Linus Rawlings), John Wayne (General William T. Sherman), Richard Widmark (Mike King). Producer: Bernard Smith; Directors: Henry Hathaway, John Ford, George Marshall; Screenplay: James R. Webb (Based on articles in *Life* magazine); Photography: Joseph LaShelle, Charles Lang Jr., William Daniels, Milton Krasner, Harold Wellman (Cinerama, Technicolor); Music: Alfred Newman, Ken Darby.

RUNNING TIME: 155 minutes.

The MGM epic moved into a new world of excitement when the studio signed a deal to produce films in Cinerama, a wide-screen process introduced in the fifties in an effort to compete with television. Cinerama had been invented in the thirties by Fred Willard. From his original eleven-camera process, it was streamlined in the fifties to use a system of three cameras operating on a single shutter. The wide-screen image captured in this way came as close as possible to the human field of vision.

In 1952, the system made its commercial debut with *This Is Cinerama*. *Cinerama Holiday* followed in 1955, becoming the top-grossing picture of its year. By the end of the decade, however, the novelty had begun to wear thin. Audiences would sit still for only so many travelogues. So, before the sun could set on Cinerama, MGM agreed to produce the first story films using the process.

They chose two subjects: *The Wonderful World of the Brothers Grimm,* which featured an all-star cast in a fanciful biography of the famed storytellers, and *How the West Was Won,* based on a series of articles in *Life* magazine. The script for the latter was entrusted to James R. Webb, a veteran writer who had started out in the late thirties penning westerns at Republic before moving up to such top films as *Trapeze, The Big Country,* and the original *Cape Fear*. Webb's story covered fifty years of American history, following the members of the Prescott family, particularly Lilith

After years of classic westerns, James Stewart was a natural choice for his role as a pioneering trapper.

HOW THE WEST WAS REALLY WON: THE NUMBERS GAME

Number of Directors	4 (3 credited)
Number of Locations	9
Cast Size (Including Extras)	12,617
Number of Technicians	400
Number of Costumes Built	5,000
Number of Buffalo	2,000
Number of Indian Tribes (Brules, Oglalas, Minnecanjous, Cheyenne, and Arapahoes)	5
Number of Horses	630
Amount of Hay Consumed	20,000 lbs./day
Number of Mules	150
Number of Covered Wagons	107
Number of Oxen	50

Prescott (Debbie Reynolds), who makes the transition from farm girl to saloon singer to San Francisco dowager, and her nephew Zeb Rawlings (George Peppard), who goes from fighting for the Union in the Civil War to fighting for the forces of law and order in the West.

With a story this big, MGM pulled out all the stops, committing $15 million. It took four directors to put the project on film. Henry Hathaway directed the first two sequences, following Lilith from her trip West on the Ohio River through life on a wagon train, then he returned for the finale, in which Zeb battles outlaws on an out-of-control lumber train. John Ford handled the re-creation of the Civil War. George Marshall took Zeb through adventures as a scout for the railroads. And Richard Thorpe offered uncredited help with the aerial shots and linking sequences that tied the film together.

Over the year it took to film *How the West Was Won,* MGM shuttled cast, crew, and extras more than a million miles to locations in eight different states. Shooting started on the Ohio River in southern Illinois, then moved to the hills of Kentucky; Custer State Park in South Dakota; Chimney Rock in the Colorado Rockies; Monument Valley, Utah; Pinnacles National Monument in California; Uncompaghre, Colorado; the desert outside Tonto, Arizona; and the National Forests near Inyo on the California-Nevada border.

Needless to say, the results were spectacular. Although critics complained about the unwieldy story and the shortcomings of Cinerama, they could not deny the film's epic sweep. Few viewers cared about the problems with Cinerama. The format was used only for first-run engagements anyway, with later bookings in 35mm. As expected, the film had tremendous pulling power, ranking fifth at the box office for its year and eventually bringing in $50 million in international rentals.

How the West Was Won was nominated for eight Oscars, including Best Picture. It won for Best Editing, Best Sound, and Best Original Screenplay, with the last a particularly popular choice. In accepting his award, veteran scripter Webb quipped, "It took me as long to win this as it took to win the West."

The Hunchback of Notre Dame

"If Only I Had Been Made of Stone Like You!"

1939. CAST: Charles Laughton (The Hunchback), Sir Cedric Hardwicke (Frolo), Thomas Mitchell (Clopin), Maureen O'Hara (Esmeralda), Edmond O'Brien (Gringoire), Alan Marshal (Phoebus), Walter Hampden (Claude). Producer: Pandro S. Berman; Director: William S. Dieterle; Screenplay: Sonya Levien, Bruno Frank (Based on the novel by Victor Hugo); Photography: Joseph August; Music: Alfred Newman. RUNNING TIME: 115 minutes.

Charles Laughton might well have wished he were made of stone during the filming of *The Hunchback of Notre Dame* in 1939. Not only did he suffer physical agonies under the massive makeup required for the role, but like many at the time, he felt the inner turmoil of watching his world erupt into war.

Laughton had wanted to play Quasimodo since 1934, when MGM production chief Irving G. Thalberg first suggested a remake of Lon Chaney's silent classic. But after completing *Mutiny on the Bounty* in 1935, the actor returned to his native England, where he launched his own production company, Mayflower Films.

Then he signed a multipicture deal with RKO Studios. His first choice for his return to American filmmaking was *The Hunchback of Notre Dame,* a perfect fit with studio president George Schaeffer's commitment to bring back quality pictures to the studio. With a budget of $1.8 million, the film would be the second most expensive RKO had made to date, topped only by the recent production of *Gunga Din*.

Laughton's protégée, Maureen O'Hara, made her U.S. debut as Esmeralda. The nineteen-year-old's beauty and natural Irish fire were assets to the role, but her presence also caused some problems. After a few minor British pictures, she had been signed by Mayflower Films to star opposite Laughton in the Alfred Hitchcock thriller *Jamaica Inn*. For *Hunchback,* O'Hara, her mother, and Laughton sailed to America on the same ship. Although he was married to Elsa Lanchester and known within the industry to be homosexual, Laughton's trip with O'Hara inspired so much speculation in the press that he finally wired his wife to join him in Hollywood just to allay the rumors.

Charles Laughton's makeup onscreen may have terrorized Maureen O'Hara, but offscreen their relationship was decidedly warmer.

> *"Sanctuary!"*
> —Charles Laughton's most famous line from The Hunchback of Notre Dame

RKO built the town square in front of Notre Dame Cathedral on its Encino Ranch, usually the location for westerns. The result was the largest set built to that day, with a price tag of $250,000. Laughton insisted the studio borrow Perc Westmore from Warner Bros. to create his makeup. Together, they worked out a grotesque creation requiring two-and-a-half hours to apply and remove. Covering the left side of Laughton's face with rubber, Westmore created the illusion that one half of his face sagged horribly, even adding a false eye socket on the actor's left cheek. The right side appeared to be pulled upward, and Laughton wore a special contact lens to give that eye a milky cast. Finally, Westmore placed a four-pound rubber hump on the actor and built up his torso to create the illusion of Quasimodo's great strength.

The makeup would have been difficult enough under normal circumstances, but the exteriors were filmed during one of the hottest Septembers in Southern California history. For ten days, temperatures climbed to 110° F as Laughton sweltered on the torture wheel under the sun. Sometimes he sweated so profusely his makeup melted. At night, he would return to his hotel room, crying from exhaustion, with welts on his legs and thighs where the whip had missed his padding—or had gone right through it.

Yet most of those on the set realized that something extraordinary was happening. Years later, director William Dieterle would write of the whipping scene, "He was not the poor crippled creature expecting compassion from the mob, but rather oppressed and enslaved mankind, suffering the most awful injustice." As happened with other films made in Hollywood before America's entry into World War II, the historical epic seemed to many an allegory of what was happening in Europe. The persecution of Esmeralda and the gypsies carried unmistakable echoes of the Nazi persecution of the Jews. When Laughton rang the cathedral bells to celebrate Esmeralda's freedom, he seemed to be ringing the bells for all of Europe. Many in the cast and crew were moved to tears, and Dieterle was so affected he forgot to yell "cut" until Laughton finally collapsed from the effort.

The Hunchback of Notre Dame was a major success for RKO. Although the film seemed lost in the shuffle at Oscar time—with a single nomination for Best Sound (it was the year of *Gone With the Wind*)—it posted $3.1 million in rentals, a fitting return to Hollywood for one of the screen's greatest actors.

Notre Dame de Encino

I Am a Fugitive from a Chain Gang

Torn from the Headlines

1932. CAST: Paul Muni (James Allen), Glenda Farrell (Marie Woods), Helen Vinson (Helen), Preston Foster (Pete), Allen Jenkins (Barney Sykes), Edward Ellis (Bomber Wells). Producer: Hal B. Wallis; Director: Mervyn LeRoy; Screenplay: Howard J. Green, Brown Holmes, Sheridan Gibney (Based on the autobiography *I Am a Fugitive from a Georgia Chain Gang* by Robert E. Burns); Photography: Sol Polito; Music: Leo F. Forbstein.

RUNNING TIME: 93 minutes.

Decades before David Janssen or Harrison Ford (depending on your medium of choice) took it on the lam, the strongest contender for Jean Valjean's title as the world's most famous fugitive was Robert E. Burns, the Georgia chain gang runaway whose story inspired an eagerly followed magazine serial, a best-seller, and one of Warner Bros.' best early films. *I Am a Fugitive from a Chain Gang* was the picture that established the studio's reputation for turning yesterday's headlines into tomorrow's hits.

Burns's 1931 book, titled *I Am a Fugitive from a Georgia Chain Gang,* created a sensation. At least three Hollywood studios were interested in the rights, much to the consternation of industry censors working for the Hays Office, who complained that the book was virtually unfilmable because its key plot points, Burns's mistreatment at the prison camp and his two escapes, violated Code injunctions against brutality, the justification of illegal activity, and the negative treatment of law enforcement methods.

Undaunted by the objections, Zanuck purchased the rights for $12,500 and assigned the film to director Mervyn LeRoy, who had directed the studio's previous headline-based hit, *Little Caesar*. Zanuck made a few changes from Burns's original account. Along with giving the main character a fictitious name, James Allen, Zanuck had him framed for a lunch-counter robbery (Burns had actually helped steal $5.29) and left the character on the lam at the end. The real Burns had settled in New Jersey and become a tax consultant.

Yet Burns was still clearly haunted by his experience. Three New Jersey governors refused demands that he be extradited. Zanuck arranged to bring Burns to Hollywood under an alias to

Paul Muni (at door) faces another day of hard labor.

work with the film's writers. During the stay, he jumped at every noise, particularly sound effects from the studio's gangster pictures.

To play Burns, Warner's signed an actor who had just scored a major hit playing a character based on Al Capone in Howard Hughes's *Scarface*. Paul Muni was starring on Broadway at the time in *Counsellor-at-Law,* but had arranged to take the summer off. At first he refused a seven-year contract with the studio, declaring it too confining. Then the Warner representative suggested a three-picture deal at $50,000 a film. They even gave him script approval, an unprecedented offer to a studio actor at the time.

Muni arrived at Warner's while Burns was still there and was able to meet with the man to get background on the role. When Burns asked if the actor planned to copy his mannerisms, Muni explained that he was more interested in capturing the feel of the character, what he called "the smell of fear." "I don't want to imitate you," Muni explained. "I want to be you."

After the first preview, Zanuck decided the ending, in which Muni carries out his second escape, wasn't strong enough. He wrote a scene

FUGITIVE TIMELINE

1920—Robert Burns arrested for stealing $5.29 so he could buy food. Sentenced to hard labor in a Georgia prison camp.

1922—Burns escapes and relocates to Chicago, where he becomes a successful businessman.

1927—Turned in by his wife, Burns waives extradition to return to Georgia on the promise that he will simply finish his sentence. On his return, he learns that he has had time added for his escape.

1930—Burns escapes for good, eventually resettling as a tax expert in New Jersey.

1931—I Am a Fugitive from a Georgia Chain Gang published first in magazine form, then in book form.

1932—Burns travels to Hollywood in secret to serve as consultant on the script for I Am a Fugitive from a Chain Gang and meet with Paul Muni.

1945—Georgia Governor Ellis Arnall finally commutes Burns's sentence to time served.

1955—Burns dies.

in which Muni returns to the woman he loves, telling her that he can never see her again, that he will be on the run the rest of his life. As he leaves, she calls after him, asking how he survives. "I steal," Muni says, as the lights fade around him.

That final fade came as an accident. LeRoy had planned to go to a black-out after the line. During rehearsals, however, a klieg light blew, taking the fuse with it. The resultant slow fade, starting just before Muni's final line, was so powerful he decided to shoot the film exactly that way.

The results were amazing. Although *Daily Variety* reported walk-outs at the previews and said the movie would appeal only to "those who enjoy suffering," most of the reviews were overwhelmingly positive, praising both the quality of the film and Warner's courage in taking on the state of Georgia. Ticket sales were surprisingly good, making the film one of the studio's biggest hits that year and turning Muni into a major screen star.

Needless to say, the film was not popular with Georgia's government. Two prison officials sued, claiming the picture defamed them. In addition, anonymous letters arrived at the studio "banning" Jack Warner and LeRoy from the state. Yet officials could not ignore the film's influence on public opinion. Within a few years, Georgia ended its chain-gang system.

I Remember Mama

"First and Foremost"

1948. CAST: Irene Dunne (Mama), Barbara Bel Geddes (Katrin), Oscar Homolka (Uncle Chris), Philip Dorn (Papa), Sir Cedric Hardwicke (Mr. Hyde), Edgar Bergen (Mr. Thorkelson), Rudy Vallee (Dr. Johnson), Ellen Corby (Aunt Trina). Producers: George Stevens, Harriet Parsons; Director: George Stevens; Screenplay: DeWitt Bodeen (Based on the play by John Van Druten and the novel *Mama's Bank Account* by Kathryn Forbes); Photography: Nicholas Musuraca; Music: Roy Webb. RUNNING TIME: 134 minutes.

The screen has presented many a self-sacrificing mother, but few have done as much to uphold simple family values as Irene Dunne in RKO's 1948 film version of Kathryn Forbes's book. In the course of just over two episodic hours, Dunne helps her sister get married, prepares her brother to enter the next world, gets two children through serious operations, and sets another on the road to a successful career as a writer, all against the backdrop of life in San Francisco before World War I. Dunne's Mama seemed to harken back to a time of simpler, all-American values in a period marked by the increasing success of social-problem pictures and more sophisticated European imports.

RKO producer Harriet Parsons discovered Forbes's collection of stories, *Mama's Bank Account,* in 1943 and convinced the studio brass to pick up the rights for her. Without telling Parsons, however, the studio sold stage rights to Richard Rodgers and Oscar Hammerstein, who then hired John Van Druten to adapt the story. One provision of the sale was that RKO could not release a competing film version until a given time after the Broadway premiere.

I Remember Mama opened to glowing reviews in 1944, eventually running 714 performances. Although that delayed work on the film until 1947, it also made the property significantly more valuable. Popularity took its toll on Parsons, however, when she had to fight off other producers for the chance to film the book she had discovered in the first place. Fortunately, Parsons had such a strong background in producing, including a successful updating of the classic weeper *The Enchanted Cottage,* that she was able to hold onto the film. Nor did she have to use family ties to keep the project—Parsons had made her mother, legendary gossip columnist Louella Parsons, swear not to use her column in her daughter's behalf.

> ***"Warm! Human! Lovable! The swellest movie anyone would ever want to see!"***
>
> **—Ad line for I Remember Mama**

With the success of *I Remember Mama* on stage, RKO upgraded the project. So Parsons went after the screen's most famous Scandinavian, Greta Garbo. The studio was also trying to hire Garbo as the murderous mother in *Mourning Becomes Electra,* but the elusive star turned down both projects with the terse telegram, "No Mamas! No Murderesses!"

Parsons's next choice was Irene Dunne, who had started her career under contract to RKO in the early thirties. Dunne was intrigued at the thought of returning to her first Hollywood home but put off at the thought of playing her first character role. Because of her uncertainties, she submitted a list of only five directors with whom she would consider making the film. From this list, the studio picked another RKO alumnus, George Stevens. This meant, however, that Parsons would have to share the producer credit with him. To get her star, she made a concession she would soon regret.

Irene Dunne discusses a scene with director George Stevens.

Stevens insisted on doing location work in San Francisco, where he lived up to his reputation for slow, meticulous shooting methods. Under his watchful eye, the schedule grew to eight months, with the budget rising above the $3 million mark. When Parsons protested that his extravagance would make it almost impossible for the film to make back its investment, new studio head Dore Schary sided with the director.

I Remember Mama was received lovingly by the press and drew some of the best preview responses in RKO history. Yet Parsons had been right about the high budget; the film failed to return a profit during its initial run. That may have also been what hurt the picture's Oscar chances. Despite five nominations—for Dunne as Best Actress; Homolka as Best Supporting Actor; Ellen Corby and Barbara Bel Geddes (in her second film, decades before she became one of television's most famous mothers on Dallas) as Best Supporting Actress; and cinematographer Nicholas Musuraca—it didn't win a single award.

Much of the competition at the 1948 Oscars came from English films, which were making a strong showing on U.S. screens toward the end of the decade. Many were predicting the end of Hollywood. But I Remember Mama provided hope according to one unlikely source, Louella Parsons's longtime rival, Hedda Hopper. She wrote, "As long as we turn out pictures like *I Remember Mama* we don't have to worry about the future of Hollywood."

Future television mom Barbara Bel Geddes (right) gets a few pointers on family life from the indomitable Irene Dunne (third from left).

MAMA FOREVER

1944—Mady Christians stars on Broadway in I Remember Mama. *Marlon Brando makes his Broadway debut as her son.*

1949—Peggy Wood, the only true rival to Dunne's popularity in the role, starts an eight-year run on television in the series Mama. *Dick Van Patten costars as her son.*

1979—Liv Ullman stars in the musical version of I Remember Mama, *with music by Richard Rodgers (his last production) and lyrics by Martin Charnin. It lasts only 108 performances.*

1983—Sally Ann Howe sings the title role in the long-awaited recording of the Rodgers-Charnin score to I Remember Mama.

The Informer

The Gutter Judas

1935. CAST: Victor McLaglen (Gypo Nolan), Heather Angel (Mary McPhillip), Preston Foster (Dan Gallagher), Margot Grahame (Katie Madden), Wallace Ford (Frankie McPhillip), Una O'Conner (Mrs. McPhillip). Producer: Cliff Reid; Director: John Ford; Screenplay: Dudley Nichols (Based on the novel by Liam O'Flaherty); Photography: Joseph H. August; Music: Max Steiner. RUNNING TIME: 91 minutes.

Director John Ford spent four years trying to get somebody in Hollywood to approve a film version of Liam O'Flaherty's tale of betrayal and redemption during the Irish Civil War of 1922. After turndowns from Fox, Warner Bros., Columbia, Paramount, and MGM, he finally convinced RKO—the little studio that could—to give him a B-movie budget and shooting schedule. In return, he gave them a surprise success that made him a critic's darling for the next two decades.

O'Flaherty had written *The Informer* for one purpose—to make money. After his first books won critical approval but generated few sales, he decided to write something more commercial, a cinematic, fast-paced novel with the feel of a detective story. The result was the tragic tale of Gypo Nolan, who turns in his best friend to the British so he can use the reward money to emigrate to America with the woman he loves.

Ford first came across the book in 1930. A year later, he picked up the film rights but still couldn't find anyone to back the picture. Then he signed a two-film deal with RKO, where he found a kindred spirit in production chief Merian C. Cooper, the pioneering documentarian who had cocreated *King Kong*. The two became lifelong friends and, years later, would form an independent production company together. Ford's promise to make *The Informer* for the relatively low cost of $243,000 provided Cooper with the ammunition he needed to get the film approved.

Even before the script was written, Ford consulted with art director Van Nest Polglase, cinematographer Joseph H. August, and composer Max Steiner. By working closely with his production chiefs, Ford created a stylized impression of Dublin at night without ever having to leave the studio. He also worked out ways to get the right feeling rapidly and cheaply.

Victor McLaglen contemplates the "twenty pieces of silver" that await him for betraying best friend Wallace Ford.

John Ford (seated, with pipe) directs himself and Victor McLaglen to Oscars.

For leading man, Ford chose Victor McLaglen, who had worked with him several times before. The RKO brass objected to the choice; McLaglen was a notorious drinker and far from Hollywood's greatest actor. But Ford wanted McLaglen's combination of hulking appearance and vulnerability and knew he could get the performance out of him. Realizing that McLaglen had a tendency to bombast, the director continually changed the shooting schedule so that the actor's uncertainty of his lines would read as the character's attempts to grasp what was going on around him. For his biggest scene, the hearing before the IRA tribunal, Ford told McLaglen he wouldn't be needed the next day. The actor went out drinking with friends only to be awakened the next morning by a call to report to the set at once. His hangover created the exact feel Ford wanted for the scene.

Among the year-end awards were Best Picture citations from the National Board of Review and the newly formed New York Film Critics Circle. At Oscar time, *The Informer* lost Best Picture to MGM's epic *Mutiny on the Bounty,* but won in four other categories: Best Actor, Best Director, Best Screenplay, and Best Score. With one film, Ford was transformed from a popular commercial director to a major screen artist. He would go on to win three more Oscars, more than any other director.

Jailhouse Rock

"C'mon, Everybody, Let's Rock!"

1957. CAST: Elvis Presley (Vince Everett), Judy Tyler (Peggy Van Alden), Mickey Shaughnessy (Hunk Houghton), Jennifer Holden (Sherry Wilson), Dean Jones (Teddy Talbot), Anne Neyland (Laury Jackson). Producer: Pandro S. Berman; Director: Richard Thorpe; Screenplay: Guy Trosper (Based on a story by Ned Young); Photography: Robert Brenner (CinemaScope); Musical Direction: Jeff Alexander; Music and Lyrics: Mike Stoller, Jerry Lieber, Roy C. Bennett, Abner Silver, Ben Weisman, Aaron Schroeder, Sid Tepper. RUNNING TIME: 96 minutes.

MGM crowned a new king when Elvis Presley brought his guitar, his hips, and his bad-boy attitude to the former home of Nelson Eddy and Jeanette MacDonald. Through his twenty-year studio stay Presley would grow increasingly domesticated, but his first explosive film there, *Jailhouse Rock,* sounded a battle cry for the rock 'n' roll revolution.

Jailhouse Rock was actually the King's third film. He had made his screen debut in the Civil War drama *Love Me Tender* at 20th Century-Fox. His second film, *Loving You,* started a long association with independent producer Hal B. Wallis. But although the film was loosely based on Elvis's rise through the music business, the virginal character he played was still a far cry from the Elvis that came through on his records.

Then came MGM and *Jailhouse Rock*. The plot—focused on a violent youth who learns to rock while doing time for manslaughter, then becomes a temperamental, swell-headed singing sensation—may not have been Elvis's life story, but it gave him his first chance to generate the kind of danger on screen that teenagers (and their parents) heard in his music. The script did borrow one event from his life. In the film, Presley starts out to record a ballad, then, unhappy with the sound, decides to get down and dirty. The same thing had actually happened at Sun Records.

Jailhouse Rock was far from a prestige film. Although the studio paid top dollar for Elvis's services—$250,000 and fifty percent of all profits—they only allowed for a budget of $650,000. Producer Pandro S. Berman was more interested in the studio's adaptation of *The Brothers Karamazov,* and he picked director Richard Thorpe solely because of his reputation for working

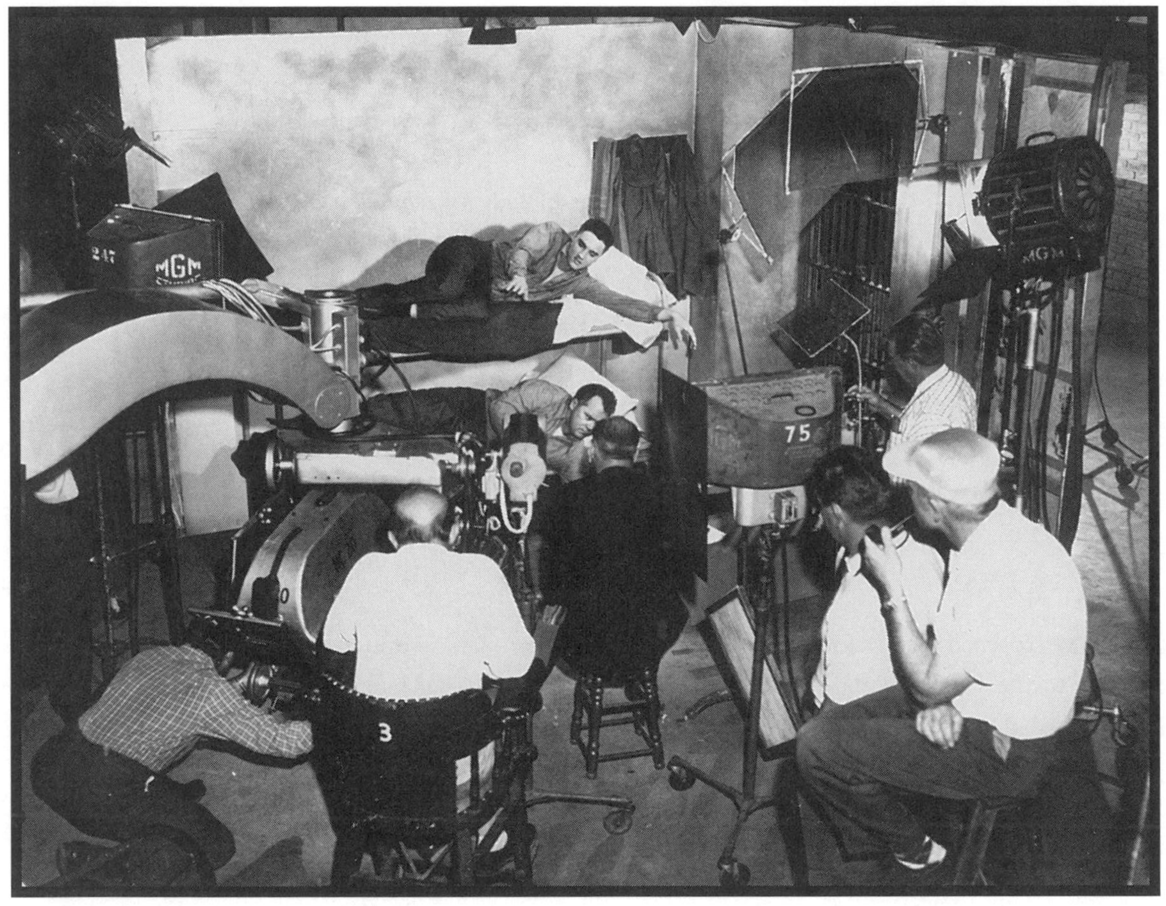

Elvis Presley (top) and Mickey Shaughnessy (bottom) bunk down for the cameras.

quickly and economically. Berman got writer Guy Trosper, who later would script such prestigious films as *Birdman of Alcatraz,* only by promising him a better assignment on his next film.

But, then, the movies were only a means to an end for Elvis's manager, Colonel Tom Parker. The Colonel never read a script. All he asked was that the picture provide a fitting showcase for the King's music—and with good reason. Parker and Presley maintained ownership of all the songs he sang on screen. That proved particularly profitable on *Jailhouse Rock,* as the film contained some of Elvis's best numbers. In addition to the title tune, rock 'n' roll songsmiths Mike Stoller and Jerry Lieber contributed such hits as "Treat Me Nice" and "Don't Leave Me Now."

Presley began work on the film on May 5, 1957, with a prerecording session. As he often did, instead of getting right down to work, he

> *"It's just the beast in me."*
> —Presley, justifying his dating style to Judy Tyler

started out at the piano, singing spirituals and asking the other musicians to join in. After lunch, he continued with the jam session. When an executive complained that they were wasting MGM's money, he walked out. Elvis's behavior wasn't any sign of star temperament. He had not recorded anything in months and had just been trying to warm up to the studio environment. The next day, he came back to record the songs.

According to some sources, Presley personally choreographed the "Jailhouse Rock" number, complete with gyrating convicts on two levels of stylized prison cells. Others suggest that the number he staged was "Treat Me Nice." Originally, the title song had not been scheduled as a major production number, but dance director Alex Romero got the idea for staging it and convinced the studio to put another $25,000 into the picture.

Jailhouse Rock did not get many good reviews, but that was hardly a problem with Elvis's film work. He dismissed the bad notices with, "Well, that's the way the mop flops," and counted his money. By November, "Jailhouse Rock" was the nation's top hit, reaching two million in sales in just two weeks. The film made $4 million at the box office on its initial release. Presley would return to the studio for ten more films—including another of his greatest, *Viva Las Vegas*—and provide the subject for the acclaimed documentary *Elvis—That's the Way It Is* in 1970.

Elvis Presley dances to the "Jailhouse Rock."

WHATEVER BECAME OF . . .

Judy Tyler seemed headed for stardom when she worked opposite Elvis Presley in* Jailhouse Rock*, only her second film. True, she didn't get to show off her vocal talents, but then her lyric Broadway style probably wouldn't have meshed with the King's combination of R&B and country-western. Besides, with a voice like hers, nobody would have believed Tyler was just a recording executive.

The Milwaukee-born singer had built a strong following among children while playing Princess Summerfall Winterspring of the Tinka Tonka tribe on* The Howdy Doody Show*. During her five-year run on the series, she also found time to star in* Pipe Dream *on Broadway, play small roles and sing on Sid Caesar's TV variety show, and guest on several other series. The result was a trip to Hollywood and a bright future. Shortly after filming* Jailhouse Rock*, however, she was killed in an automobile accident in July 1957. Tyler was only twenty-four.

The Jazz Singer

"You Ain't Heard Nothing Yet!"

1927. CAST: Al Jolson (Jake Rabinowitz), May McAvoy (Mary Dale), Warner Oland (Cantor Rabinowitz), Eugenie Besserer (Sara Rabinowitz), Bobbie Gordon (Jakie at Thirteen), William Demarest (Buster Billings), Myrna Loy (Chorus Girl). Director: Alan Crosland; Screenplay: Alfred A. Cohn (Based on the play by Samson Raphaelson); Titles: Jack Jarmuth; Photography: Hal Mohr; Music: Louis Silvers. RUNNING TIME: 89 minutes.

It was a Hollywood revolution! After years of experimenting, despite predictions by industry insiders that the public didn't want to hear actors talk, Warner Bros. and Al Jolson created a sensation with *The Jazz Singer*. The film didn't trigger the transition to talking pictures overnight. But it did prove that there was an audience for what seemed to many a brand new medium.

In fact, sound-on-film was hardly new when Warner Bros. decided to buy into the process. Experiments with talking film had begun almost with the birth of silent pictures, but there had been so many problems and so much resistance among film producers, that it developed slowly. Everybody seemed to be waiting for someone else to take the initiative, which didn't happen until Warner Bros. decided to set up its own radio station in 1927 and hired sound engineer Leonard Levenson to set up the on-lot station. During one of his visits to the old Warner's lot on Sunset Boulevard, he advised Sam Warner to check out the new sound film process being developed at the Bell Labs in New York. At the time, Warner's was considered a second-string studio. Sam and his brothers hoped that by pioneering in sound films they would be able to compete with such top contenders as MGM and Universal.

To showcase the new process, Warner's decided to record a score and sound effects for a feature already in production, *Don Juan,* with their top male star, John Barrymore. In addition, they prepared a series of classical-music shorts. Although some felt the shorts overshadowed the feature, the process, now called Vitaphone, was a big hit. So the studio followed it with a lesser film, *The Better 'Ole,* a comedy starring Charles Chaplin's brother Syd. This time the shorts featured more popular music, including "Al Jolson in a Plantation Act," featuring the great entertainer in his film debut.

The most important night in movie history: *The Jazz Singer* premieres.

Despite the excitement created by Warner's Vitaphone experiments, they hadn't begun to pay off. Most theaters couldn't afford the $23,000 required for conversion to sound film. Moreover, Fox was about to debut its own sound process, Movietone, and five other studios had entered into an agreement to develop a technology of their own. So Warner's took the process a step further, creating a feature that was essentially a string of Vitaphone shorts tied together with silent footage.

The studio had signed George Jessel on the strength of his success in the Broadway drama *The Jazz Singer,* in which he played a young

UP FROM THE CHORUS

Three members of* The Jazz Singer's *cast were destined for bigger things. Most viewers have little trouble identifying Myrna Loy as one of the chorus girls commenting on Jake's romance with dancing star Mary Dale (May McAvoy). Less recognizable is former vaudevillian William Demarest in a small role as Buster Billings. He and Jolson would become good friends during the production. Years later, Demarest would be cast at Jolson's request in* The Jolson Story. *To play Jolson's father, Cantor Rabinowitz, Warner's turned to a Swedish actor known for his ability to play a variety of nationalities. That talent would serve Warner Oland when he moved to Fox in 1931 and starred in the studio's popular Charlie Chan series.

THE OTHER JAZZ SINGERS

1925—George Jessel stars in the stage version on Broadway, then plays Jake Rabinowitz on tour.

1952—Television version on Broadway Television Theatre with Lionel Adams as Jake.

1953—Danny Thomas takes over the lead for a big-screen remake costarring Peggy Lee.

1959—Ford Star Time retells the story with Jerry Lewis in the lead.

1980—Neil Diamond stars as Jake, with Sir Laurence Olivier as his father, in a big-screen remake panned by most critics. Despite that, the film scores an impressive profit, thanks partly to sales of the soundtrack album.

man who defies family tradition to become a pop singer rather than a cantor. At the time, they had picked up the film rights for $50,000. But Jessel had not signed to perform in talking pictures and demanded an additional $10,000 to perform the songs. Instead Warner's turned to Jolson, who had actually been the model for the original play.

Contrary to legend, Jolson did not spontaneously add dialogue to the film. *The Jazz Singer* had always been planned to include a few lines along with the musical numbers. It is likely, however, that he came up with the line, "You ain't heard nothing yet," which he frequently used in his stage performances. Still, the film was only planned as a "part-talkie." In all, there are only 281 spoken words in the picture.

The Jazz Singer opened to tremendous box office, eventually producing a $3.5 million profit on an investment of $500,000. When Warner's next few part-talkies proved successful, even without Jolson's powerful on-screen presence, the rest of Hollywood embraced the new medium with startling speed. A year later, Hollywood officially recognized Warner's move into the big leagues—and the picture that had put them there—when the newly created Academy of Motion Picture Arts and Sciences honored *The Jazz Singer* with a special award as "the outstanding pioneer talking picture, which has revolutionized the industry."

Al Jolson puts over a song—and a new medium.

Jezebel

"You Can't Wear Red to the Olympus Ball"

1938. CAST: Bette Davis (Julie Marsden), Henry Fonda (Preston Dillard), George Brent (Buck Cantrell), Margaret Lindsay (Amy Bradford Dillard), Fay Bainter (Aunt Belle), Richard Cromwell (Ted Dillard). Producers: Hal B. Wallis, Henry Blanke; Director: William Wyler; Screenplay: Clements Ripley, Abem Finkel, John Huston; Adaptation by Robert Buckner (Based on the play by Owen Davis Sr.); Photography: Ernest Haller; Music: Max Steiner. RUNNING TIME: 103 minutes.

Red proved a fitting substitute for Scarlett when Warner Bros. presented diva-in-residence Bette Davis with a consolation prize for losing the lead in *Gone With the Wind*. As Julie Marston in *Jezebel*, she gave the performance that made her a major box-office star, winning a well-deserved Oscar in the process. In addition, the film introduced her to the director who would help her refine her screen acting technique and who became the great love of her life, William Wyler.

Warner Bros. had considered producing *Jezebel* as a vehicle for Davis as far back as 1935, before anybody had heard of *Gone With the Wind*. On the strength of her breakthrough performance as the vixenish Mildred in *Of Human Bondage*, the studio almost bought the rights to Owen Davis Sr.'s failed play about a southern belle whose scandalous decision to wear a red dress to New Orleans's Olympus Ball ruins her chances for happiness. But they decided the female lead was too unsympathetic and passed on it.

Jezebel looked a lot better after *Gone With the Wind* hit the bestseller lists. Davis was actually a front-runner to play Scarlett in the film version. But studio head Jack Warner insisted on a package deal that would have cast Errol Flynn as Rhett. Although she desperately wanted the role, Davis knew that Flynn could never carry off the male lead and refused the loan.

In an effort to find a vehicle that would move Davis into the top rank of film stars, the studio returned to Owen Davis's play. To complete the package, they cast Henry Fonda in the male lead and hired one of Hollywood's top directors, William Wyler.

Filming began in late October 1937, with perfectionist Wyler soon falling behind schedule as he demanded take after take.

As December drew near, Warner executives panicked. Jack Warner considered replacing Wyler with William Dieterle. When Davis got wind of this, she stormed into Warner's office, stating that she couldn't possibly keep up her level of performance with another director. She offered to work until midnight to keep the film from falling further behind.

She was right about her performance. Wyler was the first really strong director she had worked with. He showed her how to pace herself, and he toned down her famous mannerisms by threatening to put a chain around her neck to keep her from moving her head.

> ***"DARLING OF DIXIE! . . . Meanest when she's lovin' most!***
>
> ***"Half angel, half siren, all woman! The screen's greatest actress comes to you in the hit picture of her career . . . as the most exciting heroine who ever lived and loved in Dixie!"***
>
> **—Ad lines for Jezebel**

He was also doing her a great deal of good offscreen. Drawn together by their powerful personalities and dedication to filmmaking, director and star began an affair. Davis would later call Wyler the one great love of her life. When their romance burned out and he married starlet Margaret Tallichet (another Scarlett O'Hara hopeful), Davis was shattered.

Jezebel finished shooting in January 1938, twenty-eight days over schedule and almost $400,000 over budget. But the results were worth it. Davis won some of the best reviews of her career and landed on the cover of *Time* magazine. On Oscar night, Davis was a shoo-in for Best Actress and happily credited Wyler for her performance. She was also happy to see costar Fay Bainter honored as Best Supporting Actress for her quiet work as the sympathetic Aunt Belle.

GIVE THE LITTLE LADY A GREAT BIG HAND

Although William Wyler directed Bette Davis to one of her greatest performances in Jezebel, he couldn't get anywhere with another actress in the film. Margaret Lindsay, a Warner Bros. contract player, was cast as the Yankee bride Henry Fonda brings home. For the climactic scene, in which Davis begs Lindsay for permission to accompany her husband to the island where he is to be quarantined with yellow fever, Wyler shot take after take but could not get the right sense of power from the supporting player. Realizing that Davis was starting to wear out from the intense scene, he figured out the perfect way to work around Lindsay's shortcomings. By inserting a close-up of Lindsay's hand clutching the banister, with her wedding ring prominently featured, he finally got the effect he needed and could call it a night.

William Wyler (left) directs offscreen lover Bette Davis, with Henry Fonda.

Johnny Belinda

"Who Wants to See a Picture Where the Leading Lady Doesn't Say a Word!"

1948. CAST: Jane Wyman (Belinda McDonald), Lew Ayres (Dr. Robert Richardson), Charles Bickford (Black McDonald), Agnes Moorehead (Agnes McDonald), Stephen McNally (Locky McCormick), Jan Sterling (Stella McGuire). Producer: Jerry Wald; Director: Jean Negulesco; Screenplay: Irmgard von Cube, Allen Vincent (Based on the play by Elmer Harris); Photography: Ted McCord; Music: Max Steiner.

RUNNING TIME: 103 minutes.

Sometimes a single performance can turn an actor's career around. Most often, this happens with relative newcomers—Vivien Leigh as Scarlett O'Hara, for example. For Jane Wyman, the role came late, after twelve years of playing wisecracking chorus girls and tough lady reporters at Warner Bros. It took two loan-outs to other studios before Warner executives recognized Wyman's potential as a dramatic star. First, she traveled to Paramount to play Ray Milland's long-suffering girlfriend in 1945's *The Lost Weekend*. A year later she won an Oscar nomination when MGM cast her—very much against type—as the stoic backwoods woman in *The Yearling*.

The property that would clinch her position as a dramatic star had been kicking around Hollywood almost as long as Wyman had. *Johnny Belinda* started out in 1934 as a story idea proposed by Elmer Harris while under contract to MGM, then became a failed Broadway play in 1940. Few in the film capital saw the box-office potential in this tale of a deaf mute in rural Newfoundland and the doctor who teaches her to communicate. And there were censorship problems posed by the girl's rape by the town bully.

But Warner Bros. had one producer who was an expert at taming material considered too hot for the screen—Jerry Wald. He convinced the studio of the story's box-office potential and got it past the censors.

Wyman threw herself into preparation for the role as never before. She learned sign language and worked with a Mexican girl who had been born deaf. Over the next few months, Wyman filmed tests of the girl and herself, trying to duplicate what she called the "'anticipation light,' the look of one who wants so eagerly to share in things."

> *"There was temptation in her helpless silence—and then torment!"*
>
> —AD LINE FOR JOHNNY BELINDA

But for all her work, there was still something wrong—she could hear! For all her efforts, she couldn't hide her instinctive reactions to sound. A doctor fashioned wax earplugs to block out all but the loudest noises.

Helping greatly with her performance was the lengthy location shoot. Wald and Negulesco had chosen the area around Fort Bragg, two hundred miles north of San Francisco. The isolation turned cast and crew into a tight knit community.

The location shoot also minimized studio interference. Wald knew this film had to be different from the usual run of Hollywood drama and correctly feared that Warner executives wouldn't understand it. As the daily rushes were sent back to the studio, Jack Warner told Wald to cut back on shots of the local scenery and put some makeup on his star. Warner even ordered them to create a narration in which Wyman would speak the character's inner thoughts. He couldn't believe an audience would accept a silent leading lady.

One of the screen's finest acting ensembles: Agnes Moorehead, Charles Bickford, Jane Wyman, and Lew Ayres.

Three generations of McDonalds share a moment of happiness: Charles Bickford, infant, and Jane Wyman.

THE MAN THAT GOT AWAY

Jack Warner must have forgotten that he had fired director Jean Negulesco. When* Johnny Belinda *scored twelve Oscar nominations, the studio head sent him a telegram reading, "Well, kid, we did it again! Next time we do a picture we're going to get fourteen nominations!" That next time never happened. By the time* Johnny Belinda *became a hit, Negulesco had settled into a long-term contract at 20th Century–Fox.

Wald kept the film on track, but he couldn't keep the studio from firing his director. Negulesco was let go before the last shot was made. In place of a scripted scene showing Wyman and doctor Lew Ayres leading a new life together, the studio simply tacked on a long shot of the doctor driving to the girl's farm.

To Warner's surprise, *Johnny Belinda* was a major hit with audiences, who made it the studio's top-grosser of 1948. They also made Wyman Warner's number-one dramatic star.

Her Oscar nomination, one of an amazing twelve for *Johnny Belinda,* heralded Wyman's new career. Yet when it came time for the Best Actress presentation, she was certain she couldn't win. Then presenter Ronald Colman opened the envelope and read her name.

At first, she was too stunned to move. Then Wald nudged her and she stood, dumping her handbag and its contents all over the floor. She didn't have a speech ready, either. But that didn't stop her from delivering one of the all-time great Oscar acceptances: "I accept this very gratefully for keeping my mouth shut for once. I think I'll do it again."

King Kong

"The Eighth Wonder of the World!"

1933. CAST: Fay Wray (Ann Darrow), Robert Armstrong (Carl Denham), Bruce Cabot (John Driscoll), Frank Reicher (Captain Englehorn), Sam Hardy (Charles Weston), Noble Johnson (Native Chief). Producers-Directors: Merian C. Cooper, Ernest B. Schoedsack; Screenplay: James Creelman, Ruth Rose (Based on a story by Cooper and Edgar Wallace); Photography: Edward Linden, Vernon L. Laker, J. O. Taylor; Music: Max Steiner.

RUNNING TIME: 103 minutes.

On March 2, 1933, audiences at New York's Radio City Music Hall and RKO Roxy watched an eighteen-inch model of an ape terrorize beautiful Fay Wray and devastate the streets of New York. The character Willis O'Brien and his special-effects team created out of a metal skeleton, rubber muscles, and rabbit fur would become one of the most identifiable figures in screen history.

King Kong was the brainchild of Merian C. Cooper, a documentary producer just moving into fiction film during the late twenties. He was shooting location footage in Africa for *The Four Feathers* when he became fascinated with gorillas. He was also intrigued by the giant Komodo dragons a friend of his had brought to the Bronx Zoo. From those two fascinations grew the story of a giant ape brought back to civilization from an island of prehistoric creatures. Initially, however, he couldn't interest anyone in the project. Then Cooper moved to RKO Studios as assistant to his friend David O. Selznick, who had just signed as production chief there. One of his first assignments was to evaluate "Creation," a project of O'Brien's special-effects unit. O'Brien had pioneered in the development of stop-motion photography, a technique that creates an illusion of movement by filming flexible models one frame at a time. After a huge hit with *The Lost World,* he wanted to make a similar project about explorers who discover prehistoric monsters on a plateau in South America.

Cooper viewed the test footage and O'Brien's models and knew that he had found the way to realize his dream project. He pitched the costly picture to Selznick, and even though the studio had recently imposed a $200,000 limit on all film budgets, he got the go-ahead for a $400,000 picture.

O'Brien had already established himself as the screen's master of model animation, but for *King Kong* he created several new techniques that would make movie history. For each animated

Top: One of the many famous publicity images generated for *King Kong*. *Left:* Bruce Cabot (seated right), Fay Wray (seated center), and crew.

sequence, he shot one frame at a time, making minute adjustments to the models' positions between shots. It often took an entire afternoon to get the twenty-four exposures necessary to fill one second of screen time. The battle between Kong and the pterodactyl required seven weeks of shooting.

> ***"When I'm in New York, I look at the Empire State Building and feel as though it belongs to me . . . or vice versa."***
>
> **—Fay Wray, on her lifelong association with King Kong**

O'Brien used three techniques to combine the models and the actors. The one established procedure was rear projection. Other scenes involved two separate images—the model animation and the actors—brought together in an optical printer. (That's how O'Brien filmed the scene in which Fay Wray escapes from Kong during his battle with the pterodactyl.) The third method was developed by O'Brien and Cooper specifically for *King Kong,* though they lost a fortune by neglecting to patent it. This involved filming the actors first, then projecting the scene on a small screen behind the models. The models' movements were than matched to the actors' movements, as when Kong removes Wray's clothing.

The finished product took the world by storm, earning more than $100,000 during its first week and eventually grossing $1,761,000 during its initial release. That was enough to save RKO from bankruptcy. Eventually *King Kong* made more than $5 million (around $50 million in contemporary dollars).

PRETENDERS TO THE THRONE

1933*—Son of Kong—*RKO's official sequel to King* Kong *reunited Cooper, Schoedsack, and O'Brien for the story of a kinder, gentler version of Kong. The film's poor box-office showing squelched sequels.

1949*—Mighty Joe Young—*O'Brien won a long-overdue Oscar for Best Special Effects for this story of a docile ape brought to a Hollywood nightclub.

1961*—Konga—*Kong went British in this Herman Cohen production, in which mad scientist Michael Gough turns a man in a monkey suit into a giant ape threatening London.

1962*—King Kong vs. Godzilla—*Kong joined the ranks of rubber-suited Japanese monsters for this film—produced with two endings, so Kong could win in the U. S. and Godzilla in Japan.

1968*—King Kong Escapes—*Kong battled a giant robot ape and a Godzilla stand-in in his second Japanese film.

1972*—Schlock—*Director John Landis (who also plays the prehistoric monster) and makeup artist Rick Baker got their start with this comic take on the Kong legend.

1976*—King Kong—*Dino De Laurentiis's multimillion-dollar remake disappointed purists by eschewing stop-motion photography to use yet another man in a monkey suit (created by Rick Baker). Jeff Bridges, Charles Grodin, and Jessica Lange, in her film debut, took over the leads in this eco-sensitive rendition of the classic tale.

—A-P-E—*This Korean quickie, released to cash in on the De Laurentiis production, combines a tongue-in-cheek approach with bad 3-D effects to little discernible purpose.*

1986*—King Kong Lives—*In this sequel to the De Laurentiis remake, surgeon Linda Hamilton revives Kong with a mechanical heart the size of a Buick, then helps him find love with a giant lady gorilla.

Kings Row

"Where's the Rest of Me!?"

1942. CAST: Ann Sheridan (Randy Monaghan), Robert Cummings (Parris Mitchell), Ronald Reagan (Drake McHugh), Betty Field (Cassandra Tower), Charles Coburn (Dr. Henry Gordon), Claude Rains (Dr. Alexander Tower). Producers: Hal B. Wallis, David Lewis; Director: Sam Wood; Screenplay: Casey Robinson (Based on the novel by Harry Bellamann); Photography: James Wong Howe; Music: Erich Wolfgang Korngold.
RUNNING TIME: 127 minutes.

Future president Ronald Reagan delivered his most famous on-screen line and what many consider his best performance in Warner Bros.' pre–*Peyton Place* foray into small-town sin and scandal. The line could just have easily been spoken by the book's author, Harry Bellamann, considering what Hollywood's censors did to his original story.

Bellamann's novel became a scandalous bestseller in 1940. Turning *Our Town* into "sour town," he probed the sins behind a bucolic midwestern hamlet from the 1890s to the period just before World War I, exposing a hotbed of sadism, incest, premarital sex, and hypocrisy, not to mention dealing with such touchy issues as miscegenation, homosexuality, and euthanasia.

When Warner Bros. production chief Hal B. Wallis first suggested purchasing the book, he was met with massive resistance. Then writer Casey Robinson realized how to make the story work. The solution was to focus not on the town's sins, which would have to be softened considerably for the censors anyway, but on the ideals of protagonist Parris Mitchell, a sensitive young man who studies psychiatry in Vienna, then returns to help his tortured childhood friends. Even with the right focus, however, it took four drafts to get the script past Joe Breen, administrator of the industry's Production Code.

Casting proved almost as difficult as getting a suitable script. Wallis tried to get Tyrone Power or Henry Fonda to play Parris, but 20th Century–Fox studio head Darryl F. Zanuck, who held both their contracts, refused to approve the loan-out. Director Sam Wood then insisted on using Universal's Robert Cummings, even though most thought him too lightweight for the role.

On the advice of Humphrey Bogart, Ann Sheridan went after the role of Randy, the girl from the wrong side of the tracks who befriends Parris's friend Drake and stands by him after he loses his legs in an accident. Even though she had scored a hit in *Torrid Zone* and was a fan favorite as the "Oomph Girl," she still had to convince Jack Warner that she wasn't just a one-shot wonder.

> ***"Out of the hushed strangeness of these lives, and out of the shadows that hid their shame, filmdom has fashioned a drama most unusual, most touching, and most wonderful!***
>
> ***"Kings Row. . . . The town they talk of in whispers!"***
>
> **—Ad copy for Kings Row**

Completing the starring trio was Ronald Reagan, another lightweight, whose growing popularity at the box office helped him beat out such contenders as Jack Carson, Eddie Albert, and Robert Preston.

Production started in July 1941, but there were delays almost from the start. James Stephenson, who had scored a hit as Bette Davis's lawyer in *The Letter,* was originally cast as Parris's mentor, Dr. Tower. When he died suddenly, the studio had to convince Claude Rains to accept the role. This delayed the schedule so much that Cummings was forced to go to work on another film at Universal, the Deanna Durbin musical *It Started with Eve,* causing further delays as he shuttled between the two studios.

Shooting finally finished in October, but that didn't end the problems. By the time the film was ready for previews in December, the U.S. had entered World War II. Men were already returning from the front minus arms and legs. Afraid

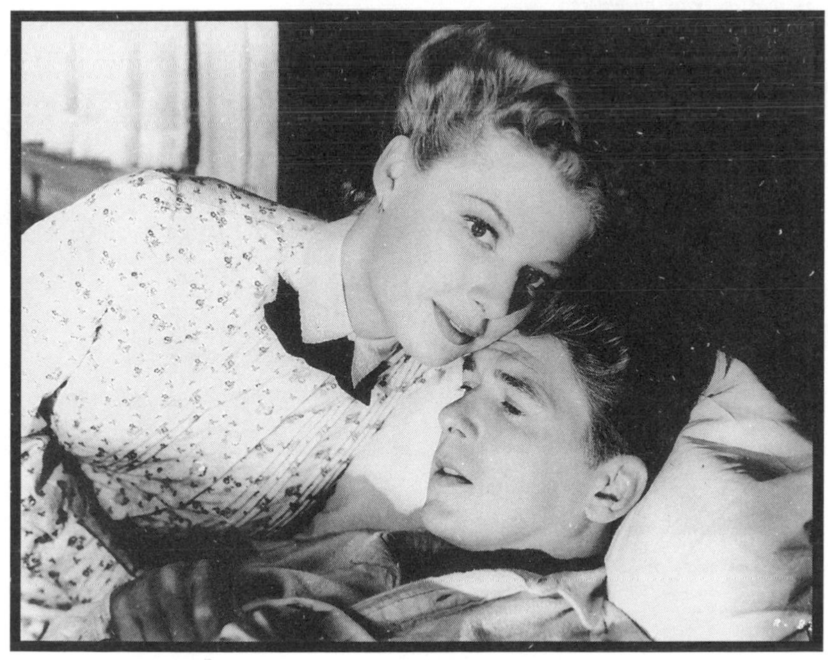

Ann Sheridan comforts an invalid Ronald Reagan.

of negative reactions to the film, some executives suggested changing Drake's double amputation to a crippling fracture, which Parris would heal.

Fortunately, Warner's decided to leave the film intact. *Kings Row* premiered in February 1942 to mixed reviews. Critics praised the film's technical accomplishments, noting that with William Cameron Menzies as production designer, James Wong Howe as cinematographer, and Erich Wolfgang Korngold writing the score, Warner's had turned the story into a quality production. But there were also quibbles about the film's view of the seamy side of life.

That aside, however, *Kings Row* emerged as a triumph of the studio system. It also proved a major boon to Sheridan and Reagan, who got the best notices. For Sheridan, the film proved her potential as an actress. Reagan's performance as Drake, progressing from schoolboy enthusiasm, to bitter defeat, to heroic determination, made him a star.

THE MAN BEHIND THE MAGIC

Much of* Kings Row's *visual power can be credited to production designer William Cameron Menzies, who supervised all visual aspects of the film, from costumes to sets to camera angles. In many cases he even designed the sets so they could only be shot the way he wanted.

***Menzies was born in Connecticut and made his movie debut as an art director for* Famous Players *in 1919. More than anyone else, he established the importance of effective production design on the screen, quickly earning a reputation for lavish sets that could do as much to sell a picture as star performances. He won the first Oscar for art direction for* The Dove *and* The Tempest *in 1928, along with a special award in 1939 for supervising the look of* Gone With the Wind.**

***Although Menzies made only occasional forays into directing, two of his films are among the most famous in the science-fiction genre: H. G. Wells's* Things to Come *and the 3-D cult classic* Invaders from Mars. *He died in 1957 after serving as Mike Todd's associate producer on* Around the World in 80 Days.**

Ann Sheridan confers with director Sam Wood.

Little Caesar

"This Game Ain't for Guys That's Soft!"

1931. CAST: Edward G. Robinson (Cesare Enrico Bandello), Douglas Fairbanks Jr. (Joe Massara), Glenda Farrell (Olga Strassoff), William Collier Jr. (Tony Passa), Ralph Ince (Diamond Pete Moran), George E. Stone (Otero). Producer: Hal B. Wallis (for Darryl F. Zanuck); Director: Mervyn LeRoy; Screenplay: Francis Edward Faragoh (Based on the novel by W. R. Burnett); Photography: Tony Gaudio; Music: Erno Rapee.

RUNNING TIME: 80 minutes.

Offscreen Edward G. Robinson was a gentle, cultured man with an impressive art collection and a love of good books. But when the script called for it, he could be tougher than tough—hard enough to rise to stardom despite his lack of stature and good looks and hard enough to create a new Hollywood genre, with the help of Warner Bros.' production machine.

Robinson's main advantage, besides his prodigious acting talents, was a resemblance to legendary underworld figure Al Capone. That likeness had helped him land a leading role in the Broadway production of *The Racket,* playing a character clearly modeled on Capone. His performance brought him a contract with Warner Bros., which put him in the right place at the right time.

While Robinson churned out six films for Warner's, writer W. R. Burnett was creating a revolutionary gangland tale. *Little Caesar* was born one night as Burnett listened to a live jazz performance from a Chicago nightclub. A friend of his was playing with the band, and Burnett sat horror-struck as he heard gangsters break into the club for a shootout, killing his friend and several other bystanders in the process. In a rage, he spent the next four weeks writing *Little Caesar.*

While the book was still in galleys, it made the rounds of Hollywood studios where somebody at Warner's—Jack Warner, producer Hal B. Wallis, and director Mervyn LeRoy have all taken credit for it—decided it was perfect picture material. There is also some disagreement over how Robinson was cast. LeRoy states he was the natural choice for the role, while the star and Wallis tell it differently. They claim Robinson was first offered the supporting role of Otero. Feeling himself better suited to the lead, he dressed as a gangster—complete with dark suit, Homburg, spats, and cigar—and confronted Wallis. "If you're going to have me in *Little Caesar* as Otero, you will completely

Edward G. Robinson discovers the wages of sin, both the material rewards (above, with Sidney Blackmer) and the final payback.

OLD CENSORS NEVER DIE

When Hollywood adopted stricter self-censorship in 1934, Little Caesar *was one of several films barred from reissue. Instead, studios like Warner Bros. had to find new ways of telling crime stories that would fit within the Code's restrictions. By 1953, however, things had loosened up enough for a reissue of* Little Caesar, *double-billed with* The Public Enemy. *Even then, Production Code staffers tried to keep Warner's from exporting the films, for fear they would create a negative image of American life overseas. Warner executives indignantly refused. The films not only did well in 1953, but also had a profitable rerelease in 1970.*

ASSASSIN OF YOUTH?

Shortly after* Little Caesar's *release, Hollywood was rocked by a report from Washington, where a judge claimed to be trying the case of a seventeen-year-old who had become a delinquent under influence of the movies. When industry kingpin Will Hays sent a representative to interview the youth, however, they turned up quite another story. The boy in question stated that he had turned to crime after falling in with a bad crowd—because his mother wouldn't let him go to the movies. He'd never even seen a film before committing his first crime at the age of twelve. And far from having his criminal pursuits reinforced by the screen, after seeing* Little Caesar *he'd been so frightened he'd tried to go straight. But his friends had taunted him into pulling off one more job, the one that had finally landed him in jail.

imbalance the picture. The only part I will consider playing is Little Caesar."

For Rico's best friend, Joe Massara, LeRoy wanted to cast an electrifying actor he'd seen in the Los Angeles company of *The Last Mile*. But when production chief Darryl F. Zanuck saw the man's test, he was outraged. How could LeRoy throw away $500 on such an unattractive actor. According to Jack Warner, the man's ears looked like windsocks. So LeRoy had to accept contract player Douglas Fairbanks Jr. as Massara, and Clark Gable went back to the stage, only to become a major star at MGM shortly thereafter.

LeRoy and Robinson never really hit it off, though each respected the other's talents. The director liked to break the tension on the set by cracking jokes or playing tricks on the cast. He was particularly fond of nailing Robinson's cigars to the furniture as a practical joke. All of this enraged the star, who took his work much more seriously. Finally, Wallis told LeRoy to quit kidding around.

But for all the toughness he mustered on screen, Robinson had one problem playing Rico. Every time he fired his gun, he blinked, weakening the moment's visual impact. Finally, LeRoy had the actor's eyelids taped open for shooting scenes.

Little Caesar created a sensation on release, triggering the start of the screen's first great cycle of gangster films. Unlike previous crime films, in which the criminal was either a supporting figure or a tortured soul who reformed in the end, the film focused primarily upon a gang leader who was totally evil. At the same time, it placed that character within the milieu of the American Depression, making it clear that, at least in Rico's eyes, crime was his only escape from a life at the bottom of the pecking order.

For Robinson, *Little Caesar* was the ticket to stardom. But it had its drawbacks. Almost immediately, people started calling him "Rico" and expecting a tough-guy act in public. Moreover, he was inescapably typed as a gangster for years, eventually leaving Warner's to escape such casting. It wasn't until he wrote his autobiography in 1973 that he could bring himself to express his gratitude to Wallis and Warner Bros. for the film that made him a star.

Little Women

"What Richness!"

1933. CAST: Katharine Hepburn (Jo), Joan Bennett (Amy), Paul Lukas (Professor Fritz Bhaer), Edna May Oliver (Aunt March), Jean Parker (Beth), Frances Dee (Meg). Producer: Kenneth MacGowan; Director: George Cukor; Screenplay: Sara Y. Mason, Victor Heerman (Based on the novel by Louisa May Alcott); Photography: Henry Gerrard; Music: Max Steiner. RUNNING TIME: 115 minutes.

Katharine Hepburn's exclamation on entering the home of her rich neighbors in *Little Women* could just as easily have come from the Depression audiences who turned this lively, intelligent adaptation of Louisa May Alcott's novel into one of RKO's biggest hits. Not only did they marvel at the best in Hollywood filmmaking—from George Cukor's accomplished direction of the solid, sometimes inspired performances, to the lavish set and costume design—but they found themselves deeply moved by the March family's struggle to survive hardship and heartache as the Civil War raged miles to the south.

The picture was David O. Selznick's brainchild. Always a great lover of the classics, he had wanted to film *Little Women* during his time as production chief at RKO. But the idea didn't coalesce until the studio signed Katharine Hepburn, the New England native who had just the right combination of independence, feistiness, and sentimentality to play Jo. Selznick had to fight for the project; conventional wisdom held that the classics didn't sell.

The first writers assigned to the project must have felt the same way, as their scripts deviated markedly from the original. Then Selznick assigned the husband-and-wife team of Sarah Y. Mason and Victor Heerman, who heeded his advice to stick to the book, simply paring down unnecessary scenes and details.

Selznick got the production but then left RKO to go to work for his father-in-law, Louis B. Mayer, at MGM. At first *Little Women* seemed a lost cause, but Selznick's replacement and close friend, Merian C. Cooper, pushed it through. He was helped greatly by positive reaction to the script. When the Heermans sent it to the steno pool, the typists loved it so much they kept breaking off work to act out the scenes.

America's first family of 1933, the March sisters: Katharine Hepburn, Jean Parker, Joan Bennett, and Frances Dee.

Hepburn had long loved the novel and immersed herself in period research as well. Her inspiration came from stories her mother had told her of grandmother Caroline Houghton, who had died before Hepburn's birth. She even asked Walter Plunkett to copy one of her grandmother's gowns for Jo.

Though Cukor had directed Hepburn's first film, *A Bill of Divorcement*, it wasn't until their work on *Little Women* that they became steadfast friends. Over the next fifty years, they would collaborate on eight more films, including the actress's big-screen comeback in *The Philadelphia Story* and her Emmy-winning turn in *Love Among the Ruins*.

Their work together wasn't always harmonious. In one scene in *Little Women,* Hepburn

TALLULAH'S TEARS

Tallulah Bankhead didn't much like Katharine Hepburn at first. After meeting her at one of George Cukor's Hollywood soirées, she wrote the director that she considered Hepburn "a New England spinster" and "a dreary opinionated college girl."

Then Cukor invited her over to watch a rough cut of Little Women. *Bankhead was so moved she went through three handkerchiefs at the screening. When it ended, she kneeled at Hepburn's feet, sobbing profusely. But Cukor wasn't impressed. "Tallulah," he said, "you're weeping for your lost innocence."*

had to run upstairs carrying a dish of ice cream. Cukor warned her not to spill anything on the dress; it was a genuine period piece and couldn't be cleaned. She spilled the ice cream nonetheless, ruining the take, then she laughed at her mistake. Cukor slapped her hard and shouted, "You amateur!" "Well, that's your opinion," was her only response as she fought back tears. Most of the time, however, the set was totally congenial. Hepburn insisted on long lunches during which she and the cast picnicked on the studio back lot. She even asked for a tea break at four o'clock.

When the film reached audiences, the RKO steno pool was proven right. It was hailed as a major breakthrough in filmmaking—and a significant break from the sex-soaked, violent films of the days before Production Code enforcement. It also proved a surprise hit, bringing the studio an $800,000 profit. *Little Women* captured three Oscar nominations, including Best Picture and Best Director, and won for Best Screenplay.

Hepburn was not nominated for *Little Women,* but her performance probably helped her win Best Actress the same year for *Morning Glory*. The film also brought her Best Actress honors at the Venice Film Festival. With the success of her fourth film, she became one of Hollywood's top female stars.

But *Little Women* was more than just a great star-making vehicle. It also helped establish the commercial potential for adaptations of the classics. Years later, Cukor would point to *Little Women* as the film that made *Gone With the Wind* possible. There have been two big-screen remakes of *Little Women* (including the very fine 1994 version starring Winona Ryder), a television movie, and even a television series, but nothing can diminish the luster of this lovingly made film, a picture that defines the word "classic."

WOMEN, WOMEN EVERYWHERE

	1933	*1949*	*1994*
Director	***George Cukor***	***Mervyn LeRoy***	***Gillian Armstrong***
Jo	***Katharine Hepburn***	***June Allyson***	***Winona Ryder***
Amy	***Joan Bennett***	***Elizabeth Taylor***	***Kirsten Dunst/Samantha Mathis***
Professor Bhaer	***Paul Lukas***	***Rossano Brazzi***	***Gabriel Byrne***
Aunt March	***Edna May Oliver***	***Lucile Watson***	***Mary Wickes***
Beth	***Jean Parker***	***Margaret O'Brien***	***Claire Danes***
Meg	***Frances Dee***	***Janet Leigh***	***Trini Alvarado***
Mr. Laurence	***Henry Stephenson***	***C. Aubrey Smith***	***John Neville***
Laurie	***Douglass Montgomery***	***Peter Lawford***	***Christian Bale***
Marmee	***Spring Byington***	***Mary Astor***	***Susan Sarandon***

Lolita

"How Did They Ever Make a Movie of Lolita?"

1962. CAST: James Mason (Humbert Humbert), Sue Lyon (Lolita Haze), Shelley Winters (Charlotte Haze), Peter Sellers (Clare Quilty), Marianne Stone (Vivian Darkbloom), Diana Decker (Jean Farlow). Producer: James B. Harris; Director: Stanley Kubrick; Screenplay: Vladimir Nabokov (Based on his novel); Photography: Oswald Morris; Music: Nelson Riddle. RUNNING TIME: 152 minutes.

The question on everybody's mind as director Stanley Kubrick readied *Lolita* for its 1962 premiere was whether any filmmaker, even Kubrick the wunderkind, could remain true to Vladimir Nabokov's vision while passing muster with both the Catholic Church's Legion of Decency and the industry's own Production Code Administration (PCA). Even though Hollywood had released successful adaptations of such scandalous novels as *From Here to Eternity* and *Peyton Place* during the previous decade, Nabokov's breakthrough bestseller was one book that seemed impossible to clean up for the screen.

Nabokov's tragicomic tale of Humbert Humbert, the middle-aged academic in love with twelve-year-old Lolita Haze, had elicited a wide range of comments from scandalized publishers. One tore his copy up. Another suggested it might not be so shocking if Lolita were a young boy. Finally, Nabokov sold the book to the only company brave enough to print it, the Paris-based Olympia Press.

Almost immediately the 1955 publication—complete with typos and disintegrating binding—became a hot item. People searched it out while visiting Paris or had it sent to them in a brown-paper wrapper. When it was finally published in the U.S. in 1958, the Cincinnati Public Library refused to buy the book. The town of Lolita, Texas, almost changed its name to Jackson. At the same time, however, readers put it on the bestseller list for fifty-six weeks.

None of this escaped Hollywood's attention, but instead of a major studio, independent producers James Harris and Stanley Kubrick picked up the screen rights.

With an independent company sticking its neck out to film *Lolita,* Hollywood could afford to be scandalized. Studio executives denounced the project, and Cary Grant announced that he had

Sue Lyon was old enough to know enough, but too young to see her own performance.

THE BOOK THAT DARE NOT SPEAK ITS NAME

When Stanley Kubrick first approached Shelley Winters about playing Lolita's mother, she was working on John F. Kennedy's presidential campaign. Kubrick asked her to read the novel before meeting with Nabokov to discuss the role in New York. That meant carrying Lolita around the country on her campaign tour and even reading it on the platform while waiting for political rallies to start. When Kennedy noticed what she was reading, he jokingly suggested she put the book in a brown-paper cover so as not to jeopardize his chances.

turned down the leading role because he thought the film would be bad for the industry. Harris countered that Grant had never been offered the role. Still, the notoriety was enough to convince Sir Laurence Olivier and Noel Coward to refuse the role. Finally, James Mason agreed to star. Although about the same age as Humbert, Mason looked ten years younger, which seemed to make the story more acceptable.

Finding the perfect Lolita was another problem. Kubrick tested several young actresses, including Tuesday Weld, before settling on Sue

LOLITA, MY FLOP

With Lolita's success and notoriety as both book and movie, adaptations to other media were inevitable. A musical version, Lolita, My Love, died during out-of-town tryouts in 1971, winning praise only for Dorothy Loudon's performance as Charlotte. A few years later, controversial playwright Edward Albee attempted a dramatic adaptation so disastrous he can only speak of it with embarrassment. More recently, director Joel Schumacher announced plans for a new film version, with Jeremy Irons and Hugh Grant mentioned at various times to play Humbert Humbert.

Lyon, a thirteen-year-old actress-model he'd spotted on *The New Loretta Young Show*. She would be fourteen by the time filming began, but looked even older.

Meanwhile, Kubrick hired Nabokov to write the script. His first draft was so suggestive the PCA refused to pass it. This posed particular problems for funding. By the sixties, most independent producers could not get financial backing without a letter from the PCA saying that the script was passable. When Nabokov's second draft passed the PCA, Kubrick and Harris had their pick of backers. They chose a consortium of Canadian businessmen whose only request was that the film be made in England, where state subsidies and lower pay scales would keep costs down. Kubrick enjoyed working there so much that he would make all his films in England from then on.

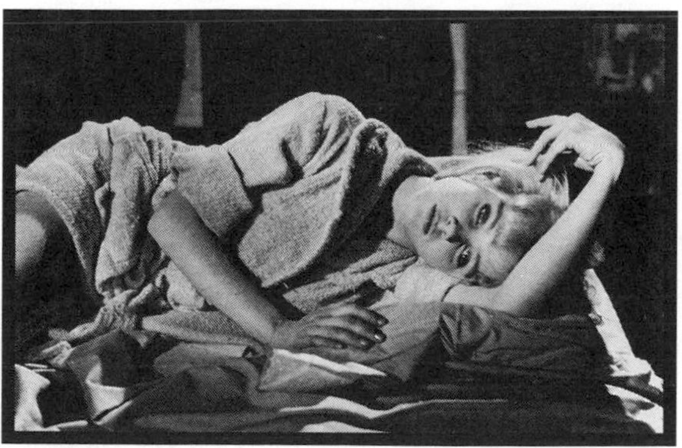

Sue Lyon

Once the film was finished, Kubrick had done such a tasteful job that he had no trouble getting it past the PCA, which only demanded two brief cuts. The Legion of Decency passed the film on condition that children under eighteen be barred from seeing it, which meant Lyon was unable to see her own performance.

With all the controversy, the film did well at the box office, though it was far from a runaway hit, grossing $4.5 million on an investment of $2 million. Still, that was enough to make *Lolita* a powerful influence. More than any other film of the early sixties, it paved the way for ever more daring assaults on audience sensitivities and the Production Code, eventually contributing to the fall of the Code in favor of the movie ratings system in 1968.

Lust for Life

"It Happens in Bright Sunlight"

1956. CAST: Kirk Douglas (Vincent Van Gogh), Anthony Quinn (Paul Gauguin), James Donald (Theo Van Gogh), Pamela Brown (Christine), Everett Sloane (Dr. Gachet), Marion Ross (Sister Clothilde). Producer: John Houseman; Director: Vincente Minnelli; Screenplay: Norman Corwin (Based on the novel by Irving Stone); Photography: F. H. Young, Russell Harlan (CinemaScope, Metrocolor, Anscocolor); Music: Miklos Rozsa. RUNNING TIME: 122 minutes.

MGM shed light on the tortured life of one of the world's great artists, Vincent Van Gogh, in 1956, creating one of the few film biographies of an artist that actually gives viewers an idea of what artistic creation is like. With a winning production team that included director Vincente Minnelli, star Kirk Douglas, and producer John Houseman, of course, they could hardly have failed to create something worth watching.

Hollywood had expressed interest in Irving Stone's historical novel about Van Gogh when it first appeared in 1934. It wasn't until 1947, however, that MGM picked up the rights, but nobody seemed able to turn the story into a workable screenplay.

When John Huston scored a surprise hit in 1953 with *Moulin Rouge,* starring Jose Ferrer as Toulouse-Lautrec, MGM's interest revived. Minnelli and Houseman won approval for the project in early 1955, but they had to move fast. The rights would revert to Stone if a film were not completed by January 1956.

That created several logistical problems. Minnelli was committed to direct the film musical version of *Kismet,* which wasn't projected to finish shooting until July. Meanwhile, Houseman tried to get a satisfactory screenplay. After several writers turned him down, he hired Norman Corwin, whose busy career as a radio writer had included many dramatizations of the lives of great artists.

Casting was an easy matter. Houseman and Minnelli had worked with Douglas on *The Bad and the Beautiful* in 1952, at which time they had noted his resemblance to the artist. Douglas's own producing company, Bryna, had announced plans to film the book until they learned MGM still held the rights. The actor eagerly accepted the assignment.

Vincent Van Gogh (Kirk Douglas) poses a model.

Much more difficult was choosing the best possible film stock. At the time, all CinemaScope films were shot in Eastmancolor, a process Minnelli felt lacked the subtlety needed to reproduce Van Gogh's work. MGM had earlier experimented with a more flexible process, Anscocolor, but faced with strong competition from Eastman, Ansco had stopped producing color motion-picture stock. The director insisted that MGM buy up all remaining Ansco stock,

VAN GOGH MEETS THE DUKE

Although most of Hollywood was in a rush to praise Kirk Douglas's performance in Lust for Life, in his autobiography, the star reports stern criticism from action star John Wayne. "Christ, Kirk!" the Duke raged after a screening. "How can you play a part like that? There's so god-damned few of us left. We got to play strong, tough characters. Not those weak queers." "Hey, John, I'm an actor," was Douglas's reply. "I like to play interesting roles. It's all make-believe, John. It isn't real. You're not really John Wayne, you know."

about 300,000 feet, and set up a special lab in Houston to process it.

Houseman sent photographers to shoot several Van Goghs being held in museums and private collections around the world. Because the original paintings would not have held up to the high-temperature lighting required for filmmaking, Houseman's crew used special portrait cameras, which shot with low light in long exposures. From these portraits, studio technicians created transparencies to be backlit and shot under studio conditions.

The company worked in many of the actual locations Van Gogh used, including a covered bridge he'd painted near Arles, the low-country mines where he'd worked as a lay minister, and the asylum at St. Rémy. They even found two elderly citizens who had known Van Gogh. One woman remembered how her friends had thrown stones at him in Arles because they thought him so strange. The main location they had to reconstruct was the yellow house Van Gogh had rented in Arles. It had been destroyed in World War II.

Adding to the authenticity was Douglas's commitment to the role. He wore the character's heavy shoes constantly, with one unlaced to give him an unkempt feeling and the other a size too large so he would shuffle as Van Gogh had. When the film was finished, he shaved off his beard in public, during a guest appearance on *The Perry Como Show*. He would later describe this as "a public retreat to help rid me of the character."

Lust for Life opened to rave reviews, helped by an intelligent publicity campaign involving department store displays of Van Gogh reproductions and special previews for the museum curators who had given Houseman access to their collections. Box office proved disappointing nonetheless, with the film only returning $1.6 million in domestic rentals, a figure offset by larger overseas returns. The poor box-office figures may have hurt Douglas's chances for the Oscar. Although the performance was acclaimed as his best ever and brought him the New York Film Critics Award and a Golden Globe, he lost a tight Oscar race to Yul Brynner, star of the much more successful *The King and I*.

Anthony Quinn (right, with Kirk Douglas), in one of the screen's shortest Oscar-winning performances.

The Magnificent Ambersons

"And Now, It Came at Last: George Amberson Minafer Had Got His Comeuppance"

1942. CAST: Joseph Cotten (Eugene Morgan), Dolores Costello (Isabel Amberson Minafer), Anne Baxter (Lucy Morgan), Tim Holt (George Amberson Minafer), Agnes Moorehead (Fanny Amberson), Ray Collins (Jack Amberson). Producer-Director-Screenplay: Orson Welles (Based on the novel by Booth Tarkington); Photography: Stanley Cortez; Music: Bernard Herrmann. RUNNING TIME: 88 minutes.

In need of a follow-up to *Citizen Kane,* which had not yet opened but was already generating positive word of mouth, Welles wrote the screenplay quickly. For his cast, Welles once again turned to his colleagues from the Mercury Theatre, providing showcase roles for Agnes Moorehead as Isabel's neurotic sister and Joseph Cotten as Eugene. But he also recruited some outsiders for notable roles, shocking the RKO brass when he cast junior-league cowboy star Tim Holt as George and retired silent star Dolores Costello as his mother.

Kane's cinematographer, Gregg Toland, was unavailable, too. On the day before shooting started, Welles surprised his bosses by picking Stanley Cortez, a cameraman who'd had most of his experience on B pictures. Although Cortez managed to capture some striking images, he couldn't match Toland's ability to realize Welles's vision, contributing to numerous production delays.

By the time Welles finished shooting *Ambersons,* he was due in Rio de Janeiro to start work on *It's All True,* an omnibus film about Latin America. Welles supervised the first cut of *The Magnificent Ambersons,* then took off, expecting editor Robert Wise to fly to Rio in March so they could create the final cut together. But the war got in the way. When a short-term ban on civilian flights to South America was imposed in March 1942, Schaeffer went ahead and previewed Welles's cut of the film—with disastrous results. The audience had just seen the Dorothy Lamour musical *The Fleet's In.* Hardly in the mood for a heavy drama, they laughed at serious scenes and even yelled "Shut up!" at the characters. Welles sent a thirty-seven-page wire outlining cuts, but by then it was too late. Schaeffer was already under pressure from RKO's New York management because of *Citizen Kane*'s poor box-office showing. To make *Ambersons* more commercial, he

A TALE OF TWO AD LINES

While RKO was still pushing The Magnificent Ambersons as a prestige film, they marketed it as a major cinematic breakthrough: "Real life screened more daringly than it's ever been before!" Once they gave up on it, though, they also abandoned the high road in an attempt to lure viewers to a hot sex drama that just wasn't there on screen: "Scandal played no favorites when that high-and-mighty Amberson girl fell in love once too often!"

instructed Wise to cut about forty minutes. He also added a happy ending.

By the time the new *Ambersons* was ready for release, Schaeffer had left RKO, to be replaced by the head of RKO's theater chain, Charles Koerner. Not only did Koerner pull the plug on *It's All True* and cancel Welles's contract, but after spotty returns on some early bookings of *Ambersons,* he buried it on a double bill with the Lupe Velez comedy *Mexican Spitfire's Elephant*. He couldn't hide the film from the press, however, which gave it mostly glowing reviews.

The Magnificent Ambersons lost about $600,000 on its initial release but proved that you can't keep a good film down—or even part of a good film—by moving into the black through reissues.

George Amberson Minafer (Tim Holt) gets his comeuppance.

The Maltese Falcon

"Here's to Plain Speaking and Clear Understanding"

1941. CAST: Humphrey Bogart (Sam Spade), Mary Astor (Brigid O'Shaugnessey), Gladys George (Iva Archer), Peter Lorre (Joel Cairo), Barton MacLane (Detective Lt. Dundy), Lee Patrick (Effie Perine), Sydney Greenstreet (Kasper Gutman), Ward Bond (Detective Tom Polhaus), Elisha Cook Jr. (Wilmer Cook), Walter Huston (Captain Jacobi). Producers: Hal B. Wallis, Henry Blanke; Director-Screenplay: John Huston (Based on the novel by Dashiell Hammett); Photography: Arthur Edeson; Music: Adolph Deutsch.

RUNNING TIME: 100 minutes.

After two less-than-successful adaptations of Dashiell Hammett's classic detective yarn, Warner Bros. hit the jackpot when writer-director John Huston did the unthinkable: He stuck to the story. The result was one of the screen's great thrillers, a precursor of the film noir that would set the style for screen detective stories for decades to come. Not only did *The Maltese Falcon* establish John Huston as one of Hollywood's top directors, it transformed Humphrey Bogart from second-string gangster to leading man.

The Maltese Falcon first appeared as a five-part serial in *Black Mask,* a detective-story magazine, then was published in book form. Warner Bros. filmed it in 1930, using the book's title. The results were steamy but lackluster. The film maintained detective Sam Spade's affairs with his partner's widow and his client Miss Wonderley, a scene in which he forces Wonderley to strip, and the depiction of Kasper Gutman, Joel Cairo, and Wilmer as homosexual, but it lacked any special spark.

The studio returned to the story in 1936 but changed the character names and transformed the jewel-encrusted Maltese Falcon into the jewel-filled Horn of Roland. The result was *Satan Met a Lady,* a notorious stinker best known as the last film Bette Davis made before attempting to walk out on her Warner's contract. Also of note was the remake's treatment of Kasper Gutman; he was turned into a woman, Madame Barrabas, well played by Alison Skipworth. Wilmer became her nephew, but the sexual implications in their relationship were still there in her reading of "He's been more than a son to me."

In 1941, John Huston was looking for a way to launch his directing career. Since arriving at

THE STUFF THAT DREAMS ARE MADE OF

The seven plaster birds created by the Warner Bros. props department have become collector's items in the decades since The Maltese Falcon, with few historians agreeing on just how many remain. In 1974, one of the statues was stolen from the Los Angeles County Museum of Art, where it had been on display. The resulting headlines generated publicity not just for the original film but for The Black Bird, a comic sequel then in production with George Segal as Sam Spade Jr. and Lee Patrick and Elisha Cook Jr. reprising their roles from the earlier film. The theft might have been more help had it occurred after the newer film's release. Met with indifferent reviews, Bird quickly sank out of sight.

PATER FAMILIAS

As a good luck gesture, John Huston's father, legendary actor Walter Huston, played a small role in The Maltese Falcon as the ship's captain who delivers the black bird to Sam Spade's office. The role required only one scene, with the man collapsing and muttering a few words before dying, but the younger Huston made his father do take after take as a practical joke. By the time they finished for the day, Walter was black and blue from doing twenty or more falls. Just to carry the joke one step further, Mary Astor called the elder Huston the next day, claiming to be his son's secretary. The film had been ruined in the lab, she told him, and he would have to come back to redo the scene. Then she held out the receiver so everybody on the set could listen to the actor's string of profanities.

Warner Bros. in 1938, he had established a reputation as one of their best writers. When it came time to renegotiate his contract, he insisted on a clause allowing him to direct one film. When the ink was dry, he suggested a third film version of *The Maltese Falcon*.

Throughout, Huston stayed as close as possible to the novel, cutting only a few scenes that either were superfluous or would not be passed by industry censors. But even though he cut overt references to homosexuality and to Spade's love affairs, he managed to slip implications into the finished film and right past the censors.

Huston didn't consider any of Warner's contract players right for the role of Gutman, The Fat Man. Then he saw Sydney Greenstreet performing with Alfred Lunt and Lynne Fontanne in the Los Angeles company of *There Shall Be No Night*. It took some persuading, however, to convince the 285-pound, sixty-five-year-old stage actor to make his film debut.

Warner's insisted that the male lead be offered to George Raft, who had recently signed with the studio. Raft, however, had other ideas. He did not think *The Maltese Falcon* would be an important picture, particularly with a first-time director at the helm. So the role went to Humphrey Bogart, who had just scored a hit in another role Raft had turned down, as Mad Dog Earle in *High Sierra*.

Shooting began in June 1941 and proceeded with few problems. Huston had planned all of his shots in advance, putting them into the screenplay to avoid any confusion. At the same time, however, he was open to suggestions from cameraman Arthur Edeson. They rehearsed so

Humphrey Bogart, Sydney Greenstreet, Peter Lorre, and Mary Astor—the kind of cast that dreams are made of.

extensively that they needed few takes. One scene between Bogart and Greenstreet lasted seven minutes, involving twenty-two camera moves. When they got it in one take, the crew applauded. As a result of Huston's planning, the film finished two days ahead of schedule and $50,000 under budget.

Wallis and Jack Warner were pleasantly surprised with Huston's first film, as were the critics, who hailed it as the sleeper of the year. With the picture's success, they continued building Huston's and Bogart's careers. By the time *The Maltese Falcon* started pulling in good reviews and strong attendance, Wallis was developing a new property designed to test Bogie's pull as a romantic star. The film was *Casablanca*. Huston would have to wait until his return from World War II to capitalize on *The Maltese Falcon*'s success, but then he would direct Bogart in two of his best pictures, *Key Largo* and *The Treasure of the Sierra Madre*.

Meet Me in St. Louis

"A Valentine in the Palm of Your Hand"

1944. CAST: Judy Garland (Esther Smith), Margaret O'Brien ("Tootie" Smith), Mary Astor (Mrs. Anne Smith), Lucille Bremer (Rose Smith), June Lockhart (Lucille Ballard), Tom Drake (John Truett), Marjory Main (Katie), Harry Davenport (Grandpa), Leon Ames (Mr. Alonzo Smith). Producer: Arthur Freed; Director: Vincente Minnelli; Screenplay: Irving Brecher, Fred F. Finklehoffe (Based on the stories by Sally Benson); Photography: George Folsey (Technicolor); Musical Director: Georgie Stoll; Songs: Hugh Martin, Ralph Blane. RUNNING TIME: 113 minutes.

MGM producer Arthur Freed first became interested in Sally Benson's "Kensington Avenue" stories when he lost his bid to make the film version of the Howard Lindsay–Russell Crouse play *Life with Father*. As an alternative, writer Fred Finklehoffe suggested Benson's stories, which had much the same flavor. At first, Freed wanted George Cukor to direct, but Cukor was called in to direct training films for the Army, so Freed gave the project to his protégé, Vincente Minnelli. Freed only had one choice in mind to play Esther Smith: Judy Garland. But Judy had other ideas. After years of juvenile roles, she wanted to move on to more dramatic fare. Nonetheless, she allowed Minnelli to talk her into sticking with the film. In her first scene, she and her older sister (played by another Freed protégée, Lucille Bremer) dressed for a dance and discussed their plans for the night. Garland insisted on spoofing the simple, naive dialogue, despite Minnelli's directions to play it sincerely. When they got to lunch without printing a single take, the near-hysterical actress called for Freed. He calmed her down and assured her that Minnelli and she could work together. But the pressure still didn't ease.

For a family dinner scene near the start of the film, Minnelli wanted the conversation to flow like a beautiful fugue, effortless but intricately structured. So he rehearsed the scene whenever he could. Garland resented the rehearsals, particularly when she couldn't even get off the lot at night without the guard at the gate telling her to report back to the set for another run-through. Finally, she complained to costar Mary Astor, who stood up for Minnelli, which made a strong impression on Judy. Sometime during production, a mutual friend set the two up on a blind date to break the ice.

Judy Garland, ripe for the wooing, both onscreen and, as events would transpire, offscreen.

Margaret O'Brien and Judy Garland perform "Under the Bamboo Tree."

Before long, Garland and Minnelli were a couple. By the time shooting finished, they were engaged.

That didn't end all of Garland's problems, however. She was already suffering from insomnia, partly as a result of insecurity, partly because of her growing addiction to pills. As a result, she was chronically late. At other times, she would hole up in her dressing room for hours, making cast and crew wait until she had worked through her anxieties.

With all the delays, *Meet Me in St. Louis* took almost a year to film, though its final cost was only about $1.7 million.

Meet Me in St. Louis opened to glowing reviews. Of the cast, Garland and Margaret O'Brien received the best notices, with the latter winning a special Oscar as outstanding juvenile performer of the year. The film grossed more than $7 million on its initial release. It would inspire a television version starring Jane Powell in 1959 and two stage productions, one premiering in St. Louis in 1960 and another reaching Broadway in 1989.

Mildred Pierce

"Don't Tell What Mildred Pierce Did!"

1945. CAST: Joan Crawford (Mildred Pierce), Jack Carson (Wally Fay), Zachary Scott (Monte Beragon), Eve Arden (Ida), Ann Blyth (Veda Pierce), Bruce Bennett (Bert Pierce). Producer: Jerry Wald; Director: Michael Curtiz; Screenplay: Ranald MacDougall (Based on the novel by James M. Cain); Photography: Ernest Haller; Music: Max Steiner. RUNNING TIME: 104 minutes.

Far from silencing film fans, Warner Bros.' ingenious ad line for *Mildred Pierce* created invaluable word-of-mouth for the film. People talked about more than just the film's heroine and her scandalous doings, however. The industry and most of the country couldn't stop discussing Joan Crawford's miraculous comeback. The talk was so strong, in fact, that it propelled her to an Oscar.

When Crawford signed with Warner's in 1943, talk of her receiving any kind of award for her first starring role there would have seemed like a cruel joke. Her last few pictures had bombed, leading MGM to cancel her contract. Two days later, Jack Warner signed her to a three-picture deal, dazzled by the thought of "stealing" one of MGM's stars.

It took him a while to get his new star on screen, however. Apart from a cameo as herself in *Hollywood Canteen,* Crawford was off the screen for two years. Nothing Jack Warner came up with seemed to offer the kind of change-of-pace role she wanted. Then she got wind of *Mildred Pierce*.

James M. Cain's 1941 novel had been a departure for the writer of crime thrillers. It told a straight-out dramatic tale of a woman using sex to give her daughter a life of luxury and promote the girl's singing career. In gratitude, the girl steals her mother's second husband and runs off to New York with him to become a radio star.

Producer David O. Selznick optioned the book in 1941, then dropped it when the industry's self-censorship organization, the Production Code Administration, told him it would never pass muster. Warner producer Jerry Wald was interested in the story, too, but couldn't get his studio to buy it because of the censorship problems.

Cain's novels had long been considered unfilmable, but then Billy Wilder came up with a treatment

Imagine Shirley Temple in this picture—if Joan Crawford hadn't helped Ann Blyth with her screen test. . . .

MICHAEL CURTIZ ON JOAN CRAWFORD

BEFORE *MILDRED PIERCE:*

"Me direct that temperamental bitch! Not on your goddamn life! She comes over here with her highhat airs and her goddamn shoulder pads! I won't work with her. She's through, washed up. Why should I waste my time directing a has-been?"

AFTER *MILDRED PIERCE:*

"When I agreed to direct Miss Crawford, I felt she was going to be stubborn as a mule, and I made up my mind to be plenty hard on her. Now that I have learned how sweet she is and how professional and talented she is, I take back even thinking those things about her."

of *Double Indemnity* that won Code approval. As word of this hot new crime story spread through Hollywood, Wald decided to give *Mildred Pierce* a try. After a meeting with Production Code chief Joe Breen, he came up with a way to sanitize the book. Mildred wouldn't sleep with anybody but would get ahead through hard work. Just to make sure there was a way to punish the story's principal wrongdoers—Mildred's second husband, Monty, and her daughter, Veda—Wald would add a murder.

> ***"Personally, Veda's convinced me that alligators have the right idea. They eat their young."***
>
> **—EVE ARDEN CRACKING WISE AND, AT LEAST FOR SOME AUDIENCES, DEMOLISHING THE PLOT OF MILDRED PIERCE**

Like Warner's other producers, Wald had met Crawford when she first signed with the studio. Something about her, possibly an air of vulnerability brought on by the decline in her career, struck him as perfect for Mildred. He sent her the script, and she loved it. Unfortunately, director Michael Curtiz was none too keen on the idea. When Wald told Crawford of Curtiz's objections, she did the unthinkable for a major star: she offered to make a screen test. The test was so good, Curtiz had to give in.

But he still wasn't completely won over. During the first days of shooting, he railed constantly against her overelaborate hairstyles and too-glamorous costumes. At one point, he went into a rage, tearing at her dress and screaming, "You and your damned shoulder pads! This stinks!" Through her tears, she replied, "Mr. Curtiz, I happened to buy this dress at Sears. There are no shoulder pads." That won him over. At the postproduction party, she presented Curtiz with a pair of giant shoulder pads.

Long before that, Wald had decided there was something special about her performance. Working with Crawford's publicist, Henry Rogers, he set up the industry's most extensive Oscar campaign ever, planting items in the gossip columns about the star's award-caliber performance before the film was even finished. Soon, everybody in Hollywood was congratulating her on her almost certain Oscar win—for a film that hadn't even been released.

Mildred Pierce was a major hit for Warner's and for Crawford, easily putting the actress back on top. But even when it picked up six Oscar nominations, Crawford didn't believe she'd win. On Oscar night, she called her publicist, claiming she was running a fever. Her health improved markedly, however, when Charles Boyer announced that she'd won the award. She was ready for the press when they arrived with Curtiz—who had accepted for her—and posed with the Oscar in her sickbed. The next day, her picture dominated newspaper coverage of the Academy Awards.

Mrs. Miniver

"A War of the People"

1942. CAST: Greer Garson (Mrs. Kay Miniver), Walter Pidgeon (Clem Miniver), Teresa Wright (Carol Beldon), Dame May Whitty (Lady Beldon), Henry Travers (Mr. Ballard), Reginald Owen (Foley), Henry Wilcoxon (Vicar), Richard Ney (Vin Miniver). Producer: Sidney Franklin; Director: William Wyler; Screenplay: Arthur Wimperis, George Froeschel, James Hilton, Claudine West (Based on the novel by Jan Struther); Photography: Joseph Ruttenberg; Music: Herbert Stothart. RUNNING TIME: 134 minutes.

MGM brought the war in Europe to the people of America with their 1942 paean to the British family under fire. Started at a time when most of America favored isolationism, *Mrs. Miniver* was either an amazing act of heroism or an astute bit of prophecy. For while the film was in production, the Japanese attack on Pearl Harbor not only changed most American minds, it made *Mrs. Miniver* a hot box-office property.

Despite MGM's steadfast refusal to depict the growing conflagration in Europe on screen, studio head Louis B. Mayer's rampant Anglophilia made some treatment of the British part of the war almost inevitable. Battle scenes were hardly the studio's forte at the time, but glamorous star vehicles were—particularly those built around a strong, beautiful female character. That's just what Mayer found when MGM picked up the rights to Jan Struther's episodic novel about an English family surviving the first months of warfare.

Mayer handed the project to Sidney Franklin, a former director who had switched to producing after Irving G. Thalberg's death.

For director, he borrowed William Wyler, by then one of the industry's most acclaimed helmsmen, from independent producer Sam Goldwyn. Born in the Alsace, one of the first areas Hitler attacked at the start of the war, Wyler had a natural sympathy for the project. Moreover, he was impressed by its potential as a vehicle for anti-Axis propaganda.

Finding a leading lady was much more difficult. Norma Shearer was Mayer's first choice, but she turned the project down because, at age thirty-nine, she did not want to play a woman with a grown son. Forty-year-old Ann Harding declined for the same reason, as did Mayer's third choice, thirty-three-

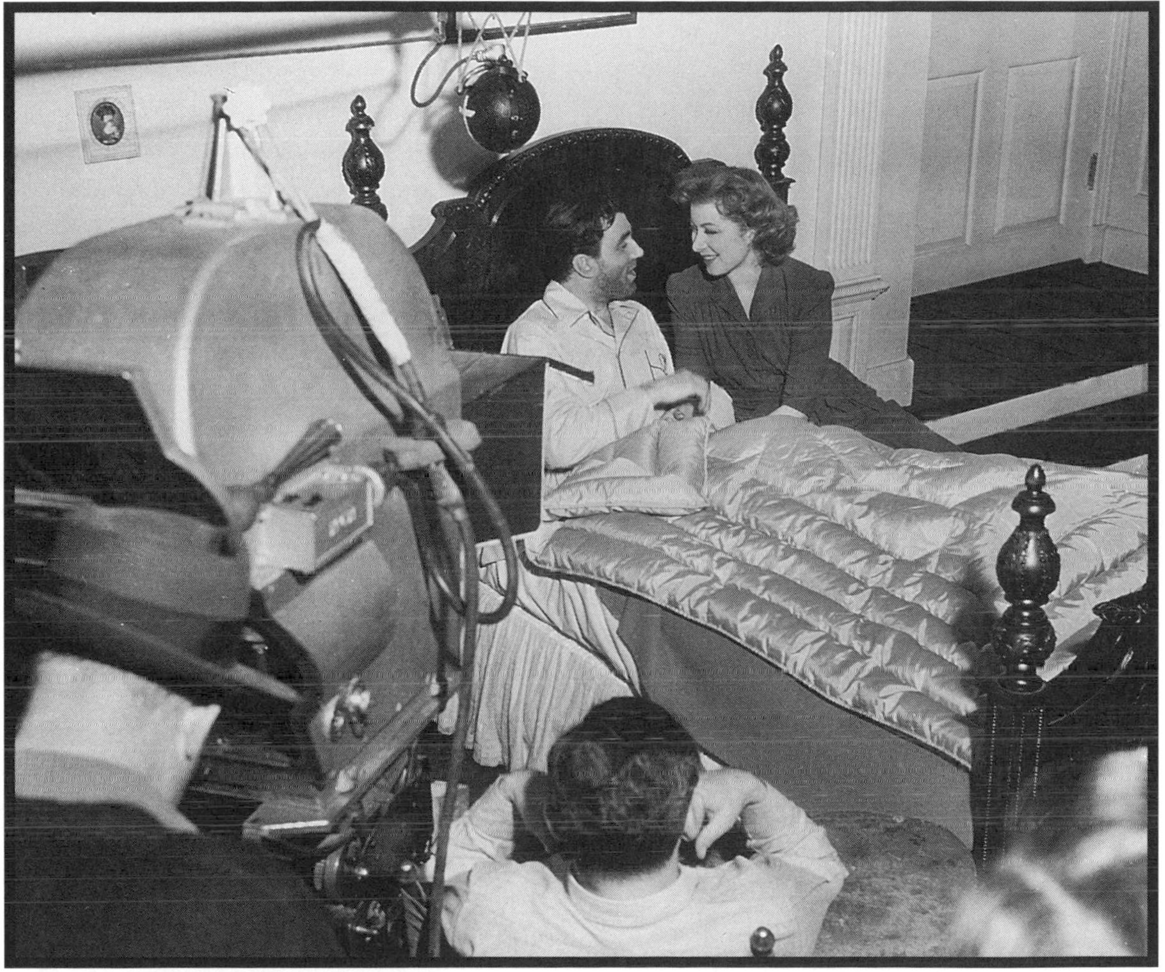

Grace under fire: Walter Pidgeon and Greer Garson endure the Blitz and director William Wyler (back to camera).

FROM *MRS. MINIVER* TO MRS. NEY

Although Greer Garson initially refused the title role in Mrs. Miniver *partly because she did not want to play a woman with a grown son, by the time shooting was finished, she had developed a more than maternal attachment to the young actor cast in that role. MGM studio head Louis B. Mayer was shocked to learn that she and actor Richard Ney, nine years her junior, wanted to get married. For the good of the film—and his favorite star's career—he advised them to postpone the wedding until after* Mrs. Miniver *had played out its first run. On July 24, 1943, the two were wed in a private ceremony, with only Garson's mother in attendance. The marriage lasted four years.*

year-old Greer Garson. Then Mayer performed the entire script for her, playing all the roles himself, driving her to such a frenzy that she agreed to play the role, then immediately fainted. Garson would later tell the press that Mayer played Mrs. Miniver much better than she.

The U.S. entry into World War II triggered one change in the *Mrs. Miniver* script. With President Roosevelt urging MGM to get the film into theaters as soon as possible, Wyler decided to reshoot the vicar's climactic speech to make it less conciliatory. Actor Henry Wilcoxon was called back from military service for two days. He and Wyler sat up all night rewriting the speech, then filmed it the next day. British Prime Minister Winston Churchill was so impressed with it that he ordered thousands of copies dropped behind enemy lines in occupied Europe.

Released early in 1942 as headlines proclaimed gallant Britain's stand against the Germans, *Mrs. Miniver* became a huge hit, posting more than $5 million in profits. Her subtle, moving performance made Garson MGM's top star, a position she would later regret when Mayer cast her in one boringly noble role after another. The film also received twelve Oscar nominations and was regarded as a shoo-in to take the major awards.

Even as *Mrs. Miniver* racked up awards for Best Screenplay, Best Director, Best Cinematography, Best Supporting Actress (Wright), and the Thalberg Award to Franklin, Garson could not believe that she would be named Best Actress. As a result, she had no speech ready when her name was called. Starting out with, "I am practically unprepared," she rambled on for more than five minutes. One audience member quipped, "Her speech is longer than her performance." Eventually, her five-and-a-half-minute speech achieved legendary status, with some claiming she spoke for over an hour.

Mrs. Miniver was a hit almost everywhere, though it fared poorly among the very people it purported to glorify, the English. Despite its propaganda value, most British audiences resented its glamorization of their lives under the Blitz. Years later, MGM tried to recapture the film's success with a sequel, *The Miniver Story*, filmed in England to use company assets frozen after the war. Despite the use of authentic locations and the addition of a terminal disease for Garson's character, the sequel bombed.

> ***"This is not only a war of soldiers in uniforms. It is a war of the people—of all the people—and it must be fought not only on the battlefield but in the cities and in the villages, in the factories and on the farms, in the home and in the heart of every man, woman, and child who loves freedom. Well, we have buried our dead, but we shall not forget them. Instead, they will inspire us with an unbreakable determination to free ourselves and those who come after us from the tyranny and terror that threaten to strike us down. This is the people's war. It is our war. We are the fighters. Fight it, then. Fight it with all that is in us. And may God defend the right."***
>
> —HENRY WILCOXON, AS THE VICAR, AT THE CONCLUSION OF MRS. MINIVER

Murder, My Sweet

Two-Fisted . . . Hardboiled. . . Terrific!

1945. CAST: Dick Powell (Philip Marlowe), Claire Trevor (Velma/Mrs. Grayle), Anne Shirley (Ann), Otto Kruger (Amphor), Mike Mazurki (Moose Malloy), Miles Mander (Mr. Grayle). Producer: Adrian Scott; Director: Edward Dmytryk; Screenplay: John Paxton (Based on the novel *Farewell, My Lovely* by Raymond Chandler); Photography: Harry J. Wild; Music: Roy Webb. RUNNING TIME: 95 minutes.

The ads for RKO's 1945 adaptation of Raymond Chandler's *Farewell, My Lovely* heralded a new kind of screen thriller, what later critics would call film noir. They also heralded a new career for star Dick Powell, who in one film made the transition from sappy boy tenor to one of Hollywood's toughest detectives.

Chandler's books had been knocking around Hollywood for years. His second Philip Marlowe mystery, *Farewell, My Lovely,* had been bought by RKO for just $2,000 back in 1941. At the time, they'd used it as the basis for one of George Sanders's "Falcon" movies. With the war years, Chandler's books grew in popularity, just as Hollywood's product began taking on a darker tone more suited to the mean streets down which Marlowe searched for stolen necklaces and missing girlfriends. In 1944 writer Adrian Scott signed a producing contract with the studio and wanted to start out with a real attention-grabber. After years of making B movies, director Edward Dmytryk wanted to break into big-budget production and stay there. They saw the possibilities in Chandler's story and convinced studio head Charles Koerner to approve it with a $400,000 budget.

Koerner made only one condition. He insisted on casting one-time singing juvenile Dick Powell as Marlowe. Powell had been a big star in Warner Bros.' Busby Berkeley musicals of the thirties, but with their decline he'd had trouble finding another onscreen niche. Koerner was eager to sign the singer for a string of low-budget musicals, but Powell wouldn't sign unless Koerner guaranteed him a wider variety of roles. Struck by the advance word on *Double Indemnity* and lightweight actor Fred MacMurray's offbeat casting as a tough-talking killer—Koerner decided to duplicate that stunt casting.

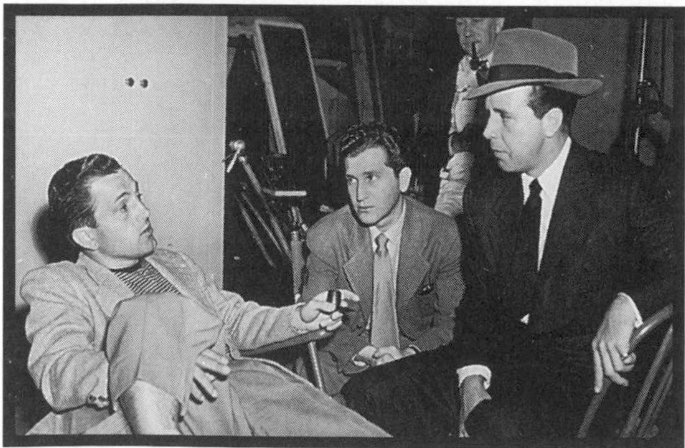

Dick Powell's new career, facing off thugs like Mike Mazurki (above center) and discussing scenes with film noir specialist Edward Dmytryk (below left).

Because of his experience in B films, Dmytryk got through the shooting easily. The main challenge he faced was making the 6′4″ Mike Mazurki, cast as the hulking Moose Malloy, tower over the 6′2″ Powell. When they had to walk down the street together, Powell walked in a trench. When they stood still, Powell had his shoes off while Mazurki stood on a box. Dmytryk even slanted the ceilings toward the camera so that Mazurki would seem to grow larger as he approached the other actors. Moose's first entrance has become a classic. As Marlowe stands in his dark office looking out the window, a neon sign just outside goes dark to reveal Mazurki's reflection in the window. When they first tried the shot, however, the actor didn't look imposing enough. So Dmytryk had the glass removed from Marlowe's window and placed between Powell and the camera lens. Mazurki stood just a few feet from the glass so his reflection would be large enough.

Everybody at RKO knew they had a winner with the Marlowe picture, but when it played its first engagements in New England and Minneapolis, the theaters were the loneliest spots in town. After some speedy market analysis, the executives realized that by using Chandler's original title, *Farewell, My Lovely,* they'd given audiences the impression that it was just another Dick Powell musical. When they changed the title to *Murder, My Sweet,* people came in droves. RKO canceled plans to star Powell in more musicals, instead giving him tough-guy roles.

More than just a hit film, however, *Murder, My Sweet* helped establish a new type of film, the film noir. With roots in the French thrillers of the late thirties and American pulp fiction, the film noir created a dark, violent world, in which corruption thrived and hardly anybody could be trusted. There had been precursors to the form—most notably *The Maltese Falcon, Casablanca, Citizen Kane,* and *Double Indemnity*—but *Murder, My Sweet* was the first film in which all of the key elements of film noir came together.

WHATEVER BECAME OF . . .

Anne Shirley retired from the screen after **Murder, My Sweet,** *deciding to bow out after playing her best role in years. The former child star (under the name Dawn O'Day) had moved into more mature roles when RKO starred her successfully in a 1934 adaptation of* **Anne of Green Gables.** *She even took the character's name as her own. With the exception of her Oscar-nominated role as Barbara Stanwyck's daughter in* **Stella Dallas,** *her career was more marked by the roles she lost out on—including Melanie in* **Gone With the Wind** *and the lead in a remake of* **A Bill of Divorcement**—*than for her actual credits. After a failed marriage to John Payne, she wed* **Murder, My Sweet** *producer Adrian Scott months before the film's release and negotiated an end to her RKO contract. She and Scott divorced three years later, possibly because of the strain of dealing with his blacklisting for refusing to testify before the House Un-American Activities Committee. She wed writer-producer-director Charles Lederer in 1949, living a comfortable existence with houses in Beverly Hills and Malibu, and refusing all comeback offers. She died in 1993.*

Mutiny on the Bounty

"We Have Beaten the Sea Itself!"

1935. CAST: Charles Laughton (Captain William Bligh), Clark Gable (1st Mate Fletcher Christian), Franchot Tone (Roger Byam), Donald Crisp (Burkitt), Henry Stephenson (Sir Joseph Banks), Spring Byington (Mrs. Byam), Movita Castaneda (Tehani). Producer: Irving G. Thalberg; Director: Frank Lloyd; Screenplay: Talbot Jennings, Jules Furthman, Carey Wilson (Based on the novels *Mutiny on the Bounty* and *Men Against the Sea* by Charles Nordhoff and James Norman Hall); Photography: Arthur Edeson; Music: Herbert Stothart.

RUNNING TIME: 132 minutes.

Captain Bligh's cry of triumph in *Mutiny on the Bounty* brought tears to the eyes of audiences who had just watched him pilot a longboat through 3,500 miles of storm-filled water. The MGM crew had been similarly moved after weeks of shooting the longboat scenes in the studio tanks. For all involved, *Mutiny on the Bounty* was a heroic triumph over the elements and human conflict—all in the name of great filmmaking.

The project started when director Frank Lloyd bought the rights to Charles Nordhoff and James Hall's three novels about the Bounty mutineers. He then began looking for a studio that would produce the film, offering to give them the rights as long as he could direct.

MGM studio head Louis B. Mayer turned Lloyd down originally, arguing that there was no love interest, that mutiny wasn't heroic, and that the whole thing would be too expensive anyway. But his production chief, Irving G. Thalberg, wanted the project, arguing, "People are fascinated by cruelty, and that's why *Mutiny* will have appeal."

Thalberg had no doubt about whom he wanted for the role of Fletcher Christian. Clark Gable was the only actor in Hollywood who could make the mutineer heroic. But Gable was afraid to appear in a period film and didn't want to shave his trademark mustache. Thalberg finally got him to do the film by promising, "If it isn't one of your greatest successes, I'll never ask you again to play a part you don't want to do."

For Captain Bligh, Thalberg considered Wallace Beery, then decided he was too American. So he went after Charles Laughton, who immersed himself in research. He visited Bligh's own tailor in

Catalina Island stood in for Tahiti in one of MGM's most lavish productions.

London and had the firm create several uniforms based on Bligh's original orders 150 years earlier. He even had a copy of Bligh's hat made —all at his own expense.

Location shooting was a rarity in thirties Hollywood, so nobody thought to send the cast and crew to Tahiti. Instead, they shot on Catalina Island, off the California coast. On one side of the island, the art department built an English shipping town. On the other, they planted coconut palms and tropic grasses, and built a Tahitian fishing village. The cast and crew lived for almost four months in barracks and bungalows on the island.

Shooting was almost as pleasant as serving under Bligh himself. The long days on the *Bounty* left Laughton and several other members of the company seriously seasick. Two technicians were almost lost when an eighteen-foot model used for special-effects sequences was blown out to sea. Another technician actually did drown when the camera barge sank. When word of this got to the mainland, newspapers reported *"Bounty* Sunk. Laughton and Gable Lost," triggering an international panic.

There were times during filming when both stars might have preferred being lost at sea. The two rarely spoke to each other offscreen. After their first scene together, Gable, complaining that Laughton hadn't even looked at him, stalked

"People are fascinated by cruelty"—especially when that meant watching onscreen battles between Clark Gable and Charles Laughton.

THE MUTINY MARRIAGE

The third leading man in* Mutiny on the Bounty *was also third choice to play the part, but he got no less of a career boost out of the film for that. After Paramount refused to loan Cary Grant to MGM to play Robert Byam, and Robert Montgomery turned down the role, Thalberg tapped former Group Theatre member Franchot Tone. Along with improving his standing at MGM and bringing the actor an Oscar nomination, the role gave him one other bonus. Tone had been dating Joan Crawford off and on for two years. Crawford's first marriage, to Douglas Fairbanks Jr., had gone on the rocks when she grew more popular than her husband. With Tone's success in* Mutiny on the Bounty *and* Lives of a Bengal Lancer, *however, they decided to take a chance. Sadly, MGM did little to advance Tone's career after that, and the marriage ended in divorce four years later. But he and Crawford would remain close friends for the rest of his life. She would even help nurse him through his final illness.

off the set. Thalberg had to fly to the location to soothe the egos of both actors. At the same time, however, Thalberg didn't really care if the two never became friends. The footage of their first scene together was, after all, electric.

Mutiny on the Bounty ended up costing almost $2 million—more than any other film since the silent *Ben-Hur*—but it grossed $4.4 million. Depression audiences, many of whom felt trapped in jobs they hated with bosses they despised, cheered Fletcher Christian's defiance of the wicked Captain Bligh. At year's end, *Mutiny on the Bounty* was high on most critics' ten-best lists, and Laughton won the first New York Film Critics Award for Best Actor.

The picture scored eight Oscar nominations, including Best Picture, Best Director, and three for Best Actor (Laughton, Gable, and Franchot Tone, the latter playing Roger Byam, the man caught between the two). On awards night, *Mutiny on the Bounty* captured Best Picture and nothing else. It would be the last Best Picture–winner to take no other Oscars.

THE REAL MUTINY

Later historians have accused Nordhoff, Hall, and MGM of distorting history in their treatment of the 1788* Bounty *mutiny. Some have suggested that Bligh wasn't really as sadistic as he was portrayed in book and film. Contradicting those claims are the changes in British maritime law in response to his cruelty. In addition, the captain suffered through another mutiny a few years later. More likely is the claim that Fletcher Christian, far from being heroic, may have been Bligh's colleague in cruelty, only turning against the captain when he decided to stay on in Tahiti. Little is known of the mutineers' fate beyond the fact that they fled Tahiti and the British Navy for the more forbidding shores of Pitcairn Island. Evidence suggests that Christian was among those murdered by Pacific tribesmen, who resented the British seamen for stealing their wives.

National Velvet

Liz Enters the Winner's Circle

1944. CAST: Mickey Rooney (Mi Taylor), Donald Crisp (Mr. Brown), Elizabeth Taylor (Velvet Brown), Anne Revere (Mrs. Brown), Angela Lansbury (Edwina Brown), Jackie "Butch" Jenkins (Donald Brown). Producer: Pandro S. Berman; Director: Clarence Brown; Screenplay: Theodore Reeves, Helen Deutsch (Based on the novel by Enid Bagnold); Photography: Leonard Smith (Technicolor); Music: Herbert Stothart.
RUNNING TIME: 125 minutes.

Although the character she played, Velvet Brown, was disqualified after winning England's Grand National, nothing could stop Elizabeth Taylor's climb to the top after she won the hearts of audiences around the world. Her sincere, deeply felt performance in *National Velvet* helped make Taylor the last great star of the studio era.

Enid Bagnold's novel about a British country girl whose determination turns an unruly stallion into a prize racehorse had brought the author more than $100,000 when it was first published. It also brought movie offers almost immediately. Pandro S. Berman, who was head of RKO Studios at the time, wanted to buy the book for Katharine Hepburn but couldn't get the project off the ground. Instead, British producer-director Victor Saville picked up the rights, turning them over to MGM as part of the deal that put him in charge of the company's British studios in 1938. Initially, studio head Louis B. Mayer wanted to cast Margaret Sullavan as Velvet, with Spencer Tracy as her father, but that project was postponed as well. When Berman moved to MGM as a producer in 1940, he wanted to revive the film but still couldn't find the right leading lady.

Then MGM executive Sam Marx discovered a beautiful little girl whose American-born parents had left England at the start of World War II. He cast the eleven-year-old Elizabeth Taylor in a small but noticeable role in *Lassie, Come Home,* then suggested her to Berman for *National Velvet*. She seemed perfect for the role except for one problem: She was too short. Although twelve years old by then, she was no taller than most six-year-olds. With no other prospects, Berman told her the part could still be hers if she grew quickly enough.

Liz would later tell the press that she willed herself to grow. In truth, she worked out constantly,

After filming was over, MGM gave King Charles, the horse cast as Pi, to Elizabeth Taylor (left of center, with Mickey Rooney, right).

BETTER THAN ANY HORSE RACE

Anne Revere was a surprise winner in the 1945 Oscar race, beating favorite Ann Blyth, who had given a breakthrough performance as vicious little Veda in Mildred Pierce. *Insiders suggested that Veda was just too nasty for Oscar. Others thought Revere benefited from being the oldest nominee for Best Supporting Actress. Or maybe her performance as the supportive mother who advised Elizabeth Taylor that, "Everyone should have a chance at a breathtaking piece of folly at least once in his life," really was the best of the lot. However it happened, hers was the name in the envelope. Her victory came as such a surprise that several papers reported the next day that she had played Veda.*

even hanging from a bar to stretch her spine. She spent hours taking riding lessons at the studio's expense, and just to push things along, increased her food intake, sometimes eating two breakfasts a day to jump-start her growth. After three months of this regimen, she had grown three inches. Her timing was perfect. Not only had she grown into the part before anybody else could beat her to it, but her growth spurt allowed Berman to cast Mickey Rooney as jockey-turned-trainer Mi Taylor, his last role before entering military service.

Shooting proceeded smoothly, with Taylor demonstrating what a good horsewoman she had become. Except for the most difficult jumps in the Grand National, which had to be doubled by Australian jockey Snowy Baker, she did all of her own riding. Her family even allowed the studio to fit her with braces, an important character element, and to pull two baby teeth to make room for them. They only drew the line when it came to Taylor's hair. Her father insisted that a wig be used for the scenes in which Velvet cuts her hair to masquerade as a male jockey.

When the picture was completed, MGM's executives were so impressed with Taylor's work and the film in general that they gave her King Charles, the horse who had played Pi in the picture, on her thirteenth birthday. They also gave her a $15,000 bonus and a new contract, raising her salary from $250 per week to $750.

National Velvet received glowing reviews, with special mention of Taylor's and Rooney's performances and the climactic horse race, which some critics called the best in film history. It grossed just over $4 million and captured five Oscar nominations, winning for supporting actress Anne Revere and for Robert J. Kern's editing. After the awards, an Academy spokesman announced that Taylor had almost won a special Oscar for best juvenile performance, but had lost out to Peggy Ann Garner for *A Tree Grows in Brooklyn.* That was the only thing Liz lost with *National Velvet,* for the film set her firmly on the road to stardom, helping her develop a devoted fan following that would stay with her through two Oscars, seven marriages, and a lifetime in the winner's circle.

AGED IN VELVET

MGM tried twice to adapt* National Velvet *for new generations—and failed. The first update was a television series that ran for two years on NBC. Lori Martin played Velvet Brown, this time an American farm girl, but the series failed to sustain interest. Despite a promising start, with a juicy role as Gregory Peck's daughter in the original* Cape Fear*, Martin's career never took off, and she retired from acting to raise a family.

In 1977, MGM tried a theatrical sequel,* International Velvet*, with Tatum O'Neal as a troubled teen who straightens herself out when her aunt, the grown-up Velvet Brown, turns her into an Olympic-caliber equestrienne. Taylor turned down the chance to play Velvet again, leaving the role to British actress Nanette Newman. But though critics praised the production's look and the performances of costars Anthony Hopkins and Christopher Plummer, audiences just weren't interested.

Network

"I'm Mad as Hell, and I'm Not Going to Take This Any More!"

1976. CAST: Faye Dunaway (Diana Christensen), William Holden (Max Schumacher), Peter Finch (Howard Beale), Robert Duvall (Frank Hackett), Wesley Addy (Nelson Chaney), Ned Beatty (Arthur Jensen), Beatrice Straight (Louise Schumacher). Producer: Howard Gottfried; Director: Sidney Lumet; Screenplay: Paddy Chayefsky; Photography: Owen Roizman (Panavision, Metrocolor); Music: Elliott Lawrence.

RUNNING TIME: 120 minutes.

After spending the fifties as the voice of the common man, with acclaimed scripts for *Marty* and *The Catered Affair,* Paddy Chayefsky unleashed a surprising torrent of anger at the changing world of the seventies in a pair of box-office winners. His first, 1971's *The Hospital,* took on the medical profession. With *Network,* in 1976, he tackled broadcasting, the field in which he had first won fame as a writer. With network news departments being taken over by entertainment divisions, talk shows erupting into violence and even leading to murder, and exploitation increasingly ruling the airwaves, history has proven Chayefsky something of a prophet.

He wrote the script in response to the growing dehumanization of life as reflected in the Vietnam War and the Watergate hearings, focusing on an out-of-control television network, where a delusional news anchor's rantings prompt executives to promote him as "an angry prophet denouncing the hypocrisies of our times." He also modeled two characters on real media figures. Fading newscaster Howard Beale's threat to kill himself on air was inspired by the on-air suicide of a California news anchor. And Faye Dunaway's soulless programming executive, Diana Christensen, was supposedly modeled on NBC vice president Lin Bolen.

At first, Chayefsky and director Sidney Lumet considered asking real-life newsmen Walter Cronkite or John Chancellor to play Beale, but they feared that their respective news departments would frown on the idea. After Henry Fonda turned the part down, they discussed casting William Holden before deciding he'd be better as Max Schumacher, the old-time news producer put out to pasture when Beale is fired.

Then they cast British actor Peter Finch as Beale. At first, Lumet and Chayefsky worried that the

Peter Finch as Howard Beale, "the mad prophet of the airwaves"—the first actor to win a posthumous Oscar.

TELEVISION EATS ITSELF

Television could hardly ignore **Network's** *surprise success at the box office, even if it was the object of the film's satirical barbs. Two years after the picture's release, NBC premiered* **W.E.B.**, *a prime-time soap opera about corporate intrigue among television executives. Heading the cast was Pamela Bellwood, following in Faye Dunaway's footsteps by playing a role modeled on the network's own Lin Bolen. And just to add to the heady mixture, the series was produced by Bolen herself. Fascinating as this Pirandellian approach to programming may have been, it wasn't enough to draw an audience.* **W.E.B.** *was canceled after only five weeks, though there were no real-life suicides or assassinations to liven up the last episode.*

two male stars would clash, but on the first day of rehearsal Finch and Holden hit it off. Both were coming off long dry spells in which they hadn't had decent roles, and both had long histories of battling entertainment executives. Through the rest of the shoot, the two got together regularly with Lumet to discuss old times, their real-life relationship paralleling the on-screen camaraderie between their characters.

The role was a particular shot in the arm for Finch. After years as a Hollywood outsider, he was ready to settle down in the film capital. Anticipating the positive response to *Network*, he even bought a house in Los Angeles and was preparing to apply for U.S. citizenship. Finch loved acting so much that he came to the set when he didn't have any scenes, just so he could watch the rest of the cast at work.

Despite an outcry from the television industry, *Network* won strong notices and did surprisingly well at the box office, helped greatly by Beale's popular catch-phrase, "I'm mad as hell, and I'm not going to take this any more!" As the year ended, the film was clearly a major contender for the Academy Awards.

Finch desperately wanted the Oscar, hiring a press agent for the first time in his life just to improve his chances. During the last half of 1976, he gave approximately three hundred interviews, including two exhausting press junkets to New York. Adding to his fatigue was his refusal to fly, which meant he had to take the train from Los Angeles both times. On January 14, he walked to the ABC studios in Century City for an appearance on *Good Morning, America*. He collapsed in the lobby at 9:00 A.M. and was pronounced dead at 10:19 A.M.

A few weeks later, Finch followed James Dean and Spencer Tracy as the third actor to receive a posthumous Oscar nomination. His was one of ten nominations for *Network*. Director William Friedkin was producer of the Oscar show that year and, wanting to get away from the ceremony's usual sentimentality, advised Chayefsky that he did not want Finch's widow accepting the award should her late husband win. Chayefsky agreed to accept in her place, but when Finch won, the writer called Mrs. Finch to the stage. She delivered a heartfelt speech—written by Chayefsky—that was the highlight of an evening in which *Network* also walked off with awards for Dunaway, Chayefsky, and supporting actress Beatrice Straight.

COMING FROM BEHIND

When Beatrice Straight started getting solid reviews for* Network*, MGM took out trade ads touting her for a Best Supporting Actress Oscar, even though her role lasted only a few minutes and consisted primarily of one long speech, denouncing her husband for walking out on their marriage. The speech was delivered so well, however, that she did indeed win one of* Network*'s ten Oscar nominations. She was far from a front-runner. Most predictions gave the Award to either Piper Laurie, returning to the screen after fifteen years to play the demented mother in* Carrie*, or thirteen-year-old Jodie Foster as a child prostitute in* Taxi Driver*. But on Oscar night, presenter Sylvester Stallone announced Straight as the winner. Accepting the award, she said, "It's very heavy, and I'm the dark horse. It's a great, great thrill and totally unexpected."

Oscar rivals, on- and offscreen friends: Peter Finch and William Holden.

A Night at the Opera

"There Ain't No Sanity Clause"

1935. CAST: Groucho Marx (Otis B. Driftwood), Chico Marx (Fiorello), Harpo Marx (Tomasso), Kitty Carlisle (Rosa Castaldi), Allan Jones (Riccardo Baroni), Walter Woolf King (Rodolfo Lasspari), Siegfried "Sig" Rumann (Herman Gotlieb), Margaret Dumont (Mrs. Claypool). Producer: Irving G. Thalberg; Director: Sam Wood; Screenplay: George S. Kaufman, Morrie Ryskind; Photography: Merritt B. Gerstad; Music: Herbert Stothart.

RUNNING TIME: 92 minutes.

The Marx Brothers might have wanted an "Insanity Clause" in their contract after they left Paramount for MGM in the mid-thirties. Not only did they find themselves faced with a producer who insisted on toning down their anarchic comedy, but they were forced to work with a director who seemed to have no sense of humor. So, of course, they wound up with the biggest hit of their careers.

Groucho, Harpo, and Chico didn't exactly choose to go to MGM. Nobody else wanted them.

Their almost surreal Paramount comedies had brought in less and less at the box office. Critics and the intelligentsia loved them, but the average ticket buyer wasn't buying. Word in Hollywood was that they were washed up in pictures, but Harpo got independent producer Samuel Goldwyn to agree to back one more picture. Zeppo decided to retire from acting to become a talent agent. Then one of Chico's bridge-playing buddies, MGM production head Irving G. Thalberg, invited the four to have lunch with him. Noting that Zeppo had retired from acting, Thalberg asked if three brothers would cost less than four. "Don't be silly," quipped Groucho. "Without Zeppo we're worth twice as much."

Thalberg had studied their pictures and suggested that they were too unstructured, with too many jokes that hadn't been planned out for movie audiences. "If you had half the jokes, the picture would be twice as good, and you'd gross three times as much." He wrapped it up by offering them a very good deal: if they made pictures his way, he'd give them fifteen percent of the gross.

Thalberg wanted a strong script with a love story to keep women interested (conventional wisdom held that women did not care for broad comedy). To maximize the effectiveness of their

The Marxes adopt a new brother, director Sam Wood, on the set of *A Night at the Opera.*

ON A CLEAR DAY YOU CAN SEE THALBERG

Thalberg's habit of missing meetings, delaying meetings, and walking out on meetings led to the above quip from a frustrated George S. Kaufman. The Marx Brothers did more than complain about the boy wonder's cavalier behavior. They fought back. When they arrived for one of their first appointments with Thalberg, his secretary informed them that they would have to wait while he finished another meeting. When they got tired of waiting, they broke up the meeting by blowing cigar smoke under his office door. Another time, they barricaded his door with file cabinets. It took Thalberg an hour to get out. Their best prank took place when Thalberg left one of their meetings for a "quick" consultation with his boss, Louis B. Mayer. He returned to find the Marxes roasting potatoes over a raging fire—in the middle of summer. According to some sources, the stars were also naked.

chaotic comedy, he decided to set them against the stuffiest, most dignified institution possible, so the film took place in the world of opera.

After several misfires, Groucho asked Thalberg to hire their favorite writing team, George S. Kaufman and Morrie Ryskind. Once they had the script in shape, Kaufman returned to Broadway, and Thalberg brought in Jack Benny's top gag man, Al Boasberg. The three-hundred pound writer punched up the jokes and wrote the famous stateroom scene, in which hordes of people cram into Groucho's miniscule room during the ocean trip to America. When Thalberg pressed him too much for the scene, Boasberg told him he had to leave, but the producer could come pick it up in his office. Thalberg and the Marxes arrived to find no script, until Groucho looked up and discovered hundreds of strips of paper, each with one line, nailed to the ceiling. It took them five hours to assemble the scene.

Rather than assign the Marxes to an established comedy director who might get too wrapped up in their routines, Thalberg picked the very serious, very right-wing Sam Wood, a man with no sense of humor. Wood started each day on the set by drinking a large glass of milk, so the brothers had his milk delivered to him in a large baby bottle—only he didn't get the joke. He imposed a fine for lateness, which Groucho supported until Harpo and Chico nailed his garage door shut, making him the first to pay the $50 penalty. After that, they turned the fine into a game, betting on who would be the next to pay up. Wood finally abandoned the system when even he had to admit it had become a big joke.

Finally, *A Night at the Opera* was ready for previews. They took it to a theater in Long Beach where the audience laughed at the titles, then shut up for the rest of the show. Undaunted, Thalberg took the picture across the street and set up an impromptu preview with the same results. The brothers were in a panic, but Thalberg was calm. The two previews had shown him exactly how to recut the film and tighten the laughs. At the third preview, the audience laughed nonstop. One line was so funny they had to cut it. In the film, the Marxes take over a performance of *Il Trovatore* and turn it into a madhouse. Then the police storm onto the stage. Watching from a box, Groucho quips, "Either there are cops in *Il Trovatore* or the jig is up." Audiences laughed so much they didn't hear the rest of the picture.

Thalberg's faith in the Marx Brothers was borne out when *A Night at the Opera* became their biggest hit, returning more than $3 million at the box office on a cost of just over $1 million. He had planned to take them with him when he left MGM to create his own independent production company, but his early death put an end to those dreams. Instead, they stayed at MGM, working for less creative producers who put so much emphasis on the romantic elements and production numbers Thalberg had added that the Marxes eventually found themselves supporting players in their own pictures.

Ninotchka

Garbo Laughs!

1939. CAST: Greta Garbo (Lena Yakushova, "Ninotchka"), Melvyn Douglas (Count Leon Dolga), Ina Claire (Grand Duchess Swana), Sig Rumann (Michael Ironoff), Felix Bressart (Buljanoff), Alexander Granach (Kopolsky), Bela Lugosi (Comissar Razinin), George Tobias (Russian Visa Official). Producer-Director: Ernst Lubitsch; Screenplay: Charles Brackett, Billy Wilder, Walter Reisch (Based on a story by Melchior Lengyel); Photography: William Daniels; Music: Werner R. Heyman. RUNNING TIME: 110 minutes.

Film historians are quick to point out that *Ninotchka* hardly marked the first time Greta Garbo laughed on screen. Even her most tragic characters had their moments of joy. Nonetheless, *Ninotchka* earned its famous advertising slogan, the brainchild of studio publicity head Howard Dietz. The film was, in fact, the first in which her character ended up neither dead nor forlorn.

As is the case with most of Hollywood history, there are divergent stories about how *Ninotchka* got made. Some sources insist that MGM decided to put Garbo into a comedy to make her more appealing to American audiences. Others suggest that the film was Garbo's idea and that she actually had to threaten retirement to get MGM to approve the project. The truth is a combination of both sources. Garbo had begun to feel the need to expand her range into comedy as early as 1935, when she threw herself in front of a train in *Anna Karenina*. According to legend, her friend, writer Salka Viertel, was charged with finding the right comic idea, and she asked Hungarian writer Melchior Lengyel if he had anything suitable. After a few days, he visited actress and writer and, while the star swam in the nude, gave Viertel the story: "Russian girl saturated with Bolshevist ideals goes to fearful, capitalistic, monopolistic Paris. She meets romance and has an uproarious good time. Capitalism not so bad, after all." According to legend, MGM paid him $15,000 just for those three sentences. In truth, he and Viertel worked on the script for months but couldn't come up with anything.

Finally, the piece was assigned to producer Gottfried Reinhardt and writer S. N. Behrman. In Behrman's script, Garbo comes to Paris and falls for a gigolo while trying to make a deal for the sale

Melvyn Douglas teaches Greta Garbo that love is blind.

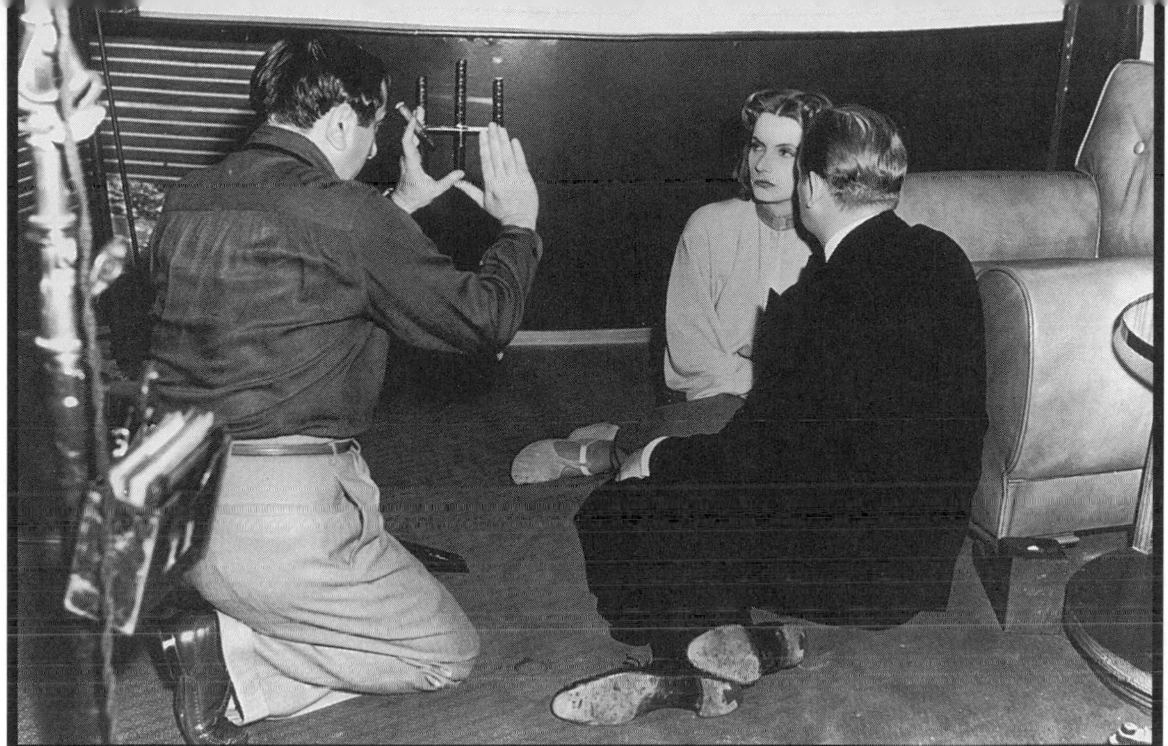

Ernst Lubitsch sizes up a scene with Greta Garbo and Melvyn Douglas.

THE MAN IN SILK STOCKINGS

George Tobias is best known to television fans as Abner Kravitz, Samantha Stevens's neighbor on Bewitched, *but he also holds the distinction of having appeared in all three versions of* Ninotchka. *In the 1939 original, he had a small role as a visa official. For the stage musical,* Silk Stockings, *he was promoted to play one of the three Soviet diplomats whose dalliance in Paris sets the plot moving. When the musical hit the screen in 1957, he didn't get to re-create his Broadway role, but he did get to take over Bela Lugosi's part as the leading lady's superior.*

of nickel from a Siberian mine. Originally George Cukor was to direct, but as scripting dragged on, he had to leave to devote full-time to another project, *Gone With the Wind*. Garbo then informed studio head Louis B. Mayer that she would only consider two directors: Edmund Goulding or Ernst Lubitsch. Both men had a reputation for extravagance. Lubitsch had not directed at MGM since 1934, when his production of *The Merry Widow* lost money because of budget overruns. Since Goulding, who had recently left MGM for Warner Bros., was considered washed up at the time, Mayer reluctantly agreed to bring in Lubitsch. (Ironically, Goulding would bounce back with *Dark Victory* the same year *Ninotchka* came out.) Lubitsch took an instant dislike to Behrman's script and brought in a friend of his, Walter Reisch, to help with rewrites. When Berhman didn't like Lubitsch's proposed changes—which included turning the Siberian nickel mine into a collection of Czarist jewels, because diamonds were more photogenic—he left. In his place, Lubitsch brought in a young writing team that had just given him a very funny script for *Bluebeard's Eighth Wife,* Charles Brackett and Billy Wilder.

Then Garbo got cold feet. The new script included a drunk scene, and she was afraid she couldn't pull it off. Lubitsch did his best to put her at ease, stopping by her dressing room to greet her each morning and to say good evening at end of day. But even though he put the drunk scene off until almost the last, Garbo still tried to get out of it. He finally had to bully her into doing the scene, then directed her carefully, praising her work and keeping notes and suggestions to a minimum. She loosened up and even managed to laugh at herself when she slipped and fell during the scene.

That anxiety aside, *Ninotchka* was one of Garbo's happiest shoots. Insiders had feared that she would clash with costar Ina Claire, a Broadway comedienne who just happened to be the widow of Garbo's former lover and costar, John Gilbert. But the two worked together flawlessly. In addition, Garbo didn't hide in her dressing room between takes, as she usually did, but hung around and joked with cast and crew.

Ninotchka finished filming in July 1939, after fifty-eight days of shooting. Because the film's carefree setting was far from the troubled Europe people were reading about in the newspapers, MGM added a prologue to distance it from real events: "This picture takes place in Paris in those wonderful days when a siren was a brunette and not an alarm . . . and if a Frenchman turned out the lights it was not on account of an air raid!" History took care of one potential problem. Before the film's release, Hitler and Stalin signed a nonaggression treaty that alienated most U.S. intellectuals from the Soviets, creating a much more favorable climate for the film on this side of the Atlantic.

The critics loved *Ninotchka,* but audiences were slightly less enthusiastic, with the film turning only a small profit. Nor did the political realities in Europe help: *Ninotchka* was banned in Italy, Estonia, Lithuania, Bulgaria and, for a while, in France. Yet its stature as Garbo's first comedy, along with the picture's sheer quality and entertainment value, have made it a classic.

OTHER TITLES CONSIDERED FOR *NINOTCHKA*

A Foreign Affair
Intrigue in Paris
A Kiss for the Commissar
A Kiss from Moscow
A Kiss in the Dark
The Love Axis
This Time for Keeps
Time Out for Love
We Want to be Alone

Nicholas Schenck, head of MGM's parent company, Loew's, Inc., finally insisted on the title* Ninotchka. *When executives worried that audiences wouldn't be able to repeat the title, the ad department came up with another line for the posters: "What makes Garbo blush and laugh in* Ninotchka? *Don't pronounce it. . . See it."

North by Northwest

"I Am But Mad North-Northwest."

1959. CAST: Cary Grant (Roger O. Thornhill), Eva Marie Saint (Eve Kendall), James Mason (Phillip Vandamm), Jessie Royce Landis (Clara Thornhill), Leo G. Carroll (Professor), Martin Landau (Leonard). Producer-Director: Alfred Hitchcock; Screenplay: Ernest Lehman; Photography: Robert Burks (VistaVision, Technicolor); Music: Bernard Herrmann.

RUNNING TIME: 136 minutes.

Like so much about Alfred Hitchcock's most popular comic thriller, the connection between *North by Northwest*'s title and the famous line from *Hamlet* was sheer accident, but appropriate nonetheless. Originally, Hitchcock signed with MGM to direct a film version of Hammond Innes's novel *The Wreck of the Mary Deare*. Lehman was under studio contract at the time, and the director requested him as writer on the strength of his strong scripts for films like *Executive Suite* and *Sabrina*. Lehman was so unimpressed with the book, however, that he turned the assignment down, only changing his mind after Hitchcock charmed him over lunch.

In daily meetings at Hitchcock's house, the two discussed everything but *The Wreck of the Mary Deare*. After a month, Lehman tried to withdraw, claiming that he couldn't see how to adapt the story. Hitchcock agreed and suggested they create an original story without telling MGM's executives until they had something concrete.

As they batted around ideas, Hitchcock brought up some suspense scenes he had always dreamed of using. He had wanted to do a chase around the presidential heads on Mt. Rushmore. He had also been intrigued by a New York journalist's suggestion for a story involving a government decoy, a nonexistent man created to confuse enemy spies. What if an innocent man were mistaken for that decoy? In addition, Hitch had imagined a scene in which a U.N. representative refuses to continue a speech until one delegate wakes up, only to discover the man has been murdered. And then there were the crop-dusting planes he'd seen while driving home. They had always looked suspicious to him.

When Lehman got the script moving, they presented the idea to MGM's executives, telling

THE GREAT WHATSIS

One of Alfred Hitchcock's great contributions to the suspense genre was his use of the "MacGuffin," his term for whatever it is the heroes and villains are fighting over. The MacGuffin—or as some people call it "The Great Whatsis"—doesn't have to make sense. It just has to be there to provide an excuse for the suspense scenes. With North by Northwest, Hitch created his favorite MacGuffin. As he told François Truffaut, the plot revolved around James Mason's character, who sells government secrets. What those secrets may be is never revealed. In the director's words, "The MacGuffin has been boiled down to its purest expression: nothing at all."

THE THINGS THEY LEFT BEHIND

Anybody planning a trip knows that you can't take along everything you want, as Alfred Hitchcock certainly discovered with North by Northwest. Originally, he had wanted the script to continue beyond the Mt. Rushmore sequence to include a breakneck chase through Alaska and into Siberia. At one point, the leading lady was to have executed a daredevil escape from the enemy agents' car by grabbing a rope dangling from a helicopter. This was cut in the scripting stage, as was a sequence set in Detroit. Cary Grant was to have played a scene while walking through an auto factory as an automobile was assembled behind him. At the end, he would open the door to discover a dead body inside. It was a great scene, but they could never figure out how to work it into the plot.

them it would take too long to develop *The Wreck of the Mary Deare,* so they wanted to do this film first. Since Lehman's script only took the protagonist as far as his escape in Grand Central Station, Hitchcock told the story to that point, then announced that he had another appointment, leaving the executives aching to hear what happened next. Once the story was approved, Hitch dropped *The Wreck of the Mary Deare*. (Michael Anderson would direct that less-than-successful picture.)

Lehman's first title for the script was "In a Northwesterly Direction," based the character Roger A. Thornhill's trip from New York to Mt. Rushmore. Also considered were "Breathless" and "The Man in Lincoln's Nose." Kenneth MacGowan, head of the MGM script department, suggested that *North by Northwest* might prove a catchier title. Only after the switch did Lehman and Hitchcock realize the connection to *Hamlet*.

Initially, they had planned the picture for James Stewart, who was starring in *Vertigo* at the time. As the story developed, however, Hitchcock realized that the befuddled advertising executive mistaken for a U.S. spy was better suited to another of his favorite stars, Cary Grant. For leading lady, Grant wanted Sophia Loren, his costar in *The Pride and the Passion* and *Houseboat*. The two had almost married, and he still may have hoped to win her away from producer Carlo Ponti. But she had other obligations. MGM wanted Hitchcock to use Cyd Charisse, but he decided he had to have another blond. So he chose Eva Marie Saint, who had won an Oscar as Marlon Brando's love interest in *On the Waterfront*.

Hitchcock took his cast across the U.S. for location shooting in Manhattan, Long Island,

Cary Grant finds love on the run with Eva Marie Saint.

Chicago, Rapid City (North Dakota), and Mt. Rushmore. U.N. rules forbade the shooting of fiction films there, so those scenes had to be shot on facsimiles built in Hollywood, though Hitchcock had one shot of Grant taken at the actual site with a concealed camera. There was no question of shooting on Mt. Rushmore. The terrain was too dangerous, and Hitchcock had already planned to have the sculpture re-created at the MGM studios. But just setting the scene there required clearance from the Department of the Interior. When a reporter leaked Hitchcock's plan for the chase scene, the bureaucrats threatened to revoke his permit, and newspaper editors around the country attacked his proposed desecration of our national heritage. Finally, the Interior Department relented, but only on condition that no actors be shown climbing over the actual faces. They also nixed a sequence in which Grant sneezes while hiding in Lincoln's nose. Hitchcock was so angry he removed a line from the credits thanking them for their cooperation.

The picture grossed more than $5 million domestically in its initial release, helping to make Grant the year's number-two box-office star. This was particularly good news to star and director, each of whom would receive ten percent of the gross over $8 million. With successful reissues, videocassette sales, and television licensing, their take from the film has been estimated as high as $20 million.

That's not the real Mt. Rushmore behind Cary Grant, James Mason, and Eva Marie Saint. In fact, Alfred Hitchcock almost had to relocate the film's climax.

Now, Voyager

"Don't Let's Ask for the Moon. We Have the Stars."

1942. CAST: Bette Davis (Charlotte Vale), Paul Henreid (Jerry D. Durance), Claude Rains (Dr. Jaquith), Gladys Cooper (Mrs. Henry Windle Vale), Bonita Granville (June Vale), John Loder (Elliott Livingstone), Ilka Chase (Lisa Vale), Lee Patrick ("Deb" McIntyre), Mary Wickes (Dora Pickford). Producer: Hal B. Wallis; Director: Irving Rapper; Screenplay: Casey Robinson (Based on the novel by Olive Higgins Prouty); Photography: Sol Polito; Music: Max Steiner. RUNNING TIME: 117 minutes.

Bette Davis gave her fans and Warner Bros. the moon and the stars and a lot more when she starred in this classic romance. The film became her biggest hit of the forties, a decade when she ruled Hollywood. In addition, her portrayal of a neurotic, overweight spinster who comes out from under her mother's thumb to become a glamorous, sensitive woman of the world gave hope to a generation of repressed females.

The 1941 novel by Olive Higgins Prouty, author of *Stella Dallas,* was the third in a tetralogy about the fictitious Vale family of New England and the only one of the four to be filmed. Warner production chief Hal B. Wallis paid $35,000 for the rights and then assigned the studio's top women's director, Edmund Goulding, to write and direct. Wallis's first choices for the leads were Irene Dunne and Charles Boyer. Since much of the film's action was set on an ocean liner, he naturally wanted to recapture the magic of their similar hit, *Love Affair*. Then Norma Shearer expressed an interest in the project. The thought of pirating away MGM's former first lady was too tempting to resist, so Wallis put off finalizing any agreement with Dunne until he heard from Shearer. By the time Shearer decided to go ahead with her retirement, Dunne was no longer available. Ginger Rogers was the third choice, and she was quite enthusiastic about the project, but then Bette Davis entered the picture. She insisted that she was the only actress to play Charlotte Vale. For one thing, she was a New Englander, just like the Vales. For another, she said it would be absurd to transform frumpy, neurotic Charlotte into a glamour girl. Her attractive but plain looks would be much more believable.

Apart from Boyer, Wallis had considered only American actors as the leading man, with Henry

Top: Bette Davis met her match romantically. *Bottom:* Davis caught between love for Paul Henreid (above) and duty to mother Gladys Cooper (left).

THE NAKED TRUTH

When Bette Davis was touring the country with a program of film clips in the seventies, she fell victim to one of the era's strangest social phenomena. She was "streaked" by a fan who ran to the stage in the nude and left her a bouquet of flowers. A card with the flowers read, "Now, Voyeur."

Fonda, George Brent, and Fredric March among those mentioned. Then he saw Austrian actor Paul Henreid in his first U.S. film, *Joan of Paris*. Here was a European charmer with a strongly masculine appeal. Davis was taken with his performance as well, and they set up a test. But somebody—Jack Warner is most often blamed for this—decided to remold Henreid for the test into a cross between Brent and Leslie Howard. His hair was slicked back, and the costume department put him into the kind of broad-shouldered, narrow-waisted suit Brent usually wore. When Davis saw the test, she shrieked that he looked like a department-store floorwalker. She insisted on a second test, with Henreid allowed to wear his hair naturally and use his own clothes. He would always be grateful to her for helping him land the star-making role, and the two remained close friends the rest of their lives.

"Untold Want, by life and land ne'er granted, Now, Voyager, sail thou forth to seek and find."
—Walt Whitman, Leaves of Grass, *the source for* Now, Voyager's *title*

Goulding had already turned his story treatment over to Casey Robinson, who wrote the screenplay. As production was about to begin, the director took ill, and Wallis considered replacing him with Michael Curtiz. Davis took exception to this. She had never particularly liked working with the autocratic Hungarian. Moreover, she didn't want to upset her own shooting schedule by having to sandwich *Now, Voyager* in between his commitments to *Yankee Doodle Dandy* and *Casablanca*. Instead, she suggested Irving Rapper, who had worked as dialogue director on several of her films before breaking into directing on his own.

There is a great deal of controversy over who created the film's famous cigarette-lighting ritual. Davis and Henreid contend that the bit as written was unplayable, involving the passing of a lit match back and forth between the two lovers. After much rehearsal, Henreid supposedly suggested something he and his wife did on motor trips. He would put two cigarettes in his mouth, light them, and pass one to Davis. Robinson contradicts that story, claiming to have created the device himself, and the script drafts on file with the Warner Bros. papers at the University of Southern California bear him out.

Now, Voyager finished production in June 1942 with a budget of just over $750,000. Its release was a triumph for Davis, who received some of the best notices of her career. The film was one of the studio's biggest hits of the year, prompting Jack Warner to give Davis, whom he hadn't wanted in the role, a well-deserved raise. But Davis's greatest reward came in the mail. Hundreds of women wrote to tell her how much they had been helped by her portrayal of a girl driven nearly mad by her possessive mother. She even got letters from domineering mothers claiming to have realized the error of their ways from watching the movie.

Out of the Past

"Build My Gallows High, Baby"

1947. CAST: Robert Mitchum (Jeff Bailey), Jane Greer (Kathie Moffett), Kirk Douglas (Whit Sterling), Rhonda Fleming (Meta Carson), Steve Brodie (Fisher), Virginia Huston (Ann), Dickie Moore (The Kid). Producer: Warren Duff; Director: Jacques Tourneur; Screenplay: Geoffrey Homes (Based on Homes's novel *Build My Gallows High*); Photography: Nicholas Musuraca; Music: Roy Webb. RUNNING TIME: 97 minutes.

Film noir is a genre noted for crooked characters, cynicism, and a sense of impending doom. Few examples of the form are as crooked, cynical, and doom-driven as *Out of the Past,* a picture often cited as the definitive film noir. It's captured postwar doubts so well that it not only performed solidly at the box office but also turned Robert Mitchum into RKO's top male star.

Daniel Mainwaring had been writing screenplays since 1942 while also publishing novels under the name Geoffrey Homes. Those two careers came together when RKO hired him to adapt his own novel *Build My Gallows High* (the film's title in Great Britain), which he did under his pseudonym. The novel dealt with a man on the run, a former detective now operating a filling station in a small town. His past catches up with him when a former partner-in-crime drives into town, forcing a confrontation with the crime boss the ex-cop had betrayed and the boss's mistress, with whom he had tried to run away. Mainwaring handed in his first draft and went off to work on another picture. Producer Warren Duff assigned James M. Cain, author of *Mildred Pierce* and *The Postman Always Rings Twice,* to finish the job, but Cain's rewrite departed too much from the original story. After finishing his other project, Mainwaring returned to put his script back into shape. On his own, he presented the material to Humphrey Bogart, who was enthusiastic about the project. Warner Bros. refused to approve the loan-out, however, so Duff offered the role to John Garfield and Dick Powell, both of whom turned it down. Finally he turned to an up-and-coming contract player at RKO who, at the very least, wouldn't cost the studio that much, Robert Mitchum. After notable supporting performances in *The Story of GI Joe* (for which he received his only Oscar nomination), *Crossfire,* and *Till the End of Time,* Mitchum was finally ready for top billing in *Out of the*

MUTE TESTIMONY

One of Out of the Past's *most striking features is the dark, unsentimental presence of former child star Dickie Moore as the deaf-mute who befriends Robert Mitchum's character and even kills to save his life. The performance was a decided change of pace for the young actor, who had starred in dozens of "Our Gang" shorts and gave Shirley Temple her first screen kiss in 1942's* Miss Annie Rooney. *Adult stardom eluded Moore, who retired from the screen to enter the world of publicity in the fifties. That did not end his connection with show business, however. In 1988 he married another former child star, MGM soprano Jane Powell.*

Robert Mitchum and Jane Greer move out of the past and into the shadows as film noir's bleakest couple.

Past. For leading lady, Webb turned to another actress who'd been coming along at the studio. Originally, Jane Greer was best known as Rudy Vallee's third wife, a marriage that had ended a few years earlier. Studio publicists had dubbed her "the girl with the Mona Lisa smile," an intriguing attribute caused by a teenage bout with Bell's palsy. Finishing off the star triangle was Kirk Douglas, playing Mitchum's criminal boss, in only his third film. He had previously worked at RKO as Rosalind Russell's passive love interest in *Mourning Becomes Electra*. *Out of the Past* gave him his first shot at a strong character—an icy mob boss who barely breaks a sweat while batting Greer around and framing Mitchum.

Astute casting helped the film tremendously, but Duff's wisest choice may have been director Jacques Tourneur. The Frenchman had made his first big splash directing low-budget horror films for RKO producer Val Lewton, including the highly influential *Cat People*. Tourneur was a master of light and shadow, using low-keyed lighting both to generate mood and disguise inexpensive sets, many of them recycled from other films.

Although *Out of the Past* started out as a B picture, Tourneur insisted on location work, taking his cast to San Francisco, Lake Tahoe, New York, Mexico City, Acapulco, and Bridgeport, California. As a result, the film was received as a major release, generating surprisingly good notices and box office. Even though critic James Agee thought Mitchum "so sleepily self-confident with the women that when he slopes into clinches you expect him to snore in their faces," his cynical, laconic performance made him a star. Even the scandal caused by his arrest a year later for smoking marijuana couldn't halt his rise to the top. Stardom would be slower coming to Douglas, who had to wait until he landed the role of the no-good prizefighter in 1949's *Champion*. But it would never come to Greer, despite solid reviews for *Out of the Past*. In the late forties, RKO was hardly the congenial home for a young dramatic actress, and by the time she broke free to work elsewhere, the studio system was declining.

> ***"It's like lightning kissing thunder when Mitchum makes love to a girl with a gun."***
>
> ***"A MAN . . . trying to run away from his past. A WOMAN . . . trying to escape her future! When they clash, it's WILDFIRE!"***
>
> —AD LINES FOR OUT OF THE PAST

Out of the Past might have faded into obscurity after its first run had it not caught on with a new generation of critics in the seventies. With the rise of auteur criticism—which exalts the director as the primary film artist—and renewed interest in film noir, the picture acquired a devoted cult following. When the picture was remade as *Against All Odds* in 1984—with Jeff Bridges, Rachel Ward, and James Woods as the starring trio—Greer was appropriately cast as her character's mother, turning in a steely performance that brought many a viewer fond memories of the earlier, much better film.

The Philadelphia Story

"I Don't Want to be Worshipped. I Want to be Loved."

1940. CAST: Cary Grant (C. K. Dexter Haven), Katharine Hepburn (Tracy Lord), James Stewart (Macaulay Connor), Ruth Hussey (Elizabeth Imbrie), John Howard (George Kittredge), Roland Young (Uncle Willie), Virginia Weidler (Dinah Lord), Henry Daniell (Sidney Kidd). Producer: Joseph L. Mankiewicz; Director: George Cukor; Screenplay: Donald Ogden Stewart (Based on the play by Philip Barry); Photography: Joseph Ruttenberg; Music: Franz Waxman. RUNNING TIME: 112 minutes.

If anybody needed to be loved by movie audiences in 1940, it was Katharine Hepburn. After poor script choices and haughty offscreen behavior sank her career, earning her the label "box-office poison," she was in desperate need of a comeback. And that's exactly what she got when playwright Philip Barry came calling. Barry and Hepburn had been friends since her early days on Broadway, when she had understudied the female lead in his hit *Holiday,* a role she would later play on screen. Hepburn had been the first actress cast opposite Leslie Howard in Barry's *The Animal Kingdom* but had been replaced during out-of-town tryouts—some say because she was stealing the star's thunder. That 1932 play had been Barry's last hit, and he needed a comeback as well. He offered Hepburn two ideas he was working on, a play about a daughter getting to know her father years after her parents' divorce and another about a haughty society girl forced to face her frailties when tabloid reporters invade her home on the eve of her second marriage. Hepburn was more enthusiastic about the latter idea, and *The Philadelphia Story* was born.

At frequent suitor Howard Hughes's suggestion, Hepburn bought the film rights for $25,000 before starting rehearsals. She also bought an interest in the play, partly because the producers were in financial trouble. She even accepted a percentage of the box office in lieu of salary. When the play became a Broadway hit, Hepburn was back on top. Naturally, Hollywood came calling. But at first, the studios only wanted the play, not Hepburn. After months of negotiation, she finally signed a contract with MGM because the studio gave her cast, script, and director approval. She also got $250,000. Warner Bros. had offered more money but with no control of the project.

Hepburn's first suggestions for costars were Clark Gable as her ex-husband, C. K. Dexter Haven,

Loving mother and ice-goddess daughter: Mary Nash and Katharine Hepburn.

"I'D LIKE TO THANK THE ACADEMY..."

***The Philadelphia Story's* two Oscars went to men named Stewart. James Stewart, who won for Best Actor, was appropriately appreciative. But the other winner, Donald Ogden Stewart, couldn't pass up the opportunity to show off his famous wit. Although in later years Stewart the writer would credit his success to the marvelous script with which he had started out, on Oscar night, he said, "There has been so much niceness here tonight, that I am happy to say that I am entirely—and solely—responsible for the success of *The Philadelphia Story*."**

and Spencer Tracy as Mac Connor, the reporter who falls for her. Gable didn't think he could play drawing-room comedy, and Tracy was desperately in need of a rest after an abortive attempt to film *The Yearling* on location in Florida. Louis B. Mayer suggested James Stewart for the reporter and director George Cukor suggested Cary Grant as Haven.

Hepburn was particularly careful in choosing a cameraman, having several come in to shoot tests of her. She picked Joseph Ruttenberg because he was the only one who made her long neck look good. For the actual filming, he developed a small light on a flexible rod, frequently carrying it around after her, just out of camera range, to fill in any shadows. When the film was finished, she sent him three cut-glass decanters from "that long string bean you made a queen."

Cukor worked quickly and efficiently, since he had only eight weeks in which to finish the film before Hepburn was due to star in the play's touring production. This still allowed for some improvisations, including a hiccuping bout Stewart developed for one of his scenes with Grant. Since the censors would not allow any implication that Stewart and Hepburn went skinny-dipping, as their characters had in the play, they had to wear bathing suits. Stewart refused to be photographed that way, stating, "If I appear in a bathing suit, I know it's the end of me. I know that, and I'm prepared to end my career, but it will also be the end of the motion picture industry." Cukor quickly substituted a long shot for his planned close-ups at the pool, and filmed the rest of the sequence with Stewart in a robe.

Shooting ended five days ahead of schedule, giving Hepburn plenty of time to make it back to the stage. Her rushes were so good, that Louis B. Mayer offered her a seven-year contract before the film was released. When it finally opened, on Christmas Day 1940, his faith was proven right. The film garnered glowing reviews and set a new box-office record at Radio City Music Hall, attracting 850,000 patrons and earning $600,000 in six weeks. *The Philadelphia Story* went on to become MGM's highest-grossing stage adaptation, bringing in well over $1 million in profits.

At awards time, Hepburn was voted Best Actress by the New York Film Critics and won an Oscar nomination, as did the film, the director, leading man Stewart, supporting actress Ruth Hussey, and the script. Although she was considered a front-runner in the race, Hepburn lost to Ginger Rogers in *Kitty Foyle*. Insiders claimed that her imperious behavior during her first reign as a star had cost her the award.

The Postman Always Rings Twice

"Their Love Was a Flame That Destroyed!"

1946. CAST: Lana Turner (Cora Smith), John Garfield (Frank Chambers), Cecil Kellaway (Nick Smith), Hume Cronyn (Arthur Keats), Leon Ames (Kyle Sackett), Audrey Totter (Madge Garland), Alan Reed (Ezra Liam Kennedy). Producer: Casey Wilson; Director: Tay Garnett; Screenplay: Harry Ruskin, Niven Busch (Based on the novel by James M. Cain); Photography: Sidney Wagner; Music: George Bassman. RUNNING TIME: 113 minutes.

Cora Smith and Frank Chambers may have burned each other with their love, but they certainly didn't do MGM any harm. Not only was *The Postman Always Rings Twice* one of the studio's biggest hits in 1946, but it made Lana Turner the decade's top sex symbol. James M. Cain's tale of love, murder, and retribution at a roadside restaurant was so hot, he even had trouble getting it published. It took a strong recommendation from Alfred A. Knopf's wife, Blanche, to get the thing into print in 1934. Hollywood was enthusiastic. Before publication, MGM had offered Cain $5,000 based on the galleys, but he held out, triggering a bidding war. Then Joe Breen entered the picture. The head of Hollywood's self-censorship organization, the Production Code Administration, decided that the story could not be adapted to his satisfaction, and suddenly the studios stopped bidding.

Fortunately, Cain's agent managed to sign an agreement with MGM for $25,000 before the studio's executives found out about Breen's objections. Unfortunately, in the rush to sell the book, the agent gave MGM complete ownership.

At first, MGM decided to try a stage version, to see if a Broadway hit wouldn't soften Breen up a bit. When the production bombed, they dropped any filming plans. Gustave Machaty, who had directed the erotic classic *Ecstasy,* came up with a treatment that passed muster in 1940, but it was so bloodless that MGM never put it into production. Then in 1944, Billy Wilder managed to get past Breen with another Cain adaptation, *Double Indemnity*. That hit revived interest in *The Postman Always Rings Twice*.

Producer Casey Wilson was best known for his work on the Andy Hardy films, but he was a great fan of Cain's work and wanted a chance to show what he could do with a more adult picture.

Lana Turner's white-hot performance may have gotten to John Garfield offscreen, too, but his bad heart kept him from following through.

He carefully presented the project to Breen so that the censor would be intrigued by the challenge of coming up with a respectable screenplay. Before long, they had solved the story's problems. Where Cain's protagonists start their adulterous affair almost as soon as they meet, the film downplays their desire for each other. With no clear indication that they are making love behind Cora's husband's back, the film gives the impression that they fall in love first. Wilson also softened the treatment of the two lawyers who conspire to get Frank and Cora off after they murder her husband, so there would be no objections from the bar association.

The story was still so hot, however, that Lana Turner turned it down. Surprisingly, it was studio head Louis B. Mayer, a noted champion of family values, who convinced her that she needed to play Cora to prove herself as a dramatic actress. John Garfield was much more enthusiastic about starring, but then he was drafted. While he was off in basic training, the studio tested the young Cameron Mitchell and almost cast him. Then Garfield was released from military service because of heart problems. When director Tay Garnett caught him playing handball during shooting, he ordered the actor to be more careful: "I don't want to louse up your fun, but I've got to finish this picture." Noting the chemistry in Garfield and Turner's love scenes, Garnett would later suggest that the only thing that kept his stars from getting involved offscreen was Garfield's bad heart.

The Postman Always Rings Twice opened to tremendous reviews, with many critics praising MGM for getting such an adult story past the Breen office. It also brought in more than $4 million at the box office. At the time, Cain praised the film vociferously. In private, however, he complained about the changes MGM had made in his book.

WHY DOES THE POSTMAN ALWAYS RING TWICE?

James M. Cain only came up with the title for* The Postman Always Rings Twice *after the book was finished. Originally, he had called it "Bar-B-Que," but his publisher didn't like that and suggested "For Love or Money." That was even worse in Cain's opinion, so he turned to screenwriter Vincent Lawrence for advice. Lawrence, recalling his own anxiety waiting for the mail after he had submitted his first play for production, not only gave Cain one of the hottest titles in publishing history but inspired a climactic speech for Frank that explained the title—sort of. For the film version, writers Harry Ruskin and Niven Busch had Garfield deliver the following: "You know, there's something about this which is like expecting a letter you're just crazy to get, and you hang around the front door for fear you might not hear 'em ring. You never realize that he always rings twice. . . . The truth is you always hear 'em ring the second time, even if you're way out in the back yard."

Pride and Prejudice

"The Middle Classes at Play"

1940. CAST: Greer Garson (Elizabeth Bennet), Laurence Olivier (Mr. Darcy), Mary Boland (Mrs. Bennet), Edna May Oliver (Lady Catherine de Brough), Maureen O'Sullivan (Jane Bennet), Ann Rutherford (Lydia Bennet), Edmund Gwenn (Mr. Bennet), Heather Angel (Kitty Bennet), Marsha Hunt (Mary Bennet). Producer: Hunt Stromberg; Director: Robert Z. Leonard; Screenplay: Aldous Huxley, Jane Murfin (Based on the play by Helen Jerome and the novel by Jane Austen); Photography: Karl Freund; Music: Herbert Stothart. RUNNING TIME: 117 minutes.

Jane Austen's brittle comic tale of class differences that almost prevent the middle-class Bennet sisters from marrying hardly seemed the kind of material at which any Hollywood studio would excel. But 1940 was the year MGM became one big drawing room, with solid adaptations of both Austen's 1813 classic and Philip Barry's elegant *The Philadelphia Story*. The studio's ability to attract top talent at every level of production turned *Pride and Prejudice* into a surprise combination of prestige picture and box-office hit.

Plans for the film started in the mid-thirties, when production chief Irving G. Thalberg bought the rights to a popular stage adaptation of the novel as a vehicle for his wife, Norma Shearer. The film was planned to follow *Marie Antoinette,* but Thalberg's sudden death in 1936 put the project on hold. When his widow finally returned to acting, Louis B. Mayer considered casting her opposite Clark Gable or Melvyn Douglas. At one point, he even penciled in plans to cast Robert Donat as Darcy with George Cukor directing. Then something went haywire. Some sources suggest that Shearer decided against the project, others that Mayer took it from her to help develop his protégée, Greer Garson. Either way, Shearer was out and Garson was in.

Cukor was still attached to the project when MGM approached Laurence Olivier about playing the male lead. Mayer's reasoning was simple. Not only did Olivier understand the high style required for the role, but his box-office allure, after hits in *Wuthering Heights* and *Rebecca,* would help expose Garson to new audiences.

Shortly before production began, Cukor was taken off the film and switched to a Joan Crawford

Laurence Olivier's cyncisim as Mr. Darcy may have horrified Greer Garson's Elizabeth Bennet, but she won out in the end, even getting the best camera angles.

picture, *Susan and God*. That did not please Olivier, particularly when the pedestrian Robert Z. Leonard took Cukor's place. Yet something about the film must have inspired Leonard, because he turned in one of his best jobs ever. Quite possibly that "something" was the finely crafted screenplay by British novelist Aldous Huxley and playwright Jane Murfin. Like Olivier, the author of *Brave New World* had accepted the assignment only for the money. He later bragged to friends that his paychecks for writing *Pride and Prejudice* supported him in the U.S. for a year, with enough left over to help out friends back in England during the war. He had recently befriended comic writer Anita Loos, herself an accomplished screenwriter. She proved a great help to him in mastering the intricacies of screenwriting, although she took no credit for the film.

Olivier was always mystified by the film's success, having convinced himself that it couldn't be any good without his choice for costar, Vivien Leigh.

"When pretty girls t-e-a-s-e-d men into marriage!"

"Five charming sisters on the gayest, merriest man-hunt that ever snared a bewildered bachelor! Girls! Take a lesson from these husband hunters!"

—AD LINES FOR PRIDE AND PREJUDICE

THOSE FABULOUS BENNET GIRLS

Heather Angel (Kitty Bennet) was a delicate ingenue in such early thirties films as **Berkeley Square** *and* **The Informer**, *then moved into supporting roles, most notably as the despondent mother in Alfred Hitchcock's* **Lifeboat**.

Mary Boland (Mrs. Bennet) was a screwball-comedy fixture, playing giddy wives in dozens of films. She had one of her best roles as the much-married Countess De Lave in **The Women**.

Greer Garson (Elizabeth Bennet) was just a few films away from becoming queen of the MGM lot in **Mrs. Miniver**, *which won her an Oscar for Best Actress. She would reign at MGM until the early fifties.*

Marsha Hunt (Mary Bennet) made her MGM debut in **Pride and Prejudice** *after years of minor roles at Paramount. Despite strong performances in* **Blossoms in the Dust** *and* **Smash-Up**, *she never became a star. Hollywood insiders have suggested she was too talented and versatile for stardom. Her career was halted by the blacklist in the late forties.*

Maureen O'Sullivan (Jane Bennet) is best known for playing Jane to Johnny Weissmuller's **Tarzan** *in MGM's first films about the jungle king and as the mother of actress Mia Farrow.*

Ann Rutherford (Lydia Bennet) played Andy Hardy's girlfriend, Polly Benedict, in most of the films in that series. She also was Scarlett O'Hara's sister Careen in **Gone With the Wind**.

The Public Enemy

"Blood and Beer"

1931. CAST: James Cagney (Tom Powers), Jean Harlow (Gwen Allen), Edward Woods (Matt Doyle), Joan Blondell (Mamie), Beryl Mercer (Ma Powers), Donald Cook (Mike Powers), Mae Clarke (Kitty). Producer: Darryl F. Zanuck; Director: William A. Wellman; Screenplay: Kubec Glasmon, John Bright, Harvey Thew (Based on the original story "Beer and Blood by Bright"); Photography: Dev Jennings. RUNNING TIME: 83 minutes.

The American gangster had started as something of a hero, a modern-day desperado defying Prohibition to bring relief to a parched America. As gang warfare spread, bootleggers and their like fell from grace, becoming, as Howard Hawks's *Scarface* labeled them, "the shame of a nation." *The Public Enemy,* one of the best and most influential pictures in Hollywood's first gangster cycle, captures that perspective perfectly. But with James Cagney in a star-making performance as Tom Powers, audiences ended up rooting for the bad guy in spite of themselves. Cagney's dynamic portrayal helped trigger a debate over crime on film that still rages today.

The Public Enemy was director William A. Wellman's brainchild. *Little Caesar* had created a new type of gangster film, in which the main hood has no redeeming qualities beyond determination and daring. When Wellman suggested a film loosely based on the exploits of Irish criminal "Deanie" O'Bannion, Warner Bros. production chief Darryl F. Zanuck turned him down. As far as he was concerned, *Little Caesar* had said it all. He changed his mind when Wellman offered him "the toughest, the most violent, most realistic picture you ever did see," but not enough to invest much time and money in it. Wellman was given a mere twenty-six days and only $151,000 to make his film.

Tom Powers might have been much less dynamic had Wellman not had a keen eye for talent. Originally, Edward Woods was cast in the lead, with Cagney as his second-in-command. Within a few days of the picture's start, Wellman knew they had made a mistake. He went to Zanuck, insisting that the two actors switch roles for the good of the picture. At first, Zanuck resisted. Like many in Hollywood at the time, Zanuck couldn't see past Cagney's height—or lack thereof—to realize how powerful he could be. Howard Hughes had recently turned him down for the role of Hildy

James Cagney and Edward Woods, after they switched roles.

Johnson, the tough-as-nails reporter in *The Front Page,* for the same reason: "He's a runt!" was his response to the actor's screen test. Besides, Woods was the son-in-law of powerful gossip columnist Louella Parsons. Taking the lead from him could spell disaster in the press. But Wellman persisted. Finally, Zanuck gave in, setting Cagney on the road to stardom.

As he would do in his other films, Cagney drew on memories of growing up in New York's

MY LIFE FOR MY ART

Filmmaking could be a dangerous proposition back when James Cagney starred in The Public Enemy. *Technicians had yet to figure out how to fake gunfire on-screen, so they used the real thing. For the film, an ace marksman named Bailey fired a real machine gun at Cagney and costar Edward Woods, actually aiming at a wall just a foot behind them. Had they been a few seconds off on their entrance, they would have been hit with a round of live ammunition.*

THE GAY DIVORCÉ

The Public Enemy's grapefruit scene was a big hit with at least one audience member, Fanny Brice's brother, Monte, who just happened to be Mae Clarke's ex-husband. The divorce must not have been a friendly one, because Monte attended the film numerous times just to see his ex-wife get it in the kisser with that high-caliber citrus. At times his laughter was so raucous people asked him to leave.

Hell's Kitchen to build the character. One of his trademark bits in the film is the way he gently taps his mother (Beryl Mercer) on the jaw with his fist, a sign of affection perfect for the character. Cagney's inspiration was his father, who would respond to his son's smart-mouthing in the same way, adding the words, "If I thought you meant that . . ."

Jean Harlow got a big career boost out of her love scenes with James Cagney.

Cast and director disagree over who came up with the film's most famous scene, in which Cagney tires of girlfriend Mae Clarke's early morning talk and pushes a grapefruit into her face. In his memoirs, Cagney claimed it was inspired by a real-life incident in which Chicago gangster Earl "Hymie" Weiss hit his girlfriend with an omelet. That was too messy to use on film, so Wellman suggested the grapefruit instead. Clarke was expecting her costar to fake it, but he really hit her with the grapefruit, triggering a surprised look that's her best moment in the film. Wellman always said he came up with the idea on the spur of the moment, because he needed something big to end the affair and didn't much like Clarke anyway.

That grapefruit would haunt Cagney for the rest of his career. Total strangers would send him a complimentary grapefruit if they saw him dining out, possibly expecting him to use it on his wife. Instead, he would simply polish off the thing before dinner, smiling genially at the disappointed fan.

The Public Enemy was a major hit, breaking box-office records set by *Little Caesar* just three months earlier. As the earlier film had done for Edward G. Robinson, *The Public Enemy* made Cagney a major star. But he never believed it would last, steadfastly refusing to settle down in Hollywood or buy anything he couldn't sell or take back to New York.

Quo Vadis?

Christians 4, Lions 7, Bottom of the 9th

1951. CAST: Robert Taylor (Marcus Vincius), Deborah Kerr (Lygia), Leo Genn (Petronius), Peter Ustinov (Nero), Patricia Laffan (Poppaea), Finlay Currie (Peter), Walter Pidgeon (Narrator). Producer: Sam Zimbalist; Director: Mervyn LeRoy; Screenplay: John Lee Mahin, S. N. Berhman, Sonya Levien (Based on the novel by Henryk Sienkiewicz); Photography: Robert Surtees, William V. Skall (Techniclor); Music: Miklos Rosza.

RUNNING TIME: 171 minutes.

With the growing threat of television in the early fifties, Hollywood studios like MGM had to think big to win back audiences quickly being lost to the small screen. The studio first met the challenge with the 1950 African adventure *King Solomon's Mines*. Their next blockbuster, 1951's *Quo Vadis?,* launched a craze for biblical epics that would dominate Hollywood filmmaking for more than a decade.

Quo Vadis? was a lavish adaptation of a turn-of-the-century bestseller about a noble Roman centurion, the beautiful slave girl who converts him to Christianity, and the wicked Emperor Nero. The story had been filmed three times before MGM got hold of it. The studio first picked up the rights in the thirties. At one point, MGM even scheduled a second-unit shoot in Italy, but World War II got in the way and the production was shelved. After the war, producer-director John Huston signed a two-picture deal with MGM and jumped at the chance to tackle the massive project. As he saw it, the story bore parallels to contemporary history, with Nero an ancient predecessor of Adolf Hitler. Studio head Louis B. Mayer wasn't too thrilled with the approach, but adopted a wait-and-see attitude. Huston cast Gregory Peck as the Roman centurion Marcus Vincius, Elizabeth Taylor as the Christian slave Lygia, and he cast his father, Walter Huston, as Saint Peter.

Trouble began when the production moved to Italy in 1949 for location shooting. The Italian film industry was still in turmoil following World War II, and union problems caused innumerable delays. When production costs rose to $2 million, with little usable footage to show for it, Mayer pulled the plug, handing the project to a pair of company men, producer Sam Zimbalist and director

Robert Taylor courted Deborah Kerr onscreen, but offscreen he kept busy with an Italian starlet, a tryst that ended his marriage to Barbara Stanwyck.

Mervyn LeRoy, dictating a more romantic, less political approach.

By this time, Peck and Taylor had become unavailable so LeRoy recast. Originally, he wanted to use unknowns, but studio executives insisted on major stars as box-office insurance. So instead of using newcomer Audrey Hepburn, LeRoy chose MGM contract star Deborah Kerr, who had just completed work on *King Solomon's Mines*. To play Marcus, they chose Robert Taylor, a dependable box-office draw who had been with MGM since his film debut in 1934. LeRoy's production was conceived on an epic scale. Though the Italian situation had not improved by the time the production returned there in 1950, he got almost everything he wanted. There were approximately two hundred speaking roles, thirty-thousand extras, and fifty-five sets, all to the tune of between $6.5 and $7.5 million, the largest budget for any movie made to that time.

For the scenes in the Coliseum, LeRoy got his assistants to round up every tame lion in Europe —one hundred twenty in all. On the first day of shooting they released the lions, but the beasts took one look at the bright, sun-filled arena and ran back into the cool shade of their cages. On the advice of the lions' trainers, LeRoy starved the animals for two weeks, but they still refused to stay in the sun. Finally, he had some dummies stuffed with raw meat. The lions tore into them, all right, but the dummies were so unconvincing that the director could only use them in a few long shots. The film's most impressive sequence was the burning of Ancient Rome. The city was constructed over a four-block area, with two miles of iron pipe used to deliver a variety of flammable liquids to key locations. Although it had only taken Nero six days to burn Rome, LeRoy and the crew labored twenty-four nights to get the sequence just right.

THEY TRIED TO TELL HER SHE'S TOO YOUNG

***It was the Los Angeles Board of Education that kept Elizabeth Taylor out of* Quo Vadis?** ***The underaged star's education fell under their jurisdiction, and they refused to allow her to leave the country again so soon after the overseas shoot for* Conspirator. *But losing* Quo Vadis? *hardly damaged her career. In fact, it may have helped, making her available for two of her biggest hits:* A Place in the Sun *and* Father of the Bride.**

For all that hard work, however, the special effects were handily upstaged by Peter Ustinov, who scored his first big hit on screen as Nero. Ustinov had tested for the role back when John Huston was still directing the picture, but he waited almost a year without any word from MGM. Then the executives told him they were still interested but thought he might be too young. He wired back, "If you wait much longer, I shall be too old. Nero died at thirty-one." They responded with another wire: "Historical research has proved you correct. The part is yours." The film's success made Ustinov an international star and brought him his first Oscar nomination for Best Supporting Actor.

And what a success *Quo Vadis?* became! It

eventually took in $25 million at the box office, ranking second only to *Gone With the Wind* as the screen's all-time box-office champion. It also picked up eight Oscar nominations, including Best Picture, but failed to win a single one. That loss was far outweighed by the film's influence. It inspired a rash of biblical epics, some successful (20th Century–Fox's *The Robe* and *David and Bathsheba,* and MGM's own *Ben-Hur*) and some laughably bad (Columbia's *Salome* and MGM's *The Prodigal*).

> ***"Ancient Rome is going to the dogs, Robert Taylor is going to the lions, and Peter Ustinov is going crazy!"***
>
> **—AD LINE FOR QUO VADIS?**

Oscar-nominated costars Leo Genn (standing left) and scene-stealer extraordinaire Peter Ustinov (seated right).

The Red Badge of Courage

"Boys with Pop Guns"

1951. CAST: Audie Murphy (Henry Fleming, The Youth), Bill Mauldin (Tom Wilson, The Loud Soldier), Douglas Dick (Lieutenant), Royal Dano (Tattered Man), John Dierkes (Jim Conklin, The Tall Soldier), Andy Devine (Fat Soldier), Arthur Hunnicutt (Bill Porter), James Whitmore (Voice). Producer: Gottfried Reinhardt; Director-Screenplay: John Huston (Based on the novel by Stephen Crane, adapted by Albert Band); Photography: Harold Rosson; Music: Bronislau Kaper. RUNNING TIME: 69 minutes.

MGM studio head Louis B. Mayer's derisive dismissal of *The Red Badge of Courage* demonstrated both the narrowness of the times and, unconsciously, an astute assessment of the film's greatest appeal to later generations. John Huston's adaptation of the Stephen Crane novel was another of Hollywood's mutilated masterpieces, shorn of more than an hour after disastrous previews. Yet it was so far ahead of its time that it is hard to fault MGM's executives for failing to get the point of a film that has only developed an audience in more recent years.

MGM producer Gottfried Reinhardt was the first to suggest a film version of the classic Civil War tale of courage and cowardice, and Huston was quick to agree to it. Directing documentaries during World War II, he had witnessed men's responses to danger on intimate terms. Afterward, he had filmed treatment sessions for shell-shocked soldiers in *Let There Be Light,* a pioneering documentary kept out of circulation by the U.S. government for almost thirty-five years. Production chief Dore Schary saw the opportunity for another prestige picture along the lines of MGM's *Battleground*. The only objections came from Mayer, who asked, "How can you make a picture of boys with funny caps and pop guns, and make people think the war they are fighting is terrible?"

Reinhardt and Schary thought the film would work commercially with an established star as Henry Fleming, the young Union soldier who panics at his first taste of battle then returns to lead his platoon to victory. Huston, however, wanted to mix new faces with nonactors, insisting that they cast Audie Murphy in the lead. Murphy had won fame as the most decorated soldier in World War II but was still relatively inexperienced as an actor. The matter finally went to arbitration, with Huston winning. Huston gave major roles to two non-actors: John Dierkes, whom he had met in London

Director John Huston got surprisingly strong performances from cartoonist Bill Mauldin and former war hero Audie Murphy.

during the war, and famed military cartoonist Bill Mauldin, cast as Murphy's closest friend.

Huston originally wanted novelist Norman Mailer to write the screenplay. When he proved unavailable, Reinhardt urged the director to try his hand at it. At the same time, Huston asked his production assistant, Albert Band, to try a straight transcription of the novel into screenplay form. When he looked at Band's work, Huston tossed his own version into the waste can.

Working with cameraman Harold Rosson, Huston modeled the film on Mathew Brady's photos of the Civil War, which had also inspired Crane's novel.

Murphy blossomed under Huston's direction, turning in one of the two best performances of his career (the other was in Huston's *The Unforgiven*). The war hero had no trouble running from battle for the camera but later clutched while shooting the scene in which he admits it to Mauldin. After almost thirty ruined takes, Mauldin told Huston, "I think Audie is having trouble confessing to a *Stars and Stripes* cartoonist that he ran from battle." Murphy agreed with his assessment, so Huston rewrote the scene, having Mauldin confess his cowardice first. After that, Murphy had no trouble.

But Huston's troubles were just beginning. He was heavily involved in preparations for *The African Queen* while *The Red Badge of Courage* was being edited, but Reinhardt and Schary tried to follow his instructions nonetheless. Mayer refused to attend the private screenings on the lot, preferring to wait for the public preview to prove him right about the picture. And it certainly did. People began walking out less than an hour into the film. They laughed at the battle and death scenes. When it was over, the preview cards were overwhelmingly negative, with some even suggesting they burn the thing. Panicked, Schary cut the two-hour-fifteen-minute film to just over one hour.

The studio sneaked the film out on the bottom of a double bill, but critics found it anyway, praising it as a major cinematic achievement.

In later life, Huston would claim that the original cut of *The Red Badge of Courage* could have been his greatest film, though he also sympathized with the executives faced with cutting it. Coming out at the height of the Korean War, in a period when Hollywood glamour was still a dominant factor on screen, it was simply the wrong picture at the wrong time. Ten years later, the film's strong visual sense and Huston's intermingling of professional and nonprofessional actors would have fit perfectly with the move towards independent production in the sixties. Twenty years later, its debunking view of wartime heroism would have matched the mood of a country still torn apart by the Vietnam War.

Little wonder, then, that the film, though a dismal failure on its initial release, has found its audience over the years. *The Red Badge of Courage* is now regarded as a classic, albeit a flawed one. Sadly, the original will never be seen. The first cut was burned by the studio, while a 16mm print of it made by Huston has long since been lost.

A STAR IS NOT BORN

Of all the performances in* The Red Badge of Courage*, Huston was probably most impressed with Royal Dano's Tattered Man, whom Murphy meets among the wounded. For his death scene, Huston simply told the actor to walk alongside Murphy and try to talk himself out of dying. The result was one of the film's best scenes and a performance many predicted would make Dano's reputation as a film actor. Huston was so impressed with his work, he hailed the man as a great actor, as good as the director's father, the great Walter Huston. Schary decided to cut the scene, however, because at the end it showed Murphy running away from a dying man, an act of cowardice he didn't think audiences would stomach. Everyone involved with the film thought Dano had been betrayed. As Dano said, "They removed the turning point of the story. It was like removing the baby and leaving the afterbirth."

Red Dust

"They Were Born to Costar"

1932. CAST: Clark Gable (Dennis Carson), Jean Harlow (Vantine), Gene Raymond (Gary Willis), Mary Astor (Barbara Willis), Donald Crisp (Guidon), Tully Marshall (Mr. Quarg). Producer-Director: Victor Fleming; Screenplay: John Lee Mahin (Based on the play by Wilson Collison); Photography: Harold G. Rosson.

RUNNING TIME: 83 minutes.

The MGM publicity department certainly had it right when they set out to sell the studio's steamy 1932 tale of love and desire on an Indonesian rubber plantation. Teamed for the first time as leading players (they had previously worked together in *The Secret Six*), Clark Gable and Jean Harlow shot to stardom.

Wilson Collison's play had been batting around Hollywood since 1927, when studio readers filed their first reports about a story most felt was too hot for the screen. The tale of a rugged, brutal plantation foreman torn between a lady of the streets and a married woman was guaranteed to raise the censors' ire, but MGM bought it nonetheless. Originally they planned the film as a Greta Garbo vehicle. With her in mind, the story was refined. The streetwalker, Vantine, became a "kept woman" who falls in love with a young plantation worker. In early treatments, Clark Gable was mentioned for the latter role, with Adolphe Menjou considered for Garbo's sophisticated sponsor. That approach to the script was ultimately abandoned.

After considering Norma Shearer or Joan Crawford to play Vantine, production chief Irving G. Thalberg decided the role would be the perfect follow-up to Jean Harlow's sizzling performance as an amoral but funny social climber in *Red-Headed Woman*. He wanted former silent heartthrob John Gilbert to costar, figuring that his polished presence would take off Harlow's rough edges while her sensuality could help reestablish the now-fallen idol at the box office. Studio head Louis B. Mayer hated Gilbert, however, and was receptive to writer John Lee Mahin's suggestion that they cast Gable instead. "He's got the eyes of a woman and the build of a bull," Mahin reasoned.

Studio technicians built a miniature rain forest, complete with the manager's cabin, on Soundstage Six, then turned it into a tropical hell. When the actors complained about how much

Director Victor Fleming (seated with script) helps bring out Jean Harlow's comedic talents while Clark Gable (center) watches.

they were sweating under the hot lights, director Victor Fleming dismissed it, reminding them that everybody sweats in the jungle.

> "He treated her rough—and she loved it!"
>
> —AD LINE FOR RED DUST

A little discomfort was a minor matter compared to the catastrophe that struck Harlow part way through production. Her husband, MGM executive Paul Bern, killed himself under mysterious circumstances. The bookish, sophisticated executive and his blonde bombshell wife were hardly born to costar. Gossips contended that the marriage had never been consummated, that Bern was impotent or homosexual or had underdeveloped sex organs. In one bizarre story, he was supposed to have been a hermaphrodite. More likely, their marriage was threatened when a common-law wife, Dorothy Minnette, arrived in Los Angeles and threatened to expose Bern as a bigamist.

For whatever reason, Bern shot himself in the early morning hours of Labor Day 1932. Studio efforts to avoid a scandal probably made matters worse. At first, Harlow was viewed as the villainess in the piece, a platinum blonde slut who had driven one of Hollywood's best minds to despair. Harlow's grief-stricken appearance at Bern's funeral began to turn public opinion in her favor. So did her insistence on returning to work a week after his death. As she explained to Thalberg, "Staying around here is driving me crazy. I've got to get busy." But when she arrived on the set, Fleming was so shocked at the deadness in her eyes that he scheduled only long shots for the first few days. On her second day back, Harlow had to do a retake of the scene in which she tantalizes Gable while bathing in a rain barrel. When she'd first done the scene, the ever-ebullient Harlow had stood up at the end to reveal her naked breasts, shouting, "Something for the boys in the lab!" Now she asked that they cut one line that struck too close to home: "I'm La Flamme, the gal that drives men mad." That was the only time she asked for special treatment because of her tragedy.

MGM's publicity department quickly caught on to the star's bravery, and by the time *Red Dust* opened later that year, Harlow was something of a national heroine. Even that wouldn't have been enough for a hit if the film hadn't been any good, but it was. Audiences delighted in her wisecracks, particularly when she scrapes the bottom of a parrot's cage and asks, "Whadda ya been eatin', cement?" And they positively swooned over her love scenes with Gable.

Jean Harlow shot retakes of her bawdy rain-barrel scene (with Clark Gable) shortly after her husband's suicide.

Ride the High Country

"All I Want Is to Enter My House Justified"

1962. CAST: Randolph Scott (Gil Westrum), Joel McCrea (Steve Judd), Mariette Hartley (Elsa Knudsen), Ronald Starr (Heck Longtree), R. G. Armstrong (Joshua Knudsen), Edgar Buchanan (Judge Tolliver), L. Q. Jones (Sylvus Hammond), Warren Oates (Henry Hammond). Producer: Richard E. Lyons; Director: Sam Peckinpah; Screenplay: N. B. Stone Jr.; Photography: Lucien Ballard (CinemaScope, Metrocolor); Music: George Bassman.

RUNNING TIME: 94 minutes.

By the time *Ride the High Country* finished filming, aging western hero Steve Judd wasn't the only one who could "enter his house justified," as he put it in one of the film's most famous lines. So could stars Randolph Scott and Joel McCrea and director Sam Peckinpah. The actors capped their careers as western legends with performances playing two aging gunfighters going out in a blaze of glory as they transport gold from a remote mining town to the bank. In only his second feature, the director helped usher the western into a new era while also paying tribute to his father, one of the last great frontiersmen.

The project started with producer Richard E. Lyons, who saw Randolph Scott as a natural choice to star. But Lyons initially asked him to play Judd, the more honest of the two partners. Scott liked the script but wouldn't do it unless he had just the right costar. If Lyons could get Joel McCrea to come out of retirement to play Gil Westrum, who gives in to greed and tries to steel the gold, Scott would make the film. McCrea liked the script, too, but not the role. Having played only one villain in his career, he wasn't about to tarnish his image. Lyons took Scott to lunch to discuss the change, but before he could bring it up, Scott asked if he could play Westrum. He was tired of playing the hero and wanted a change of pace.

With his stars in place, Lyons went in search of a director. After looking at some episodes of *The Westerner* and *Rifleman,* two television series directed by the young Sam Peckinpah, Lyons made him an offer. Peckinpah rewrote the script and suggested a new title, *Ride the High Country* (the film would retain its original title, *Guns in the Afternoon,* in England), and asked to make one other major change. In the original, Scott's character was killed in the climactic shoot-out. Peckinpah

Randolph Scott and Joel McCrea take the West by storm one more time.

thought it would work better if McCrea were killed, leaving a reformed Scott to take his place and bring in the gold safely.

In reworking the script, Peckinpah drew on his memories of growing up in the West. The mining town of Coarsegold became a mirror of the town where his father had worked as a judge, and Steve Judd became so much like Peckinpah's father that family members wept at the film's previews. The final shot of McCrea looking off into the mountains with his back to the camera was inspired by the last photo ever taken of the director's father. Judd's statement of his moral code, "All I want is to enter my house justified," was a paraphrase of the father's favorite Bible verse.

For the rest of the cast, Peckinpah drew on actors he'd worked with in television, including L. Q. Jones, R. G. Armstrong, and James Drury. He was so impressed with newcomer Mariette

Hartley that he cast her for her film debut over the objections of MGM executives who wanted a contract starlet in the role of Elsa Knudsen. It helped that Hartley had just had her hair cut short for a stage production of St. Joan. As she would reveal later, her own family situation—both her parents were alcoholics and her husband was physically abusive—gave her an instant rapport with the character, a sheltered child living with an abusive, religious fanatic father.

The film wrapped four days over schedule and about $50,000 over budget, partly because Peckinpah had decided to film the final shootout from every conceivable angle, one hundred fifty setups in all. Unlike other great directors, who preferred to shoot a film so it could only be edited in one way, Peckinpah wanted to leave himself as many options as possible. Yet when the film got back to MGM, Margaret Booth, the veteran head of the editing department, declared the picture uncuttable—a pronouncement that turned out to the film's advantage. Rather than scrap the project on Booth's say-so, MGM production head Siegal let Peckinpah cut it himself. Siegel loved the rough cut, but before they could prepare the final cut, MGM underwent a change in management. Siegel was out, and Joseph Vogel, formerly head of the studio's East Coast business offices, had decided to run the studio as well. When he screened *Ride the High Country,* he fell asleep. On waking, he declared it the worst film he'd ever seen. When Peckinpah protested, Vogel barred him from the lot. Fortunately, Lyons was still on his director's side. He supervised the final cut carefully, even calling Peckinpah up to play the sound mixes for him over the phone. At the studio preview, the audience stood up and cheered.

Ride the High Country has remained a favorite among film critics and western fans. Its revisionist view of the West—combining the lonesome morality of heroes like Judd, the squalor of life in the mining camps, and the cynical view of civilization's encroachment on the frontier—gave it a special appeal to new generations of film fans. The film marked the end of the road for Scott and McCrea, with the former retiring from pictures and the latter making just one more film. For Peckinpah, it was the start of a brilliant, if controversial, career.

THE PECKINPAH CONNECTION

Like John Ford before him, director Sam Peckinpah created a virtual stock company of cast and crew members who traveled with him from one film to another. For many, **Ride the High Country** *was the start of their association with the controversial director:*

R. G. Armstrong (Joshua Knudsen)—**Major Dundee, The Ballad of Cable Hogue, Pat Garrett,** *and* **Billy the Kid**

Lucien Ballard (Photography)—**The Wild Bunch, The Ballad of Cable Hogue, Junior Bonner,** *and* **The Getaway**

L. Q. Jones (Sylvus Hammond)—**Major Dundee, The Wild Bunch, The Ballad of Cable Hogue, Pat Garrett,** *and* **Billy the Kid**

Warren Oates (Henry Hammond)—**Major Dundee, The Wild Bunch,** *and* **Bring Me the Head of Alfredo Garcia**

Rose Marie

"When I'm Calling You-ou-ou-ou-ou-ou-ou"

1936. CAST: Jeanette MacDonald (Marie de Flor), Nelson Eddy (Sergeant Bruce), James Stewart (John Flower), Reginald Owen (Myerson), David Nivens [later Niven] (Teddy), Allan Jones (Romeo/Mario Cavaradossi). Producer: Hunt Stromberg; Director: W. S. Van Dyke II; Screenplay: Francis Goodrich, Albert Hackett, Alice Duer Miller (Based on the operetta by Otto A. Harbach, Oscar Hammerstein II, Rudolf Friml, Herbert Stothart); Photography: William Daniels; Music: Friml, Stothart; Musical Director: Stothart. RUNNING TIME: 110 minutes.

MGM sent out a call to romantics everywhere with its second and most profitable teaming of Jeanette MacDonald and Nelson Eddy. Although some at the studio dubbed them "The Iron Butterfly" and "The Singing Capon"—in reference to her steely business sense and his stiffness as an actor—their fans adored them.

MacDonald was already a star when she reached MGM, having appeared in several lavish Paramount musicals, the best of them directed by Ernst Lubitsch. MGM bought the rights to *I Married an Angel* for her studio debut, but when censors at the Breen Office refused to pass the story of a deflowered seraph, they put her into *The Cat and the Canary* instead. Then Metropolitan Opera star Grace Moore dropped out of *The Merry Widow* over a contract dispute, and studio head Loius B. Mayer cast McDonald opposite Maurice Chevalier in the risqué Lubitsch operetta. For her next project, the studio picked Victor Herbert's *Naughty Marietta* but needed a leading man who could match both her classical singing and her sparkling personality.

Mayer's secretary, Ida Koverman, had spotted Nelson Eddy when he got eighteen encores from the audience at his Los Angeles concert debut in 1933. She convinced her boss to sign him to a contract, but at first he just had brief singing spots, most notably in the Joan Crawford musical *Dancing Lady*, which also introduced Fred Astaire. Koverman suggested Eddy to Mayer for *Naughty Marietta;* Mayer in turn passed him on to producer Hunt Stromberg. Mayer wanted Eddy to dye his hair black. When Stromberg protested, Mayer demanded, "Show me a blonde leading man." "I will when this picture is over," was Stromberg's answer.

> **"A Pampered Pet of the Opera Who Meets a Rugged Canadian Mountie!"**
> —AD LINE FOR ROSE MARIE

Naughty Marietta was a huge hit, with audiences swooning as MacDonald and Eddy crooned to "Ah, Sweet Mystery of Life." Mayer immediately ordered the story department to come up with a new vehicle for his new stars, but he also decided to put Eddy into a property to which they already owned the rights, *Rose Marie*. The Otto Harbach operetta had been filmed as a silent in 1928 with Joan Crawford and James Murray in the leads. Back then, the plot had stayed closer to the original tale about a French-Canadian gamine torn between a prospector and a Mountie. The screenwriters created a new story about a runaway opera singer searching for her criminal brother in the Canadian Rockies. Mayer's first choice for the female lead was Grace Moore. When she couldn't free up time from her busy concert schedule,

Recently published rumors have suggested that Jeanette MacDonald and Nelson Eddy were offscreen lovers.

TOGETHER FOREVER

1935—*Naughty Marietta*—Jeanette MacDonald and Nelson Eddy team for the first time, to tremendous box-office results.

1936—*Rose Marie*—With their second teaming, the pair score their biggest hit ever.

1937—*Maytime*—Nelson and Jeanette share a lifetime of sorrow as singers kept apart by fate, but John Barrymore, as Jeanette's jealous husband, steals the show.

1938—*Girl of the Golden West*—Generally regarded as the weakest MacDonald-Eddy film, this adaptation of the David Belasco stage hit bears little resemblance to Puccini's opera.

—*Sweethearts*—MacDonald shows her ability to deliver a barbed line in this tale of a bickering stage team, cowritten by Dorothy Parker. This was MGM's first Technicolor film.

1940—*New Moon*—The team returns to the New Orleans setting of their first film to share two of their most popular duets, "Wanting You" and "Lover Come Back."

1940—*Bitter Sweet*—MacDonald and Eddy's popularity starts to fade when they star in this Technicolor rendition of the popular Noel Coward operetta, with most of the Coward songs cut out.

1942—*I Married an Angel*—MGM finally gets the Richard Rogers–Lorenz Hart musical past the censors, but nobody seems to care as Nelson and Jeanette team for the last time.

1957—*The Gordon MacRae Show*—After only a few radio appearances together over the years, romance returns to the high Cs when MacDonald and Eddy reunite on television.

1958—*Jeanette MacDonald and Nelson Eddy Favorites*—As a follow-up to their reunion, the team record some of their most popular numbers. The album goes gold in 1967.

MacDonald inherited another role from her. It would be the role that changed her career.

Rose Marie shot on location near Lake Tahoe during the summer of 1935. Director W. S. Van Dyke—nicknamed "One-Shot" for his rapid filming methods—was almost stymied by Eddy. He would later say that he could make anything act, human or animal, except Nelson Eddy.

In addition to cementing MacDonald and Eddy's popularity as a screen team, *Rose Marie* featured two other screen newcomers. James Stewart, in only his second film, played MacDonald's criminal brother, earning solid reviews for his one scene toward the end of the film. Less noticeable was David Niven, billed as "Nivens," playing one of MacDonald's suitors back in the big city.

For all the beautiful music Eddy and MacDonald made together, the team barely got along. But that couldn't diminish the magic spell they wove in six more films. For their fans, their personal difficulties became just an ironic footnote to two careers linked from the first moment they appeared on screen together.

San Francisco

"Open Your Golden Gates"

1936. CAST: Clark Gable (Blackie Norton), Jeanette MacDonald (Mary Blake), Spencer Tracy (Father Tim Mullin), Jack Holt (Jack Burley), Ted Healy (Matt), Jessie Ralph (Maisie Burley). Producers: John Emerson, Bernard H. Hyman; Director: W.S. Van Dyke II; Screenplay: Anita Loos (Based on a story by Robert Hopkins); Photography: Oliver T. Marsh; Music: Edward D. Wood. RUNNING TIME: 115 minutes.

MGM opened the gates to its best box office since the coming of sound when the studio put together two top stars and Hollywood's finest actor for this rousing action romance. For those who love San Francisco, the city possesses a magical hold that keeps calling people back. It was this magic that inspired MGM writers Anita Loos and Robert Hopkins to create a screenplay set on the eve of the great earthquake and fire of 1906. Both had lived in the city, and Hopkins used to delight Loos with stories about his days as a Western Union messenger working along the Barbary Coast. From his reminiscences, they created the story of a minister's daughter who gets a saloon singing job and falls for the owner. They even threw in a local priest to trigger the leading man's redemption through suffering.

Loos showed the screenplay to the studio's top singer at the time, Jeanette MacDonald, who took it to production chief Irving G. Thalberg. Thalberg loved the screenplay and agreed with her choice of leading man, Clark Gable. Only Gable didn't want any part of his new leading lady. For one thing, he didn't want to stand around while she sang at him. As he told Thalberg, "It's one thing if you have a voice and can sing back and defend yourself. It's another if you don't, and I don't." In addition, MacDonald simply wasn't his type of woman. He considered her too ladylike and had heard that she was a bit of a prima donna. Even when Loos rewrote the script to build up his part and make the character even more masculine, he refused. Then MGM executive Eddie Mannix informed him that MacDonald had gone off salary rather than be caught in the middle of another film, should Gable decide to make *San Francisco.* That impressed Gable, who was notorious for his penny-pinching, and he finally accepted the role. But it didn't make him go easy on

CALL ME JEANETTE

In the third book of that other great paean to San Francisco, Armistead Maupin's* Tales of the City *series, the author explains how the City by the Bay can have two theme songs. According to one of the characters, Michael Tolliver, there are two types of people living in San Francisco, Tonys and Jeanettes. The Tonys consider "I Left My Heart in San Francisco" the city's theme. The Jeanettes prefer "San Francisco." Although nobody in the book says which of these is the superior viewpoint, the suggestion that Tonys keep pet rocks and call women "chicks" would suggest that they lack the timeless, classical taste associated with being a Jeanette.

MacDonald. Before shooting their first love scene, he chewed garlic just to needle her. The result was a believable look of shock from MacDonald that fit the scene perfectly.

Gable wasn't the only actor who balked at his role in *San Francisco*. Spencer Tracy's father had wanted him to become a priest, and the actor had never gotten over the feeling that he had disappointed his old man. As he would two years later, when asked to play Father Flanagan in *Boys Town,* Tracy turned the role down. Director W. S. Van Dyke had to beg him to take the part, insisting that only Tracy could give the film the humanity it needed to become a hit. Once Tracy agreed to play Father Tim Mullin, he struck up an instant rapport with his male costar. Gable admired and envied Tracy's acting abilities. Tracy felt the same about Gable's star power. The two would reteam twice more, for *Test Pilot* and *Boom Town*.

During shooting, movie pioneer D. W. Griffith visited MGM and asked if he might direct a scene. Van Dyke had started his career as an assistant on *Intolerance* and was only too happy to oblige. Although there is no record of which scene or scenes Griffith directed, historians have suggested that some of the earthquake sequences, particularly the use of a spinning wagon wheel that finally stops as the tremors end, bear the mark of the master.

San Francisco became Thalberg's highest-grossing movie since *The Big Parade,* showing a profit of more than $2 million. It garnered four Oscar nominations—including Best Picture, Best Director, and Best Actor (Tracy)—winning for Douglas Shearer's masterful sound effects. After just one year at MGM, Tracy was clearly on the road to stardom with his performance as Father Mullin.

> ***"San Francisco, guardian of the Golden Gate, stands today as a queen among seaports . . . industrious . . . mature . . . respectable . . . but perhaps she dreams of the queen and city she was . . . splendid and sensuous, vulgar and magnificent . . . that perished suddenly with a cry still heard in the hearts of those who know her at exactly 5:13 AM, April 18, 1906."***
>
> **—INTRODUCTORY TITLE FOR SAN FRANCISCO**

With her stirring rendition of the film's title song, Jeanette MacDonald would find herself permanently welcome in San Francisco.

She Wore a Yellow Ribbon

"Lest We Forget"

1949. CAST: John Wayne (Captain Nathan Brittles), Joanne Dru (Olivia Dandridge), John Agar (Lieutenant Flint Cahill), Ben Johnson (Sergeant Tyree), Harry Carey Jr. (Lieutenant Ross Pennell), Victor McLaglen (Sergeant Quincannon), Mildred Natwick (Mrs. Abby Alshard). Producers: John Ford, Merian C. Cooper; Director: John Ford; Screenplay: Frank Nugent, Laurence Stallings (Based on the stories "War Story" and "The Big Hunt" by James Warner Bellah); Photography: Winton C. Hoch, Charles P. Boyle (Technicolor); Music: Richard Hageman.

RUNNING TIME: 103 minutes.

Director John Ford never considered his three films about the U.S. cavalry a trilogy, though they all starred Wayne and were all adapted from stories by James Warner Bellah. The "trilogy" title was added later by cinema historians struck by the similar themes in the three films. In many ways, actually, *She Wore a Yellow Ribbon* does not fit in with the other two pictures: *Fort Apache* and *Rio Grande*. It is the only one of the three in color, and while the other two cast Wayne as the same character, cavalry officer Kirby York, *She Wore a Yellow Ribbon* places him in a character role, the first serious acting challenge Ford had ever offered his most frequent star.

When they started working together in the last days of silent pictures, Ford had not thought much of Wayne's acting, describing him as "a lucky stiff with a minimum of talent but a lot of drive in his acting." Then he saw him in director Howard Hawks's *Red River,* in which the Duke more than held his own against fiery young star Montgomery Clift. "I didn't know the son-of-a-bitch could act," was Ford's assessment of the picture. That revelation inspired him to cast Wayne in his first character role, as the gentle but tough sixty-year-old cavalry captain who helps avoid a war with the Indians in the last days before his retirement.

Wayne's performance as Captain Nathan Brittles pointed the way to the roles he would play as he grew older: rugged men of the West, with a barely concealed soft spot beneath the surface. But the film almost cost him dearly. During the scene in which he leads his men on a raid of a nearby Indian camp, the cinch belt on Wayne's saddle came loose and he fell from his horse. The fall knocked him

John Wayne (right) faces his first character role, with the help of the John Ford "stock company": Victor McLaglen, Ben Johnson, and George O'Brien.

out in the middle of about fifty other horses. Fortunately, one of the wranglers on the crew headed off the stampede and saved his life.

Ford had a particularly difficult time working with cinematographer Winton C. Hoch. Often the actors had to stand baking in the hot sun of Utah's Monument Valley while Hoch fiddled with lights and other equipment to get just the right shot. During one sequence, the sky clouded over as a thunderstorm moved in. Hoch wanted to call it a day, but Ford insisted he get the shot of the cavalry crossing the plains. The cameraman was so angry he lodged an official complaint with his union. Some historians have claimed that Hoch was worried about the danger of shooting in a lightning storm. In truth, he simply did not want to take the blame if the loss of light ruined the shot. The result, however, was a spectacular vista that helped Hoch win the Academy Award for Best Color Cinematography.

> "So here they are, the dog-faced soldiers, the regulars, the fifty-cents-a-day professionals, riding the outposts of a nation. From Fort Reno to Fort Apache, from Sheridan to Stark, they were all the same. Men in dirty shirt blue, and only a cold page in the history books to mark their passing. But wherever they rode, and whatever they fought for, that place became the United States."
>
> —CLOSING NARRATION FROM SHE WORE A YELLOW RIBBON

Despite Hoch's slowness, Ford managed to complete *She Wore a Yellow Ribbon* ahead of schedule and under budget. The film was finished in just thirty-one days at a cost of about $1.3 million (it had been budgeted at $1.8). Although it received only mixed reviews, later critics would hail it as one of Ford's masterpieces. Audiences didn't need the perspective of time to appreciate the picture. *She Wore a Yellow Ribbon* grossed $5.2 million on its initial release.

Joanne Dru and John Wayne, showcased in one of cameraman Winton C. Hoch's Oscar-winning compositions.

The Shop Around the Corner

"Dear Friend"

1940. CAST: James Stewart (Alfred Kralik), Margaret Sullavan (Klara Novak), Frank Morgan (Huto Matuschek), Joseph Schildkraut (Ferencz Vardas), Sara Haden (Flora), Felix Bressart (Perovitch). Producer-Director: Ernst Lubitsch; Screenplay: Samson Raphaelson (Based on the play *Parfumerie* by Nikolaus Laszlo); Photography: William Daniels; Music: Werner R. Heymann. RUNNING TIME: 97 minutes.

Like a letter from an old friend, *The Shop Around the Corner*—with its timeless tale of coworkers who hate each other without realizing they're romantic pen pals—is the kind of movie fans return to again and again. Its gentle comedy about simple working folk was made particularly touching by the warm, sincere performances of costars James Stewart and Margaret Sullavan. Yet it was the last thing audiences of the day would have expected from the master of continental sophistication, director Ernst Lubitsch.

Lubitsch had signed with MGM to direct *Ninotchka* and one other film. For the second picture he chose a Hungarian play about life among the employees at a perfume shop. Both Lubitsch and writer Samson Raphaelson drew on experience to create the script. The director had worked in his father's tailor shop during his youth. Raphaelson had helped out in a shop during the World's Columbian Exposition in Chicago just before the turn of the century. With an uncredited polish by playwright Ben Hecht, one of Hollywood's most sought-after rewrite men, they created a simple tale, now set in a department store. Previously, Lubitsch's leading men had been suave continental charmers, but this time that type became the villain of the piece—the philandering salesman played by Joseph Schildkraut—and he cast James Stewart as the lead, precisely because the young actor was the antithesis of the old-time matinee idol.

Stewart was thrilled to be working with the great director but even more excited about another chance to team with one of his best friends and favorite leading ladies, Margaret Sullavan. The two had started out in the theater in the late twenties, and some biographers have suggested that unrequited love for Sullavan was the reason Stewart didn't marry until 1949. Yet their friendship couldn't save him from Sullavan's famous temper. In one scene, the secret pen pals are supposed to

meet for dinner. Arriving at the restaurant late, Stewart realizes that Sullavan is his "dear friend" at Box #237. He approaches her at the restaurant but keeps that discovery a secret. For some reason, the actor simply couldn't wrap his mouth around the dialogue. After he ruined more than twenty takes, Sullavan threw one of her feared tantrums and stormed off the set. As she usually did, she returned in a few hours, all smiles, charming everybody into forgetting that anything had happened.

The Shop Around the Corner was a surprise hit, returning international profits of $380,000 at a time when the European market was drying up. American audiences adored the touching love story and the chance to escape for ninety-seven minutes from the frightening news about what was really going on in Europe. Years later, Lubitsch would cite the picture as the most human of all his films. Stewart claimed *The Shop Around the Corner* as one of his favorites. Coupled with his earlier success in 1939's *Mr. Smith Goes to Washington* and his Oscar for *The Philadelphia Story,* it played a key role in making him a major star.

CONTINENTAL GLAMOUR?

For her first scene in The Shop Around the Corner, Margaret Sullavan bought a simple dress off the rack for $1.98, but that was not enough for director Ernst Lubitsch. Departing from the glamorous films that had made his name, he ordered the dress left out in the sun to fade and had it altered to fit poorly.

SHOPPING AROUND

The Shop Around the Corner's plot would seem to be a foolproof crowd pleaser, at least as evidenced by its two reincarnations. At MGM, the story was remade in 1949 as a turn-of-the-century musical. In the Good Old Summertime starred Judy Garland as the troublesome sales clerk and Van Johnson as her secret pen pal and public enemy. It even featured the film debut of Garland's daughter, Liza Minnelli, in the final sequence showing the two leads living happily ever after. The story hit Broadway in 1963 as She Loves Me, a musical with songs by Jerry Bock and Sheldon Harnick. She Loves Me failed to become a hit, but it lived on the hearts of theater lovers, inspiring a popular revival in 1993 that brought Boyd Gaines a Tony Award for his performance in the leading role.

Ernst Lubitsch (opposite, center) directs the scene in which James Stewart discovers that he and Margaret Sullavan are secret pen pals.

Singin' in the Rain

"What a Glorious Feeling!"

1952. CAST: Gene Kelly (Don Lockwood), Donald O'Connor (Cosmo Brown), Debbie Reynolds (Kathy Selden), Jean Hagen (Lina Lamont), Millard Mitchell (R. F. Simpson, Studio Head), Rita Moreno (Zelda Zanders), Cyd Charisse (Dancer), Kathleen Freeman (Phoebe Dinsmore, Diction Coach). Producer: Arthur Freed; Directors: Gene Kelly, Stanley Donen; Screenplay: Adolph Green, Betty Comden (Suggested by the song "Singin' in the Rain"); Photography: Harold Rosson (Technicolor); Musical Director: Lennie Hayton; Music and Lyrics: Arthur Freed, Nacio Herb Brown, Betty Comden, Adolph Green, Robert Edens, Al Hoffman, Al Goodhart. RUNNING TIME: 103 minutes.

S*ingin' in the Rain* is the kind of timeless feel-good movie that still sends fans dancing through the streets after screenings. It all started in 1949 when the dean of Hollywood musical producers, Arthur Freed, decided it was time to make another songbook musical in the tradition of *Easter Parade*. Whereas that film had been built around the work of Broadway tunesmith Irving Berlin, this new feature would be inspired by the work of a songwriter Freed knew particularly well: himself. Before he had signed on as an MGM executive, Freed and his partner, composer Nacio Herb Brown, had written a string of hits, including "You Were Meant for Me," "You Are My Lucky Star," and, of course, "Singin' in the Rain." Freed didn't want to produce an autobiography, so he set to work looking for a story that could incorporate his and Brown's best numbers. He turned the project over to Betty Comden and Adolph Green, who had scored with scripts for *Good News* and *On the Town,* also supplying lyrics for the latter. After listening to several selections from the Freed songbook, they decided to do a story set during the transition from silent to talking pictures.

Their first plot concerned a two-bit western actor who becomes a singing cowboy, with Howard Keel mentioned for the lead. They also looked at other films of the period, including such Jean Harlow hits as *Platinum Blonde* and *Bombshell*. Then they came up with the idea of a song-and-dance man who had become a silent-screen swashbuckler. With the arrival of talking pictures he would revert to his roots to become a musical star. With that change in plots, they decided to

Donald O'Connor, Debbie Reynolds, and Gene Kelly share a "Good Morning."

WHATEVER BECAME OF . . .

Jean Hagen was a natural choice to play Lina Lamont, the vain, dimwitted silent star threatened by the coming of sound. Comden and Green had modeled the character on routines they had worked up with Judy Holliday back when they were part of a satirical group called The Revuers in New York. By the time **Singin' in the Rain** *started shooting, Holliday had become a star in* **Born Yesterday** *and wasn't available for the supporting role. So they turned to Hagen, Holliday's understudy during* **Born Yesterday's** *Broadway run. She almost stole the film with her dumb blonde routine, even winning an Oscar nomination for Best Supporting Actress.*

But Hagen may just have been too versatile for Hollywood stardom, as effective in dramatic films like **The Asphalt Jungle** *as she was in* **Singin' in the Rain.** *She spent three years playing Danny Thomas's wife on* **The Danny Thomas Show,** *winning two Emmy nominations, but she grew so dissatisfied with the role's limitations that they killed off her character. After that, Hagen had a hard time getting her career back on track. A long illness confined her to a nursing home in the sixties, but she came back for one more performance, a strong character turn as the title character's landlady in the television movie* **Alexander: The Other Side of Dawn.** *Because the character was a retired actress, the set for her apartment was appropriately decorated with glamour portraits from Hagen's days as an MGM star.*

approach Gene Kelly, even though he was busily involved in preparations for *An American in Paris*.

Kelly loved the idea and agreed to codirect with Stanley Donen, with whom he'd done *On the Town*. Freed suggested giving Kelly a best friend in the film, to be played by Oscar Levant. The writers and directors then decided that they really needed another male dancer in the film, so they convinced Freed to borrow Donald O'Connor from Universal. The part of Cosmo Brown would turn out to be the best in his career. For leading lady, Freed pushed for a young actress who had only recently started at MGM. Debbie Reynolds had scored with small

Gene Kelly cavorts through one of MGM's stock street sets for the classic title number. *Opposite:* Cyd Charisse finally got a leg up on stardom with her provocative appearance in the "Broadway Melody Ballet."

roles in *Three Little Words* and *Two Weeks with Love*. Freed felt it was time to try her in a starring role, even though it took some convincing to get the MGM brass to accept the idea.

An inexperienced dancer, Reynolds had to study tap dancing rigorously to be able to keep up with her costars. After they finished the number, Reynolds had to be carried to her dressing room. She had burst the blood vessels in her feet. O'Connor did his share of suffering as well. For the "Make 'em Laugh" number, Kelly asked O'Connor to revive a trick he'd done as a young dancer, running up a wall and turning a somersault. The number was so strenuous that O'Connor, who was smoking four packs a day at the time, went into the hospital for a week after its completion. When he got out, he was told that there had been a problem with the film, and he'd have to do it all over again.

Originally, Comden and Green had indicated that the film would have a big musical finale, but nobody knew what it would be. Kelly didn't want to do another ballet, having used the device in both *On the Town* and the recently finished *An American in Paris*. But when the latter film became a big hit, he decided to go for another number. The fourteen-minute ballet rehearsed for four weeks, then shot for two. Although originally budgeted at $80,000, the number came in at $600,000, almost one fifth of the film's $2.5 million cost. The expense was quickly forgotten, however, when the film grossed $7.6 million on its initial release.

BACK TO THE PAST

***Singin' in the Rain's* production crew dressed the film's sets with relics from MGM's earlier days. For Kelly's mansion, they used furnishings from the Greta Garbo–John Gilbert silent classic *Flesh and the Devil*. Debbie Reynolds's car in the film was the jalopy from the old Andy Hardy films. When they couldn't find all the vintage cameras and sound recording equipment they needed, they built duplicates from specifications in the studio's files and behind-the-scenes photos.**

Costume designer Oliver Plunkett drew on Hollywood history, too, particularly for Lina Lamont's outrageous wardrobe. Most of her gowns were copies of dresses that he had designed for actress Lilyan Tashman in the early thirties. In fact, they were the same outfits that had helped establish Tashman's reputation as one of Hollywood's best-dressed women.

Tarzan, the Ape Man

Swinging to Stardom

1932. CAST: Johnny Weissmuller (Tarzan), Neil Hamilton (Harry Holt), Maureen O'Sullivan (Jane Parker), C. Aubrey Smith (James Parker), Doris Lloyd (Mrs. Cutten), Forrester Harvey (Beamish). Producer: Irving G. Thalberg; Director: W. S. Van Dyke II; Screenplay: Cyril Hume, Ivor Novello (Based on the characters created by Edgar Rice Burroughs); Photography: Harold Rosson, Clyde De Vinna. RUNNING TIME: 99 minutes.

In 1932, Johnny Weissmuller became a Hollywood anomaly, the only star to build his career almost entirely around a single role. Weissmuller was Tarzan, a character he played in eleven films over a sixteen-year span. He made only two other pictures outside the Tarzan series before moving on to the low-budget Jungle Jim films at Columbia.

Ralph Rothmond, the general manager of Edgar Rice Burroughs, Inc., gave MGM production chief Irving G. Thalberg the idea of tackling a Tarzan film. The studio had just scored a big hit with *Trader Horn,* an African adventure featuring the first location scenes with sound ever shot on that continent. The production team had brought back about two hundred thousand feet of usable footage, and there was still a great deal left over. Rothmond suggested the new subject as a means of capitalizing on *Trader Horn*'s success and recycling the African backgrounds.

British writer Cyril Hume went to work on the script, initially creating a story in which Trader Horn meets Tarzan while on the trail of a lost African tribe. When the studio decided to drop Horn from the storyline, they substituted the search for the elephant graveyard and put British explorer James Parker in charge of the expedition.

Having directed *Trader Horn* and built a solid reputation for speedy work, W. S. Van Dyke was assigned to make the first Tarzan film. The most difficult part of the job was finding the perfect star. Among those considered were Joel McCrea, Clark Gable, Charles Bickford, and two future Tarzans, Olympic swimming champion Buster Crabbe and the gold medalist in the shot-put, Herman Brix.

Weissmuller was perfect for the role. The twenty-eight-year-old swimmer had won five gold

Maureen O'Sullivan and Johnny Weissmuller enjoy the seclusion of jungle life, despite the presence of the film crew.

medals in the 1924 and 1928 Olympics, in addition to sixty-seven world and fifty-two national titles. He had broken 174 individual records, including every free-style record from one-hundred yards to the half-mile.

There was only one problem. Weissmuller was under exclusive contract to BVD—the underwear people. They worked out a deal with MGM, releasing him from his contract in exchange for MGM's providing its top stars—everyone from Greta Garbo to Marie Dressler—for appearance in BVD ads. The studio signed Weissmuller at $500 a week. Casting Jane was another problem. Nobody seemed to have the right blend of sophistication and innocence. Then somebody got hold of new photos of Irish-born Maureen O'Sullivan. The portraits won her a contract at MGM, with Jane as her first role there.

Van Dyke proved true to his nickname—"One-Shot Woody"—by finishing *Tarzan, the Ape Man* in only eight weeks at a cost of just over $652,000. Added to the stock footage from Africa were scenes shot in the then-undeveloped Toluca Lake region north of Hollywood. The only production delay occurred when the trainers of two rhinos being used in the film asked if the animals could bathe in the lake. It took them three weeks to get the animals out of the water while Van Dyke feverishly shot around them as much as possible.

Tarzan, the Ape Man was a huge hit on its initial release, bringing in almost $1 million in profits. It also made Weissmuller one of Hollywood's hottest young stars. Censors around the nation, however, objected to the scanty costumes, not to mention Tarzan and Jane's common-law marriage. And as the Tarzan series progressed, O'Sullivan felt progressively stifled by her identification with Jane. She demanded that the character be killed off at the end of *Tarzan Finds a Son* (1939), but when audiences objected, the studio changed the film's final scene to bring her back. They lured her into making *Tarzan's New York Adventure* in 1942 only by promising to let her wear the latest fashions for the couple's trip to America. By then, MGM had pretty much tired of the series as well and sold it to RKO. Weissmuller and Johnny Sheffield, who played Boy, went along for the ride, but O'Sullivan decided to retire from the screen to devote more time to her family.

TARZAN YELLS

Carol Burnett still delights fans with her imitation of the legendary Tarzan yell, but that's more than Johnny Weissmuller ever could have done. Although his voice was the starting point for the jungle king's famous cry, the final product was the work of MGM's pioneering sound technician Douglas Shearer, brother of leading lady Norma Shearer. Shearer amplified Weissmuller's yell, even adding a few seconds played backward. His handiwork has stayed with the character for almost fifty years.

The Thin Man

The Perfect Couple

1934. CAST: William Powell (Nick Charles), Myrna Loy (Nora Charles), Maureen O'Sullivan (Dorothy Wynant), Nat Pendleton (Lieutenant John Guild), Minna Gombell (Mimi Wynant), Porter Hall (Mac Cauley), Cesar Romero (Chris Jorgenson). Producer: Hunt Stromberg; Director: W. S. Van Dyke II; Screenplay: Albert Hackett, Frances Goodrich (Based on the novel by Dashiell Hammett); Photography: James Wong Howe; Music: William Axt. RUNNING TIME: 93 minutes.

Director W. S. Van Dyke created one of the screen's most popular couples when he cast William Powell and Myrna Loy as Nick and Nora Charles, the wisecracking sleuths in Dashiell Hammett's classic detective story. They were so successful that the studio would team them for eleven more films, five of them sequels to *The Thin Man*. As a novel, *The Thin Man* was one of Hammett's biggest hits, hailed when it came out as "the best detective story yet written in America." Hammett had modeled the characters on his unmarried relationship with playwright Lillian Hellman. She would later say that some of the book's dialogue was taken verbatim from their own verbal sparring matches. If so, their conversation was decidedly racier than what middle America was used to. After Nick has a wrestling match with a female suspect, Nora asks, "Didn't you have an erection?" The question shocked many readers, but that didn't stop the publisher from alluding to it in ads for the book, which became a runaway hit in January 1934.

Fortunately for MGM, producer Hunt Stromberg fell in love with the story while it was still in galleys. As a result, they got the rights for just $21,000. Stromberg had no problem interesting Van Dyke in the project. A happily married man, the director was fed up with most big-screen treatments of holy matrimony. He saw the story as the perfect means of making marriage on screen look like fun. And he had the perfect stars to drive the point home. Van Dyke had just directed William Powell and Myrna Loy in the gangster film *Manhattan Melodrama,* which costarred Clark Gable. He had felt the tremendous chemistry between the two and knew they would be ideal for Hammett's couple.

Along with Powell and Loy, another hit of the film was their dog, Asta, played by a wire-haired

The screen's most popular married couple—William Powell and Myrna Loy as Nick and Nora Charles—had to sleep in twin beds to satisfy British censors.

MARITAL MIX-UP

William Powell and Myrna Loy were so convincing as Nick and Nora Charles that fans just assumed they were husband and wife, even sending letters to "Mr. and Mrs. William Powell." That case of mistaken identity created an embarrassing problem when the two traveled to San Francisco to do location work for After the Thin Man *and found themselves booked into the same hotel room. The mix-up provided an unexpected cover-up as well. Powell was traveling with his current flame, Jean Harlow, but nobody noticed while Loy was around. After a quick conference, the two women decided to share the suite, while Powell took the smaller room booked for his lady love. The arrangements did nothing to hurt the romance and even led to a strong friendship between the star's on- and offscreen leading ladies.*

terrier named Skippy. But for all the rapport he had with his masters on-screen, he didn't go near them between takes. The dog had been trained to perform tricks for a toy mouse and a dog biscuit. Just to keep Skippy under control, his trainers forbade anybody to play with him or pet him between scenes. When Loy disobeyed orders and tried to get friendly with the pooch, he bit her.

The Thin Man was one of the surprise hits of 1934. Critics raved about Powell and Loy and their witty repartee, and fans flocked to the theaters to the tune of $729,000 in profits. The film picked up four Oscar nominations—Best Picture, Best Actor, Best Director, and Best Screenplay—though it lost all four to *It Happened One Night*. These two comedy surprises helped establish screwball stories at the box office, leading the way for dozens of comedies about wealthy characters carrying on in madcap ways.

MGM continued the series, using the films to showcase such rising stars as James Stewart, Donna Reed, and Gloria Grahame.

William Powell, Skippy, and Myrna Loy.

TRAIL OF THE THIN MAN

1934—**The Thin Man**—*MGM launches one of its most popular series.*

1936—**After the Thin Man**—*James Stewart gets a career boost out of his involvement with Nick and Nora and a murder in San Francisco's Chinatown.*

1939—**Another Thin Man**—*The last Hammett written sequel gives Ruth Hussey and Tom Neal some early exposure.*

1941—**Shadow of the Thin Man**—*Donna Reed and Barry Nelson are mixed up with the stars in a racetrack murder.*

1944—**The Thin Man Goes Home**—*This time Gloria De Haven is the resident newcomer as a visit to Nick's parents leads to another mystery.*

1947—**Song of the Thin Man**—*For MGM's last feature in the series, Dean Stockwell plays Nick and Nora's son, while Gloria Grahame and Jayne Meadows are among the suspects.*

1957—**The Thin Man**—*MGM launches a half-hour television series based on their popular detectives, with Peter Lawford and Phyllis Kirk starring. The program lasts two seasons.*

1975—**Nick and Nora**—*ABC's pilot for a new* **Thin Man** *series, starring Craig Stevens and Joanne Pflug, goes nowhere fast.*

1991—**Nick and Nora**—*The long-awaited Broadway musical based on Hammett's classic finally opens—and bombs. Barry Bostwick and Joanna Gleason star.*

To Have and Have Not

"It's Even Better When You Help"

1944. CAST: Humphrey Bogart (Harry Morgan), Walter Brennan (Eddie), Lauren Bacall (Marie Browning), Dolores Moran (Helene De Brusac), Hoagie Carmichael (Cricket), Marcel Dalio (Gerard). Producer-Director: Howard Hawks; Screenplay: Jules Furthman, William Faulkner (Based on the novel by Ernest Hemingway); Photography: Sidney Hickox; Music: Franz Waxman (uncredited). RUNNING TIME: 100 minutes.

Sultry, sexy Lauren Bacall got the best help any nineteen-year-old actress could ask for in her screen debut—solid direction by Howard Hawks, a script tailor-made to turn her into a star, and the backing of the Warner Bros. publicity department, which dubbed her "The Look" to capitalize on her insolent appeal. Most important, in addition to her own natural talent and common sense, she had the support of a leading man who would eventually take over a similar role in her private life—the great Humphrey Bogart.

According to legend, the film version of *To Have and Have Not* resulted from an argument between director Howard Hawks and novelist Ernest Hemingway. Hawks was trying to talk Hemingway into coming to Hollywood to write for the movies. Faced with the writer's resistance, Hawks bet that he could make a good film out of his worst novel. Hemingway asked which novel he meant, to which Hawks responded, "That goddamned piece of junk called *To Have and Have Not.*" When the author protested that it was unfilmable, Hawks shot back, "Okay, I'll get Faulkner to do it. He can write better than you, anyway."

In many ways, Hemingway's novel was unfilmable. The hero, Harry Morgan, runs a fishing boat between the Florida Keys and Cuba, taking on an occasional smuggling job to support his family when money runs low. This was a little downbeat for Hollywood, so Hawks, supposedly with Hemingway's help, moved the action back in time, showing how Harry meets his wife, Marie. More changes became necessary when the U.S. State Department stepped in. Concerned that the story would offend the Cuban government, they pressured Warner's to drop the picture altogether, ultimately threatening to deny the film an export license. To make them happy, Hawks moved the action

HOW LITTLE WE KNOW

Controversy has raged for decades over exactly who did Lauren Bacall's singing in* To Have and Have Not. *The actress has always maintained that she did it herself, while other sources claim that her singing was dubbed. Making the story even more colorful is the contention that the dubbing was done by the fourteen-year-old Andy Williams, later the popular performer of such hits as "Moon River" and "Days of Wine and Roses." For his part, Williams has always contended that the studio cut together bits of his singing with bits of Bacall's.

***Toward the end of his life, director Howard Hawks finally straightened things out. According to him, he had hired Williams to dub the song when he couldn't find a woman singer whose voice matched Bacall's throaty tones. As was the custom, Williams's voice track for Hoagy Carmichael's "How Little We Know" was played back while they shot the scene, and Bacall sang along just to make it look convincing. Hearing her voice, Hawks decided to go ahead and let her do the number on her own. He would let her sing again in* The Big Sleep, *but Bacall's vocal talents would be long forgotten by the time she transformed herself into a Broadway musical star for* Applause.**

to the only Caribbean Island not allied with the United States in World War II, Martinique.

Bogart appears to have been Hawks's choice for leading man from the start, but there was some controversy over the leading lady. Hawks's wife, model and novelist Nancy Raye Gross, had spotted a young model named Betty Bacal on the cover of *Vogue*. Impressed with the eighteen-

Lauren Bacall provided an extra spark to Warner's *Casablanca* reunion, with Humphrey Bogart and the croupier from "Rick's Café Américain," Marcel Dalio.

"You know you don't have to act with me, Steve. You don't have to say anything, and you don't have to do anything. Not a thing. Oh, maybe just whistle. You know how to whistle, don't you, Steve? You just put your lips together and blow."

—BACALL'S FAMOUS COME-ON TO BOGART IN *TO HAVE AND HAVE NOT*

year-old beauty, he had signed her to a personal contract, changing her first name to Lauren and adding an "l" to her second name. He also advised her to develop a lower speaking voice. To do so, she drove every day to a remote spot and read *The Robe* aloud, using the deepest voice she could muster. She also worked with a voice coach who made her speak while holding a two-by-four against a wall with her chest. The result was a deep, throaty voice that radiated sex appeal. But there was some resistance among Warner executives to casting an unknown in such an important role. Hawks instructed Faulkner's cowriter, Jules Furthman, to prepare two versions of the script, one in which Marie was as important as Harry, another in which the other female character, a Resistance fighter named Helene, shared the limelight. After Bacall's screen test, all doubts vanished, and the alternative script was left unfinished.

When Bogart met Bacall for the first time, he simply said, "I've just seen your test. We'll have a lot of fun together." Initially, the admiration was all one-sided. Bacall would later write that she thought of Bogart as just a "dese, dem, dose" kind of guy. Once they started working together, she realized just how good an actor he was. She also began to appreciate him in other ways. About three weeks into filming, the two fell in love. Bogart was trapped in an unhappy marriage to alcoholic actress Mayo Methot at the time, and a relationship with Bacall seemed hopeless. But the two couldn't keep away from each other. Within a year after filming *To Have and Have Not,* they were married.

Although Hawks objected to the developing romance between his stars, he wasn't above exploiting the electricity. As Bacall's performance improved, he cut back further on Dolores Moran's role as Helene. By the time the film was finished, Helene had moved from a meaty supporting role to a minor character, whose main function was to make Bacall's Marie look good by contrast. Helping Bacall greatly was the distinctive posture she developed early in the shooting. She was so nervous that she couldn't keep her head from shaking. Finally, she learned to hold her chin against her chest, which seemed to keep her still. It also meant that she played almost all of her scenes looking up at Bogart, even when he was sitting. Her cure for nerves turned out to be amazingly sexual, leading the publicity department to dub her "The Look."

When all of these lucky accidents came together on screen, it spelled a major hit for Warner Bros. and turned Bacall into a major star overnight. The film's first reviews concentrated mainly on her, dismissing the picture. It was not until 1952, when Jean-Luc Godard published his famous appreciation of the film in *Cahiers du Cinema,* that critics began taking the film seriously.

Top Hat

"Heaven, I'm in Heaven"

1935. CAST: Fred Astaire (Jerry Travers), Ginger Rogers (Dale Tremont), Edward Everett Horton (Horace Hardwick), Helen Broderick (Madge Hardwick), Erik Rhodes (Albert Beddini), Eric Blore (Bates, the Butler), Lucille Ball (Flower Clerk). Producer: Pandro S. Berman; Director: Mark Sandrich; Screenplay: Dwight Taylor, Allan Scott (Based on the musical *The Gay Divorce* by Dwight Taylor and Cole Porter, from the play *The Girl Who Dares* by Alexander Farago and Aladar Laszlo); Photography: David Abel, Vernon L. Walker; Musical Director: Max Steiner; Music and Lyrics: Irving Berlin. RUNNING TIME: 101 minutes.

Film fans and the RKO executive suite were certainly in heaven when Fred Astaire and Ginger Rogers danced through London and Venice in the fourth of their ten films together. In later years, dance critic Arlene Croce would describe their pairing as the great American courtship. The stars, however, were far from ecstatic about *Top Hat,* even if it was their highest-grossing picture together. Fred quickly tired of Ginger and her outlandish costumes, while Ginger wanted to prove she could do more than dance backwards in high heels.

For all their popularity, Fred Astaire and Ginger Rogers seemed an unlikely screen team. Nobody in Hollywood would have expected his sophistication to match with her everyday, working-girl directness or his combination of tap and ballet to work with the moves she'd picked up as a chorus girl and Broadway headliner. Yet his elegance smoothed out her rough edges; her earthiness gave him sex appeal.

Astaire hadn't been happy with film. After viewing his screen debut as Joan Crawford's dancing partner in *Dancing Lady,* he'd commented on himself, "Ponderous dancer, grotesque face." Meanwhile, Ginger was floundering in Hollywood without a studio berth. Her test at Columbia was a notorious disaster, but something about it intrigued RKO production chief Merian C. Cooper, and he signed her.

It was a lucky move on his part. Dorothy Jordan had been slated to team with Astaire in *Flying Down to Rio,* but when she married Cooper, the only time they could get away for their honeymoon coincided with the film's production dates. So, Cooper put Rogers into the picture in her

Watch out for flying feathers: Fred Astaire and Ginger Rogers dance "Cheek to Cheek."

place. Choreographer Hermes Pan had come up with a great gimmick for the film's "Carioca" number: Fred and Ginger would try to keep their foreheads together for the entire dance, sometimes bumping heads for comic effect.

Exhibitors were clamoring for more films with this hot new dancing team, but Astaire wasn't. When new RKO head Pandro S. Berman asked Astaire for a film version of *The Gay Divorce,* retitled *The Gay Divorcée* to appease the censors, he objected to the choice of Rogers as his costar. He gave in only when Berman offered him ten percent of the film's profits.

With *The Gay Divorcée*'s success, Fred and Ginger were a hot item at the box office. *Top Hat* was the first film specifically written for the pair.

Like *The Gay Divorcée,* it was built around a mistaken identity plot: Ginger finds herself falling for Fred but thinks he's her best friend's husband. Astaire's main problem was with Rogers's costume for their romantic pas de deux, "Cheek to Cheek." The dress was covered with ostrich feathers, and during the first day of rehearsals they kept flying off and making him sneeze. Finally, he had enough and demanded the dress be changed. This led to a huge fight with Rogers and, worst of all, her domineering mother. The crew called it "the battle of the feathers." Finally, the costume designer had to stay up all night and sew every feather in place. They got the number the next day, but observant fans have noticed that some feathers still fly from the dress, sticking to Fred's pants legs.

More comfortable for Astaire was his performance of the title song. He had used a similar routine, in which he shot down chorus boys with his cane, in the 1930 Broadway musical *Smiles*. Originally, he'd wanted a number like that in *The Gay Divorcée,* but director Mark Sandrich had suggested holding off until they could better showcase the routine. They did just that in *Top Hat*, helped by the great Irving Berlin song. In fact, "Top Hat, White Tie and Tails" would become Astaire's trademark.

Berlin's score—which also included "Isn't This a Lovely Day to Be Caught in the Rain," "Fancy Free," and "The Piccolino"—was an important factor in the film's success. During the week of September 20, 1935, all five songs from the film were featured on radio's "Your Hit Parade," the first time a single composer had had that many songs on one show. "Cheek to Cheek" also set a record by staying in the top ten for eleven weeks. *Top Hat* naturally emerged as a box-office winner. It took in $3 million, making it the second-highest-grossing film of 1935 (MGM's *Mutiny on the Bounty* captured the top spot).

CHEEP TO CHEEP

After surviving the battle of the feathers, Fred Astaire and choreographer Hermes Pan serenaded Ginger with their own version of the hit tune:

Feathers—I hate feathers—
And I hate them so that I can hardly speak,
And I never find the happiness I seek
With those chicken feathers dancing
Cheek to cheek.

The Treasure of the Sierra Madre

"I Know What Gold Does to Men's Souls"

1948. CAST: Humphrey Bogart (Fred C. Dobbs), Walter Huston (Howard), Tim Holt (Curtin), Bruce Bennett (Cody), Barton MacLane (McCormick), Alfonso Bedoya (Gold Hat), Bobby Blake (Mexican Boy), John Huston (American Tourist), Ann Sheridan (Unbilled Bit). Producer: Henry Blanke; Director-Screenplay: John Huston (Based on the novel by B. Traven); Photography: Ted McCord; Music: Max Steiner. RUNNING TIME: 126 minutes.

The power of gold to destroy men's souls is one of the oldest themes in literature. When B. Traven's tale of gold lust in the Mexican wilderness first appeared in 1935, critics were quick to identify its roots in myth and literature, most notably Chaucer's "The Pardoner's Tale." John Huston became intrigued with the novel when it was first published. At the time, he dreamed of directing a film version with his father, Walter Huston, starring as Fred C. Dobbs, a prospector overcome with paranoia when he finally strikes it rich. Huston was in no position to get any film financed back then, but after he moved into directing with the sleeper hit *The Maltese Falcon* in 1941, he urged Warner Bros. to pick up the rights for him.

Huston started working on the script in 1941. By that time, he was considering Edward G. Robinson for the lead with his father as Howard, the older, experienced prospector who joins Dobbs and his partner, Curtin, in their quest for gold. With the outbreak of World War II, however, the project was put on hold as the younger Huston entered the service to direct military documentaries. When Huston returned to Hollywood after the war, *The Treasure of the Sierra Madre* was the first project on his plate. Robinson had long since left the studio, so Huston offered the lead to Humphrey Bogart, whom he had directed in *The Maltese Falcon* and *Across the Pacific*. The director wanted Ronald Reagan to play Curtin, but it didn't work out. Huston would later contend that Reagan had turned him down when he learned the director was still testing other actors; Reagan would state that the studio had pulled him from the project to film *The Voice of the Turtle*. Either way, the role went to Tim Holt, an underappreciated actor whose only previous relief from the B westerns he was churning out at RKO had been Orson Welles's *The Magnificent Ambersons*.

Gold fever heats up when Bruce Bennett (back to camera) arrives at the claim staked by Tim Holt, Humphrey Bogart, and Walter Huston.

WE AIN'T GOT NO STINKING BADGES—WE JUST WANT OUR LUNCH

One of the most memorable characters in The Treasure of the Sierra Madre *is Gold Hat, the Mexican bandit chief who seems to dog Fred C. Dobbs's trail throughout the movie. The character wasn't as important in the novel, in which he simply leads the attack on the train Dobbs and his colleagues are riding, but John Huston built up the character to give the story a stronger sense of doom.*

Huston cast Alfonso Bedoya in the role after spotting him among a crowd of locals out to land extra work on the film. The actor performed wonderfully in the part, particularly with his rendition of Gold Hat's most famous line: "Badges? We ain't got no badges. I don't have to show you any stinking badges." But he also became a running joke with the company by always being the first in line at mealtime. One day, Huston asked the actor to pose for publicity shots in his saddle just before lunch. As a practical joke, the director had coated the saddle with glue so that, when the lunch call came, Bedoya couldn't move. When the actor burst into tears, Huston ordered technicians to cut his pants off so he could eat.

After scouting much of the Mexican countryside, Huston settled on a remote location in Jungapao. The elder Huston enjoyed roughing it with his son, but Bogart and many of the crew members were less than thrilled. They nicknamed their director "Hard-Way Huston." Bogie's suffering, however, was nothing compared to what Warner was going through back at the studio. With Huston out of reach in Mexico, the studio head could only fume as the production ran over schedule and over budget. He cabled Huston with demands that the actors shave, so they'd look more like stars, and he fought unsuccessfully to get Huston to change the ending so that Bogart wouldn't die. As Warner watched seemingly endless rushes of the prospectors searching for gold, he quipped, "Yeah, they're looking for gold, all right—mine!" Later, while screening Bogart's desperate battle with thirst in the desert, he jumped up and said, "If that s.o.b. doesn't find water soon, I'll go broke!" When he finally saw the film fully assembled, Warner changed his tune. He cabled his sales manager in New York that it was "the greatest motion picture we have ever made." The critics echoed his approval, with James Agee hailing the film as "one of the most visually alive and beautiful movies I have ever seen" and calling Huston "next only to Chaplin . . . the most talented man working in American pictures."

> ***"Greed, gold and gunplay on a Mexican mountain of malice!"***
>
> ***"The nearer they got to their treasure the further they got from the law!"***
>
> **—Ad lines for The Treasure of the Sierra Madre**

Many critics hailed Bogart's performance as the best of his career, but much of his thunder was stolen by Walter Huston in a role widely perceived as the heart of the film. Critics were astounded at the one-time matinee idol's transformation into the grizzled prospector. *The Treasure of the Sierra Madre* was the big winner in the New York Film Critics Awards that year, capturing Best Picture and Best Director. It had not been a winner with audiences, however, who resented buying tickets to a western that turned out to be a serious psychological study. The film's poor box-office showing may account for its meager representation in the year's Oscar nominations. It was only up for four awards: Best Picture, Best Director, Best Screenplay, and Best Supporting Actor (Huston). It won in three categories, with John Huston taking home a pair of Oscars and his father scoring as well. To date, the Hustons remain the only father and son to win Oscars in the same year. When Anjelica Huston won Best Supporting Actress in 1985 for *Prizzi's Honor,* the Hustons became the only family to place three generations of filmmakers in the winner's circle.

2001: A Space Odyssey

The Ultimate Trip

1968. CAST: Keir Dullea (David Bowman), Gary Lockwod (Frank Poole), William Sylvester (Dr. Heywood Floyd), Daniel Richter (Moonwatcher), Leonard Rossiter (Smyslov), Douglas Rain (voice of HAL). Producer-Director: Stanley Kubrick; Screenplay: Stanley Kubrick, Arthur C. Clarke (Based on the short story "The Sentinel" by Clarke); Photography: Geoffrey Unsworth, John Alcott (Super Panavision, Cinerama, Technicolor, Metrocolor). RUNNING TIME: 160 minutes.

Time may be running out for the prophecies Arthur C. Clarke and Stanley Kubrick made for the year 2001, but the changes the film wrought in Hollywood are still going strong. After years of films with rubber monsters and cardboard spaceships, *2001: A Space Odyssey* was the first big-budget, bigger-box-office science-fiction spectacular. It set new standards for special effects with its monumental, carefully detailed spacecraft and its dazzling climactic cosmic ride. Most important of all, however, it revealed the tastes of a new generation of filmgoers. Defying conventional rules of storytelling, it appealed to audiences primarily through the senses, demonstrating the potency of the youth market and pointing the way to the rise of the MTV generation.

The plot took off from an Arthur C. Clarke short story called "The Sentinel," in which astronauts on the moon discover a black monolith transmitting a radio beacon. Triggered by their presence, the beacon shuts off, signaling some unknown race that humanity has finally developed space travel. Working with Clarke, Kubrick created a story in which monoliths on the earth and the moon—along with another, orbiting Jupiter—trigger major developments in human evolution.

Financing came from MGM, which initially committed $6 million to the picture. As shooting dragged on at the company's Boreham Wood Studio in England, the budget rose to $10.5 million. In all, three years elapsed between the start of production in December 1965 and the film's 1968 release. Kubrick spent six months in preproduction, four-and-a-half months shooting, and over a year-and-a-half on the special effects. The finished film would include 205 effects shots.

To supervise the film's effects, Kubrick discovered Douglas Trumbull, a young painter who had been working on NASA recruiting films, and put him in charge of a team of veteran effects men.

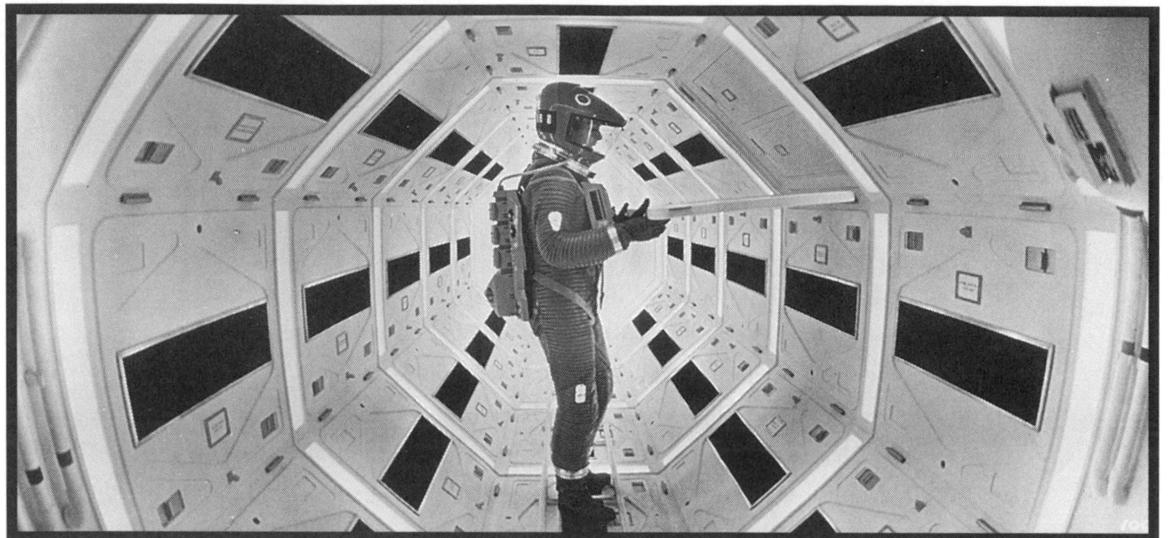

Kubrick wanted to get away from the sterile, artificial look of most movie spaceships, so his crew raided a European toy fair, buying up hundreds of model kits. Using the plastic pieces, they gave the ships a more realistic, detailed look.

The director also wanted to avoid traveling matte shots, which often left a discernable line around the objects that were added to background shots in the lab. As a result, the special-effects team wound up inventing their own techniques. *2001* was the first film to use front projection, which had a more vibrant look than the usual rear projection. Using large transparencies, they projected background shots for the Dawn of Man on a large screen behind the actors. They also used that technique for the moon landing, projecting the ship's descent on a screen behind actors watching from the surface.

The film's most spectacular special-effects sequence was the "cosmic ride." For this, Trumbull combined aerial shots of Monument Valley, Utah, shot through colored filters with footage using a split-scan effect. For the latter, he kept the camera shutter open on a single frame of film while moving the light source toward the camera, sometimes creating fantastic patterns. The result was the impression that Dullea was flying through vast reaches of space.

WHAT'S IN A NAME?

Stanley Kubrick came up with the name for 2001's computer by using the first letters of "heuristic" and "algorithmic," the two principal computer learning systems. After the film's release, a code-breaker informed him that the word "HAL" was also one letter away from the name of the world's most famous computer company, IBM. The connection was a one-in-a-million coincidence, yet fans have ever since credited Kubrick with consciously creating one of the cleverest names in film history. Some years after the release of the film, a real-life computer programming language was developed and reverently christened HAL.

With all the film's technical effects, the human element was minimized. Only one character emerged as fully realized: the computer, HAL 9000. HAL's rebellion against his human masters paralleled the human evolution triggered by the monoliths and provided suspense for the Jupiter trip sequence. Helping tremendously was the voice of Canadian actor Douglas Rain. Initially, HAL was to have been called "Athena" and would have had a woman's voice. When the computer was changed to a male voice, Martin Balsam was hired to record the lines. Meanwhile, Rain was hired to provide narration. When Kubrick scrapped the narration, he also scrapped Balsam's performance, putting Rain in his place.

By the time *2001* was finished, MGM's executives didn't know what they'd gotten themselves into. The film defied all the rules of conventional storytelling. Though early critics hailed its breakthrough special effects, which would bring the film its only Oscar, many complained that the movie made no sense. There was some fear that *2001* would not make back its investment.

THE WHOLE SCORE

Producer-director Stanley Kubrick created another minor revolution when he scuttled the original score for* 2001: A Space Odyssey *and replaced it with classical pieces. Many films had used classical themes in the past, but* 2001 *was the first to create a bestselling score entirely pasted together from the classical canon, including—Aram Khatchaturian, "Gayana Ballet Suite;" Gyorgy Ligeti, "Atmospheres," "Lux Aeterna," "Requiem for Soprano, Mezzo-Soprano, Two Mixed Choirs and Orchestra;" Johann Strauss, "Blue Danube Waltz;" and, most notably, the opening fanfare from Richard Strauss's "Thus Spake Zarathustra."

Then the youth audience discovered it. Raised on television and, in some cases, attending under the influence of "recreational" drugs, younger audiences embraced the film as a total visual experience, often returning several times simply to relish the climactic cosmic ride. Not only did they turn *2001* into a hit, with about $23 million in profits, they opened Hollywood's eyes to a whole new audience. In the next few years, the major studios would all but destroy themselves in a scramble to cash in on the youth market.

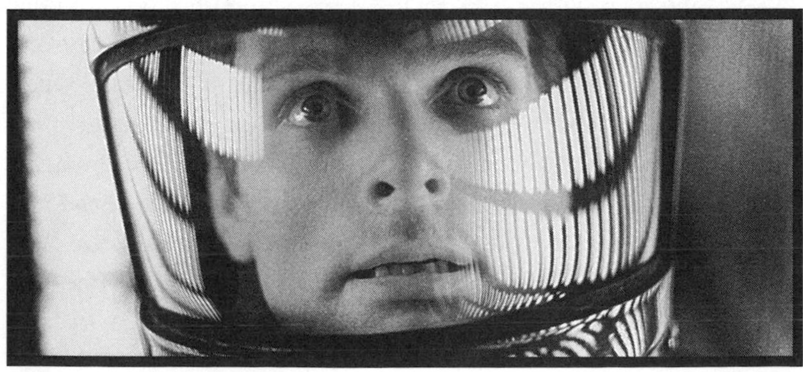

Keir Dullea may have been the human star of *2001*, but most audiences found themselves identifying with the computer HAL.

White Heat

"Made It, Ma. Top of the World!"

1949. CAST: James Cagney (Arthur Cody Jarrett), Virginia Mayo (Verna Jarrett), Edmond O'Brien (Hank Fallon/Vic Pardo), Margaret Wycherly (Ma Jarrett), Steve Cochran (Big Ed Somers), John Archer (Philip Evans). Producer: Louis F. Edelman; Director: Raoul Walsh; Screenplay: Ivan Goff, Ben Roberts (Based on a story by Virginia Kellogg); Photography: Sid Hickcox; Music: Max Steiner. RUNNING TIME: 114 minutes.

Like Cody Jarrett in *White Heat,* James Cagney made it to the top of the world with his 1949 return to gangster films. But, whereas the character's triumph blew up in his face, Cagney's carried him to the top of the box office.

Cagney's role was not even in the original story. Virginia Kellogg, a onetime journalist for the *Los Angeles Times,* sold Warner Bros. a plot about the Secret Service tracking down a hood named Blackie Flynn, with all the focus on the intelligence agency's new crime-fighting methods. She then moved on to research her most famous film, the seminal women's prison drama *Caged.* The first two script drafts followed Kellogg's story closely but did nothing to excite the studio's executives. Then they handed it over to Ivan Goff and Ben Roberts, a writing team who had just done an impressive rewrite on the missing-persons story *Backfire.* They decided to focus the Kellogg idea on the gangster, renamed Cody Jarrett, and throw in a Freudian angle that hadn't been tried before. They gave the crook a mother, modeled on Ma Barker, and a fixation on her that, in their opinion, "played like Greek tragedy." Studio head Jack Warner was so impressed with the results that he even asked them to suggest a star. His generosity must have felt like a big mistake when they suggested Cagney. Even though Warner had liked the money made by Cagney's pictures, he did not like the star. Warner thought him too independent, and whenever they had an argument, which was quite often, the Irish-born actor would rattle off a string of Yiddish profanities he had learned growing up in New York's Hell's Kitchen. By the late forties, however, Warner's was losing many of its biggest stars, so the studio head swallowed his pride and made Cagney an offer.

Cagney had an ally in director Raoul Walsh, with whom he had worked on *The Roaring*

Edmond O'Brien was the leading man, but audience sympathies were squarely with James Cagney as criminal Cody Jarrett.

"Pick up the pieces, folks, Jimmy's in action again!"
—AD LINE FOR WHITE HEAT

Twenties, one of the best of his early gangster films. Walsh came naturally to his credentials as an action director. As a young man, he had ridden with Pancho Villa. But he also had a knack for getting extra psychological depth into his work. He proved particularly open to Cagney's suggestions on how to put the part over more effectively. For one scene, in which the gangster's mother (Margaret Wycherly) soothes him after an epileptic-type seizure, Cagney suggested having Cody sit in his mother's lap—one of the film's most famous images. Walsh also let Cagney add Jarrett's insane laughter as the police gun him down at the finish.

The script's biggest acting challenge was probably the prison mess hall scene, in which Cody learns that his mother has died. With no dialogue, the actor had to stage a convincing breakdown. Jack Warner's legendary stinginess made matters even worse. Where others could appreciate the scene's dramatic power, all he saw was a large set with six hundred extras, and just one line of dialogue.

Walsh agreed to cut the extras to three hundred and stage the scene at the studio mill, which could be quickly made over as a mess hall. He also agreed to do the entire scene in one morning. During the blocking, Cagney simply marked the scene. He then asked the writers how far they wanted him to go. They deferred to him on the matter, but added, "If you make people's spines tingle, so much the better." As a child, Cagney had visited a mental institution on Ward's Island in the East River and had been deeply affected by the cries of the insane. Once the cameras started rolling, he drew on those memories so well that some of the extras thought he really had gone mad. They got the scene, one of the best in his career, in a single take.

MY BROTHER THE PROPHET—NOT!

Nobody had even thought of* White Heat *back when Cagney and his producer-brother, William, were working on the script for* Yankee Doodle Dandy. *The first drafts had worked well as long as the Four Cohans were together as a vaudeville team but lost focus when George M. Cohan went off on his own. Arguing that the script needed to move beyond the early family problems, Bill Cagney wrote to producer Hal B. Wallis, "It would be hard to swallow Jimmy Cagney as a guy with a mother or father complex." With his performance in* White Heat, *however, the star would prove that he could make audiences swallow just about anything he wanted to dish out to them.

The Wizard of Oz

"Are You a Good Witch or a Bad Witch?"

1939. CAST: Judy Garland (Dorothy), Ray Bolger (Hunk/The Scarecrow), Bert Lahr (Zeke/The Cowardly Lion), Jack Haley (Hickory/ The Tin Woodman), Billie Burke (Glinda), Margaret Hamilton (Miss Gulch/ The Wicked Witch), Charles Grapewin (Uncle Henry), Clara Blandick (Auntie Em), Frank Morgan (Professor Marvel/The Wizard/Guard/ Coachman), The Singer Midgets (Munchkins), Terry the Dog (Toto). Producer: Mervyn LeRoy; Director: Victor Fleming; Screenplay: Noel Langley, Florence Ryerson, Edgar Allen Woolf (Based on the novel by L. Frank Baum); Photography: Harold Rosson (Technicolor); Music: Herbert Stothart; Music and Lyrics: Harold Arlen, E. Y. Harburg. RUNNING TIME: 101 minutes.

THE ULTIMATE *WIZARD OF OZ* QUIZ

1. Where did *The Wonderful Wizard of Oz* come from?
2. How many dramatic and film versions of *The Wonderful Wizard of Oz* preceded the MGM classic?
3. What film's success inspired MGM to pick up the rights to *The Wizard of Oz?*
4. One of MGM's most important producers got his start on *The Wizard of Oz*. Who was he?
5. How many different directors worked on the film?
6. Who was the first choice to play Dorothy?
7. Three different actors were signed for one role in *The Wizard of Oz*. Who were they, and why was the casting changed?
8. What breed of dog is Toto, and where did MGM find him?
9. Who were the Singer Midgets?
10. Why don't Auntie Em and Uncle Henry have time to listen to Dorothy's story about what happened to Miss Gulch?
11. What are the first words the Tin Woodman speaks to Dorothy and the Scarecrow?
12. What does the Wicked Witch of the West threaten to do with the Scarecrow and the Tin Woodman?
13. Where do Dorothy and her companions go when they first enter the Emerald City?

14. What are the words written on the balloon the Wizard uses to leave Oz?
15. Why did MGM transform the silver slippers in the original novel into ruby slippers for the movie?
16. What technical innovation was made during the shooting of *The Wizard of Oz?*
17. How did the special effects department get the shot of the farmhouse being sucked up in the twister?
18. What was used to create the "horse of a different color?"
19. Which musical numbers did MGM want to cut from the film during previews? Which did they finally cut?
20. What element of the film caused problems with the censors?
21. How long did it take *The Wizard of Oz* to turn a profit?
22. Which two songs from *The Wizard of Oz* became favorites during World War II?
23. When did *The Wizard of Oz* become one of the most popular family films of all time?
24. How many pair of ruby slippers remain today? What are they worth?
25. Who played or supplied the voice for the Dorothy character in the following projects: a) The 1925 silent version of *The Wonderful Wuzard of Oz?* b) "The Land of Oz" segment of television's *Shirley Temple's Storybook?* c) *Journey Back to Oz?* d) *Kentucky Fried Movie?* e) *The Wiz*—stage and screen?

18. Jello, which you can see the horse licking off in one shot.
19. Studio executives wanted to cut "The Jitterbug," which Dorothy and her friends sang on the way to the Wicked Witch's castle, and "Over the Rainbow." Freed fought to keep the latter number in, helped greatly by the fact that it had already become popular on the radio. Eventually, they cut "The Jitterbug" and a reprise of "Ding, Dong the Witch is Dead" sung after Dorothy accidentally kills the Wicked Witch of the West.
20. Hollywood's Production Code Authority warned that the Wicked Witch might be considered too frightening for young children, and MGM actually did cut down some of her scenes after previews. There were no other censorship problems in this country, but there were in Europe. Sweden and Denmark made further cuts in the Witch's scenes, while the English censors rated the film for adults only.
21. *The Wizard of Oz* returned only $3,335,000 on its first release. With print and advertising costs added to the budget of $2.7 million, that put the film almost $1 million in the red. When the picture's 1949 reissue took in another $1.5 million, it finally turned a small profit.
22. "Over the Rainbow" became a huge hit in England during the days of the Blitz. "We're Off to See the Wizard" became the official marching song of the Australian Army.
23. It took television to make *The Wizard of Oz* a perennial favorite. The film made its network television debut on CBS in 1956, with the network paying $225,000 for broadcast rights. The picture's average television viewership per year is estimated at sixty million.
24. Four of the seven pairs created for the film remain. A pair was sold for $15,000 at MGM's 1970 auction of props and costumes. It is believed that this is the pair on display at the Smithsonian. Three pairs have surfaced since then. One was won by Memphis, Tennessee, schoolteacher Roberta Bauman in a 1940 contest. The other two may have been stolen by a costumer working on the auction. In 1988, Ms. Bauman's pair was auctioned off by Christie's. The shoes sold for $165,000, setting a record for a single piece of Hollywood memorabilia. Originally, the slippers only cost MGM $20 a pair.
25. a) Dorothy Dwan; b) Nobody, the telefilm was adapted from Baum's second Oz book in which the leading character is Tip, an orphan boy who is actually the enchanted Princess Ozma; Shirley Temple played the role; c) Liza Minnelli supplied the voice for the animated Dorothy; d) martial-arts expert Evan Kim, in a parody of *Enter the Dragon* that turns into *The Wizard of Oz*; e) Stephanie Mills on stage and Diana Ross on film.

ANSWERS

1. L. Frank Baum, a former actor and failed businessman who had achieved some success writing children's stories, took his mother-in-law's advice and wrote down the bedtime stories he had been telling his children.
2. A musical version of *The Wonderful Wizard of Oz* became a stage hit in 1902, thanks partly to the comic performances of Fred Stone as the Scarecrow and David Montgomery as the Tin Woodman. There also was a silent-film version in 1925 starring Oliver Hardy as the Tin Woodman.
3. *Snow White and the Seven Dwarfs.*
4. Arthur Freed. The former songwriter had been working his way into production through the thirties and was instrumental in getting Mayer to buy *The Wizard of Oz*. When the budget was set at $2.7 million, Mayer decided to give the film to a more experienced producer, Mervyn LeRoy, with Freed as his associate.
5. Four. Richard Thorpe, who had done some of the early Tarzan films, shot for a few days but was let go because his footage didn't have a strong enough sense of fantasy. None of his work was used. George Cukor supervised some tests and was instrumental in giving Judy Garland a more natural look (originally she was to have worn a blonde wig and exaggerated makeup). Victor Fleming became director of record and filmed all of the Oz sequences. When Fleming took over *Gone With the Wind*, King Vidor came in to finish the film, working on most of the Kansas sequence, including "Over the Rainbow."
6. Freed always wanted Judy Garland as Dorothy, but with the film's high budget, other executives insisted they try to get Shirley Temple. When 20th Century–Fox head Darryl F. Zanuck refused to loan her to MGM, Garland got the part.
7. Ray Bolger was originally cast as the Tin Woodman, with Buddy Ebsen as the Scarecrow. Since he had always idolized Fred Stone, Bolger begged to switch roles and play the Scarecrow. That was fine with Ebsen until nine days into filming, when he developed an allergic reaction to the aluminum dust in his makeup. While he was in the hospital recuperating, the makeup man developed an aluminum paste that wouldn't damage anybody's lungs, and the studio recast the role with Jack Haley.

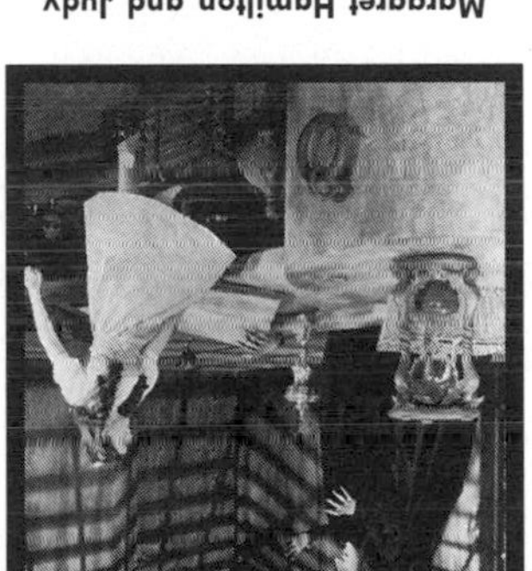

Margaret Hamilton and Judy Garland, in roles originally envisioned for Edna Mae Oliver and Shirley Temple.

8. Toto was a Cairn Terrier. Freed and LeRoy wanted a dog that matched the book's original illustrations, but at first nobody could figure out what the dog's breed was. Animal trainer Carl Spitz had the answer and also had the dog, a shy terrier named Terry. Not realizing how desperate they were, he contracted to supply and train the dog for $125 a week. Contrary to legend, that was not more than Judy Garland made for the film. Her contract stipulated $500 per week.
9. The Singer Midgets were a troop of German and Austrian performing midgets under the direction of Leon Singer. He did not have enough midgets for *The Wizard of Oz*, so he issued a national casting call, assembling 124 little people, many of them nonprofessionals. The studio also used six to eight children to fill in as needed. Contrary to legend, the Munchkins did not terrorize the set with wild behavior but were models of professionalism. Their main problem on the film was that they were too small to use the studio rest rooms. After one of them fell into the toilet and couldn't get out until someone missed him forty-five minutes later, attendants were delegated to help lift them into position.
10. Because the incubator has broken down, and they're racing to save the baby chicks.
11. "Oil can."
12. She threatens to stuff a mattress with the Scarecrow and turn the Tin Woodman into a beehive.
13. The Brush and Scrub Co., to clean up after their long journey.
14. "State Fair, Omaha."
15. When the studio decided to film the Oz scenes in Technicolor, they changed the shoes from silver to ruby to take advantage of the color process. The early script draft on display at the Smithsonian Institute is opened to the page on which the change was first penciled in.
16. To get the right sound for the Munchkins' voices, vocal arranger Ken Darby recorded their numbers (performed by other vocalists, not the Singer Midgets) at a slower tempo. He then had the MGM Sound Department build a special gear for the recording equipment so that the tape would play at the proper speed. This was the first time anybody had used that trick.
17. They dropped the model farmhouse to the floor, then played the film back upside down.

The Women

Cat Fight of the Century

1939. CAST: Norma Shearer (Mary Haines), Joan Crawford (Crystal Allen), Rosalind Russell (Sylvia Fowler), Mary Boland (Countess De Lave), Paulette Goddard (Miriam Aarons), Joan Fontaine (Peggy Day), Lucile Watson (Mrs. Moorehead), Virginia Weidler (Little Mary), Ruth Hussey (Miss Watts), Margaret Dumont (Mrs. Wagstaff), Marjorie Main (Lucy), Hedda Hopper (Dolly Depuyster). Producer: Hunt Stromberg; Director: George Cukor; Screenplay: Anita Loos, Jane Murfin (Based on the play by Clare Boothe); Photography: Oliver T. Marsh, Joseph Ruttenberg (Part Technicolor); Music: Edward Ward, David Snell.

RUNNING TIME: 132 minutes.

In one corner was Norma Shearer, the glamorous, dignified queen of the MGM lot. In the other was Joan Crawford, feisty young upstart with a bone to pick after more than a decade of fighting her way to stardom while Shearer seemed to have everything handed to her. The battle started when the cameras rolled. When the dust had settled, the winner was . . . Rosalind Russell.

Clare Boothe had written *The Women* after overhearing a gaggle of society types indulging in some earthy ladies' room gossip. The result was a Broadway smash that eventually earned her $2 million. Norma Shearer had seen *The Women* on Broadway and instantly felt a rapport with the leading role. Mary Haines was one of the few honest, good-hearted characters in the play. Under the influence of her malicious friends, she allows her husband's infidelity to end their marriage, then uses the tricks she's learned from them to put it all back together.

As soon as the project was announced, Joan Crawford mounted a campaign to win the role of Crystal Allen, the ruthless shopgirl who steals Mary's husband but can't hold him. Studio head Louis B. Mayer warned her that playing such an out-and-out villainous role could sink her career. But Crawford was adamant. "I'll play Wally Beery's grandmother if it's a good role," she said.

Everybody on the lot was waiting for the fireworks when the two divas played their first scene together. The showdown came as the two were rehearsing their dressing-room confrontation. Like many other Hollywood actresses, Crawford kept busy between scenes by knitting, which she did

THE MEN

MGM got a publicity gold mine out of the fact that* The Women *had a cast of one hundred thirty with nary a man in sight. But there was one man in the picture, at least in spirit. Until she played showgirl Miriam Aarons in* The Women*, Paulette Goddard had specialized in bouncy coquettes. When she kept trying to play Miriam that way, director George Cukor suggested she model her performance on one of Hollywood's most respected stars—Spencer Tracy.

during the rehearsal. And these weren't baby booties she was creating, but a full-sized afghan, with large, noisy needles. Shearer was so distracted, she finally turned to director George Cukor and said, "I think Miss Crawford can go home now, and you can feed me my lines." The enraged director followed Crawford outside to tell her off and insist she apologize the next day. Instead, Crawford sent the woman a scathing telegram that night with words so strong Western Union almost refused to transmit them. The pair never spoke to each other again, and when Shearer threw the film's wrap party, Crawford and her best buddy on the picture, Paulette Goddard, boycotted it.

Had the two stars been more aware of what was happening on the picture, however, they might have focused their rancor on Rosalind Russell, who quite simply walked off with the

The smiles hide the offscreen battles among the film's cast: Florence Nash, Phyllis Povah, Rosalind Russell, Joan Crawford, Norma Shearer, Paulette Goddard, Mary Boland, and Joan Fontaine.

"The women who inspired this play deserved to be smacked across the head with a meat ax, and that, I flatter myself, is exactly what I smacked them with. They are vulgar and dirty-minded and alien to grace, and I would not, if I could, which I hasten to say I cannot, cross their obscenities with a wit which is foreign to them and guild their futilities with the glamour which by birth and breeding and performance they do not possess."

—CLARE BOOTHE ON THE INSPIRATION FOR THE WOMEN

"There's a name for you ladies, but it isn't used in high society—outside of a kennel."

—JOAN CRAWFORD'S PARTING SHOT IN THE WOMEN

Manicurist Dennie Moore spills the beans to Rosalind Russell.

film. Russell had had to fight for the role of malicious society gossip Sylvia Fowler. At the time, she was typed in much more docile roles and had not had much experience with comedy.

The first day of filming, Russell tried playing the role realistically, but then Cukor told her to use the exaggerated style from her screen test. When she protested that that would make her a laughing stock, he explained that Sylvia had to be a clown in the film version, which would play to much less sophisticated audiences than those in New York. "Sylvia's breaking up a family," he said, "and there's a child involved, and if you're a heavy, audiences will hate you. Don't play it like a heavy. Just be ridiculous."

Russell rarely indulged in star temperament, but as she realized how important she was to the picture, she put in a bid for billing above the title. Initially, however, Shearer would not agree to it. Her contract stipulated that no other woman could share star billing with her. She had already made an exception for Crawford, but she wouldn't do it again. So Russell called in sick, carefully planning her strike to fall five weeks into shooting, when it would be too expensive to replace her. After four days, Shearer gave in, and Russell got better.

With its all-star cast and a dazzlingly funny script by Anita Loos and Jane Murfin, *The Women* couldn't help but be a hit. It provided Shearer with her best reviews ever and gave solid career boosts to almost everybody involved. But the biggest winner was Russell, who suddenly found herself acclaimed as one of the screen's best comediennes, partly because of the business Cukor had invented for her. She would follow with inspired comic turns in such films as *His Girl Friday* and *My Sister Eileen.*

Yankee Doodle Dandy

"Born on the Fourth of July"

1942. CAST: James Cagney (George M. Cohan), Joan Leslie (Mary), Walter Huston (Jerry Cohan), Richard Whorf (Sam Harris), George Tobias (Dietz), Irene Manning (Fay Templeton), Rosemary DeCamp (Nellie Cohan), Jeanne Cagney (Josie Cohan), S. Z. Sakall (Schwab). Producer: Hal B. Wallis; Director: Michael Curtiz; Screenplay: Robert Buckner, Edmund Joseph (Based on a story by Buckner); Photography: James Wong Howe; Musical Director: Leo F. Forbstein. RUNNING TIME: 126 minutes.

Warner Bros. and James Cagney sent America a love letter in 1942, just when the nation needed it most. Even before America's entry into World War II, Hollywood had been gearing up for the war effort with a string of patriotic pictures. Shooting for *Yankee Doodle Dandy* started just four days before the Japanese attack on Pearl Harbor. By the time the film premiered in May 1942, the country was primed for a loving salute to the greatest flag waver in American history.

George M. Cohan had ruled Broadway in the early decades of this century, but despite his prodigious talents, he hadn't had much to do with Hollywood. As he entered old age, however, Cohan decided that he would like to see his life story filmed while he was still around to supervise it. The first producer he approached was Samuel Goldwyn, who had a one-picture contract with Fred Astaire. Astaire rejected the role, however, feeling himself miscast. Then Jack Warner came calling with an offer of $125,000 against ten percent of the gross, plus script and cast approval.

Writer Robert Buckner researched material by interviewing Cohan and his colleagues in New York, then wrote an exhaustive treatment of the man's life. The main problem he had was the limitations Cohan imposed on the writing: he did not want either of his wives represented on screen, partly to protect his privacy, partly out of fear that his first wife might sue. After six months of almost daily work, Buckner handed in a script inspired by Cohan's life, using his fight to succeed on Broadway, his family loyalty, his patriotism, and a fictitious marriage to an aspiring actress to drive the action. Cagney took one look at the script and threatened to walk. At his insistence, Julius and Philip Epstein, twin brothers who had worked on the scripts for *The Bride Came C.O.D.* and *The Strawberry Blonde,* were asked to do a rewrite.

The writers poured on the schmaltz, but the actors made it real: Walter Huston's famous death scene, with James Cagney.

> "I've always maintained that in this business you're only as good as the other fellow thinks you are. It's nice to know that you people thought I had done a good job. And don't forget it was a pretty good part, too. My mother thanks you, my father thanks you, my sister thanks you, and I thank you."
>
> —James Cagney's Oscar acceptance speech, echoing George M. Cohan's famous curtain line from *Yankee Doodle Dandy*

Cagney had seen Cohan's stage work and screened some of his films to capture the man's mannerisms: his stiff-legged dancing, his monkey-like stance, the way he stuck his chin out, and the wink and nod he used to register approval. To get back into shape for the musical numbers, Cagney started practicing two months before shooting began. He worked four hours a day, then added the four-hour regimen to his time on the set.

Cagney made some important additions to the film on the set. When Joan Leslie, who played his wife, arrived to shoot the scene in which they auditioned the song "Harrigan," he worked out the routine with her on the spot, then showed it to Curtiz. His most inspired improvisation occurred five minutes before he shot the scene in which Cohan walked down the White House stairs after receiving a medal from President Roosevelt. Without telling the director, he started tap-dancing down the steps, providing the movie with one of its best-remembered moments. Another high spot was the death of Cohan's father, played by Walter Huston, a long-time friend of Cohan's who had worked under his direction years earlier. Curtiz kept pushing the Epsteins to make the scene more moving. Finally they wrote a scene so over-the-top they considered it hilarious, but when Cagney and Huston played it, they reduced the normally hard-nosed Curtiz to tears.

Cohan had asked that Warner's premiere *Yankee Doodle Dandy* on his birthday, July 4. Then he learned that he was dying of cancer. To be sure that he would be around for his last great triumph, the studio pushed the premiere date up to May 29, 1942. Like many other films of the period, *Yankee Doodle Dandy* premiered with a War Bonds rally. Bonds were priced at \$25 to \$25,000. In one night, the film raised \$5,750,000 for the war effort—almost as much as it made for Warner Bros. during its entire first release.

Yankee Doodle Dandy was the top-grossing film of its year and Warner's top-grosser to that time. It put Cagney in a very strong position from which to start his career as an independent producer, earning him \$500,000 from his percentage of the profits. It also brought him the New York Film Critics Award and the Oscar for Best Actor. But his greatest praise probably came from Cohan himself, who lived long enough to screen the film in his home. According to legend, after the picture was over, Cohan's wife, who also was in poor health, turned to her husband and said, "George, you were fine." Cohan's immediate response to Cagney's performance was, "My God, what an act to follow!" He then sent Cagney a wire the actor would always treasure: "Dear Jim, How's my double? Thanks for a wonderful job. Sincerely, George M. Cohan."

The Yearling

"They Tamed a Tropic Wilderness!"

1946. CAST: Gregory Peck (Pa Baxter), Jane Wyman (Ma Baxter), Claude Jarman Jr. (Jody Baxter), Chill Wills (Buck Forrester), Clem Bevans (Pa Forrester), Margaret Wycherly (Ma Forrester), Henry Travers (Mr. Boyles), Forrest Tucker (Lem Forrester), June Lockhart (Twink Weatherby). Producer: Sidney Franklin; Director: Clarence Brown; Screenplay: Paul Osborn (Based on the novel by Marjorie Kinnan Rawlings); Photography: Charles Rosher, Leonard Smith, Arthur Arling (Technicolor); Music: Herbert Stothart, Themes from Frederick Delius. RUNNING TIME: 134 minutes.

MGM's ad line for *The Yearling* may have referred to the Baxter family's onscreen fight to eke out a meager living from the Florida soil, but to most Hollywood insiders it represented the studio's own struggles to adapt Marjorie Kinnan Rawlings's novel. To film the story of a young boy's love for the pet deer he will one day have to kill, the studio went to the Florida Everglades not once, but twice. It took nine years to get the novel onto the screen, but the result was one of the most beloved family films of all time.

The studio picked up rights to the novel for $30,000 in 1938, then watched its investment grow when the book won the Pulitzer Prize and became a bestseller. Rather than re-create the setting on the back lot, they leased a farm in Florida's Ocala National Forest. Producer Sidney Franklin then sent director Victor Fleming, stars Spencer Tracy and Anne Revere, and the film crew there in the dead of summer. It was not the wisest move. Following quarrels between Fleming and Tracy, impossible weather, and almost unbearable insect invasions, the company returned to Hollywood after only three weeks. Fleming left the picture and was replaced by King Vidor, who asked for a break so he could familiarize himself with the story and its setting before shooting resumed. Meanwhile, the fawns cast in the title role grew into adulthood, and young Gene Eckman, who had been cast as Jody after a national talent search, started growing, too. The latter change didn't bother anybody. The young Atlantan's southern dialect had proven so strong that he was virtually indecipherable on film. Nor did his native dialect match up with that of the professional actors in the cast. Finally, the production was abandoned at a cost of $500,000.

Former chorus girl Jane Wyman probably would have sewn the costumes for the chance to play Ma Baxter with Claude Jarman Jr. and Gregory Peck.

> "The Yearling has a quality most other films cannot claim. It is something born of the open air; of fields and rivers and forest; of the primal issues of life and survival as they are there encountered; of the poverty of humble, hard-driven people; and of man's courage and patience in his endless struggle with nature."
>
> —John Mason Brown's review in Saturday Review

There was some talk of reviving *The Yearling* in 1942 with Roddy McDowall as Jody, but the idea was dropped. With the end of World War II, Franklin convinced studio head Louis B. Mayer to revive the production, partly in hopes of recovering the money they had already spent. Clarence Brown was picked to direct.

Brown searched the nation to find just the right child to play Jody, looking at more than twelve thousand children. Finally, he spotted a blonde boy in a Nashville school taking valentines down from the bulletin board. At first, he told ten-year-old Claude Jarman Jr. that he was scouting future football talent for the University of Tennessee. The child had never even seen a movie, much less considered acting in one, and it took some convincing to get his parents' approval.

When Franklin screened the film for the stars and their families, they were so moved they couldn't say anything after the lights came back up. Finally, Brown asked, "Will someone say something?" Jane Wyman's husband, Ronald Reagan, could only say, "I don't know if I should go to church, or if I've just been there."

The Yearling opened in Los Angeles in December 1946 to qualify for the Academy Awards, then premiered at the Radio City Music Hall in January 1947. At the request of the Music Hall's managing director, some of the animal violence was toned down, though the change came so late that the studio couldn't edit all of the prints in time. About ninety went into circulation uncut. The film won ecstatic reviews and strong box office, becoming MGM's top picture of the year, with $5.2 million in box-office returns. It also scored seven Oscar nominations, including Best Picture, Best Director, Best Actor (Peck), and Best Actress (Wyman). It won for Best Color Cinematography and Best Color Art Direction in addition to receiving a special award for Claude Jarman Jr. as the year's best child actor.

Claude Jarman Jr., Gregory Peck, and the Florida Everglades.

Index by Star

Index by Genre

$3.00 discount per movie!

Adam's Rib

For pricing and ordering information, call 1-800-4-MOVIES.
Be sure to mention "TURNER CLASSIC MOVIES" to receive your discount.

$3.00 discount per movie!

The Adventures of Robin Hood

For pricing and ordering information, call 1-800-4-MOVIES.
Be sure to mention "TURNER CLASSIC MOVIES" to receive your discount.

$3.00 discount per movie!

An American in Paris

For pricing and ordering information, call 1-800-4-MOVIES.
Be sure to mention "TURNER CLASSIC MOVIES" to receive your discount.

$3.00 discount per movie!

Angels with Dirty Faces

For pricing and ordering information, call 1-800-4-MOVIES.
Be sure to mention "TURNER CLASSIC MOVIES" to receive your discount.

$3.00 discount per movie!

The Band Wagon

For pricing and ordering information, call 1-800-4-MOVIES.
Be sure to mention "TURNER CLASSIC MOVIES" to receive your discount.

$3.00 discount per movie!

Battleground

For pricing and ordering information, call 1-800-4-MOVIES.
Be sure to mention "TURNER CLASSIC MOVIES" to receive your discount.

$3.00 discount per movie!

Ben-Hur

For pricing and ordering information, call 1-800-4-MOVIES.
Be sure to mention "TURNER CLASSIC MOVIES" to receive your discount.

$3.00 discount per movie!

The Big Parade

For pricing and ordering information, call 1-800-4-MOVIES.
Be sure to mention "TURNER CLASSIC MOVIES" to receive your discount.

$3.00 discount per movie!

The Big Sleep

For pricing and ordering information, call 1-800-4-MOVIES.
Be sure to mention "TURNER CLASSIC MOVIES" to receive your discount.

$3.00 discount per movie!

The Blackboard Jungle

For pricing and ordering information, call 1-800-4-MOVIES.
Be sure to mention "TURNER CLASSIC MOVIES" to receive your discount.

$3.00 discount per movie!

Blow Up

For pricing and ordering information, call 1-800-4-MOVIES.
Be sure to mention "TURNER CLASSIC MOVIES" to receive your discount.

$3.00 discount per movie!

Boys Town

For pricing and ordering information, call 1-800-4-MOVIES.
Be sure to mention "TURNER CLASSIC MOVIES" to receive your discount.

$3.00 discount per movie!

Bringing Up Baby

For pricing and ordering information, call 1-800-4-MOVIES.
Be sure to mention "TURNER CLASSIC MOVIES" to receive your discount.

$3.00 discount per movie!

Cabin in the Sky

For pricing and ordering information, call 1-800-4-MOVIES.
Be sure to mention "TURNER CLASSIC MOVIES" to receive your discount.

$3.00 discount per movie!

Camille

For pricing and ordering information, call 1-800-4-MOVIES.
Be sure to mention "TURNER CLASSIC MOVIES" to receive your discount.

$3.00 discount per movie!

Captain Blood

For pricing and ordering information, call 1-800-4-MOVIES.
Be sure to mention "TURNER CLASSIC MOVIES" to receive your discount.

$3.00 discount per movie!

Captains Courageous

For pricing and ordering information, call 1-800-4-MOVIES.
Be sure to mention "TURNER CLASSIC MOVIES" to receive your discount.

$3.00 discount per movie!

Casablanca

For pricing and ordering information, call 1-800-4-MOVIES.
Be sure to mention "TURNER CLASSIC MOVIES" to receive your discount.

$3.00 discount per movie!

Cat on a Hot Tin Roof

For pricing and ordering information, call 1-800-4-MOVIES.
Be sure to mention "TURNER CLASSIC MOVIES" to receive your discount.

$3.00 discount per movie!

Cat People

For pricing and ordering information, call 1-800-4-MOVIES.
Be sure to mention "TURNER CLASSIC MOVIES" to receive your discount.

Coupon expires March 31, 1998.

Coupon can only be redeemed by calling the telephone number printed on the opposite side of this coupon. Not valid in retail stores. All orders fulfilled by Movies Unlimited. Coupon valid only for title indicated. Offer subject to title availability. Shipping and handling charges extra. Terms and conditions subject to change without notice.

Coupon expires March 31, 1998.

Coupon can only be redeemed by calling the telephone number printed on the opposite side of this coupon. Not valid in retail stores. All orders fulfilled by Movies Unlimited. Coupon valid only for title indicated. Offer subject to title availability. Shipping and handling charges extra. Terms and conditions subject to change without notice.

Coupon expires March 31, 1998.

Coupon can only be redeemed by calling the telephone number printed on the opposite side of this coupon. Not valid in retail stores. All orders fulfilled by Movies Unlimited. Coupon valid only for title indicated. Offer subject to title availability. Shipping and handling charges extra. Terms and conditions subject to change without notice.

Coupon expires March 31, 1998.

Coupon can only be redeemed by calling the telephone number printed on the opposite side of this coupon. Not valid in retail stores. All orders fulfilled by Movies Unlimited. Coupon valid only for title indicated. Offer subject to title availability. Shipping and handling charges extra. Terms and conditions subject to change without notice.

Coupon expires March 31, 1998.

Coupon can only be redeemed by calling the telephone number printed on the opposite side of this coupon. Not valid in retail stores. All orders fulfilled by Movies Unlimited. Coupon valid only for title indicated. Offer subject to title availability. Shipping and handling charges extra. Terms and conditions subject to change without notice.

Coupon expires March 31, 1998.

Coupon can only be redeemed by calling the telephone number printed on the opposite side of this coupon. Not valid in retail stores. All orders fulfilled by Movies Unlimited. Coupon valid only for title indicated. Offer subject to title availability. Shipping and handling charges extra. Terms and conditions subject to change without notice.

Coupon expires March 31, 1998.

Coupon can only be redeemed by calling the telephone number printed on the opposite side of this coupon. Not valid in retail stores. All orders fulfilled by Movies Unlimited. Coupon valid only for title indicated. Offer subject to title availability. Shipping and handling charges extra. Terms and conditions subject to change without notice.

Coupon expires March 31, 1998.

Coupon can only be redeemed by calling the telephone number printed on the opposite side of this coupon. Not valid in retail stores. All orders fulfilled by Movies Unlimited. Coupon valid only for title indicated. Offer subject to title availability. Shipping and handling charges extra. Terms and conditions subject to change without notice.

Coupon expires March 31, 1998.

Coupon can only be redeemed by calling the telephone number printed on the opposite side of this coupon. Not valid in retail stores. All orders fulfilled by Movies Unlimited. Coupon valid only for title indicated. Offer subject to title availability. Shipping and handling charges extra. Terms and conditions subject to change without notice.

Coupon expires March 31, 1998.

Coupon can only be redeemed by calling the telephone number printed on the opposite side of this coupon. Not valid in retail stores. All orders fulfilled by Movies Unlimited. Coupon valid only for title indicated. Offer subject to title availability. Shipping and handling charges extra. Terms and conditions subject to change without notice.

Coupon expires March 31, 1998.

Coupon can only be redeemed by calling the telephone number printed on the opposite side of this coupon. Not valid in retail stores. All orders fulfilled by Movies Unlimited. Coupon valid only for title indicated. Offer subject to title availability. Shipping and handling charges extra. Terms and conditions subject to change without notice.

Coupon expires March 31, 1998.

Coupon can only be redeemed by calling the telephone number printed on the opposite side of this coupon. Not valid in retail stores. All orders fulfilled by Movies Unlimited. Coupon valid only for title indicated. Offer subject to title availability. Shipping and handling charges extra. Terms and conditions subject to change without notice.

Coupon expires March 31, 1998.

Coupon can only be redeemed by calling the telephone number printed on the opposite side of this coupon. Not valid in retail stores. All orders fulfilled by Movies Unlimited. Coupon valid only for title indicated. Offer subject to title availability. Shipping and handling charges extra. Terms and conditions subject to change without notice.

Coupon expires March 31, 1998.

Coupon can only be redeemed by calling the telephone number printed on the opposite side of this coupon. Not valid in retail stores. All orders fulfilled by Movies Unlimited. Coupon valid only for title indicated. Offer subject to title availability. Shipping and handling charges extra. Terms and conditions subject to change without notice.

Coupon expires March 31, 1998.

Coupon can only be redeemed by calling the telephone number printed on the opposite side of this coupon. Not valid in retail stores. All orders fulfilled by Movies Unlimited. Coupon valid only for title indicated. Offer subject to title availability. Shipping and handling charges extra. Terms and conditions subject to change without notice.

Coupon expires March 31, 1998.

Coupon can only be redeemed by calling the telephone number printed on the opposite side of this coupon. Not valid in retail stores. All orders fulfilled by Movies Unlimited. Coupon valid only for title indicated. Offer subject to title availability. Shipping and handling charges extra. Terms and conditions subject to change without notice.

Coupon expires March 31, 1998.

Coupon can only be redeemed by calling the telephone number printed on the opposite side of this coupon. Not valid in retail stores. All orders fulfilled by Movies Unlimited. Coupon valid only for title indicated. Offer subject to title availability. Shipping and handling charges extra. Terms and conditions subject to change without notice.

Coupon expires March 31, 1998.

Coupon can only be redeemed by calling the telephone number printed on the opposite side of this coupon. Not valid in retail stores. All orders fulfilled by Movies Unlimited. Coupon valid only for title indicated. Offer subject to title availability. Shipping and handling charges extra. Terms and conditions subject to change without notice.

Coupon expires March 31, 1998.

Coupon can only be redeemed by calling the telephone number printed on the opposite side of this coupon. Not valid in retail stores. All orders fulfilled by Movies Unlimited. Coupon valid only for title indicated. Offer subject to title availability. Shipping and handling charges extra. Terms and conditions subject to change without notice.

Coupon expires March 31, 1998.

Coupon can only be redeemed by calling the telephone number printed on the opposite side of this coupon. Not valid in retail stores. All orders fulfilled by Movies Unlimited. Coupon valid only for title indicated. Offer subject to title availability. Shipping and handling charges extra. Terms and conditions subject to change without notice.

Coupon expires March 31, 1998.

Coupon can only be redeemed by calling the telephone number printed on the opposite side of this coupon. Not valid in retail stores. All orders fulfilled by Movies Unlimited. Coupon valid only for title indicated. Offer subject to title availability. Shipping and handling charges extra. Terms and conditions subject to change without notice.

$3.00 discount per movie!

Citizen Kane

For pricing and ordering information, call 1-800-4-MOVIES.
Be sure to mention "TURNER CLASSIC MOVIES" to receive your discount.

$3.00 discount per movie!

Crossfire

For pricing and ordering information, call 1-800-4-MOVIES.
Be sure to mention "TURNER CLASSIC MOVIES" to receive your discount.

$3.00 discount per movie!

Dark Victory

For pricing and ordering information, call 1-800-4-MOVIES.
Be sure to mention "TURNER CLASSIC MOVIES" to receive your discount.

$3.00 discount per movie!

David Copperfield

For pricing and ordering information, call 1-800-4-MOVIES.
Be sure to mention "TURNER CLASSIC MOVIES" to receive your discount.

$3.00 discount per movie!

The Dawn Patrol

For pricing and ordering information, call 1-800-4-MOVIES.
Be sure to mention "TURNER CLASSIC MOVIES" to receive your discount.

$3.00 discount per movie!

Dinner at Eight

For pricing and ordering information, call 1-800-4-MOVIES.
Be sure to mention "TURNER CLASSIC MOVIES" to receive your discount.

$3.00 discount per movie!

The Dirty Dozen

For pricing and ordering information, call 1-800-4-MOVIES.
Be sure to mention "TURNER CLASSIC MOVIES" to receive your discount.

$3.00 discount per movie!

Dr. Jekyll and Mr. Hyde

For pricing and ordering information, call 1-800-4-MOVIES.
Be sure to mention "TURNER CLASSIC MOVIES" to receive your discount.

$3.00 discount per movie!

Doctor Zhivago

For pricing and ordering information, call 1-800-4-MOVIES.
Be sure to mention "TURNER CLASSIC MOVIES" to receive your discount.

$3.00 discount per movie!

Easter Parade

For pricing and ordering information, call 1-800-4-MOVIES.
Be sure to mention "TURNER CLASSIC MOVIES" to receive your discount.

$3.00 discount per movie!

Executive Suite

For pricing and ordering information, call 1-800-4-MOVIES.
Be sure to mention "TURNER CLASSIC MOVIES" to receive your discount.

$3.00 discount per movie!

Father of the Bride

For pricing and ordering information, call 1-800-4-MOVIES.
Be sure to mention "TURNER CLASSIC MOVIES" to receive your discount.

$3.00 discount per movie!

Flesh and the Devil

For pricing and ordering information, call 1-800-4-MOVIES.
Be sure to mention "TURNER CLASSIC MOVIES" to receive your discount.

$3.00 discount per movie!

Footlight Parade

For pricing and ordering information, call 1-800-4-MOVIES.
Be sure to mention "TURNER CLASSIC MOVIES" to receive your discount.

$3.00 discount per movie!

Forbidden Planet

For pricing and ordering information, call 1-800-4-MOVIES.
Be sure to mention "TURNER CLASSIC MOVIES" to receive your discount.

$3.00 discount per movie!

Fort Apache

For pricing and ordering information, call 1-800-4-MOVIES.
Be sure to mention "TURNER CLASSIC MOVIES" to receive your discount.

$3.00 discount per movie!

42nd Street

For pricing and ordering information, call 1-800-4-MOVIES.
Be sure to mention "TURNER CLASSIC MOVIES" to receive your discount.

$3.00 discount per movie!

Freaks

For pricing and ordering information, call 1-800-4-MOVIES.
Be sure to mention "TURNER CLASSIC MOVIES" to receive your discount.

$3.00 discount per movie!

Gaslight

For pricing and ordering information, call 1-800-4-MOVIES.
Be sure to mention "TURNER CLASSIC MOVIES" to receive your discount.

$3.00 discount per movie!

Gigi

For pricing and ordering information, call 1-800-4-MOVIES.
Be sure to mention "TURNER CLASSIC MOVIES" to receive your discount.

Coupon expires March 31, 1998.

Coupon can only be redeemed by calling the telephone number printed on the opposite side of this coupon. Not valid in retail stores. All orders fulfilled by Movies Unlimited. Coupon valid only for title indicated. Offer subject to title availability. Shipping and handling charges extra. Terms and conditions subject to change without notice.

Coupon expires March 31, 1998.

Coupon can only be redeemed by calling the telephone number printed on the opposite side of this coupon. Not valid in retail stores. All orders fulfilled by Movies Unlimited. Coupon valid only for title indicated. Offer subject to title availability. Shipping and handling charges extra. Terms and conditions subject to change without notice.

Coupon expires March 31, 1998.

Coupon can only be redeemed by calling the telephone number printed on the opposite side of this coupon. Not valid in retail stores. All orders fulfilled by Movies Unlimited. Coupon valid only for title indicated. Offer subject to title availability. Shipping and handling charges extra. Terms and conditions subject to change without notice.

Coupon expires March 31, 1998.

Coupon can only be redeemed by calling the telephone number printed on the opposite side of this coupon. Not valid in retail stores. All orders fulfilled by Movies Unlimited. Coupon valid only for title indicated. Offer subject to title availability. Shipping and handling charges extra. Terms and conditions subject to change without notice.

Coupon expires March 31, 1998.

Coupon can only be redeemed by calling the telephone number printed on the opposite side of this coupon. Not valid in retail stores. All orders fulfilled by Movies Unlimited. Coupon valid only for title indicated. Offer subject to title availability. Shipping and handling charges extra. Terms and conditions subject to change without notice.

Coupon expires March 31, 1998.

Coupon can only be redeemed by calling the telephone number printed on the opposite side of this coupon. Not valid in retail stores. All orders fulfilled by Movies Unlimited. Coupon valid only for title indicated. Offer subject to title availability. Shipping and handling charges extra. Terms and conditions subject to change without notice.

Coupon expires March 31, 1998.

Coupon can only be redeemed by calling the telephone number printed on the opposite side of this coupon. Not valid in retail stores. All orders fulfilled by Movies Unlimited. Coupon valid only for title indicated. Offer subject to title availability. Shipping and handling charges extra. Terms and conditions subject to change without notice.

Coupon expires March 31, 1998.

Coupon can only be redeemed by calling the telephone number printed on the opposite side of this coupon. Not valid in retail stores. All orders fulfilled by Movies Unlimited. Coupon valid only for title indicated. Offer subject to title availability. Shipping and handling charges extra. Terms and conditions subject to change without notice.

Coupon expires March 31, 1998.

Coupon can only be redeemed by calling the telephone number printed on the opposite side of this coupon. Not valid in retail stores. All orders fulfilled by Movies Unlimited. Coupon valid only for title indicated. Offer subject to title availability. Shipping and handling charges extra. Terms and conditions subject to change without notice.

Coupon expires March 31, 1998.

Coupon can only be redeemed by calling the telephone number printed on the opposite side of this coupon. Not valid in retail stores. All orders fulfilled by Movies Unlimited. Coupon valid only for title indicated. Offer subject to title availability. Shipping and handling charges extra. Terms and conditions subject to change without notice.

Coupon expires March 31, 1998.

Coupon can only be redeemed by calling the telephone number printed on the opposite side of this coupon. Not valid in retail stores. All orders fulfilled by Movies Unlimited. Coupon valid only for title indicated. Offer subject to title availability. Shipping and handling charges extra. Terms and conditions subject to change without notice.

Coupon expires March 31, 1998.

Coupon can only be redeemed by calling the telephone number printed on the opposite side of this coupon. Not valid in retail stores. All orders fulfilled by Movies Unlimited. Coupon valid only for title indicated. Offer subject to title availability. Shipping and handling charges extra. Terms and conditions subject to change without notice.

Coupon expires March 31, 1998.

Coupon can only be redeemed by calling the telephone number printed on the opposite side of this coupon. Not valid in retail stores. All orders fulfilled by Movies Unlimited. Coupon valid only for title indicated. Offer subject to title availability. Shipping and handling charges extra. Terms and conditions subject to change without notice.

Coupon expires March 31, 1998.

Coupon can only be redeemed by calling the telephone number printed on the opposite side of this coupon. Not valid in retail stores. All orders fulfilled by Movies Unlimited. Coupon valid only for title indicated. Offer subject to title availability. Shipping and handling charges extra. Terms and conditions subject to change without notice.

Coupon expires March 31, 1998.

Coupon can only be redeemed by calling the telephone number printed on the opposite side of this coupon. Not valid in retail stores. All orders fulfilled by Movies Unlimited. Coupon valid only for title indicated. Offer subject to title availability. Shipping and handling charges extra. Terms and conditions subject to change without notice.

Coupon expires March 31, 1998.

Coupon can only be redeemed by calling the telephone number printed on the opposite side of this coupon. Not valid in retail stores. All orders fulfilled by Movies Unlimited. Coupon valid only for title indicated. Offer subject to title availability. Shipping and handling charges extra. Terms and conditions subject to change without notice.

Coupon expires March 31, 1998.

Coupon can only be redeemed by calling the telephone number printed on the opposite side of this coupon. Not valid in retail stores. All orders fulfilled by Movies Unlimited. Coupon valid only for title indicated. Offer subject to title availability. Shipping and handling charges extra. Terms and conditions subject to change without notice.

Coupon expires March 31, 1998.

Coupon can only be redeemed by calling the telephone number printed on the opposite side of this coupon. Not valid in retail stores. All orders fulfilled by Movies Unlimited. Coupon valid only for title indicated. Offer subject to title availability. Shipping and handling charges extra. Terms and conditions subject to change without notice.

Coupon expires March 31, 1998.

Coupon can only be redeemed by calling the telephone number printed on the opposite side of this coupon. Not valid in retail stores. All orders fulfilled by Movies Unlimited. Coupon valid only for title indicated. Offer subject to title availability. Shipping and handling charges extra. Terms and conditions subject to change without notice.

Coupon expires March 31, 1998.

Coupon can only be redeemed by calling the telephone number printed on the opposite side of this coupon. Not valid in retail stores. All orders fulfilled by Movies Unlimited. Coupon valid only for title indicated. Offer subject to title availability. Shipping and handling charges extra. Terms and conditions subject to change without notice.

Coupon expires March 31, 1998.

Coupon can only be redeemed by calling the telephone number printed on the opposite side of this coupon. Not valid in retail stores. All orders fulfilled by Movies Unlimited. Coupon valid only for title indicated. Offer subject to title availability. Shipping and handling charges extra. Terms and conditions subject to change without notice.

$3.00 discount per movie!

Gone With the Wind

For pricing and ordering information, call 1-800-4-MOVIES.
Be sure to mention "TURNER CLASSIC MOVIES" to receive your discount.

$3.00 discount per movie!

Gold Diggers of 1933

For pricing and ordering information, call 1-800-4-MOVIES.
Be sure to mention "TURNER CLASSIC MOVIES" to receive your discount.

$3.00 discount per movie!

The Good Earth

For pricing and ordering information, call 1-800-4-MOVIES.
Be sure to mention "TURNER CLASSIC MOVIES" to receive your discount.

$3.00 discount per movie!

Goodbye, Mr. Chips

For pricing and ordering information, call 1-800-4-MOVIES.
Be sure to mention "TURNER CLASSIC MOVIES" to receive your discount.

$3.00 discount per movie!

Grand Hotel

For pricing and ordering information, call 1-800-4-MOVIES.
Be sure to mention "TURNER CLASSIC MOVIES" to receive your discount.

$3.00 discount per movie!

Greed

For pricing and ordering information, call 1-800-4-MOVIES.
Be sure to mention "TURNER CLASSIC MOVIES" to receive your discount.

$3.00 discount per movie!

Gunga Din

For pricing and ordering information, call 1-800-4-MOVIES.
Be sure to mention "TURNER CLASSIC MOVIES" to receive your discount.

$3.00 discount per movie!

How the West Was Won

For pricing and ordering information, call 1-800-4-MOVIES.
Be sure to mention "TURNER CLASSIC MOVIES" to receive your discount.

$3.00 discount per movie!

The Hunchback of Notre Dame

For pricing and ordering information, call 1-800-4-MOVIES.
Be sure to mention "TURNER CLASSIC MOVIES" to receive your discount.

$3.00 discount per movie!

I Am a Fugitive from a Chain Gang

For pricing and ordering information, call 1-800-4-MOVIES.
Be sure to mention "TURNER CLASSIC MOVIES" to receive your discount.

$3.00 discount per movie!

I Remember Mama

For pricing and ordering information, call 1-800-4-MOVIES.
Be sure to mention "TURNER CLASSIC MOVIES" to receive your discount.

$3.00 discount per movie!

The Informer

For pricing and ordering information, call 1-800-4-MOVIES.
Be sure to mention "TURNER CLASSIC MOVIES" to receive your discount.

$3.00 discount per movie!

Jailhouse Rock

For pricing and ordering information, call 1-800-4-MOVIES.
Be sure to mention "TURNER CLASSIC MOVIES" to receive your discount.

$3.00 discount per movie!

The Jazz Singer

For pricing and ordering information, call 1-800-4-MOVIES.
Be sure to mention "TURNER CLASSIC MOVIES" to receive your discount.

$3.00 discount per movie!

Jezebel

For pricing and ordering information, call 1-800-4-MOVIES.
Be sure to mention "TURNER CLASSIC MOVIES" to receive your discount.

$3.00 discount per movie!

Johnny Belinda

For pricing and ordering information, call 1-800-4-MOVIES.
Be sure to mention "TURNER CLASSIC MOVIES" to receive your discount.

$3.00 discount per movie!

King Kong

For pricing and ordering information, call 1-800-4-MOVIES.
Be sure to mention "TURNER CLASSIC MOVIES" to receive your discount.

$3.00 discount per movie!

Kings Row

For pricing and ordering information, call 1-800-4-MOVIES.
Be sure to mention "TURNER CLASSIC MOVIES" to receive your discount.

$3.00 discount per movie!

Little Caesar

For pricing and ordering information, call 1-800-4-MOVIES.
Be sure to mention "TURNER CLASSIC MOVIES" to receive your discount.

$3.00 discount per movie!

Little Women

For pricing and ordering information, call 1-800-4-MOVIES.
Be sure to mention "TURNER CLASSIC MOVIES" to receive your discount.

Coupon expires March 31, 1998.
Coupon can only be redeemed by calling the telephone number printed on the opposite side of this coupon. Not valid in retail stores. All orders fulfilled by Movies Unlimited. Coupon valid only for title indicated. Offer subject to title availability. Shipping and handling charges extra. Terms and conditions subject to change without notice.

Coupon expires March 31, 1998.
Coupon can only be redeemed by calling the telephone number printed on the opposite side of this coupon. Not valid in retail stores. All orders fulfilled by Movies Unlimited. Coupon valid only for title indicated. Offer subject to title availability. Shipping and handling charges extra. Terms and conditions subject to change without notice.

Coupon expires March 31, 1998.
Coupon can only be redeemed by calling the telephone number printed on the opposite side of this coupon. Not valid in retail stores. All orders fulfilled by Movies Unlimited. Coupon valid only for title indicated. Offer subject to title availability. Shipping and handling charges extra. Terms and conditions subject to change without notice.

Coupon expires March 31, 1998.
Coupon can only be redeemed by calling the telephone number printed on the opposite side of this coupon. Not valid in retail stores. All orders fulfilled by Movies Unlimited. Coupon valid only for title indicated. Offer subject to title availability. Shipping and handling charges extra. Terms and conditions subject to change without notice.

Coupon expires March 31, 1998.
Coupon can only be redeemed by calling the telephone number printed on the opposite side of this coupon. Not valid in retail stores. All orders fulfilled by Movies Unlimited. Coupon valid only for title indicated. Offer subject to title availability. Shipping and handling charges extra. Terms and conditions subject to change without notice.

Coupon expires March 31, 1998.
Coupon can only be redeemed by calling the telephone number printed on the opposite side of this coupon. Not valid in retail stores. All orders fulfilled by Movies Unlimited. Coupon valid only for title indicated. Offer subject to title availability. Shipping and handling charges extra. Terms and conditions subject to change without notice.

Coupon expires March 31, 1998.
Coupon can only be redeemed by calling the telephone number printed on the opposite side of this coupon. Not valid in retail stores. All orders fulfilled by Movies Unlimited. Coupon valid only for title indicated. Offer subject to title availability. Shipping and handling charges extra. Terms and conditions subject to change without notice.

Coupon expires March 31, 1998.
Coupon can only be redeemed by calling the telephone number printed on the opposite side of this coupon. Not valid in retail stores. All orders fulfilled by Movies Unlimited. Coupon valid only for title indicated. Offer subject to title availability. Shipping and handling charges extra. Terms and conditions subject to change without notice.

Coupon expires March 31, 1998.
Coupon can only be redeemed by calling the telephone number printed on the opposite side of this coupon. Not valid in retail stores. All orders fulfilled by Movies Unlimited. Coupon valid only for title indicated. Offer subject to title availability. Shipping and handling charges extra. Terms and conditions subject to change without notice.

Coupon expires March 31, 1998.
Coupon can only be redeemed by calling the telephone number printed on the opposite side of this coupon. Not valid in retail stores. All orders fulfilled by Movies Unlimited. Coupon valid only for title indicated. Offer subject to title availability. Shipping and handling charges extra. Terms and conditions subject to change without notice.

Coupon expires March 31, 1998.
Coupon can only be redeemed by calling the telephone number printed on the opposite side of this coupon. Not valid in retail stores. All orders fulfilled by Movies Unlimited. Coupon valid only for title indicated. Offer subject to title availability. Shipping and handling charges extra. Terms and conditions subject to change without notice.

Coupon expires March 31, 1998.
Coupon can only be redeemed by calling the telephone number printed on the opposite side of this coupon. Not valid in retail stores. All orders fulfilled by Movies Unlimited. Coupon valid only for title indicated. Offer subject to title availability. Shipping and handling charges extra. Terms and conditions subject to change without notice.

Coupon expires March 31, 1998.
Coupon can only be redeemed by calling the telephone number printed on the opposite side of this coupon. Not valid in retail stores. All orders fulfilled by Movies Unlimited. Coupon valid only for title indicated. Offer subject to title availability. Shipping and handling charges extra. Terms and conditions subject to change without notice.

Coupon expires March 31, 1998.
Coupon can only be redeemed by calling the telephone number printed on the opposite side of this coupon. Not valid in retail stores. All orders fulfilled by Movies Unlimited. Coupon valid only for title indicated. Offer subject to title availability. Shipping and handling charges extra. Terms and conditions subject to change without notice.

Coupon expires March 31, 1998.
Coupon can only be redeemed by calling the telephone number printed on the opposite side of this coupon. Not valid in retail stores. All orders fulfilled by Movies Unlimited. Coupon valid only for title indicated. Offer subject to title availability. Shipping and handling charges extra. Terms and conditions subject to change without notice.

Coupon expires March 31, 1998.
Coupon can only be redeemed by calling the telephone number printed on the opposite side of this coupon. Not valid in retail stores. All orders fulfilled by Movies Unlimited. Coupon valid only for title indicated. Offer subject to title availability. Shipping and handling charges extra. Terms and conditions subject to change without notice.

Coupon expires March 31, 1998.
Coupon can only be redeemed by calling the telephone number printed on the opposite side of this coupon. Not valid in retail stores. All orders fulfilled by Movies Unlimited. Coupon valid only for title indicated. Offer subject to title availability. Shipping and handling charges extra. Terms and conditions subject to change without notice.

Coupon expires March 31, 1998.
Coupon can only be redeemed by calling the telephone number printed on the opposite side of this coupon. Not valid in retail stores. All orders fulfilled by Movies Unlimited. Coupon valid only for title indicated. Offer subject to title availability. Shipping and handling charges extra. Terms and conditions subject to change without notice.

Coupon expires March 31, 1998.
Coupon can only be redeemed by calling the telephone number printed on the opposite side of this coupon. Not valid in retail stores. All orders fulfilled by Movies Unlimited. Coupon valid only for title indicated. Offer subject to title availability. Shipping and handling charges extra. Terms and conditions subject to change without notice.

Coupon expires March 31, 1998.
Coupon can only be redeemed by calling the telephone number printed on the opposite side of this coupon. Not valid in retail stores. All orders fulfilled by Movies Unlimited. Coupon valid only for title indicated. Offer subject to title availability. Shipping and handling charges extra. Terms and conditions subject to change without notice.

$3.00 discount per movie!

Lolita

For pricing and ordering information, call 1-800-4-MOVIES.
Be sure to mention "TURNER CLASSIC MOVIES" to receive your discount.

$3.00 discount per movie!

Lust for Life

For pricing and ordering information, call 1-800-4-MOVIES.
Be sure to mention "TURNER CLASSIC MOVIES" to receive your discount.

$3.00 discount per movie!

The Magnificent Ambersons

For pricing and ordering information, call 1-800-4-MOVIES.
Be sure to mention "TURNER CLASSIC MOVIES" to receive your discount.

$3.00 discount per movie!

The Maltese Falcon

For pricing and ordering information, call 1-800-4-MOVIES.
Be sure to mention "TURNER CLASSIC MOVIES" to receive your discount.

$3.00 discount per movie!

Meet Me in St. Louis

For pricing and ordering information, call 1-800-4-MOVIES.
Be sure to mention "TURNER CLASSIC MOVIES" to receive your discount.

$3.00 discount per movie!

Mildred Pierce

For pricing and ordering information, call 1-800-4-MOVIES.
Be sure to mention "TURNER CLASSIC MOVIES" to receive your discount.

$3.00 discount per movie!

Mrs. Miniver

For pricing and ordering information, call 1-800-4-MOVIES.
Be sure to mention "TURNER CLASSIC MOVIES" to receive your discount.

$3.00 discount per movie!

Murder, My Sweet

For pricing and ordering information, call 1-800-4-MOVIES.
Be sure to mention "TURNER CLASSIC MOVIES" to receive your discount.

$3.00 discount per movie!

Mutiny on the Bounty

For pricing and ordering information, call 1-800-4-MOVIES.
Be sure to mention "TURNER CLASSIC MOVIES" to receive your discount.

$3.00 discount per movie!

National Velvet

For pricing and ordering information, call 1-800-4-MOVIES.
Be sure to mention "TURNER CLASSIC MOVIES" to receive your discount.

$3.00 discount per movie!

Network

For pricing and ordering information, call 1-800-4-MOVIES.
Be sure to mention "TURNER CLASSIC MOVIES" to receive your discount.

$3.00 discount per movie!

A Night at the Opera

For pricing and ordering information, call 1-800-4-MOVIES.
Be sure to mention "TURNER CLASSIC MOVIES" to receive your discount.

$3.00 discount per movie!

Ninotchka

For pricing and ordering information, call 1-800-4-MOVIES.
Be sure to mention "TURNER CLASSIC MOVIES" to receive your discount.

$3.00 discount per movie!

North by Northwest

For pricing and ordering information, call 1-800-4-MOVIES.
Be sure to mention "TURNER CLASSIC MOVIES" to receive your discount.

$3.00 discount per movie!

Now, Voyager

For pricing and ordering information, call 1-800-4-MOVIES.
Be sure to mention "TURNER CLASSIC MOVIES" to receive your discount.

$3.00 discount per movie!

Out of the Past

For pricing and ordering information, call 1-800-4-MOVIES.
Be sure to mention "TURNER CLASSIC MOVIES" to receive your discount.

$3.00 discount per movie!

The Philadelphia Story

For pricing and ordering information, call 1-800-4-MOVIES.
Be sure to mention "TURNER CLASSIC MOVIES" to receive your discount.

$3.00 discount per movie!

The Postman Always Rings Twice

For pricing and ordering information, call 1-800-4-MOVIES.
Be sure to mention "TURNER CLASSIC MOVIES" to receive your discount.

$3.00 discount per movie!

Pride and Prejudice

For pricing and ordering information, call 1-800-4-MOVIES.
Be sure to mention "TURNER CLASSIC MOVIES" to receive your discount.

$3.00 discount per movie!

The Public Enemy

For pricing and ordering information, call 1-800-4-MOVIES.
Be sure to mention "TURNER CLASSIC MOVIES" to receive your discount.

Coupon expires March 31, 1998.

Coupon can only be redeemed by calling the telephone number printed on the opposite side of this coupon. Not valid in retail stores. All orders fulfilled by Movies Unlimited. Coupon valid only for title indicated. Offer subject to title availability. Shipping and handling charges extra. Terms and conditions subject to change without notice.

Coupon expires March 31, 1998.

Coupon can only be redeemed by calling the telephone number printed on the opposite side of this coupon. Not valid in retail stores. All orders fulfilled by Movies Unlimited. Coupon valid only for title indicated. Offer subject to title availability. Shipping and handling charges extra. Terms and conditions subject to change without notice.

Coupon expires March 31, 1998.

Coupon can only be redeemed by calling the telephone number printed on the opposite side of this coupon. Not valid in retail stores. All orders fulfilled by Movies Unlimited. Coupon valid only for title indicated. Offer subject to title availability. Shipping and handling charges extra. Terms and conditions subject to change without notice.

Coupon expires March 31, 1998.

Coupon can only be redeemed by calling the telephone number printed on the opposite side of this coupon. Not valid in retail stores. All orders fulfilled by Movies Unlimited. Coupon valid only for title indicated. Offer subject to title availability. Shipping and handling charges extra. Terms and conditions subject to change without notice.

Coupon expires March 31, 1998.

Coupon can only be redeemed by calling the telephone number printed on the opposite side of this coupon. Not valid in retail stores. All orders fulfilled by Movies Unlimited. Coupon valid only for title indicated. Offer subject to title availability. Shipping and handling charges extra. Terms and conditions subject to change without notice.

Coupon expires March 31, 1998.

Coupon can only be redeemed by calling the telephone number printed on the opposite side of this coupon. Not valid in retail stores. All orders fulfilled by Movies Unlimited. Coupon valid only for title indicated. Offer subject to title availability. Shipping and handling charges extra. Terms and conditions subject to change without notice.

Coupon expires March 31, 1998.

Coupon can only be redeemed by calling the telephone number printed on the opposite side of this coupon. Not valid in retail stores. All orders fulfilled by Movies Unlimited. Coupon valid only for title indicated. Offer subject to title availability. Shipping and handling charges extra. Terms and conditions subject to change without notice.

Coupon expires March 31, 1998.

Coupon can only be redeemed by calling the telephone number printed on the opposite side of this coupon. Not valid in retail stores. All orders fulfilled by Movies Unlimited. Coupon valid only for title indicated. Offer subject to title availability. Shipping and handling charges extra. Terms and conditions subject to change without notice.

Coupon expires March 31, 1998.

Coupon can only be redeemed by calling the telephone number printed on the opposite side of this coupon. Not valid in retail stores. All orders fulfilled by Movies Unlimited. Coupon valid only for title indicated. Offer subject to title availability. Shipping and handling charges extra. Terms and conditions subject to change without notice.

Coupon expires March 31, 1998.

Coupon can only be redeemed by calling the telephone number printed on the opposite side of this coupon. Not valid in retail stores. All orders fulfilled by Movies Unlimited. Coupon valid only for title indicated. Offer subject to title availability. Shipping and handling charges extra. Terms and conditions subject to change without notice.

Coupon expires March 31, 1998.

Coupon can only be redeemed by calling the telephone number printed on the opposite side of this coupon. Not valid in retail stores. All orders fulfilled by Movies Unlimited. Coupon valid only for title indicated. Offer subject to title availability. Shipping and handling charges extra. Terms and conditions subject to change without notice.

Coupon expires March 31, 1998.

Coupon can only be redeemed by calling the telephone number printed on the opposite side of this coupon. Not valid in retail stores. All orders fulfilled by Movies Unlimited. Coupon valid only for title indicated. Offer subject to title availability. Shipping and handling charges extra. Terms and conditions subject to change without notice.

Coupon expires March 31, 1998.

Coupon can only be redeemed by calling the telephone number printed on the opposite side of this coupon. Not valid in retail stores. All orders fulfilled by Movies Unlimited. Coupon valid only for title indicated. Offer subject to title availability. Shipping and handling charges extra. Terms and conditions subject to change without notice.

Coupon expires March 31, 1998.

Coupon can only be redeemed by calling the telephone number printed on the opposite side of this coupon. Not valid in retail stores. All orders fulfilled by Movies Unlimited. Coupon valid only for title indicated. Offer subject to title availability. Shipping and handling charges extra. Terms and conditions subject to change without notice.

Coupon expires March 31, 1998.

Coupon can only be redeemed by calling the telephone number printed on the opposite side of this coupon. Not valid in retail stores. All orders fulfilled by Movies Unlimited. Coupon valid only for title indicated. Offer subject to title availability. Shipping and handling charges extra. Terms and conditions subject to change without notice.

Coupon expires March 31, 1998.

Coupon can only be redeemed by calling the telephone number printed on the opposite side of this coupon. Not valid in retail stores. All orders fulfilled by Movies Unlimited. Coupon valid only for title indicated. Offer subject to title availability. Shipping and handling charges extra. Terms and conditions subject to change without notice.

Coupon expires March 31, 1998.

Coupon can only be redeemed by calling the telephone number printed on the opposite side of this coupon. Not valid in retail stores. All orders fulfilled by Movies Unlimited. Coupon valid only for title indicated. Offer subject to title availability. Shipping and handling charges extra. Terms and conditions subject to change without notice.

Coupon expires March 31, 1998.

Coupon can only be redeemed by calling the telephone number printed on the opposite side of this coupon. Not valid in retail stores. All orders fulfilled by Movies Unlimited. Coupon valid only for title indicated. Offer subject to title availability. Shipping and handling charges extra. Terms and conditions subject to change without notice.

Coupon expires March 31, 1998.

Coupon can only be redeemed by calling the telephone number printed on the opposite side of this coupon. Not valid in retail stores. All orders fulfilled by Movies Unlimited. Coupon valid only for title indicated. Offer subject to title availability. Shipping and handling charges extra. Terms and conditions subject to change without notice.

Coupon expires March 31, 1998.

Coupon can only be redeemed by calling the telephone number printed on the opposite side of this coupon. Not valid in retail stores. All orders fulfilled by Movies Unlimited. Coupon valid only for title indicated. Offer subject to title availability. Shipping and handling charges extra. Terms and conditions subject to change without notice.

Coupon expires March 31, 1998.

Coupon can only be redeemed by calling the telephone number printed on the opposite side of this coupon. Not valid in retail stores. All orders fulfilled by Movies Unlimited. Coupon valid only for title indicated. Offer subject to title availability. Shipping and handling charges extra. Terms and conditions subject to change without notice.

$3.00 discount per movie!
Quo Vadis?
For pricing and ordering information, call 1-800-4-MOVIES.
Be sure to mention "TURNER CLASSIC MOVIES" to receive your discount.

$3.00 discount per movie!
The Red Badge of Courage
For pricing and ordering information, call 1-800-4-MOVIES.
Be sure to mention "TURNER CLASSIC MOVIES" to receive your discount.

$3.00 discount per movie!
Red Dust
For pricing and ordering information, call 1-800-4-MOVIES.
Be sure to mention "TURNER CLASSIC MOVIES" to receive your discount.

$3.00 discount per movie!
Ride the High Country
For pricing and ordering information, call 1-800-4-MOVIES.
Be sure to mention "TURNER CLASSIC MOVIES" to receive your discount.

$3.00 discount per movie!
Rose Marie
For pricing and ordering information, call 1-800-4-MOVIES.
Be sure to mention "TURNER CLASSIC MOVIES" to receive your discount.

$3.00 discount per movie!
San Francisco
For pricing and ordering information, call 1-800-4-MOVIES.
Be sure to mention "TURNER CLASSIC MOVIES" to receive your discount.

$3.00 discount per movie!
She Wore a Yellow Ribbon
For pricing and ordering information, call 1-800-4-MOVIES.
Be sure to mention "TURNER CLASSIC MOVIES" to receive your discount.

$3.00 discount per movie!
The Shop Around the Corner
For pricing and ordering information, call 1-800-4-MOVIES.
Be sure to mention "TURNER CLASSIC MOVIES" to receive your discount.

$3.00 discount per movie!
Singin' in the Rain
For pricing and ordering information, call 1-800-4-MOVIES.
Be sure to mention "TURNER CLASSIC MOVIES" to receive your discount.

$3.00 discount per movie!
Tarzan, the Ape Man
For pricing and ordering information, call 1-800-4-MOVIES.
Be sure to mention "TURNER CLASSIC MOVIES" to receive your discount.

$3.00 discount per movie!
The Thin Man
For pricing and ordering information, call 1-800-4-MOVIES.
Be sure to mention "TURNER CLASSIC MOVIES" to receive your discount.

$3.00 discount per movie!
To Have and Have Not
For pricing and ordering information, call 1-800-4-MOVIES.
Be sure to mention "TURNER CLASSIC MOVIES" to receive your discount.

$3.00 discount per movie!
Top Hat
For pricing and ordering information, call 1-800-4-MOVIES.
Be sure to mention "TURNER CLASSIC MOVIES" to receive your discount.

$3.00 discount per movie!
The Treasure of the Sierra Madre
For pricing and ordering information, call 1-800-4-MOVIES.
Be sure to mention "TURNER CLASSIC MOVIES" to receive your discount.

$3.00 discount per movie!
2001: A Space Odyssey
For pricing and ordering information, call 1-800-4-MOVIES.
Be sure to mention "TURNER CLASSIC MOVIES" to receive your discount.

$3.00 discount per movie!
White Heat
For pricing and ordering information, call 1-800-4-MOVIES.
Be sure to mention "TURNER CLASSIC MOVIES" to receive your discount.

$3.00 discount per movie!
The Wizard of Oz
For pricing and ordering information, call 1-800-4-MOVIES.
Be sure to mention "TURNER CLASSIC MOVIES" to receive your discount.

$3.00 discount per movie!
The Women
For pricing and ordering information, call 1-800-4-MOVIES.
Be sure to mention "TURNER CLASSIC MOVIES" to receive your discount.

$3.00 discount per movie!
Yankee Doodle Dandy
For pricing and ordering information, call 1-800-4-MOVIES.
Be sure to mention "TURNER CLASSIC MOVIES" to receive your discount.

$3.00 discount per movie!
The Yearling
For pricing and ordering information, call 1-800-4-MOVIES.
Be sure to mention "TURNER CLASSIC MOVIES" to receive your discount.

Coupon expires March 31, 1998.

Coupon can only be redeemed by calling the telephone number printed on the opposite side of this coupon. Not valid in retail stores. All orders fulfilled by Movies Unlimited. Coupon valid only for title indicated. Offer subject to title availability. Shipping and handling charges extra. Terms and conditions subject to change without notice.

Coupon expires March 31, 1998.

Coupon can only be redeemed by calling the telephone number printed on the opposite side of this coupon. Not valid in retail stores. All orders fulfilled by Movies Unlimited. Coupon valid only for title indicated. Offer subject to title availability. Shipping and handling charges extra. Terms and conditions subject to change without notice.

Coupon expires March 31, 1998.

Coupon can only be redeemed by calling the telephone number printed on the opposite side of this coupon. Not valid in retail stores. All orders fulfilled by Movies Unlimited. Coupon valid only for title indicated. Offer subject to title availability. Shipping and handling charges extra. Terms and conditions subject to change without notice.

Coupon expires March 31, 1998.

Coupon can only be redeemed by calling the telephone number printed on the opposite side of this coupon. Not valid in retail stores. All orders fulfilled by Movies Unlimited. Coupon valid only for title indicated. Offer subject to title availability. Shipping and handling charges extra. Terms and conditions subject to change without notice.

Coupon expires March 31, 1998.

Coupon can only be redeemed by calling the telephone number printed on the opposite side of this coupon. Not valid in retail stores. All orders fulfilled by Movies Unlimited. Coupon valid only for title indicated. Offer subject to title availability. Shipping and handling charges extra. Terms and conditions subject to change without notice.

Coupon expires March 31, 1998.

Coupon can only be redeemed by calling the telephone number printed on the opposite side of this coupon. Not valid in retail stores. All orders fulfilled by Movies Unlimited. Coupon valid only for title indicated. Offer subject to title availability. Shipping and handling charges extra. Terms and conditions subject to change without notice.

Coupon expires March 31, 1998.

Coupon can only be redeemed by calling the telephone number printed on the opposite side of this coupon. Not valid in retail stores. All orders fulfilled by Movies Unlimited. Coupon valid only for title indicated. Offer subject to title availability. Shipping and handling charges extra. Terms and conditions subject to change without notice.

Coupon expires March 31, 1998.

Coupon can only be redeemed by calling the telephone number printed on the opposite side of this coupon. Not valid in retail stores. All orders fulfilled by Movies Unlimited. Coupon valid only for title indicated. Offer subject to title availability. Shipping and handling charges extra. Terms and conditions subject to change without notice.

Coupon expires March 31, 1998.

Coupon can only be redeemed by calling the telephone number printed on the opposite side of this coupon. Not valid in retail stores. All orders fulfilled by Movies Unlimited. Coupon valid only for title indicated. Offer subject to title availability. Shipping and handling charges extra. Terms and conditions subject to change without notice.

Coupon expires March 31, 1998.

Coupon can only be redeemed by calling the telephone number printed on the opposite side of this coupon. Not valid in retail stores. All orders fulfilled by Movies Unlimited. Coupon valid only for title indicated. Offer subject to title availability. Shipping and handling charges extra. Terms and conditions subject to change without notice.

Coupon expires March 31, 1998.

Coupon can only be redeemed by calling the telephone number printed on the opposite side of this coupon. Not valid in retail stores. All orders fulfilled by Movies Unlimited. Coupon valid only for title indicated. Offer subject to title availability. Shipping and handling charges extra. Terms and conditions subject to change without notice.

Coupon expires March 31, 1998.

Coupon can only be redeemed by calling the telephone number printed on the opposite side of this coupon. Not valid in retail stores. All orders fulfilled by Movies Unlimited. Coupon valid only for title indicated. Offer subject to title availability. Shipping and handling charges extra. Terms and conditions subject to change without notice.

Coupon expires March 31, 1998.

Coupon can only be redeemed by calling the telephone number printed on the opposite side of this coupon. Not valid in retail stores. All orders fulfilled by Movies Unlimited. Coupon valid only for title indicated. Offer subject to title availability. Shipping and handling charges extra. Terms and conditions subject to change without notice.

Coupon expires March 31, 1998.

Coupon can only be redeemed by calling the telephone number printed on the opposite side of this coupon. Not valid in retail stores. All orders fulfilled by Movies Unlimited. Coupon valid only for title indicated. Offer subject to title availability. Shipping and handling charges extra. Terms and conditions subject to change without notice.

Coupon expires March 31, 1998.

Coupon can only be redeemed by calling the telephone number printed on the opposite side of this coupon. Not valid in retail stores. All orders fulfilled by Movies Unlimited. Coupon valid only for title indicated. Offer subject to title availability. Shipping and handling charges extra. Terms and conditions subject to change without notice.

Coupon expires March 31, 1998.

Coupon can only be redeemed by calling the telephone number printed on the opposite side of this coupon. Not valid in retail stores. All orders fulfilled by Movies Unlimited. Coupon valid only for title indicated. Offer subject to title availability. Shipping and handling charges extra. Terms and conditions subject to change without notice.

Coupon expires March 31, 1998.

Coupon can only be redeemed by calling the telephone number printed on the opposite side of this coupon. Not valid in retail stores. All orders fulfilled by Movies Unlimited. Coupon valid only for title indicated. Offer subject to title availability. Shipping and handling charges extra. Terms and conditions subject to change without notice.

Coupon expires March 31, 1998.

Coupon can only be redeemed by calling the telephone number printed on the opposite side of this coupon. Not valid in retail stores. All orders fulfilled by Movies Unlimited. Coupon valid only for title indicated. Offer subject to title availability. Shipping and handling charges extra. Terms and conditions subject to change without notice.

Coupon expires March 31, 1998.

Coupon can only be redeemed by calling the telephone number printed on the opposite side of this coupon. Not valid in retail stores. All orders fulfilled by Movies Unlimited. Coupon valid only for title indicated. Offer subject to title availability. Shipping and handling charges extra. Terms and conditions subject to change without notice.

Coupon expires March 31, 1998.

Coupon can only be redeemed by calling the telephone number printed on the opposite side of this coupon. Not valid in retail stores. All orders fulfilled by Movies Unlimited. Coupon valid only for title indicated. Offer subject to title availability. Shipping and handling charges extra. Terms and conditions subject to change without notice.

Coupon expires March 31, 1998.

Coupon can only be redeemed by calling the telephone number printed on the opposite side of this coupon. Not valid in retail stores. All orders fulfilled by Movies Unlimited. Coupon valid only for title indicated. Offer subject to title availability. Shipping and handling charges extra. Terms and conditions subject to change without notice.